THE PHILOSOPHY OF INDIA AND ITS IMPACT ON AMERICAN THOUGHT

Publication Number 772

AMERICAN LECTURE SERIES®

A Monograph in

The BANNERSTONE DIVISION *of*
AMERICAN LECTURES IN PHILOSOPHY

Edited by

MARVIN FARBER
State University of New York at Buffalo
Buffalo, New York

THE PHILOSOPHY OF INDIA AND ITS IMPACT ON AMERICAN THOUGHT

By

DALE RIEPE

Department of Philosophy
State University of New York at Buffalo
Buffalo, New York

CHARLES C THOMAS · PUBLISHER
Springfield · *Illinois* · *U.S.A.*

Published and Distributed Throughout the World by

CHARLES C THOMAS · PUBLISHER

BANNERSTONE HOUSE

301–327 East Lawrence Avenue, Springfield, Illinois, U.S.A.

NATCHEZ PLANTATION HOUSE

735 North Atlantic Boulevard, Fort Lauderdale, Florida, U.S.A.

© *1970, by* CHARLES C THOMAS · PUBLISHER

Library of Congress Catalog Card Number: 75–97533

With THOMAS BOOKS *careful attention is given to all details of manufacturing and design. It is the Publisher's desire to present books that are satisfactory as to their physical qualities and artistic possibilities and appropriate for their particular use.* THOMAS BOOKS *will be true to those laws of quality that assure a good name and good will.*

Printed in the United States of America

K–8

For Charleine Harriet Williams Riepe

Uxori carissimae quae parentibus suis devota,
maritum liberosque suo corde amans, erudita,
ordinata, firma, diligens, modesta, clemens
gaudium pacemque semper fovet.

Female Goddess, South India

INTRODUCTION

I

HERE IS THE first attempt to render an account of the influence of Indian thought on American philosophy. American *speculation* might be a more correct word because it includes perhaps more than is nowadays commonly thought of as philosophy. Philosophy, as I use it, is a broader and more inclusive term than what is meant by it in academic circles; it may include wisdom literature and religious philosophy, as well as what generally falls under ethics, theory of knowledge, metaphysics, aesthetics, and logic.

To find out what American philosophers have thought about Indian philosophy, I have examined the views of the clergy of the eighteenth century, of the Transcendentalists in the nineteenth, of the philologists in the nineteenth and twentieth centuries, and of the academic philosophers from the time of James and Royce to the present.

In this examination of Indian speculative influence it is of importance to note that Americans had little commercial or military interest in India during most of the period with which we deal until after World War II. This period covers a time span of more than 200 years—from 1721 to 1945.[1] After 1945, however, the pattern of Indian influence has undergone enormous change as the behavioral sciences, agronomy, medicine, military science, and commercial interests far above all, have shown awareness of India's past, present, and especially its future posture in relation-

[1] But even earlier, Christopher Newport (1584–1617), who founded Jamestown in 1601–07 and who served with Sir Francis Drake, made three voyages for the East India Company (1613–16) during which time he is believed to have visited India. He died in Java.

vii

ship to the United States. They have brought with them a practical and professional intensity unknown during the leisurely and amateurish pace of idle curiosity for five quarter centuries.

II

Orientalism in Europe was an attack on conventional Christianity and monarchy. It was an assault on the economic, moral, and aesthetic foundations of Europe. Examples of this are to be seen in the *Arabian Nights* and Voltaire's *Zadig* and *The Good Brahmin*. Orientalism provided social and political satire, exotic sentimentalism, and "polemical expedients for use against national tradition." [2]

At first Europeans used Middle Eastern and Chinese sources because they were more available, but they turned at the end of the eighteenth century to India as the great literature of that country became known. Learned Oriental societies sprang up with Indo-European studies, and slightly later anthropology and Darwinism showed the futility of traditional doctrinal positions making possible an escape from the oppression of the industrial expansion and capitalism. Philosophically this was to be seen in Leibniz's concern with Confucian ethics, especially in his *De Novissima Sinica* (1697), and in the "De Sinarum Philosophia Practica" of Christian Wolff. This was an oration delivered June 12, 1721 on the occasion of his resignation from the Prorectorship of the University of Halle. Wolff, in claiming that philosophy had encouraged the Chinese to be lovers of the truth as opposed to what usually was being loved in Prussia, so enraged the local authorities that he was ordered under pain of immediate death by the King of Prussia to quit the University of Halle within twenty-four hours and to quit the kingdom within forty-eight. Goethe also interested himself in occultism all of his life, and was one of the first Europeans to become enamored of the literature of India.

III

American awareness of Indian thought came through several routes. First, it came through the literature and philological stud-

---

[2] Paul Masson-Oursel: *Comparative Philosophy*. London, Kegan Paul, Trench, Trubner, 1926, p. 20.

ies of Western Europe—from England, France and Germany. Second, it came via the reports of missionaries, ship captains and sailors. Third, it came by means of American scholars who studied Indian languages and thought, mostly in Germany and infrequently in France or England. And fourth, it came from scholars who themselves went to India to teach or study.

What Americans needed from Europe they also needed from India, although it was more inaccessible and costly. For, as Lewis Mumford has said in his critique of American civilization as it turned to Europe:

> America may be defined by its possessions, or by the things that it lacks. On the second count our country is plainly a place without a long past, without a court and an aristocracy, without a stable tradition and definite connections, without the graces and souvenirs of an old and civil community. . . . [it turned] away from Nature, externalized and unassimilated, the new generation turned towards an equally foreign and externalized culture.[3]

Despite American need for tradition, important segments of *homo liber et solutus* wished to sever European ties, and hence non-European cultures provided a wider scope for historical attachment. Some Americans found these things in India which had been a civilization three thousand years before England, Germany, or France.

Part of the unstated attraction of Indian philosophy was its narcissistic view of the self, a self easily transformed into the Great Self of cosmic proportion. This is the perfect confluence of egotism with egoism raised to the infinite. Such Americans as the Transcendentalists, disillusioned and alienated, "for reality . . . substituted a fiction, the center of which is himself [as the Oversoul or Brahman]"[4] Americans turned to Indian philosophy, from the Transcendentalists to the Theosophists, because they felt cut off from community, severed from past traditions and existing conventions. Christianity's inability to cope with the economic

[3] Lewis Mumford: *The Golden Day*. The White Oak Library, New York, Norton, 1933, pp. 203–4.
[4] Arnold Hauser: *Mannerism*. London, Routledge & Kegan Paul, 1965, vol. I, p. 113.

and social changes in American life after 1800 led to moral leadership going to other forces. These forces were economic-political, Transcendental and literary. Unitarianism, Universalism, Mormonism, Christian Science, Theosophy, all took some or considerable moral captaincy from Christian churches which had been so powerful during the Colonial Era.

Between 1820, when Unitarian doctrines became increasingly attractive, and 1878, when Charles Sanders Peirce enunciated the pragmaticist method, Indian philosophy played a number of differing roles in the complicated web of American theophilosophical thought. On the one hand were the first faint stirrings of rationalism (freedom of inquiry), scientism (sensationalism), naturalism (Darwinism, deism, and pantheism); on the other, theism, intuitionism, antimechanism, and antidogmatism revealed somewhat more conservative traits. Conservative though they appeared to some freethinkers, they still were quite radical compared to the continuing "orthodox" Protestant main tide. While the first tendency moved towards naturalism and materialism, the second enhanced spiritualism. These movements were frequently interwoven and orchestrated in such a way that probably no history will ever be detailed enough to untangle them. The one direction, however, was towards naturalism while the other led to religious concerns—and hence to the study of Hinduism and Buddhism. Pragmatism never completely extricated itself from these bifurcating nuances. As it moved leftwards it tended to become positivistic or naturalistic; rightwards it merged with heterodox religious developments.

From the root of Calvinism, Unitarianism arose; from Unitarianism, free thought branched. Transcendentalism shot off towards the religious pole in the 1840's while social radicalism focused on abolition and working conditions in the 1850's. By 1866 the Free Religion Association moved leftward from Transcendentalism which it found too constraining. It was the fundamental assumption of Free Religion that the individual have absolute freedom. His freedom would only be circumscribed by a rationalism bound by the universal manifestation of the laws of nature. Nothing could be more illuminating, Free Religionists believed, than the scientific study of man's religious history. As a consequence, adherents to Free Religion pioneered the introduction of the study of comparative religion, including Hinduism and Buddhism. Instead of heavenly perfection, mundane perfection was envisioned. In this progressive movement towards perfection every aspect of life became religious in their eyes. A contemporary movement in India—Brahmō-Samaj—also attempted to emphasize this very thing.

Farther to the left of Free Religion, the main impetus in American philosophical dialogue proved more impatient of religious considerations. This group included agnosticism, positivism, naturalism, atheism, and materialism. That this direction smacked too much of heresy for the academic temper of the time was obvious from the treatment of the teachings as well as the bodies of Thomas Paine, Thomas Cooper, and Col. Robert Ingersoll. A major factor here was the powerful grip exercised by the clergy on American education. Americans, then, who espoused the study of Indian thought, were among those addicted to intuitionism in method, individualism in ethics, and theosophy in metaphysics. After the appearance of pragmatism and naturalism, the philosophers concerned with Indian philosophy and religion still had spiritualistic, idealistic, theological, or theosophical ties right up to World War II. After that the situation altered somewhat revealing a slight shift towards naturalism. Thereafter Indian thought was seen as a fruitful field not only for religion, ethics, and metaphysics, but also for behavioral science and methodology.

Besides these deeply underlying causes of interest in Orientalism in general and India in particular, Americans were also filled with philological curiosity; they were searching for evidences of universal thought and speech; they were bored with industrialism and the late Protestant ethic which had rid itself of mysticism regarding economics and political practice. Americans were filled with self-doubts as well as lust for wealth. This made them hunger, even as they do today, for alternative paths of life.

Indians were themselves appealing because they were skeptical of the ultimate value of reason and scientific method which they well might be if they associated these with the results of European imperialism. Also enchanting was the idea that Indians had little belief in the panacea of progress. India seemed to demonstrate, in addition, a kind of primitivity and down-to-soul awareness of human values often overlooked in the American scramble for markets and exploitation of everything appearing to possess commercial value.

The Chinese outlook was more congenial to the French and the British. Outside of Germany and the United States men found less wisdom than raw materials and markets in India. Britons usually viewed Indian thought with cool detachment or outright hostility. Nevertheless, by 1813, they did set aside one lakh or 100,000 rupees for the revival and improvement of literature and learning for "the inhabitants of the British territories in India." Americans, on the other hand, were more open to Indian influences, particularly for religious reasons. Also Americans were more prone to succumb to novelties which spread among their ever-shifting frontiers like brush fires.

Indian thought made direct impact upon the cultivated American public in 1893 during the World's Parliament of Religions held concurrently with the Columbia Exposition at Chicago. But even though by 1897 American Manifest Destiny and Open Door Policy were firmly established, their impact was at first in Latin American and other vestiges of the Spanish Empire and second in China rather than in India where British control remained unquestioned until the independence of India in 1947. Not until the Second World War did Americans have any important trade or military relations with India and then of a scattered nature in such military bases as Bangalore and Calcutta. Americans generally favored Indian independence. When it came, the commercial interests of the United States for the first time became seriously concerned about our relations with India.[5] With the death of President Franklin Roosevelt the Cold War ideology changed all American relations, and by 1950 the Fulbright program in India initiated far-ranging cultural and intellectual events. Foreign trade, loans, and even gifts to India became more common al-

[5] Whereas in 1938 the United States provided only 6.4 percent of imports to India, by 1966 this figure had risen to 41.7 percent as calculated from data in *International Trade Statistics, 1938*, Geneva, League of Nations, 1939 and *Direction of Trade, 1962–66*, Washington, D. C., International Monetary Fund, 1966.

though the United States did not at first attain to anything like the height of British involvement.

Societies involving India sprang up as early as the 1870's with the formation of the New York Theosophical Society. Some of the fugitive journals before the turn of the twentieth century included *The Path, Theosophical Magazine, Theosophical Forum, The Pacific Theosophist* and *The New Californian.* All these were extant in 1894 and all were tied up with Indian philosophy and religion. The Ramakrishna-Vivekananda Centres were initiated in 1894. After World War I a number of Indian-American societies appeared, such as the Hindustan Association of America (1922) with its bimonthly *Oriental Magazine.* Out of this the India Society developed, founded in 1924. Pandit Jagadish Chandra Chatterji became the Director of the International School of Vedic and Allied Research in the same decade, with Dr. George C. O. Haas (1881–   ), the Sanskritist, as its secretary. In 1930 the New Orient Society of America was incorporated in Illinois to further cultural relations between the Orient and Occident. Like the International School and the Hindustan Association, it was dominated by scholars. Ananda K. Coomaraswamy was the founder and first president of the India Cultural Centre in New York and was the first honorary president of the National Committee for India's Freedom with headquarters in Washington, D. C. The Vedanta Society of Southern California is today probably the most active of the Indian societies, with an estimated 400 members. Its journal, *Vedanta for the West* was established in 1951.

At the same time an increasing number of journals in the nineteenth century carried articles about Indian thought and customs, such as the *Journal of the American Oriental Society, Journal of Speculative Philosophy* (in its first issue), *The Open Court, The Monist,* and *The Platonist.* Others continued the practice into the twentieth century, including *Athenaeum, Atlantic Monthly, Asia, Century, Contemporary Review, Fortune, Forum, Harper's Monthly Magazine, The Nation, Outlook,* and the *Review of Reviews.* Topics varied from translations of the sacred Indian scriptures to the explication of principles of Brahmō-Samaj.[6]

[6] See Kurt Leidecker: Oriental Philosophy in America. In Winn, Ralph B. (Ed.) : *American Philosophy,* New York, Philosophical Lib., 1955.

IV

Americans enamored of language studies founded Indian studies on Indo-European philology. With the translations of Indian wisdom by the English, French, and Germans, Hinduism and Buddhism slowly penetrated. Sanskrit studies began with Isaac Nordheimer teaching its intricacies at The City University of New York as early as 1836. At Yale Edward Elbridge Salisbury (1814–1901 taught Sanskrit as early as 1841. From 1836 to 1890 nearly all instruction in Indian studies was carried on by men whose primary concern was either Indian languages and literature or Asian religion. Theological seminaries found it useful as well as stimulating to institute the study of Hinduism and Buddhism.

V

After 1890 courses in Indian philosophy began at Harvard University under the persuasion of James H. Woods, for many years chairman of its philosophy department. By the end of World War I, Indian thought was taught in departments of Sanskrit at Johns Hopkins, Yale, Columbia, Chicago, and California at Berkeley and in courses of comparative religion at such institutions as Union Theological Seminary. Sporadic teaching of Indian thought occurred in the philosophy departments at the following universities: Pennsylvania, Nebraska, Washington, and at Oberlin College. Between the two World Wars no philosophy department offered advanced work in Indian philosophy. But after World War II some work could be had at the Universities of Hawaii and Virginia (at Mary Washington College). In the past few years Indian thought has been taught at the graduate level at the State University of New York at Buffalo, at the University of Hawaii, Minnesota, Wisconsin, and at Harvard University where a joint degree in Indian philosophy and Sanskrit has been available since the 1950's.

We have seen the development, then, from idle curiosity about Indian thought in the eighteenth century to professional expertness in the last half of the twentieth. More Americans today read the Indian scriptures in Sanskrit or translations than perhaps read the classics in the eighteenth century. It can no longer be said that Americans are ignorant of the rich philosophical literature of India.

ACKNOWLEDGMENTS

I wish to thank the following journals for permitting me to use the material I had originally published in their pages. They include *The Journal of the History of Ideas, The Personalist, Philosophy East and West,* and *Philosophy and Phenomenological Research.*

My research has been made possible by a grant from the Penrose Fund of the American Philosophical Society, by a grant from the Research Foundation of the State University of New York, and by a fellowship from the American Institute of Indian Studies. I am greatly indebted to these funding sources.

I also owe many thanks to W. Norman Brown of the University of Pennsylvania, Solomon Katz of the University of Washington, Karl Potter of the University of Minnesota, John C. Plott of Marshall University, and the following scholars at the State University of New York at Buffalo: Willard H. Bonner, Marvin Farber, Peter Hare, and W. T. Parry.

The staffs of Lockwood Memorial Library in Buffalo and the Library of Congress have been of continuous assistance to me in locating research material, especially Mrs. W. Dzewenietsky and Mrs. Ellen Mack Schultz, for which I am truly grateful.

For the preparation of the manuscript I am indebted to Miss Donna Aiple.

D.R.

Buffalo

CONTENTS

THE PHILOSOPHY OF INDIA AND ITS IMPACT ON AMERICAN THOUGHT

Chapter I

SEARCH FOR THE EARLIEST INDIAN
INFLUENCES

I

ONE OF THE earliest references to India by an American intellectual is to be found in Cotton Mather's *India Christiana* [1]
published in Boston in 1721. Mather learned very little Indian
thought from his correspondence with the German missionaries
Bartholomew Ziegenbalg (d. 1719) and Heinrich Gründler (d.
1720), but he at least heard that the people of South India had
opinions that he not only found extraordinary but that he could
feel superior to. How Ziegenbalg heard of Mather we do not
know. He felt it urgent, however, that he and Mather correspond
since they were both somehow involved in Indian missionary
work: the one with the East Indian, the other with the West
Indian. Ziegenbalg with Heinrich Plutschau was the first Protestant missionary in India, landing there in 1706. The earliest
American missionaries to attempt to convert the East Indians
were Judson and Newell in 1812, but since the British government "had not yet learned that the Christian religion was a
greater force to preserve India to England than the army itself,
ordered their expulsion from the country." [2] Judson subsequently
served long in Burma.

---

[1] The full title of this work is: India Christiana, A Discourse, Delivered unto the
Commissions for the GOSPEL among the American Indians Which is accompanied
with several Instruments relating to the Glorious Design of Propagating our Holy
Religion in the Eastern as well as the Western India An Entertainment which they
are waiting for the Kingdom of GOD will receive as Good News from a far Country. Boston in New England, B. Green, 1721.

[2] John Fletcher Hurst: *Indika.* New York, Harper & Brothers, 1891, p. 435. See
also *Biographie Universelle Ancienne et Moderne.* Paris, L. G. Michaud, 1828, vol.
52, pp. 325–328.

Ziegenbalg addressed Mather at "Boston, West Indies" asking
for advice and information in dealing with the Indians of the
West.

According to Mather:

> We rejoice in what our Dutch [German?] Brethren have done in the
> East-Indies, where the Schoolmasters have taught some Hundreds of
> Thousands, to recite the Lords-Prayer, the Creed, the Ten Command-
> ments, a Morning-Prayer, and Evening-Prayer, a Blessing before eating
> and after.[3]

To have reached hundreds of thousands in fifteen years was no
small feat. Mather also states that:

> We shall Remember our dear Brethren, of the Danish Mission as far
> off as Malabar. . . . I shall recite a passage in one of their Letters:
> "Whenever the Sun riseth in these Eastern Parts of the world, it is
> always Surrounded with Thick Clouds, the common People of the
> Malabarians tell us that these Clouds are huge overgrown Giants, thro'
> which the Sun every Morning must fight his way." [4]

This report of what may well be South Indian epic poetry indicates that the Malabarians who were dealing with the Dutch
[German?] missionaries had retained at least a touch of the early
naturalistic worship. Or is it possible that they were not quite
serious with the earnest Dutch [German?]?

We are interested to note that the reaction of the Indians of the
South to the blandishments of the Dutch [German?] missionaries
is described as:

> The Pagans were generally possessed with an utter aversion to the
> Christian Religion; and this for no other Reason, but because they saw
> so much Impiety and Profaneness abounding among those that Call
> themselves by This Name.[5]

If the Indians knew as little about Christianity as they did
about English trade, this is easy to comprehend from an intellectual as well as moral point of view. According to Richard

---

[3] Mather: *India Christiana*, p. 35.

[4] *Ibid.*, p. 44. Matthew Ricci, first Christian missionary to China, was informed
that "They say that at night they hide the sun under a mountain, named Siumi,
which has its base twenty-four thousand miles under the sea." *China in the Six-
teenth Century: The Journals of Matthew Ricci: 1583–1610.* Louis J. Gallagher,
Trans., New York, Random House, 1953, p. 328.

[5] *Ibid.*, p. 58.

Whately (1787–1863) ". . . it is positively stated that the Hindoos at this day believe the honorable East India Company to be a venerable old lady of high dignity, residing in this country [England]." [6] The author of the earlier comment on the resistance of the Indians is John Ernest Gründler, responding to Mather instead of Ziegenbalg, who had "been taken from the vineyard" by the time he was ready to answer all of Mather's inquiries from Boston. Gründler's simplicist analysis of the resistance of the Indians must be at least partially attributed to his relative ignorance of Hindu religion.

It is worthy of notice at this time that John Parker Boyd (1764–1830), representing a military interlude to the predominantly missionary activity, went to India in 1789. There he equipped three battalions of native troops to the satisfaction of the then nizam, Ali Khan of Hyderabad. Ali Khan then gave Boyd command over 10,000 men. Boyd left India in 1808 and became a brigadier general in the War of 1812. And John Lowell (1799–1836), another American to visit India at this time, inherited a fortune from his father Francis Cabot Lowell (a pioneer in cotton manufacturing), attended Harvard and made voyages to India in 1816–17. After the death of his wife and two daughters in 1830–31 he spent the rest of his short life traveling in Europe and Asia, dying in Bombay.

At the time early European Protestant missionary efforts in India were under way, the Great Revival of 1798–1801 swept the colonies. The effects of it were noticeable from 1786 to 1840 at which time most of the accomplishments of the English Baptist cobbler, William Carey, in India served as an inspiration to such men as Samuel J. Mills (1783–1818), a young Congregationalist who felt the call to become active in the foreign field. And in 1812 Adoniram Judson, Luther Rice, and three other men set sail for India as agents of the American Board of Commissioners for Foreign Missions. En route to India, Judson and Rice were converted to Baptist principles and upon arriving in Calcutta they were immersed.[7] The missions in Ceylon and Hawaii were estab-

[6] Richard Whately, Historic doubts relative to Napoleon Bonaparte. In Houston Peterson (Ed.) : *Essays in Philosophy*. New York, Pocket Bks., 1959, p. 169.

[7] Baptist missionaries of Serampore offered to begin a series of Sanskrit publications at the time the Asiatic Society of Bengal was founded by thirty men, January 15, 1784.

lished in 1814.[8] Judson (1788–1850) graduated from Brown University, entered Andover Theological Seminary, and there headed a group of students who petitioned the General Association of Massachusetts to send them abroad as missionaries. As a result the American Board of Commissioners for Foreign Missions was created. Judson translated the Bible into Burmese and made a Pāli dictionary.

The Great Awakening seemed overdue according to the view of Lyman Beecher in the 1790's, for in those years Yale College, unjustly famous for its impeccable conservatism, had a class made up of infidels who called each other such names as Voltaire, Rousseau, and D'Alembert. This infidelity might also be applied to the classes at Dartmouth and the University of Georgia at the time.[9] It is said that attendance at services of worship declined noticeably in those days, and many congregations averaged no more than four or five new members a year. In many parts of the South, Sunday became a day of "riot and drunkenness." The Presbyterian General Assembly of 1798 noted with apprehension "a general dereliction of religious principles and practices among our fellow citizens . . . and an abounding infidelity, which in many instances tends to atheism itself." [10] And as Lewis Mumford expressed it,

> For a whole generation the classical myth held men in its thrall; the notion of returning to a pagan polity, quaintly modified by deism, was a weapon of the radical forces in both America and France.[11]

By 1813, nearly a hundred years after Ziegenbalg, the British had decided that missionary work was not strictly objectionable and so allowed the American Board entry to India. After the American Board, followed the American Presbyterian Mission in 1834, the American Baptist Missionary Union in 1836, the American Evangelic Lutheran Mission in 1842, the American Reformed Mission in 1853, and by 1883 the Disciples of Christ. Besides the rather sparse reports of the heathenish philosophy from these

[8] Clifton E. Olmstead: *Religion in American Past and Present.* Englewood Cliffs, Prentice-Hall, 1961, pp. 70–71.
[9] Olmstead, p. 54.
[10] *Ibid.,* p. 55.
[11] Mumford: *Sticks and Stones.* New York, Dover, 1955/1924, p. 59.

vigorous Christian organizations, there was information emanating from the Baptist Missionary Society of England founded in 1793 and the London Missionary Society, which began converting the heathen in India in 1798. The American Board of Commissioners for Foreign Missions sent Gordon Hall and Samuel Nott to Western India, who arrived in Bombay February 11, 1813. They assumed the name American Marathi Mission after they were once asked to leave and then allowed to return by the East India Company.[12] Roman Catholic missions to India had of course been instituted much earlier, by Francis Xavier who landed in Goa on May 6, 1542, with the consequence that scattered information about Indian thought such as that reported in French by the missionary Abbé J. A. Dubois [13] was available.

II

Besides missionary activity, there was the Indian trade of the American sailing ships, begun as early as 1787 [14] from Salem to Boston—usually to Calcutta. The American ships brought back spices, indigo, and fine cloth as well as some notion of Indian culture and thought.[15]

Official American intercourse with India began in 1794 when the East India Company allowed the American shippers to trade directly with India provided that they did not undertake a circuitous commerce via Europe.[16] Within eleven years, however, even though the India trade was lucrative, the Jefferson Embargo soon

[12] Samuel Macauley Jackson (Ed.) : *The New Schaff-Herzog Encyclopedia of Religious Knowledge.* New York, Funk, 1909, vol. V, p. 477.

[13] Abbé Dubois: *Hindu Manners, Customs and Ceremonies,* 3rd. ed. Oxford, Clarendon Press, 1943. (1st ed. 1815[?].)

[14] The year that William Duane (1760–1835) went to Calcutta to establish the *Indian World.* Because of resistance to the East India Company he was deported from India. Upon returning to the United States he became co-editor of the Philadelphia *Aurora* which became a powerful Jeffersonian paper. When he was arrested under the Sedition Act, Jefferson saw that the charges against him were dropped.

[15] John T. Reid: Indian Influence in American Literature and Thought. *Hyphen,* Nov.–Dec., 1962, p. 19. There are many interesting artifacts in the Salem Museum showing what the American sailors brought back with them from India during those early days.

[16] American trade was called "clandestine and illicit," but was encouraged by British private merchants who had more than a million dollars invested in American ships. C. H. Philips: *The East India Company 1784–1834.* Manchester, Manchester Univ. Press, 1961, p. 106.

crippled it.[17] Ironically enough Jefferson himself lost money by his own embargo.[18] But missionary work made some commerce still possible during the embargo and indeed, as reported April 30, 1808, by Rev. William Bentley, an outstanding worthy of Salem, "Several of our vessels that pushed out at first notice of the Embargo have returned."[19] Bentley (1759–1819) was Thomas Jefferson's choice for the first president of the University of Virginia and Jefferson regretted that Bentley was so attached to Salem that he could not leave. It is said that "He sought for truth in the Orient and found much long before 'The Light of Asia' appeared."[20] It is true that Bentley had a

> liberal and investigating mind and a catholic view of Christianity. . . . A man of great linguistic and philological gifts, he is said to have read more than twenty languages, including Arabic and Persian. . . . The credentials of the Tunisian Ambassador were sent from Washington to be translated by him.[21]

Bentley reveals himself an astute observer of the human comedy and tragedy, yet is of interest to us primarily because of his comments on events relating to India during these early days. We learn from the diary of 1790–92 that Bentley,

> had the pleasure of seeing for the first time a native of the Indies from Madras. He is of very dark complexion [*sic*], long black hair, soft countenance, tall, and well proportioned. He is said to be darker than Indians in general of his own cast [*sic*], being much darker than any native Indians of America. I had no opportunity to judge of his abilities, but his countenance was not expressive. He came to Salem with Capt. J. Gibaut and has been in Europe.[22]

There are so few other references to India in Bentley that it will not take up much space to quote most of them.

[17] The embargo was put into effect on December 22, 1807.

[18] See Paul K. Padover: *Jefferson*. New York, New Am. Lib., 1955, pp. 132, 162.

[19] William Bentley: *The Diary of William Bentley, D.D.* Salem, Mass., Essex Institute, 1905, vol. III, p. 356.

[20] Marguerite Dalrymple: An address on Rev. William Bentley, November 26, 1897 [this when she was eighty-seven]. In Bentley, vol. I, p. xxiii.

[21] Joseph G. Waters: Biographical Sketch of Rev. William Bentley. In Bentley, vol. I, p. xviii.

[22] Bentley, vol. I, p. 228.

Capt. Gibaut arrived after a voyage of three years from India having been detained and embargoed in different ports 17 months. . . . Stopped at the Cape of Good Hope long enough to have a share of British Insolence, and has been safely returned. [May 1, 1794.] [23]

Mr. Nathanial Bowditch Lately arrived from a Voyage to India. [January 4, 1804.] [24]

Each of the brethern bore some Indian curiosity and the palanquin was borne by the negroes dressed in nearly the Indian manner. [January 4, 1804.] [25]

This morning arrived Capt. B. Crowninshield of this Town from India in the New Ship America. He is in health with all his crew. Good voyage. [June 8, 1805.] [26]

This day the Ship America of the firm of Crowninshield sailed for Europe and thence for India. [June 26, 1805.] [27]

In 1793, 23 Jan. went in same ship Henry for India. In 1794 returned, 12 Nov. from Calcutta. This is Jacob Crowninshield, Salem merchant and Member of Congress.[28]

A leopard is shown in Salem 4' long and 2' high from India about 8 mos. old.[29]

The eldest son of Dr. Lathrop in India. A man of abilities but eccentric, bred to the law and now an editor of a paper in Calcutta.[30]

Yesterday we had the annual dinner of the East India Society. It began in 1799. The Circumnavigation of Africa is the condition of admittance. [November 5, 1818.] [31]

[23] *Ibid.,* vol. II, p. 88.

[24] *Ibid.,* vol. III, p. 68. It is noteworthy that in 1801 Ramdoolal Dey, Calcutta merchant, was sent a gift of a portrait of George Washington painted by Gilbert Stuart in return for his help to American merchants of Boston and Salem. Jack Anderson: The Washington merry-go-round. *Buffalo Courier Express,* February 22, 1964.

[25] Bentley, vol. III, p. 68.

[26] *Ibid.,* vol. III, p. 164.

[27] *Ibid.,* vol. III, p. 168. It may interest the reader to know that one ship mentioned was 337 tons (vol. IV, p. 547) and that a three-masted schooner of Salem was about 100 feet long.

[28] *Ibid.,* vol. III, p. 356.

[29] *Ibid.,* vol. III, p. 408.

[30] *Ibid.,* vol. III, p. 414.

[31] *Ibid.,* vol. IV, p. 558.

Finally, the last quotation of interest to us runs as follows:

> By the news we have from India we learn that the Missionaries which
> went in a Salem Vessel had not had a kind reception and had been
> forbidden a landing, and even bonds had been required that all
> persons associated with such a Mission should not be landed.
> [December 13, 1812.] [32]

William Bentley House, Salem, Massachusetts (courtesy Peter Hare).

It is not clear whether the missionaries here referred to are English or American. That their intent was "the universal dissemination of Christianity in India," [33] despite such strong evidence that the Hindus and other Indians were indifferent to any form of Christian teaching, attests to their zeal.

Ralph Waldo Emerson was introduced to Indian thought in the 1820's by his aunt, Mary Moody Emerson, who wished him to

[32] *Ibid.*, vol. IV, p. 138.
[33] C. H. Philips, p. 158.

read about Ram Mohun Roy and his broad views on religion. It is not clear to what extent Mary Moody Emerson assented to the opinions of Ram Mohun Roy, yet one might suppose that as long as his remarks were addressed to the English they would not stir much American hostility except in the exceptionally narrow. In answering a common charge of the day, Roy states:

> Before "A Christian" indulged in a tirade about persons being "degraded by *Asiatic* effeminacy," he should have recollected that almost all the ancient prophets and patriarchs venerated by Christians, nay even Jesus Christ himself, a Divine Incarnation and the *founder* of the Christian Faith, were Asiatics. So that if a Christian thinks it degrading to be born or to reside in Asia, he directly reflects upon them. . . . It is unjust in the Christian to quarrel with Hindoos because (he says) they cannot comprehend the sublime mystery of his religion; since he is equally unable to comprehend the sublime mysteries of ours, and since both these mysteries equally transcend the human understanding, one cannot be preferred to the other.[34]

Many Americans came to associate India with the half savage, half decadent peoples described by antagonistic British writers who became extremely critical from about 1836.[35] Part of the reason for the shift from mild approval to marked disapproval was that whereas eighteenth century Europe had much in common with India, this was no longer true after the second decade of the nineteenth century, because Europe was so fast industrializing and because Indians were becoming more critical of their colonial servility.

III

Americans were receiving information not only directly from Calcutta [36] and from Great Britain, but also from Western Europe, where Goethe first stirred enthusiasm for Kalidāsa in the eighteenth century. Soon followed the scholarship of Friedrich von Schlegel (1772–1825) and his older brother Charles August

[34] Louis Renou (Ed.) : *Hinduism*. New York, Braziller, 1961, p. 225. Evidently Roy had a touch of Hume.

[35] G. T. Garratt; Indo-British Civilization. In G. T. Garratt (Ed.) : *The Legacy of India*. Oxford, Clarendon Press, 1938, p. 410.

[36] Charles Brewer (1804–1885) made a voyage to Calcutta in 1821–24. When he returned he brought the night-blooming cereus to Hawaii.

Schlegel who died in Madras on September 9, 1789. F. von Schlegel's first acquaintance with Indian thought came through his reading of Heinrich Noth, who studied Sanskrit in 1664 and the Jesuit Hanxleden (d. 1793) who went to India in 1699 and later worked in the Malabar mission.[37] The work of Wilford "of the English service" was also known to Schlegel as it was to a few select Americans. It appeared in the collection of the British Society of Calcutta. Most of all Schlegel, whose work was known to Americans as early as 1809, praised the great endeavors of Sir Charles Wilkins (1750–1833) and Sir William Jones (1746–1794) and his own teacher of Sanskrit, Mr. Alexander Hamilton of the British Society of Calcutta, who later was a professor of Persian and Indic in London.[38]

Sir William Jones in 1786 announced the birth of a comparative grammar based upon his newly acquired knowledge of Sanskrit. Thereafter Friedrich von Schlegel wrote his *Über die Sprache und Weisheit der Indien* (Heidelberg, 1808) and a little later, a second brother, August Wilhelm von Schlegel (1767–1849) became the first professor of Sanskrit in a German university, at Bonn.[39] F. Schlegel's aesthetic works and his *Lectures on the History of Literature* became known to American readers through the editions of Henry G. Bohn. As early as 1815 the *Lectures* were published in German and hence available to Americans who commanded that tongue.

IV

While American intellectuals with religious, literary, and linguistic sensitivities of a certain scope welcomed any knowledge of Indian thought that proved edifyingly spiritualistic, it was also true that the more hardheaded like Benjamin Franklin and Cadwallader Colden found little in the ideas of the "Hindoos" to praise.

[37] Friedrich Schlegel: *The Aesthetic and Miscellaneous Works of Friedrich von Schlegel.* E. J. Millington, Trans. London, Bohn, 1860, p. 428.

[38] He also mentions in this account his indebtedness to M. de Langles, Keeper of the Oriental MSS. of the Imperial Library. Schlegel, p. 424.

[39] Holger Pedersen: *Linguistic Science in the Nineteenth Century.* J. W. Spargo, trans. from Danish. Cambridge, Harvard, 1931, pp. 18–19. America produced its own Sanskritists somewhat later in William Dwight Whitney and Charles Rockwell Lanman, the first at Yale and the second at Harvard, and Maurice Bloomfield at Johns Hopkins.

These philosophers and others like them, who founded the American Philosophical Society in 1744, thought of philosophy rather strictly as natural philosophy, by which they meant what we today mean by science, both applied and pure. By "American Philosophy" was meant the electrical experiments of Franklin, astronomical and meteorological observation, soil improvement, sheep and horse breeding, cartography, and botanical studies.[40] There were other Americans closely allied to natural philosophy whose work was later to reappear in American naturalistic philosophy such as Cadwallader Colden (1688–1776). By contemporary standards, even in the United States, Colden was not a materialist, although he inveighed against priests and held that knowledge is not passive as Locke suggested, but active. But he held that what men knew was the quality of phenomena and not substance itself. He was no idealist either and shared with Samuel Johnson of Boswell fame the view of Berkeley's philosophy that: "Can any thing be more ridiculous in all the following exploded School learning than this?" If Colden had any opinion of the Indian thought first made known to Europe during his lifetime he surely would have felt repelled by it with the possible exception of the Indian Sāṁkhya philosophy which was consistent in some way with his own dualism. In fact his own words are exceedingly close to Later Sāṁkhya:

> God in the beginning created a certain being, to which he gave the power of motion; and distributed this being, in certain proportions, in the several parts of the universe. The granting of this is not negative to the existence of spirits; they may, and undoubtedly both exist, without including any contradiction.[41]

Joseph Priestley (1733–1804) left England not to teach philosophy but as a subversive, fleeing persecution. When he examined the concept of immaterial substance which at that time created a furor because of Berkeley and his defenders, he found no truth in it. Like Colden he held that matter has dynamic qualities that

[40] Michael Kraus: Science and Curiosity. *Intercolonial Aspects of American Culture on the Eve of the Revolution.* New York, Columbia University Press, 1928. Although Franklin was a correspondent of the famous Orientalist, Sir William Jones (1746–1794), there is no record of their discussion of Indian thought. American Independence was their topic.

[41] Colden in Joseph Blau (Ed.) : *American Philosophic Addresses 1700–1900.* New York, Columbia, 1946, p. 303.

bring mind and body closely together. By implication, his critics thought, Priestley taught the mortality of the soul and seemed to be quite unclear as to what properties to attribute to God. How he differed from his naturalistic friends in his concern for Indian thought we shall presently see.

Joseph Priestley's son-in-law, Thomas Cooper, perpetuated his teachings,[42] epitomizing them in his *View of the Metaphysical and Physiological Arguments in Favor of Materialism*. He first described the philosophy of idealism (Berkeley and others) and then dismembered it in a fashion that would have made his father-in-law proud. He showed that immaterial substance is without causal efficacy, that perception may be explained mechanically through physiology, and indeed that the mind must be material because of its modifications by the body. What he has added to Lucretius' argument is largely examples from the then recent discoveries in biology. According to Cooper we must study external factors to find out ideals and habits, the environmental factors must be studied.

As President of the College of South Carolina, Thomas Cooper was tried for being a shameful atheist and forced to resign in 1833. Surely, such a man would not be enamoured of the systems of Hinduism being slowly disseminated from the salons of Paris or the *Bierstuben* of German idealism. These men were by no means alone in their opposition to the labyrinths of epistemological and metaphysical idealism. One ought to mention that as unalterably opposed as they would be to such flagrant misuse of intellect, they would not be far ahead of Benjamin Rush (1745–1813) who wrote a speech entitled "An Inquiry into the Influence of Physical Causes on the Moral Faculty," and stated that questions of conscience are beyond scientific investigation, although he was certain that physiological factors influenced man's moral faculty, an interesting behavioral contradiction that persists to this day. Christianity for Rush had its charms, but these may not be very clear to us, he thought, until science or philosophy extends the scope of human understanding.[43] Anything that would appear to

---

[42] Frederick Mayer: *A History of American Thought*. Dubuque, Wm. C. Brown, 1951, p. 71.

[43] *Ibid.*, p. 75.

restrict the human understanding in the way that Rush would have meant it, would doubtless be anathema to him and surely this might well include the Hinduism known to the Europe of this day. Ethan Allen, another tough-minded naturalist and patriot of the Revolution, was described by Alexander Graydon as having a "style which was a singular compound of local barbarisms, scriptural phrases, and oriental wildness," [44] but this wildness did not refer to anything in East or Southeast Asia, but rather to Persia and the Middle East. Emerson and the Transcendentalists frequently used "Oriental" to mean Hebrew or pertaining to the region appearing in Old Testament writing. Allen of course would doubtless agree with the views of Jefferson and John Adams with regard to the utility of such views as appeared in the sacred writings of the Hindus.

A general reaction that could be called peculiarly irreverent toward reports coming from Calcutta and other Indian ports via clipper ship indicated qualities that Commager attributes to the nineteenth century American mind. These attributes included a quantitative cast of mind, dislike of abstruseness and piety, and an aversion to tradition and precedent. [45] The hardheaded rejected the to them patent absurdities of "Hindooism" while some of their more idealistic American brethren took them to their bosoms. But as G. T. Garratt has pointed out concerning the English reaction to Indian thought, most Americans who knew anything of it probably found it repellent for reasons we shall soon discover. [46]

Despite the hardheaded company he kept, Joseph Priestley was the first "American" to reconstruct Indian thought for English readers. Like Alfred North Whitehead, he was an American by adoption in his later years. His work, entitled *A Comparison of the institutions of Moses with those of the Hindoos and the ancient nations . . .* , was published in Northumberland by Kennedy in 1799. Just slightly over three hundred pages, it is mostly an account of the religion, philosophy, and customs of the Indians

[44] John H. G. Pell: *Ethan Allen.* Boston, Houghton, 1929, p. 127.
[45] Henry Steele Commager: *The American Mind: An Interpretation of American Thought and Character Since the 1880's.* New Haven, Yale, 1950, pp. 4–13.
[46] Garratt, pp. 410–12.

through the sources available to him in English and French. Although slighter than the work of the Abbé Dubois it perhaps comes to grips more with modern ideas. Jefferson claims that it was done in a state of anxiety lest Priestley be unable to finish it. But considering this suggestion of haste, it is remarkable as to the number and quality of sources at his command.[47]

Priestley begins the introductory chapter by stating:

> The institutions of the Hindoos, civil and religious, are the most respectable for their antiquity of any that now subsist, at least of any that are extant in writing. The fundamental principles of these were probably prior to those of Moses . . .[48]

We are not surprised to find that Priestley has some sharp comments to make on the Hindu view of the physical world: "The Hindoo philosophy of the physical or corporal world is not more rational than that of the intellectual world. According to the Vedas the moon is much higher than the sun." [49] Yet, we are surprised to learn that "wild and confused as is the Hindoo account of the universe, it is far preferable to that which was generally adopted by the Greeks" [50] because "according to the Hindoos, the world has a creator; but according to the Greeks it had none." [51] Along this same vein Priestley quotes La Croze as saying that there are atheists in India [despite their theogony] and there are treatises in defense of atheism. As a parting shot, Priest-

---

[47] These include Ezourvedam: *Ancient Commentaire du Vedam* (Iverdun, 1778); La Croze: *Histoire du Christianisme des Indes,* 2 vols. (1758); *Sketches chiefly relating to the History, Religion, Learning and Manners, of the Hindoos,* 2 vols. (1792); Mr. Philips, *An Account of the Religion, Manner, and Learning of Malabar . . .* (1717); Henry Lord, trans.; *Histoire de la Religion des Banians & C.* (1667); B. Picart, *The Ceremonies and Religious Customs of the various Nations of the known World* (abridged 1741); *A Relation of the Voyage to Siam performed by six Jesuits, sent by the French King in 1685* (London, 1688); Alexander Hamilton, *A new Account of the East-Indies,* 2 vols. (1727); Donald Campbell of Barbree, *A Journey over Land to the East Indies* (Philadelphia, 1778). In addition, the authors and translators most cited are Sir William Jones, Langles, Wilkins, Holwell, Sonnerat, Dow, Bernier, Fablonski, Bogle, P. Della Valle, Delaport, Boulanger, and Chambers.

[48] Priestley: *A Comparison of the institutions of Moses with Those of the Hindoos and the Ancient Nations,* p. 1.

[49] *Ibid.,* p. 66.

[50] Priestley, pp. 71–72.

[51] *Ibid.,* p. 72.

ley quotes La Croze as also maintaining that in Malabar there are some who "live like brutes" with no religion at all.[52]

Ex-President John Adams' comment on Priestley is interesting even if he was unacquainted with the literature. He seems, first of all, to be loath to ascribe any virtues to a person taking a position that has materialistic overtones, despite Priestley's obvious Unitarianism. Ex-President Thomas Jefferson told John Adams on August 22, 1831, that he would procure a copy of Priestley's book in Philadelphia and he did send it to Adams in Quincy, Massachusetts. Jefferson assessed the work as "executed with learning and candor, as was everything Priestley wrote, but perhaps a little hastily; for he felt himself pressed by the hand of death." [53] By September 14, 1813, John Adams received the Priestley book, but judging by his feelings concerning Priestley as evidenced by a letter to Jefferson on July 22, 1813, he had certain reservations concerning it:

> If Priestley had lived, I should certainly have corresponded with him. His friend Cooper, Thomas Cooper, the American materialistic, pre-revolutionary philosopher who, unfortunately for him and men and you, had as fatal an influence over him as Hamilton had over Washington . . .[54]

But Adams was not solely against *Indian* philosophy as one might draw from his letter to Jefferson on July 16, 1814 when he says:

> In short, philosophers, ancient and modern, appear to me as mad as Hindoos, Mahometans, and Christians, No doubt they would all think me mad, and for all I know, this globe may be the Bedlam, Le Bicatre [*sic*] of the universe.[55]

For Adams admits that the madness of the Hindus does not compare with that of Grimm, Diderot, Frederick the Great, and D'Alembert.[56] Yet, when making comparisons to heighten what he believes to be ridiculous effect, he thinks readily of Hinduism as he does in a letter to Jefferson on June 20, 1815:

---

[52] *Ibid.,* p. 92.
[53] Thomas Jefferson: *The Writings of Thomas Jefferson,* Albert Ellery Bergh (Ed.) . Washington, D. C., Thomas Jefferson Mem. Assoc., 1907, vol. XIII, pp. 350–51.
[54] *Ibid.,* vol. XIII, p. 323.
[55] *Ibid.,* vol. XIV, p. 157.
[56] *Ibid.,* vol. XIV, p. 440.

> Who shall take the side of God and Nature? Brahmans? Mandarins?
> Druids? or Techumseh and his brother the prophet? [57]

He makes slighting reference to "Birma, Vitsnou, and Siv" in the
same year and in relation to superstitious practices of "the worship of cows and crocodiles in Egypt and elsewhere." [58] Perhaps
that Priestley had introduced Adams to Indian thought was unfortunate considering that he had such a low opinion of Priestley.
But his vinegar extended in many directions as we can see by his
beliefs that:

> Metaphysics I would leave in the clouds with the materialists and
> spiritualists, with Leibnitz, Berkley [sic], Priestley, and Edwards, and I
> might add Hume and Reed [Reid?] . . .[59]

Adams is even in doubt as to whether Priestley really has proved
what he set out to, indicated by the following sentence from a
letter to Jefferson in February, 1814:

> Priestley has proved the superiority of the Hebrews to the Hindoos, as
> they appear in the Gentoo laws, and institutes of Menu; but the
> comparison remains to be made with the Shasta [and the "original
> Vedams" of which Adams had heard], but had not yet seen.[60]

Jefferson's attitude concerning Hindu philosophy is probably
more sceptical than Adams', for whereas Adams admits that his
favorite reading is theology, it is clear that Jefferson would rather
read something of a scientific or technological nature that could
somehow be useful in government, farming or trade.

V

It was somewhat different with the Germans who found in
Indian religion and philosophy justification for a universal idealism of the most luxuriant kind. At first this German idealism was
not sympathetically received in America, but its uses became

---

[57] *Ibid.*, vol. XIV, p. 320.

[58] *Ibid.*, vol. XIV, p. 40.

[59] *Ibid.*, vol. XIV, p. 160. It is most unlikely that he is referring to Emerson's
mentor, Sampson Reed the druggist-philosopher born in 1800. It appears that Jefferson is the only American President to have much patience with philosophy.

[60] *Ibid.*, vol. XIV, pp. 106–108. Adams uses the form used by Priestley, the Shastas
rather than the śastras. Gentoo is used by Priestley as a synonym for Hindu. Some
of the synonyms for Brahma used by Priestley, based on earlier sources of course,
are Birma, Burmha, Brumma. See Priestley, p. xvi.

clearer just at the time that Emerson's aunt, Mary Moody Emerson, was introducing him to its esoteric lore. The American scene, dominated by Calvinism in the North and Neoclassicism in the South mellowing to a riper and fruitier philosophy blowing from Germany, was at least partially ready for the rich systems manured in the Indian subcontinent for three thousand years.

Despite negative reactions on the part of some of the leading intellectuals of the United States, Indian thought was eagerly studied, especially in New England which was soon to be struck like a hurricane by the Second Awakening. Transcendentalists around and in Boston hungrily picked at the available scraps provided in translations from India and Europe. Minute study of Asian thought began in France in the eighteenth century with scholars like Anquetil-Duperron and Bailly, the counterparts of Sir William Jones, Charles Wilkins, and Warren Hastings in England. It was fostered further by the foundation of the École des Langues Orientales Vivantes and the Asiatic societies in Paris, Calcutta, and London. In the nineteenth century, Chézy, Langlois, Fauche and above all Eugene Burnouf (1801–52) [61] carried on Indic studies which were transmitted to American readers. Burnouf, whose work was known to the New England Transcendentalists, was the teacher of Littre, Renan, J.J. Ampere, Barthélemy Saint-Hilaire and other philologists.[62] Americans who read French were able to procure Burnouf's *Introduction à l'histoire du bouddhisme* (1844), Saint-Hilaire's *Le Bouddha et sa religion* (1858–60), or translations such as *Sacountala* by Chézy (1820), *Bhagavata Purana* by Burnouf (1940–47), *Rig Veda* by Langlois (1849–51), *Bhagavad Gita* by Burnouf (1861), *Ramayana* by Fauche (1854–58) in nine volumes paid for by himself. It is note-

[61] The year of Burnouf's birth, Anquetil-Duperron published his Oupnek'hat [Upaniṣad] in two volumes (Strassburg, Levrault, 1801–1802), a translation into Latin of a translation into Persian from the Sanskrit of fifty Upaniṣads. The primary translation was made at Delhi in 1656–1657 by Pandits who had been brought from Banaras by the Moslem Prince Dara Shukoh, the son of Shah Jahan who had the Taj Mahal built. This same translation (read by Schopenhauer) was translated into German by Franz Mischel (Dresden, Heinrich, 1882). Burnouf credits Brian Houghton Hodgson (1800–1894), upon whose MS collection his own work was based, with being the founder of Buddhistic studies based on texts and monuments.

[62] Burnouf's *Gita* was translated into English by Charles Wilkins in 1846 with a preface by Warren Hastings. Hastings in 1786 recommended a translation of the *Gita* to the president of the East India Company and wrote a preface to it.

worthy that Victor Cousin, the so-called eclectic French philosopher, left out Buddhism from his famous lectures of 1829 because
Colebrooke's study was not yet available to him. This may be
thought curious because Hegel had read Colebrooke on Hinduism as early as 1823.

The French interest in Indian thought had several causes besides Aristotelian curiosity. According to E. M. Grant,

> It is by no means a novelty to assert that the philosophy of the
> Romantic school was essentially one of escape and protest oppressed by
> the indifference and incomprehension of society, writers celebrated in
> prose and verse their own "otherwiseness" and took refuge in a
> melancholy exoticism. Thus do we explain the extraordinary vogue in
> Romantic literature of Ossian, of the Middle Ages, of Spain and the
> Orient, even of America.[63]

But this of course is an explanation without an explanation. It is
not genetic, economic, manneristic or anything else. It states a
fact and then states another fact but does not bring them together
with a contextual tie. Nevertheless it confirms our knowledge that
Indian philosophy appealed to the alienated. Foremost was the
French concern with supernaturalism in religion, the Indian
treatment of which was peculiarly attractive.[64] Victor Cousin re-
flected the moderate view that whereas the *Bhagavad Gītā* is a
"monument du plus haut prix, et qui renferme tout le mysticisme
indien," nevertheless he felt that Indian sensualistic thought
might end in the bogs of fatalism, atheism, and materialism.[65]
Buddhism appealed to French naturalists also: to Vigny, Hilaire,
Michelet, Leconte de Lisle, and Taine.[66] There can be little doubt
that American Transcendentalists were influenced most by the
work of Burnouf, but that they were also influenced by other
French philologists as well, as by later lectures of Cousin, is
acknowledged.

[63] Elliot Mansfield Grant: *French Poetry and Modern Industry*. Harvard Studies
in Romance Language, vol. VI. Cambridge, Harvard, 1927, pp. 173–174.

[64] See D. G. Charlton: *Secular Religions in France 1815–1870*. London, Oxford,
1963, p. 146.

[65] *Ibid.*, p. 147.

[66] Burnouf, interestingly enough, gives an atheist as well as theist interpretation
of *nirvana* in his *Introduction à l'histoire du buddhisme indien*, 2e ed. Paris, Mai-
sonneuve, 1876, pp. 16–17.

German was scarcely known in Boston around 1815 although Dr. Bentley of Salem and Professor Moses Stuart of Andover both owned collections of German books.[67] Emerson began the study of German so that he could read *Wilhelm Meisters Lehrjahre* [on December 5, 1828].[68] Emerson owned Friedrich von Schlegel's *The Philosophy of History* in two volumes which was published in London in 1835. When Emerson was a child of twelve, George Ticknor (1791–1871) met A. W. Schlegel, the Sanskritist, while both scholars were in Paris. Ticknor remained in Europe from 1815 to 1819, during which time he met most of the intellectuals of international celebrity.[69] Emerson himself was influenced by A. W. Schlegel's Indianism through Coleridge—unfortunately, diluted Coleridge. Even though most American philosophers at this time were influenced largely by Scottish and English philosophy, there were some like James Marsh, who were influenced by Herder, Jacobi and Fichte.[70]

It would appear that Americans were chiefly influenced in their Indic awareness by the English, the Germans and the French. At the same time they got their information at first hand from the East Indians who were rapidly mastering English and beginning to write in that language. The first such to be mentioned is Ram Mohun Roy, a founder of Neo-Hinduism. In tracing the influence of Indian conceptions from the eighteenth to the middle of the nineteenth century, one striking fact is that whereas the British and French generally regarded Indian thought from a naturalistic (deistic or atheistic) point of view, the Germans and Americans regarded it from an idealistic and theistic or pantheistic perspective. The philosophers in each country used Indian thought to satisfy their own hearts' desire. Presumably the American Transcendentalists "needed" Indian philosophy as did the later Harvard idealists to a lesser degree. On the other hand, the Colonial Deists, the Evolutionists, and the Later Naturalists (after Santayana) did not "need" Indian thought.

[67] Van Wyck Brooks: *The Flowering of New England 1816–1865.* New York, Dutton, 1940, p. 76 n.

[68] Kenneth Walter Cameron, *Emerson the Essayist.* Hartford, Transcendental Books, 1945, p. 320.

[69] Brooks, *The Flowering of New England 1816–1865,* pp. 88, 190.

[70] *Ibid.,* p. 191.

VI

American thinkers who could not read German were treated to a translation of Friedrich Schlegel's lectures in 1818 and to August Wilhelm von Schlegel's extracts in Dennie's Portfolio in 1833.[71] These included material on Indian metaphysics and ethics and it may well be the source of the knowledge possessed by Emerson's aunt. By the 1840's, called by some the fabulous forties, some of the movements afoot were Abolition and Fourierism (called by Edgar Allan Poe, Furrierism), esoteric anthropology, spiritualism, mesmerism, pantheism, and phrenology. With such illustrious developments, the interest in Orientalism could not lag. Albert Pike (1809–1891) of Little Rock, Arkansas, the author of *Dixie* and *The Fine Arkansas Gentlemen,* had been a teacher of Greek in New England. As an ex-Confederate general he studied Sanskrit in later years and made a translation of the *Rig-Veda.*[72] As early as 1810, however, Philip Freneau, the New Jersey Huguenot, Jacobin, friend of Jefferson, and poet composer of *The Wild Honeysuckle, The Indian Burying Ground, Eutaw Springs,* had traveled to Calcutta as a skipper.[73] Even though we do not know the immediate effect, that a well-known American traveled to India in those early days is noteworthy.

I cannot ascertain precisely who first taught Sanskrit in an American institution of higher learning, but certainly one of the earliest was Isaac Nordheimer (1809–1842), professor of Arabic, Syriac, Persian, and Ethiopic in the University of the City of New York. In 1836 he taught "Sanscrit" on Wednesday and Friday from 7 to 8 P.M. Other members of this distinguished faculty of but eighteen were Samuel F. B. Morse, professor of literature and the arts of design; Rev. Henry P. Tappan, professor of intellectual and moral philosophy and belles-lettres, later president of the University of Michigan; and Willard A. Norton, acting professor of natural philosophy and astronomy.

[71] Brooks: *The World of Washington Irving.* New York, Dutton, 1944, p. 355 n.

[72] *Ibid.,* p. 369. Pike's *Indo-Aryan Deities and Worship as Contained in the Rig-Veda* appeared in Louisville, The Standard Printing Co. in 1930. It was a reissue of the first edition of 1872.

[73] *Ibid.,* p. 56.

Indian thought must have had the greatest influence upon those agreeing with it when they could understand it. And although no American thinker seems to have swallowed it whole, its influence was considerable with the Transcendentalists. Their interest was not only in exotica, but also in religious thought that could fill the vacuum created by disillusionment with Christianity, rejection of trinitarianism, and boredom with the old theological riddles concocted in Europe. Not only did Indian spiritualism fill a vacuum; it also provided weapons to strike out against the "sinister" inroads of science, scientism, materialism, naturalism, and a general indifference to the prestige of spiritual claims of both organized and unorganized Christianity. Although it must be pointed out that the sectarian self-satisfaction of most Christians was such that they might well be the last to look into the writings of notorious heathen. The Jews were far enough from the truth without American Christians searching among the fallacies of the Hindus. Perhaps another reason for the interest in Indian thought was to use it as a knife to skin away the analogous absurdities of Christianity—a Bayle-Voltaire approach. As fascinating as such speculation is, when we turn to the actual acceptance of Indian thought by the New England Transcendentalists, no other figure dominates the canvas like Emerson.

New England Transcendentalism was the first important attempt in America to formulate an idealistic philosophy. Every form of romanticism, idealism and mysticism before the nineteenth century had been rigidly held in check either by puritan or other religious dogmas or enlightenment sentiments. The Transcendentalists first abandoned Locke for Plato. Then they became susceptible to the charms of English and German idealism. In England they discovered Coleridge; in Germany, Schelling, Kant, Fichte, Goethe, and Schleiermacher. American Unitarianism was the soil that nourished Transcendentalism; German idealism was its sun. Schelling's starting point was Fichte's doctrine of the ego, to which he added a touch of Spinozism, incorporating the two into a system of identity. He meant by this that object and subject, real and ideal, nature and spirit, are identical in the absolute. This identity is perceived by intuition. According to Schelling nature is a negative, real, pole, in which resides a vital principle uniting all inorganic and organic existences in one complete organism. Opposed to nature is spirit representing the positive, ideal, pole. What Emerson was to call the "Oversoul," Schelling called the soul of the world, or the complete organism uniting the negative and positive poles. What this Transcendentalism had in common with nineteenth century Indian thought besides its metaphysics was that it was moral philosophy in action, a protest against philistine usage. Visitors to America at this time, such as Charles Dickens, were told that whatever was unintelligible would be certainly transcendental.

Emerson's bare-bone philosophy may be summed up in three theses: first, he believed in the unity of being in God and man; second, he believed that the material world was created by mind; and, third, he believed in the identity and universality of moral law in the material and spiritual universe. These are certainly consistent with Indian philosophy as popularly understood, and it is congruent with Indian philosophy in several of its *darśanas* or viewpoints. There is not an overwhelming amount of speculation in the famous six systems of Indian philosophy that would contradict Emerson's three axioms. Vedānta particularly is receptive in one of its three major forms to each of Emerson's theses. Little wonder then that gurus and yogis reading his essays for the past one hundred years have believed that they have hit upon an Indian philosopher with an Anglo-Saxon name who happened by chance to have resided in Massachusetts instead of Conjeeveram or reasonably near the birthplace of Śankarachārya. In what manner Emerson was able to synthesize Indian philosophy with that of his transcendentalism we shall now examine.

What is fascinating and instructive here are the tenuous threads by which the thought of one civilization is passed to another. Although Americans have had some direct contact with India, they rely almost exclusively on the scholarship of Western Europe for their knowledge. One thinks of the introduction of Buddhism into Tibet, which is on the borders of India, through the mediation of China, but there are few instances one can easily recall of such indirect influence. This has allied Indian thought in the United States with German idealism. French eclecticism, and English spiritualism.

Chapter II

EMERSON AND INDIAN PHILOSOPHY

I

TWO QUITE DIFFERENT American philosophers looked upon Emerson's concern with Indian philosophy as a kind of aberation: William Torrey Harris (1835–1909) and Charles Sanders Peirce (1839–1914). Peirce and Harris both wished to disassociate themselves from such concerns, but of the two, Peirce showed himself the more impatient. He says:

> I was born and reared in the neighborhood of Concord—I mean Cambridge—at the time when Emerson, Hedge,[1] and their friends were disseminating the ideas they had caught from Schelling, and Schelling from Plotinus, from Boehm, or from God knows what minds stricken with the monstrous mysticism of the East.[2]

Ralph Waldo Emerson (1803–1882), however, seemed of tougher stuff than his younger friend Peirce, for he could read the works of the mystical East without annoyance, yet without devouring it all uncritically.

Harris tried to explain Emerson's deviation in the following way:

> What Emerson says of Plato we may easily and properly apply to himself. But he goes farther than Plato towards the Orient, and his pendulum swings farther West into the Occident. He delights in the all-absorbing unity of the Brahman, in the all-renouncing ethics of the Chinese and Persian, in the measureless images of the Arabian and

[1] Frederic Henry Hedge (1805–1890) was a Unitarian minister and professor of ecclesiastic history at Harvard Divinity School.

[2] C. S. Peirce: *Collected Papers,* C. Hartshorne and Paul Weiss (Ed.). (Cambridge, 1931–35), VI, 86.

Hindoo poets. . . . It is the problem of evil that continually haunts him, and leads him to search its solution in the Oriental unity which is above all dualism of good and evil. . . . Finally, it is his love of beauty, which is the vision of freedom manifested in matter, that leads him to Oriental poetry.[3]

Emerson became the leading exponent of Indian thought among the Transcendentalists, many of whom saw it as not only curious and interesting but also as an antidote to the rising American materialism. It is a curious fact throughout history that materialism keeps rising whereas spiritualism seldom descends.

It had been hoped that New England would provide a kind of Christ's Kingdom in the Wilderness; instead rationalism, deism, and worldly concerns in Boston and elsewhere were setting a tone described at that time as low thinking and money-grubbing.[4]

That a number of the Transcendentalists themselves were coupon-clippers was scarcely recognized as a serious consideration in their rendering moral and economic judgments. Theodore Parker (1810–1860), for example, who was certainly not much taken with Indian thought, finds it convenient to purge Christianity by reference to some of the sects commonly compared to in the days of Unitarian and Transcendentalist influence. He says:

Of the five great world sects, the Brahmins, the Jews, the Buddhists, the Christians, and the Mohammedans, none started with such humane ideas, with such pious moral feelings in its originators, none had such a magnificent character in its founder, as the Christian sect, but no one has taught such absurd doctrines, none has practiced such wanton and monstrous cruelty, and I think there is none at the present day in which so great fraud is imposed upon the people by the priesthood.[5]

About 1836, several years after Emerson had begun reading the Indian classics,[6] and two years before he had read Heeren's *India,*

[3] Harris: Emerson's Orientalism, in F. B. Sanborn (Ed.): *The Genius and Character of Emerson.* Boston, James R. Osgood, 1885, pp. 372–73.

[4] George F. Whicher (Ed.): *The Transcendentalist Revolt Against Materialism.* Boston, Heath, 1940, p. vi.

[5] Theodore Parker: *Lessons from the World of Matter and the World of Man,* selected from notes of unpublished sermons by Rufus Leighton. Chicago, Charles H. Kerr, 1887, p. 400. This work was copyrighted in 1865.

[6] Emerson began reading borrowed copies of *The Edinburgh Review* between 1820 and 1825 so that he could read about India among other fascinating topics. He →

a group of intellectuals "with high moral aim" met together in Emerson's study in Concord to discuss new developments in philosophy, literature, and theology. At first called Mr. Hedge's Club, this association was born July 20, 1836. Soon thereafter it became known as the New England Transcendentalists. They were the first body in America, however loosely knit, to pay serious attention to Indian thought. Besides Emerson, the Transcendentalists included Theodore Parker, George Ripley, F. H. Hedge, Amos Bronson Alcott, Henry David Thoreau, William Ellery Channing, Margaret Fuller,[7] Elizabeth Peabody, Nathaniel Hawthorne, and Orestes W. Brownson. These New England spirits, with strong clerical backgrounds, or fideist leanings, found in Indian thought not only ideas with which they agreed, but suggestions as to the possible shape future spiritual developments might take if they were to be universalistic in appeal.

---

was between seventeen and twenty-two at this time, already a graduate of Harvard College. Emerson mentions "tasting" the *Bhagavadgītā* in Victor Cousin's *Cours des philosophies* (1828) in a letter to his brother William (1831) in his *Letters,* Ed. Ralph L. Rusk. New York, Columbia 1939, I, 322. His reading after 1836 included Sir William Jones, *To Narayena,* "Hindu Mythology and Mathematics," in *The Edinburgh Review,* and Vyasa's Ramayana. Jones was unanimously elected a corresponding member of the Historical Society of Massachusetts in 1795 but "the society had soon the mortification to learn that, nine months before the date of thir votes, the object of their intended distinction was no more," according to Lord Teignmouth, *The Life, Writings, and Correspondence of Sir William Jones.* Philadelphia, Classic Press, Wm. Poyntell & Co., 1805, pp. 416–17.

[7] Margaret Fuller as editor of the *Dial* after 1850 published some translations of Indian classics. Caleb Wright published in Boston in 1848 his *Lectures on India,* illustrated by ninety-two engravings. It stated on its title page that Wright had traveled more than 40,000 miles in collecting the material, most of it gathered in Hindustan "or India within the Ganges." This region, with a population of 130,000,-000 in 1846 [more than simply speculative?], has more inhabitants than England, Scotland, Ireland, Russia, plus the continent of America according to Wright. It described the people, their customs, their houses, temples, artifacts, festivals and the philosophical literature of the "Shasters." For much of the account, Wright depended upon his own experience including descriptions of ascetic postures, results of the caste system, yet he also quotes the findings of a few other people, mostly Anglo-American missionaries.

Appended to the work of Wright is a chapter by J. J. Weitbrecht on "A Description of the Shasters." This includes the four Vedas, the Upanisads and "Purannes," "Mahabharat," Bhagavadgītā, "Ramayun," "Nyay Shasters," the "Smritis," "the Mimangsa." Treated briefly are such prephilosophical topics as a description of Brahman, the inception of the world in the golden egg, followed by specimens from the Shastras such as the "Shiva Puran," Part II and others.

II

Emerson and the other Transcendentalists found Indian wisdom attractive because it was profound without being gloomy. The "puritan's harsh insistence on the preeminent importance of salvation was suited to the exigencies of reform, or of revolution, or of migration and settlement" [9] and was simply not sufficient to appeal to the spiritual hunger of Emerson. Emerson, of all the Transcendentalists, rose above the melancholy of New England and its relative emptiness of sun and a warm sea. His valiant cry in "The Method of Nature," read at Waterville College [10] in 1841, was that:

> We ought to celebrate this hour by expression of manly joy. Not thanks, not prayer seem quite the highest or truest name for our communication with the infinite,—but glad and conspiring reception. . . . When all is said and done, the rapt saint is found the only logician. Nor exhortation, not argument becomes our lips, but paeans of joy and praise. [11]

It is worth noting that early Buddhist sculpture contained most of the joy that was the heritage of Hinduism. Gradually the juice was wrung out of it until we end with the husk-like Bodhisattvas that frequently depress at least the nonbeliever. Emerson's fondness for Persian wisdom and literature also attests to his almost pathetic drive towards sunlight and the joy that mankind derives from it, not bundled up in storm coats, but naked and stretching with bare feet planted on the warm sand or the cool grass. Such was the naturalistic aesthetic charm of Hinduism for the Transcendentalists who were often unaware of it except for Thoreau who smelled it out. Thoreau's naturalist grasp was more scientific than Emerson's poetic and metaphysical embrace. Emerson's moral Hinduism consisted as much in his refusal to use the puritan homeopathy as it did in his delight in the emphasis upon *māyā*. His sense of depravity refused to bend to the ultimate

[9] Ralph Barton Perry: The moral athlete. In *Puritanism in Early America*. Boston, Heath, 1950, p. 101.

[10] Today Colby College.

[11] Milton Konvitz & Stephen Whicher: *Emerson: A Collection of Critical Essays*. Englewood Cliffs, Prentice-Hall, 1962, p. 59.

depravity of man. Emerson was not morbid. His sense of realism gave him balance in the judgment of the human condition. Here he may be contrasted with Jonathan Edwards, America's foremost puritan philosopher. Edwards made a business of moral virtue and was a death's head at a naturalist feast. Buddhism has also this quality when it is not cajoled out of it by the Taoists in China and the Shintoists in Japan who bring it light, sunshine, and fresh air. Emerson could never tolerate fanaticism or obstinacy and it was this that led him to adhere to the teachings of the *Bhaga-vadgītā* rather than to a more ascetic call.

An unrecorded appeal of Indian philosophy is the feeling of sympathy Americans had with Indians who were still under the heavy hand of the English oppressor. This became more noticeable after the World Parliament of Religion in Chicago in 1893 where the delegates from India were able in a personal yet unobtrusive way to gain sympathy for the cause of Indian independence. But earlier, Americans were delighted to observe that after his defeat in America, General Cornwallis was again beaten at least once near Madras at the ancient city of Kāñchī (Conjeeveram) by Dravidian soldiers.

Emerson called Sampson Reed (1800–1880) his "early oracle." With his friend John H. Wilkins, Reed founded Swedenborgian studies in the United States after resigning from his theological studies at Harvard. Reed began teaching in a small school in Boston and then became a druggist's apprentice. On August 21, 1821 Reed delivered a commencement address at Harvard entitled "Oration on Genius" which pointed out that genius is divine, but not necessarily of the church. Emerson heard this address. The church concentrates too much on death, no fault of the divine which one must listen to. Locke is not a sufficient guide, according to Reed. In 1826 Reed wrote 'Observations on the Growth of the Mind" in which he maintained that the spiritual world is real, that there is a spiritual as well as a natural sun, and that the divine and human are united within. That there is a supervoluntary power is evident in infancy and sleep, a notion that Reed reaches without any access to Indian philosophy. Reed's viewpoint is one not without parallels in Indian philosophy. That Emerson was impressed by Reed indicates in a somewhat different way how he might easily be receptive to Vedānta conceptions, although the notion that "the kingdom of heaven is within you" could well be the source of the idea for Reed or for Swedenborg without any access to Stoical or Indian metaphysics. Perhaps it is this background of Emerson that explains what has been described as

> Philosophy for him was rather moral energy flowering into sprightliness of thought than a body of serious and defensible doctrines. In practicing transcendental speculation only in this poetic and sporadic fashion, Emerson retained its true value and avoided its greatest danger.[12]

Comparing Emerson to the German system-makers, Santayana says that

> Emerson cannot rival them in the sustained effort of thought by which they sought to reinterpret every sphere of being according to their chosen principles. But he surpassed them in an instinctive sense of what he was doing. He never represented his poetry as science, nor countenanced the formation of a new sect that should nurse the sense of private and mysterious illumination.[13]

If we change "sects" to "academic schools" we might have the equivalent in Germany and the United States to what would readily come to mind when considering the growth of a spiritual school in India. In the one the ritual is highly circumscribed and unimaginative, appealing more to antagonism and a sense of virulent rightness than to the tinkle of bells and the gentle waving of incense smoke. In one passage in "Compensation" Emerson refers to the incorporation of the divine: "A plain confession of the in-working of the All, and of its moral aim. The Indian mythology ends in the same ethics."[14] Emerson himself found in Vedānta[15] an answer to his quest for absolute being, as illustrated in the Chandogya-Upanishad by the dialogue on the soul (soul which is equal to reality) between Svetaketu and his father. In his

---

[12] George Santayana: *Interpretations of Poetry and Religion.* New York, Scribner, 1911, p. 223.

[13] *Ibid.*, p. 223.

[14] Emerson, *The Works of R. W. Emerson.* New York, Tudor, n.d., p. 71.

[15] This was the non-dualistic Vedānta of Gauḍapada and Śaṁkara.

Ralph Waldo Emerson

journal at this time Emerson records, "Blessed is the day when the youth discovers that Within and Above are synonymous." [16]

Friendship and love are closely related in Emerson to Ātman. "Every friend whom not thy fantastic will but the great and tender heart in thee craveth, shall lock thee in his embrace." [17]

[16] Emerson: *Journals of Ralph Waldo Emerson*, E. W. Emerson and W. E. Forbes (Eds.). Boston, Houghton, 1910, vol. III, p. 399 (1833–35).

[17] Emerson, *Works*, vol. II, p. 294.

And if it is the duty of intellect not only to analyze and dissect, but also its duty to discover unity, parallelism, analogies, and similarities, then Emerson found these in Indian philosophy. Nevertheless, as Swami Paramananda has pointed out,

> This does not mean that Emerson borrowed, I believe that there cannot be any borrowing in the higher realms of knowledge . . . A gentleman once said to Emerson that he had studied all the different philosophies and religions of the world, and he was now convinced that Christianity was the only one; to which Emerson replied: "That only shows, my friend, how narrowly you have read them." [18]

According to Emerson, the intellect discovers behind polarity, behind the positive-negative, behind the laws on earth, the centrality of truth, the centrality of mind. To Emerson, "My dreams are not me; they are not Nature, or the Not-me: they are both." [19]

III

Besides being highly receptive to the Vedānta view of deity, Emerson was greatly influenced by the notions of *māyā* and *karma,* although transmigration seems to have left him a trifle chilled. Emerson's own understanding of *māyā* may best be shown by quoting his own short poem having that word as its title:

Maya
Illusion works impenetrable,
Weaving webs innumerable,
Her gay pictures never fail,
Charmer who will be believed
By man who thirsts to be deceived.
Illusions like the tints of pearl,
Or changing colors of the sky,
Or ribbons of a dancing girl
That mend her beauty to the eye.[20]

As Ram Mohan Singh has reminded us, Emerson frequently used books for their quotations alone. Even if this is true, then the mass of quotations concerning *māyā* that he gathered is evidence

[18] Swami Paramananda: *Emerson and Vedanta.* Boston, Vedanta Centre, 1918, p. 9.
[19] Emerson, *Works,* vol. X, p. 8.
[20] *Ibid.,* vol. IX, p. 348.

of his preoccupation with *māyā* as interpreted by the ancient
Indian philosophers. Some of these quotations carrying the kernel
of Emerson's beliefs, include the following:

> Hindoo theology teaches that the . . . supreme good is to be attained
> . . . by perception of the real and unreal . . . and thus arriving at the
> contemplation of the one eternal Life.[21]

> Truth is the principle, and the moral of the Hindoo theology,—truth
> as against Maya.[22]

Emerson goes on to say that:

> The first illusion that is put upon us in the world is the amusing
> miscellany of colours, forms, and properties.[23] Our education is
> through surfaces and particulars . . . as infants are occupied wholly
> with surface-differences, so attitudes of adults remain in the infant or
> animal estate, and never see or know more.[24]

For Emerson too, God is a reality and his method is illusion.[25] After
Emerson had composed "hamatreya," [26] according to Leyla Goren,
he was still playing with the idea of illusions. In 1861 he wrote
about the legends surrounding the successive *māyās* of Viṣṇu.[27]

Turning from Emerson's view of *māyā* to his view of *karma*, we
again note his great perceptiveness. Writing in his journal, Emerson says:

> The Indian system is full of fate, the Greek not. The Greek uses the
> word, indeed, but in his mind the Fates are three respectable old
> women who spin and shear a symbolic thread,—so narrow, so limitary
> is the sphere allowed them, as it is with music. We are only at a more
> beautiful opera, or at private theatricals. But in India, it is the dread
> reality, it is the cropping-out in our planted gardens of the core of the
> world: it is the abysmal Force, untameable and immense.[28]

[21] Emerson, *Journals*, vol. X, p. 162.
[22] *Ibid.*, vol. X, pp. 123–24.
[23] See Plato's *Symposium:* Socrates, Diotima, and the Ladder of Love.
[24] Emerson, *Journals*, vol. X, pp. 123–24.
[25] *Ibid.*, vol. VII, p. 505.
[26] A minor poem which includes a minor poem, called "Earth-Song."
[27] See Goren: *Elements of Brahminism in the Transcendentalism of Emerson.* New
York, Columbia, 1959, p. 39.
[28] Emerson, *Journals*, vol. VII, p. 123.

Not only does he bring out what Indian artists have symbolized through the cosmic dance of Śiva. For comparative philosophy [29] here is a splendid example of what awareness of a philosophy from the other side of the globe can bring to understanding of a "familiar" philosophy. Yet in his essay on "Compensation," Emerson shows his nineteenth century Yankeeism in the following lines:

> You think me the child of my circumstances: I make my circumstances
> . . . As I am, so shall I associate, and so shall I act.[30]

Universal law is unconscious and inscrutable with no act of grace possible on the part of God, since God for Emerson has been absorbed into Brahman. Universal law is both physical and moral; whatever will be, will be. Yet there are innate qualities in the individual waiting to be unfolded. Later, the pragmatists, first James and then Dewey, were to give this innate unflowering a specifically biological or biopsychological interpretation. For Emerson the individual seems to have more freedom to act than perhaps the Vedāntin will allow. And yet, having heard many pleas to the effect that Vedānta and other Indian outlooks are not fatalistic nor really pessimistic, I am possibly taking unwarranted liberties in holding that Emerson's notion of compensation here is more optimistic, as a child of American upward mobility, than is the Indian.

IV

A fourth influence of Indian thought on Emerson is to be found in his doctrines of the Oversoul, certainly an atypical conception in the history of American thought.[31] Kurt Leidecker has examined Carpenter's belief that this notion was not based upon an Indian prototype. It was believed by William Torrey Harris and John Smith Harrison that *Bhagavadgītā,* 8.3 was the prototype Emerson used, in which *adhyatman* easily yields "Oversoul."

[29] A distinguished medievalist from Arkansas claims that "comparative philosophy" has the same intellectual status as "comparative potato."

[30] Emerson, *Works,* vol. I, pp. 334–35.

[31] Yet it did attract adherence even in Jacksonville and Quincy, Illinois, and other Platonic centers along the Mississippi. See Paul Russell Anderson: *Platonism in the Midwest.* New York, Temple U. 1963.

That Emerson did not know Sanskrit is adduced by Leidecker to show the unlikelihood that Emerson did in fact borrow his notion from the *gītā*. Various translations with which Emerson was familiar, such as Ram Mohun Roy's or Sir William Jones', might have stirred his imagination more, Leidecker believes, than the Neoplatonic concept of emanation.[32] After scrutinizing the "Self-Reliance" essay of Emerson, Leidecker concludes that no sense can be made of *it* without seeing it "against the philosophical or metaphysical background of the 'Indian Self.' "[33] Relevant to this discussion is Emerson's poem published in the *Dial* magazine called "The Three Dimensions" in which he expresses an image of Creative Principle manifesting itself in diversity:

> Room room [*sic*] willed the opening mind, And found it in Variety.[34]

This aspect of vision is closer to Neoplatonism than to Indian views. Still many have said something important about Emerson's Oversoul; and nearly all have found passages to substantiate that both Brahmanism and Neoplatonism entered into Emerson's notion of Oversoul, and perhaps more besides.[35]

V

It is worthy of note that Emerson was much less influenced by Buddhism than Hinduism, although the reverse proved to be the case with Josiah Royce. Emerson first mentions Buddhism in a letter to Margaret Fuller, September 8, 1841, in which he makes the cryptic remark that "Buddhism cometh in like a flood Sleep is better than waking: Death than life."[36] It seems clear from his letters in 1835 that he is not certain as to the difference between Hinduism and Buddhism, or whether the *Bhagavadgītā* is Bud-

---

[32] See Goren, p. 41.

[33] Leidecker: Emerson and East-West Synthesis. In *Philosophy East and West*, vol. I, no. 2 (July, 1951), p. 43. With a conciliatory flourish John S. Harrison concludes that "A Hindoo term has thus been filled with Greek thought: or Greek thought has been capped with a Hindoo name. *The Teachers of Emerson*. New York, Sturgis & Walton, 1910, pp. 277–278.

[34] Goren, p. 42.

[35] According to Sarvepalli Radhakrishnan, for example, "Emerson's Oversoul is the *paramatman* of the Upanisads," for which he produces no evidence. See his *Eastern Religions and Western Thought*. New York, Oxford 1959, p. 249.

[36] Emerson, *Letters*, vol. II, p. 445.

dhistic in its message. By May 30, 1845, in a letter to John Chapman, Emerson seems to have cleared up this problem for he says:

> There is a book which I very much want of which this is the title.
> "The Bhagavat Geeta, or Dialogues of Kreeshna & Arjoon; in eighteen
> lectures; with notes. Translated from the original in Sanskreet, or
> ancient language of the Brahmins, by *Charles Wilkins;* London: C.
> Nourse; 1835." [37]

In the same volume of letters Emerson mentions that he read the Purana on a trip to Vermont [38] and that he thought of Thoreau as "Our Spartan-Buddhist Henry." [39] In 1843 Emerson asked the question, "Buddhism or Occidentalism, which is best?" [40] Perhaps this would be tantamount to asking today "Orientalism or pragmatism, which is best?" Obviously neither pair is mutually exclusive. It is curious that in 1835 when Emerson mentions "Orientalism" he is speaking of the following: That "God is a petty Asiatic king" is obstinate Orientalism.[41] Here by the Oriental man he means Abraham, Seth, and Job.[42]

Emerson's knowledge of Indian and Buddhist philosophy came from a variety of sources, but he owed a major debt to a translation of Victor Cousin's work under the title *Course of the History of Modern Philosophy* (1852) in two volumes. These were based on lectures delivered at Paris in 1828–29. What Emerson thought of Cousin's opinion that "The Vedan philosophy is the idealistic philosophy of India; it is, therefore, the most obscure," [43] we can only guess. What was Cousin's source of information? He derived his knowledge from Colebrooke's work (London, 1837) in Vol-

---

[37] *Ibid.*, vol. III, p. 288. See also vol. III, p. 290, 291 n and *Journals,* vol. VII, p. 68.

[38] Emerson, *Letters*, vol. III, p. 293.

[39] *Ibid.*, p. 455.

[40] *Ibid.*, vol. III, p. 153.

[41] *Ibid.*, pp. 505–6.

[42] *Ibid.*, p. 566.

[43] Victor Cousin: *Course of the History of Modern Philosophy,* O. W. Wight, Trans. New York, D. Appleton & Co., MDCCCLVI [sic], vol. I, p. 386. According to the Scottish historian J. D. Morell, in *An Historical and Critical View of the Speculative Philosophy of Europe*, 2nd. ed. London, John Johnstone, 1847, vol. II, p. 248: "America, too, has recently been arousing herself from the dream of practical utilitarianism and giving birth to a school of philosophy (grounded chiefly upon the writings of Cousin) which bids fair to prove as productive though not certainly as profound as the European sources from which it springs."

ume I, consisting of around 75,000 words. Colebrooke's essays in eight volumes first appeared in the *Transactions of the Asiatic Society of London* (1824–1828). It is interesting to note that Burnouf got his material from Houghton, an English resident in Nepal who communicated it to the Asiatic Society of Paris, having translated it from the Sanskrit. Cousin's roughly 14,000 words on Indian philosophy comprising Lectures V–VI of his *Course* also refer to the opinions of M. B. Saint-Hilaire concerning the *nyāya* logic. But it must be conceded that French Indianists were heavily indebted to Colebrooke.

The last known letter of Emerson to mention Indian thought was to Max Müller on August 4, 1873. It indicates the excellent mileage that Emerson had got out of his rather sparse sources. He says:

> All my interest in the Aryan is old reading of Marsh's Menus [there was no such work. Emerson probably confused this with Joshua Marshman, an editor of the work of Confucius], then Wilkin's [*sic*] Bhagavat Geeta; Burnouf's Bhagavat Purana; and Wilson's Vishnu Purana—yes and a few other translations.[44]

Emerson owned at least four of Müller's books, including *A History of Sanskrit Literature* (London, 1860, 2nd ed.), the *Works* of Sir William Jones (6 vols. 1799), Schlegel's *Lectures on the History of Literature* (2 vols. Edinburgh 1818), and H. H. Wilson's translation of the Rig-veda-sanhita (4 vols. London, 1850–1866).[45]

That Emerson was deeply influenced by Indian thought cannot be doubted. Furthermore it must be said that his writing would have been different if he had not known it. And this is not meant in the trivial or obvious sense. Not only American scholars have been aware of this, but Indians have discovered in Emerson a kindred spirit to which a voluminous literature attests. Protap Chunder Mozoomdar in "Emerson as Seen from India," points out shortly after Emerson's death in 1882, that:

---

[44] Emerson, *Letters*, vol. VI, pp. 246, 246 n.
[45] Kenneth Walter Cameron: *Ralph Waldo Emerson's Reading*. Raleigh, Thistle Press, 1941.

Yes, Emerson had all the wisdom and spirituality of the Brahmans . .
In whomsoever the eternal Brahma breathed his unquenchable fire, he
was the Brahman. And in that sense Emerson was the best of Brahmans.[46]

Herambachandra Maitra has said that Emerson's writings represent a union of the modern spirit with what was noblest in
ancient times.[47] And the literature on Emerson continues to be
written as I sit here myself writing it. When Principal A. S.
Narayana Pillai visited me in Grand Forks, North Dakota eight
winters ago (1962) he told me of a venerable scholar not far from
Trivandrum who is in the process of writing a voluminous work
on Emerson's philosophy in its relation to Indian thought; perhaps he is the same scholar of whom I heard when I lived in
Mylapore, Madras, in the early 1950's.

Emerson shared with many other American idealists the desire
to have the advantages of a spiritual community in a pragmatic
and practical world. Like John Dewey, fifty years later, he promoted attitudes and insights rather than develop a utopia. Neither could envision a political straightjacket for a country devel-
oping with the rapidity of America. So he emphasized what
Americans could learn from other civilizations. He believed we
could learn much from the wisdom of the Indians, especially in
those affairs where they kept a firm hold on the realities that
transcend the phenomenal. Although he found the epistemic useful and engaging in its own ephemeral right, he also wanted no
one to think that what gave the phenomenal its qualitative dimension was the ocean of the constitutive. It was awareness and
understanding of this spiritual being that would lead men to
appreciate Indian philosophy.

How Emerson's enthusiasm for Indian wisdom and its expan-
sive horizons was to affect Henry David Thoreau we shall next
consider.

[46] Quoted by Goren, p. 46.

[47] *Ibid*. "With Emerson it is ever the special capacity for moral experience—
always that and only that." Henry James: *Partial Portraits*. London, Macmillan,
1888, p. 46.

Chapter III

THE LATER TRANSCENDENTALISTS AND THE ST. LOUIS AND CHICAGO PHILOSOPHERS

I

HENRY DAVID THOREAU (1817–1862) was a member of the Transcendentalist Club between 1840 and 1841. In the summer of 1841 he spent considerable time reading the Hindu philosophy available in Emerson's library as well as other works including that of Paley. Thoreau had earlier mentioned in a letter to Helen Thoreau on October 6, 1838 that in his opinion the systems of Locke, Stewart, and Brown in comparison with an intuitionist approach must yield to it. He had been dried out by the Scotch common sense of Edward T. Channing, the Stewartism of Joel Giles and Francis Bowen. Other works read by Thoreau and found unsatisfying to him were Locke's *Essay on Human Understanding*, Paley's *The Principles of Moral and Political Philosophy*, Jean-Baptiste Say's *Political Economy,* Paley's *Evidences of Christianity* and Butler's *The Analogy of Religion. . . .* By his senior year at Harvard College there was a sudden inrush of Oriental and transcendental material. It is the belief of Joseph J. Kwiat that the Scotch school smoothed the way from the materialism of Locke to Coleridge and the Germans and its attendant transcendentalism.[1] Whether this proved its function for Thoreau is simply a surmise.

Emerson created no greater enthusiasm for India in his friends than in Thoreau whose first recorded impression of Indian

[1] Joseph Kwiat, Thoreau's philosophical apprenticeship. *New Eng. Quar.*, XVIII, 1, 1945, p. 69.

thought is found in his journal of 1841, the decade during which the American Oriental Society was founded (1842). Thoreau makes his imaginative experience of India concrete by referring it to objects of nature. In his journal he records that:

> I cannot read a sentence in the book of the Hindoos without being elevated as upon the table-land of the Ghauts. It has such a rhythm as the winds of the desert, such a tide as the Ganges, and seems as superior to criticism as the Himmaley Mounts. . . . The great thought is never found in mean dress, but is of virtue to ennoble any language.[2]

After his summer of 1841 in Emerson's library reading the Hindu material to be found there, Thoreau read widely as well as deeply in the Indian wisdom literature, religion and philosophy, but frequently with more an eye to the enjoyment of new modes of description than for philosophical concepts. Not that Thoreau was without capability in abstract thought, but rather that his love of nature expresses itself as it did one hundred years later for Llewelyn Powys in the visual sense, smells, sounds, and tactility. As Christy has pungently said:

> The sulphur-like pollen of the pitch pine covering Walden pond, the stones and rotted shore-strewn wood brought back his [Thoreau's] thoughts of Kalidasa.[3]

In a letter to H. G. O. Blake in 1849 [4] Thoreau writes:

> Free in this world as the birds in the air, disengaged from every kind of chains, those who practice the *yoga* gather in Brahma the certain fruit of their works . . . Depend upon it that, rude and careless as I

---

[2] Henry Thoreau: *Journal,* Bradford Torrey and Francis H. Allen (Ed.). Boston, Houghton, 1949, vol. I, p. 266.

[3] Arthur Christy, *The Orient in American Transcendentalism, A Study of Emerson, Thoreau, and Alcott.* New York, Columbia, 1932, p. 192.

[4] Charles Eliot Norton (1827–1908), a Harvard graduate and editor of *North American Review* with James Russell Lowell travelled in India in 1849 after he entered a Boston firm trading with the orient.

Two years earlier Maurice Barrymore (1847–1905) was born at Agra with the name, Herbert Blythe, went to London in 1872 to become an actor. Three years later he came to the United States as an actor and to father three more famous than himself: Ethel, Lionel, and John.

am, I would fain practice the yoga faithfully. . . . To some extent, and at rare intervals, *even I am a yogi.*[5]

By the most exacting standards of India, Thoreau did not of course live an ascetic life. From Thoreau's meditations at Walden Pond, on Emerson's woodlot, another great poet was inspired to act in such a way as to inspire the freeing of millions of semi-slaves. This was Gandhiji. As with Emerson and India, there was reciprocity between Thoreau and India, and in this respect, Thoreau may be considered an important avatar of Indian wisdom in the United States.

There is some reason to believe that Thoreau's

"skepticism about the future of our [American] culture" was chiefly received through the influence of the *Bhagavadgita,* early voiced in *A Week on the Concord and Merrimack Rivers* and more completely in *Walden.* It was at Walden Pond, an attractive tiny lake surrounded by woods near Concord, Massachusetts that Thoreau tested "the validity of the doctrines of the Bhagavad Gita." [6]

At the same time, according to Stein, he was proving to his contemporaries that "money is not required to buy one necessary for the soul." [7] It is in his *A Week on the Concord* that Thoreau pays honor to Charles Wilkins who first put the *gītā* into English. Thoreau's own reaction to the *gītā* is as enthusiastic as that of Wilkins [8] and Warren Hastings who correctly foresaw that it would outlast the English imperial rule in India. Rhapsodizes Thoreau:

In the morning I bathe my intellect in the stupendous and cosmogonal philosophy of the Bhagavat Geeta, since whose composition years of the gods have elapsed, and in comparison with which our modern world and its literature seem puny and trivial; and I doubt if that

[5] Arthur Christy: *The Orient in American Transcendentalism, A Study of Emerson, Thoreau, and Alcott.* New York, Columbia, 1932, p. 201.

[6] William Bysshe Stein: Thoreau's *Walden* and the Bhagavad Gita. *Liberal Arts,* No. 6, 1963, p. 39.

[7] Stein, Thoreau's *Walden* . . . , p. 40.

[8] On October 8[?], 1854 Thoreau wrote to Harvard librarian Thaddeus W. Harris asking him to deliver Wilkins' *Bhagavad Geeta* to the bearer. The changing book shows it to have gone out October 23, 1854. Cameron: *Companion to Thoreau's Correspondence.* Hartford, Transcendental Books, 1964, pp. 201–202.

philosophy is not to be referred to a previous state of existence, so remote is its sublimity from our conceptions. I lay down the book and go to my well for water, and lo! there I meet the servant of the Brahmin, priest of Brahma, and Vishnu and Indra, who still sits in his temple on the Ganges reading the Vedas, or dwells at the root of a tree with his crust and water-jug. I meet his servant come to draw water for his master, and our buckets as it were grate together in the same well.[9]

According to Stein, Thoreau rightly conceives of this vast spiritual amalgamation in the *gītā* under the symbolic aspect of water. According to Thoreau, "The pure Walden water is mingled with the sacred water of the Ganges." As I stood on the bank of the Ganges near Banaras in 1951 I hoped that Walden Pond was more pure for I was not to visit it for the first time until the summer of 1963. Although I could not see bottom then, I felt relieved that there was no picnic garbage about nor beer cans bobbing on the surface to attest to advanced technical development. Speaking of his diet at Walden Pond, Thoreau says, "It was fit that I should live on rice mainly, who loved so well the philosophy of India." [10] In addition he had Indian meal, potatoes, salt pork (clearly not a Hindu delicacy), molasses and salt "and my drink of water." In his chapter in *Walden* on "Reading" Thoreau says:

> that in dealing with truth we are immortal, and need fear no change nor accident. The oldest Egyptian or Hindoo philosopher raised a corner of the veil from the statue of the divinity.[11]

And perhaps prescient of the age of paperbacks he says, "The modern cheap and fertile press, with all its translations, has done little to bring us nearer to the heroic writers of antiquity."

> The Vishnu Purana says, "The house-holder is to remain at eventide in his courtyard as long as it takes to milk a cow, or longer if he pleases, to await the arrival of a guest." I often performed this duty of hospitality, waited long enough to milk a whole herd of cows, but did not see the man approaching from the town.[12]

[9] Thoreau: *Walden.* New York, Grosset, 1910, pp. 393–4.
[10] *Ibid.,* p. 78.
[11] *Ibid.*
[12] *Ibid.,* p. 358.

Thoreau's spiritual development was perhaps such that others felt that they would be intruding on Swami or Guru Henry. Yet, this thought is made more pleasant by reference to the spirit of the *gītā*.

> In proportion as he simplifies his life, the laws of the universe will appear less complex, and solitude will not be solitude, nor poverty, poverty, nor weakness, weakness.[13]

And sexual desires will not be sexual desires, and the biological and social needs of man will not be the biological and social needs of man . . . and so on. . . . One feels a certain impatience with such logomachy, necromancy, and a spiritualized necrophilosophidealaphagia—the devouring of imported idealistic philosophical corpses. It is the disease labelled by John Dewey as anti-naturalism-in-extremis. But this mood passes and Thoreau says in a moment of earthbound insight:

> Why level down to our dullest perception always, and praise what is common sense? The commonest sense is the sense of men asleep, which they express by snoring . . . Some would find fault with the morning red if they ever got up early enough. "They pretend," as I hear, "that the verses of Kabir have four different senses: illusion [*māyā*], spirit, intellect, and the exoteric doctrine of the Vedas;" but in that part of the world it is considered a ground for complaint if a man's writings admit of more than one interpretation. While England endeavors to cure the potato-rot, will not any endeavor to cure the brain-rot, which prevails so much more widely and fatally?[14]

Thoreau believes that one path to enlightenment away from brain-rot is to become released from the bondage of ignorance. This may be achieved, he thinks, by renunciation of concern for the gains and losses of temporal endeavors.[15] It is expressed in the *gītā* as "He who abandons all desires and acts free from longing without any sense of mineness of egotism—he attains peace." [16]

Thoreau's asceticism has been splendidly drawn by Stein [17] as

[13] Quoted in *Walden*, p. 427.
[14] *Ibid.*, p. 429.
[15] Stein, Thoreau's *Walden* . . . , p. 43.
[16] *Bhagavadgītā*, vol. II, p. 71.
[17] Stein, *ibid.*, p. 45.

he shows the ethical iconography of "vital heat" as opposed to "animal heat"; the chimney as the symbol of vital heat even when the fleshly animal body is absent. Stein quotes Thoreau as saying:

> Before we adorn our houses with beautiful objects the walls must be stripped, and our lives must be stripped, and beautiful housekeeping and living be laid for a foundation.[18]

Stripping denotes the sacrifice of egotism; vital heat in Thoreau represents tapas in Hinduism. Heat or ardor becomes the ascetic effort of the little self to join without, *māyā* the great self (*ātman*).[19] But the message of the *gītā* to Thoreau is not simply renunciation. There is also work to be done for as the *gītā* says: from exertion come wisdom and purity; from sloth come ignorance and sensuality. "Snipes and woodcocks also may afford rare sport; but I trust it would be nobler game to shoot one's self." [20] And according to Stein:

> Paragraph after paragraph is no more than [in *A Week*] paraphrase of the thought of the Upanishads and of transforming power of yoga. His stress is always on the encumbering of the flesh and on the capacity of the mind to transcend this condition: "I see men with infinite pain endeavoring to realize to their bodies, what I, with at least equal pains, would realize to my imagination . . . ; for certainly there is a life of the mind above the wants of the body." [21]

Thoreau uses the "imagery of cloud, eye, ray, and sun, the boat metaphor, the liturgical sounds, the allegorical rivers and oceans," [22] these elements that are derived from *devayana* (the path of and to God) in *A Week*.

I cannot resist including in this account an assessment of the *gītā* made by a leading Indian scholar. If what he says is true, Thoreau built into that classic what he needed for his own purposes. If what he says is true, then most Indian and Western

[18] Stein, *ibid.*, p. 45.

[19] Stein, Thoreau's *Walden* . . . , pp. 45–46.

[20] *Walden*, p. 423.

[21] Stein: *Thoreau's First Book: A Spoor of Yoga: The Orient in a Week on the Concord and Merrimack Rivers.* Hartford, Emerson Society, 1965, p. 18.

[22] *Ibid.*, p. 5.

interpreters have simply misread one of the most influential books of all time. But does that surprise us? Says D. D. Kosambi:

> To put it bluntly, the utility of the Gītā derives from its peculiar fundamental defect, namely dexterity in seeming to reconcile the irreconcilable [with all due respect to Kosambi, if this were to be considered "peculiar" in what way could we separate this fault from the same fault found in every major system of philosophy East or West?]. The high god repeatedly emphasizes the great virtue of non-killing (ahimsā), yet the entire discourse is an incentive to war . . . . The soul merely puts off an old body as a man his old clothes, in exchange for new; it cannot be cut by weapons, nor suffer from fire, water, or the storm. . . . The moral is pointed by the demoniac god himself: that all the warriors on the field had really been destroyed by him; Arjuna's killing them would be a purely formal affair whereby he could win the opulent kingdom. Again, though the yajna sacrifice is played down or derided, it is admitted to be the generator of rain, without which food and life would be impossible. This slippery opportunism characterizes the whole book. Naturally, it is not surprising to find so many Gītā lovers imbued therewith. Once it is admitted that material reality is gross illusion, the rest follows quite simply; the world of "doublethink" is the only one that matters.[23]

It may be said that the incredulity of men, from the dull-witted to genius is so great that we must constantly be on guard. And it appears that even when we are on guard we are likely to be gulled by those who while pointing out dangerous crevices to save us from, are preparing us for their own tar pits.

II

Living down the road a piece from Emerson, and sometimes Thoreau, Amos Bronson Alcott (1799–1888) stands out among the Transcendentalists as the only one of them to have read the

---

[23] Damodar Dharmanand Kosambi: *Myth and Reality: Studis in the Formation of Indian Culture.* Bombay, Popular Prakashan, 1962, p. 17. Franklin Edgerton's comments are worth quoting here also: "The curious many-sidedness, tolerance or inconsistency—whichever one may choose to call it—of the *Bhagavad Gītā.*" Edgerton: *The Bhagavad Gītā.* New York, Harper, 1944, p. 179. Of equal interest is Edgerton's remark in the same volume: "The Gītā's morality . . . does include . . . nonviolence (ahimsā) in several of its lists of virtues. But it never singles it out for special emphasis. . . . One gets the impression that it was too prominent and well-recognized a virtue to be ignored; so some lip-homage is paid to it." *Ibid.,* p. 185.

Tao Te Ching, often attributed to Laotzu.[24] Besides this the
Bhagavad Gītā was "easily domesticated in his hospitable mind."
He states in his *Journal* May 6, 1846 that if he had time he would
transcribe the section entitled "The Principles of Nature and the
Vital Spirit." [25] Again, Alcott mentions the *Bahgvat Geeta* [*sic*] as

Concord School of Philosophy (courtesy Peter Hare) .

being just what he would like to read one day, but then he was
prevented by "various little chores." [26] We are glad to know that it
was on his mind at any rate. Ten years later, on May 12, 1856,
Alcott enthusiastically describes a present to Thoreau which presumably was one of the first Oriental libraries in the United

[24] Odell Shepard (Ed.) : *The Journals of Bronson Alcott.* Boston, Little, 1938, p.
xxiii.
[25] *Ibid.,* p. 179.
[26] Shepard, *Journals,* p. 181.

States; "I see Thoreau, and Cholmondeley's magnificent present of an Oriental library, lately come to hand from England—a gift worthy of a disciple to his master, and a tribute of admiration to Thoreau's genius from a worthy Englishman." [27] Six years later, after Thoreau was dead, Alcott records that "Emerson brings me books left me by Thoreau: Bhagav Gita 2 Vols., translated by Thompson and given to Thoreau by Chelmondly [sic] of England. Budhism [sic] 2 Vols., Eastern Monachism and Manual of Budhism, translated by Hardy . . . also from Chelmondley [sic]." [28]

Alcott's next reference to Eastern thought is to be found in his *Journal* describing his visit to the St. Louis Hegelians on February 9, 1866:

> Evening: Harris takes me to an informal meeting of the Philosophical Society at Mr. Hill's rooms. Here meet Brokmeyer, President of the Society, Dr. Watters, formerly professor in St. Louis Medical College, Dr. Hall, Mr. Hill, Counsellor at Law, and others. I received a friendly greeting, and we discourse on Faust, Hegel, Fichte, eastern and western life and thought.[29]

But does Alcott mean Eastern United States or the thought of India and the East? What of course matters is that one enthusiast of Indian thought visited a group that was to try briefly to encourage its growth in the American Middle West, particularly in the direction of Chicago.

III

Bayard Taylor, the American poet, visited India, China, Russia, Palestine, Arabia and Turkey in the early 1850's. While Taylor was in Delhi an old wandering minstrel sang in the streets "O Suzanna" and "Old Dan Tucker" which he had picked up in Madras from young English officers.[30] Thus India, indirectly, was subject to American aesthetic concerns.

In the United States in 1850 the leading themes were Abolition,

[27] *Ibid.,* p. 282.

[28] *Ibid.,* p. 349. Thomas Cholmondeley visited Concord in 1854 and upon his return to England sent Thoreau a collection of Oriental classics in forty-four volumes. See Romain Rolland: *Prophets of the New India.* London, Cassell, 1930, p. 269.

[29] *Ibid.,* p. 378.

[30] Brooks: *The Times of Melville and Whitman.* New York, Dutton, 1947, p. 86.

the Mexican War, expansionism. the forty-niners, and the social revolution in Europe. Whitman, Bellamy, Howells, and Henry George were aware of them, as were Emerson and Thoreau, but few of the other Indianophiles seemed to be. Spiritualism of the day is mentioned by Van Wyck Brooks as flourishing as far West as Indiana and there were spirit rappers in Rochester, New York.[31] In such an atmosphere Indian influence might thrive.

Before Alcott met Hiram K. Jones (1818–1903), one of the Midwest Platonists, in Jacksonville, Illinois in the 1860's, he discovered that Jones was faintly interested in Oriental thought but more in Emerson, Harris, and Snider of St. Louis. Jones, co-founder of the American Akademe (1883) and its journal, *The Platonist,* was instrumental in encouraging the Plato Clubs of Jacksonville, Decatur and Bloomington, Illinois. The Illinois College annual, dedicated to Jones, was called *The Rig Veda.* After Alcott visited Dubuque, Iowa, he praised the culture of the ladies of that town for their keen interest in spiritual and intellectual matters. He also met "The Sage of the Osage," Thomas M. Johnson (1851–1919), a Neoplatonist with the finest philosophical library in the middle western states. Johnson was a member of the Theosophical Society and was probably instrumental in encouraging the articles on yoga and theosophy that appeared in *The Platonist.* Johnson collected nearly a thousand works on Plato and Plotinus. In all, 1,200 volumes later were presented by one of his sons to the University of Missouri at Columbia. Johnson, it is curious to note, named his sons: Waldo Plato, Ralph Proclus, and Franklin Plotinus.[32]

It is pointed out by Anderson that by 1890: (1) amateur philosophers gave way to the professional; (2) philosophy found its major task to hold its own with science; (3) the amateur and professional schools, societies, and clubs dealing with philosophy attracted no young people and hence withered away.[33]

---

[31] *Ibid.,* p. 143.

[32] See Anderson, *Platonism in the Midwest,* especially p. 176. Johnson's daughter, Helen Moore, became an Indologist. She is best known for her translation of Hemacandra's *Triṣaṣṭiśalākāpuruṣacaritra* (1949). It was Franklin Plotinus who gave the books to the University of Missouri Library, *Letter* from R. P. Johnson to the author, Osceola, Missouri, (June 6, 1968).

[33] *Ibid.,* pp. 200–201.

IV

At the end of the same summer Alcott was West, Emerson was a guest at Alcott's house. They agreed that "The Oriental Scriptures . . . are to be given to the people along with the Hebrew Books, as a means of freeing their faith from the Christian superstitions." [34] Thus we see in this meeting of Transcendentalists an aim for using Indian thought for a cause not different from that of the French naturalists.

It is recorded that on February 11, 1851, Alcott brought home from the Athenaeum Library in Boston a full armload of Asian classics. Although most of Alcott's enthusiasm was based upon English and European translations and commentaries, by 1855 we know that there were Americans such as William Healey Dall, the first foreign missionary of the Unitarian Church to go to India, sending information from Calcutta to Massachusetts; his wife was a member of the Transcendentalists to whom she passed her husband's news from India.

It is likely that Alcott's enthusiasm and talking influenced not only William T. Harris, first of Connecticut and then of St. Louis who was involved in the Concord Summer School of Philosophy,[35] but also Charles de Bernard Mills of Syracuse, New York who wrote *The Indian Saint: or Buddha and Buddhism,* and *The Tree of Mythology* (1889).[36] His *The Indian Saint: or Buddha and Buddhism* was published in Northampton, Massachusetts. Although published six years before Emerson's death, he probably never saw it. After expressing his love and admiration for the Buddha in the preface Mills writes an account based largely on European sources.[37]

Mills mentions that renunciation was preached by Thoreau "in our own time; None could argue its claims with more eloquence

[34] Shepard: *Journals,* p. 383.

[35] The School which stands [in 1969] in good condition, behind and to the side of Alcott's house in Concord is a monument to the early development of philosophy in the United States.

[36] Christy: *The Orient in American Transcendentalism,* pp. 237–59.

[37] Sources such as Hardy, *Legends and Theories of the Buddhists,* Müller's *Lectures on Buddhist Nihilism,* Bignandet's *Legend of Gaudama,* St. Hilaire's *Bouddha,* Koeppen's *Buddha,* Beal's *Catena,* Wasseljew, and Wuttke's *Geschichte des Heidenthums.*

and force than he." [38] But "very deep is the debt we owe to the Oriental, particularly the Indian thinkers. . . ." [39] Mills does not believe that all is perfect with Buddhism since it contains a "morbid, chilly element." Its scripture is "grim and ghastly," so that "with out Western temperament and habits we cannot abide it." Doubtless such a gloomy view would not have been maintained had Mills visited Ceylon and Burma to see the lighter side of Buddhism, perhaps something comparable to a Baptist Sunday School picnic which reveals that there is some grass as well as blood in the consciousnesses of stern communicants. Yet Mills also admits that Judaism and Christianity are not all hedonism and joy either. What is wrong with the Buddha was his "dark temperament." Such a temperament may lead us to abdicate our relations, to withdraw from the post of life.[40] Buddhism fails to see that "Life itself is . . . a battle, there is no escape from victorious doing." [41] It would seem that Mills is more Emersonian and Jamesian than Thoreauvian in this judgment of the inaction and negativity of Buddhism. Yet it must be remarked that he finds this same note in all the world's great religions. He continues,

> No man may rightfully forget, while in a body, that he has a body, and that he primarily should serve and feed his own. It is to be suspected that Buddhism made its grave, its fatal shortcoming here.[42]

The greatest gift of the Buddha, despite such a drawback, is to help us attempt the eternal drive to "escape the bounds of limitation."

Mills writes of the myths in the Vedas and well-known tales: of the glass palace surrounded by seven hedges of spears; of King Bali who expands to the size of Vishnu; of Indra throttling Ahi,

[38] Charles Mills: *The Indian Saint or Buddhism and Buddhism*. Northampton, Journal and Fress Press, 1876, p. 185. In 1877, Seth Pancoast (1823–1889) who received his M.D. from the University of Pennsylvania Medical School in 1852, and collected the largest library of the occult ever assembled in the United States, published *An Introduction to the Philosophy and Theosophy of the Present Sages*.

[39] *Ibid.*, p. 186.

[40] *Ibid.*, p. 156.

[41] *Ibid.*, p. 156.

[42] Had Mills been a professional philosopher, he might have been called one of the early founders of American naturalistic philosophy. He sounds like a Lucretian twenty years before Santayana discovered that worthy.

the serpent; of the story of Apala, the water-maiden, and Indra who "frees her from her ugly and deformed appearance, and she shines a princess." [43] He also speaks of the retributions of souls under Hinduism:

> The stealer of food shall be dyspeptic; the scandal-monger shall have foul breath; the thief who stole perfumes, shall become a musk-rat.[44]

He also wrote *Pebbles, Pearls, and Gems of the Orient* (1876) .[45]

V

We read in the journal entry of August 8, 1867 that Alcott was with Weiss and Wasson at the Emerson house.

> We consider the aspects of religion and its instrumentalities. 'Tis thought much may be done by private clubs and conversations for inspiring a nobler divinity into the students, thus complementing the defects of the teaching at the schools. . . . The books of thoughts, the Bibles of the races, specially invite the deepest study. . . . Homer, Zoroaster, Vishnu, Gotama, Confucius, Mencius, Mahomet, the mystics of the Middle Ages.[46]

This is the well-known seed of the projected Bibles of The World series that several of the Transcendentalists wished to publish. Eventually such a set was produced in England, called the *Sacred Books of the East,* to be followed by a shorter American Edition in twelve volumes appearing in 1897 (New York, The Christian Literature Company) .

On August 19, 1879 Alcott wrote in his journal that he and William T. Harris of St. Louis and F. B. Sanborn of Concord had received from Edwin Arnold, its author, *The Light of Asia.* Oliver Wendell Holmes, writer, and father of the famous jurist, wrote an exhaustive review of it which favorably effected the sale of the book. It was first published in Boston, January 1880. Besides Holmes' account, Ripley, W. E. Channing, and Sanborn gave it highly favorable notices, and as dean of the Concord

---

[43] Mills: *The Tree of Mythology.* Syracuse, C. W. Bardeen, 1889, p. 98.
[44] *Ibid.,* p. 252.
[45] Reviewed by George A. Ripley for the *New York Tribune.*
[46] Shepard, *Journals,* p. 388.

Summer School of Philosophy, Alcott impressed upon the reading public of Boston the value of Arnold's work as well as many others casting a favorable light on the classics of India.

Of the Concord School of Philosophy, Austin Warren wrote: "its members grew old and died just as did persons innocent of metaphysics," [47] showing a positivistic bias no doubt. What concerns us here is that at the Hillside Chapel behind the Orchard House of Alcott lectures on the "Genesis of the Maya" and the "Philosophy of the Bhavad Ghita [*sic*]" were delivered during the session of 1882, the latter by W. T. Harris. The Concord School of Philosophy was opened in 1879 and lasted the first year for about twenty-five days during the months of July and August. Its meetings were held in the chapel about fifty yards from Alcott's house on his land. Accommodating 125 people, it was built for less than the $1,000 bequeathed by Mrs. Elizabeth Thompson of New York City. The staff included several philosophers from Concord as well as academics like Benjamin Peirce, F. H. Hedge, Noah Porter, G. S. Morris, John Bascom, Thomas Davidson, and W. T. Harris, and William E. Channing who gave a lecture on "True Buddhism."

VI

Concern for Indian thought passed from Alcott and the New England Transcendentalists westward until it reached at least halfway across the continent to St. Louis. W. T. Harris visited Emerson on July 18, 1865, at which time he presumably persuaded Emerson to consider lecturing in St. Louis, which Emerson did in 1867, the year that Harris founded the *Journal of Speculative Philosophy*. There along the American Indus, William T. Harris (1835–1909) and other American idealists like Henry C. Brokmeyer (1826–1906) sent out further waves and eddies to quicken Middle Western interest in India. This culminated in the World Parliament of Religions held at the Chicago Columbian Exposition in 1893.

With Brokmeyer, Harris founded the St. Louis Philosophical

[47] Austin Warren: The Concord School of Philosophy. *New Eng. Quar.*, II, 1929, p. 229. Raymond L. Bridgman (Ed.): *Concord Lectures on Philosophy* [1882]. Cambridge, Moses King, 1882, is the most complete current account of that school that we possess.

Society and also *The Journal of Speculative Philosophy,* reputed to be the first philosophical periodical published regularly in the English language. The first issue contained a translation of Indian philosophy, but thereafter Indian thought seems to have waned in the minds of the editor or board of the journal. It was on Philosopher's Row or Targee Street in St. Louis that the *St. Louis Journal of Speculative Philosophy* was conceived in 1866 and begun the next year. The journal began as an attack on Herbert Spencer as well as a platform for a personal vendetta of Harris against the Eastern American publisher-monopolists who were not enthusiastic to publish Harris' writings.[48] The St. Louis Movement, as it showed its Hegelian features, was at first reluctantly recognized by Thomas Davidson, William James, and other "Easterners." Even George Howison, a professor of philosophy at Washington University in St. Louis, was not ardent about its Orientalism or its Hegelianism.

The ferment in St. Louis came about by the confluence of unitarian, scholastic, Transcendentalistic elements, and other influences such as Southern antebellum manners soon to be larded in with German beer and potato salad. St. Louis produced in this period several eminent Americans, including Joseph Pulitzer, the famous journalist; W. T. Harris, later to become the first national Commissioner of Education; Carl Schurz, Senator from Missouri; and Brokmeyer, a seminal figure who ended his days living with Missouri Indians having devoted years of loving care to translating Hegel. Harris and the St. Louis School of Philosophy introduced Western America to Indian thought. The movement was most vital from 1867 to 1869 whereupon Harris moved to Concord, Massachusetts to help run the Concord School of Philosophy situated in Alcott's orchard. Although Harris had moments when Indian philosophy attracted him, the reaction of Denton Snider, the historian of the St. Louis School, was less hospitable to it. Frances B. Harmon says, for example, that:

> The final stage of negativity is reached in the religious institution which no longer actualizes God's will, but rejects God completely. This is perverted religious institution of which there are many examples.

[48] Denton Snider: *The St. Louis Movement.* St. Louis, Sigma, 1920, p. 118.

Buddhism has neither God, nor immortality, nor freedom in the institutional sense.[49]

Presumably this is not only Harmon's view but roughly that of Denton Snider.

Harris was converted to Kantianism in December 1858. In 1859–60 Brokmeyer translated Hegel's *Logic* for his friends, including Harris who by 1866 arrived at his early Hegelian insight.[50] It took another thirteen years before Harris claimed to be in possession of "the true outcome of the Hegelian system." Soon he rejected Hegel's pantheism, for his own tastes were more personalistic as has been pointed out by Werkmeister.[51] Although Harris occasionally found a sympathetic tune in the plucking of Oriental strings, Snider as we have already anticipated held that:

So it comes that Philosophy is distinctly and creatively European, hardly Oriental, in spite of numerous Oriental philosophies of which we read in many a book. The Orient is fundamentally and genetically religious . . .[52]

More orthodox Christian scholars like the Frothinghams were also critical of the Transcendentalist's assessment of Indian philosophy. They said,

With regard to the Hindoo nation . . . which is the highest Malay race . . . philosophical incapacity has not . . . readily been acknowledged. Indeed, by some of the leading transcendentalists, the Hindoo writings have been considered as containing the highest and most spiritual of all philosophies.[53]

[49] Frances B. Harmon: *The Social Philosophy of the St. Louis Hegelians.* New York, Columbia, 1943, p. 72.

[50] W. H. Werkmeister: *A History of Philosophical Ideas in America.* New York, Ronald, 1949, pp. 74–75.

[51] *Ibid.*, pp. 75, 79. Also at this time Moncure Daniel Conway (1832–1907) allowed that Hinduism noted the conception of an absolute idea represented in Nature, but that Hegel said it better. Loyd D. Easton: *Hegel's First American Followers.* Athens, Ohio Univ. Press, 1966, p. 137.

[52] Snider, p. 117. This erroneous view, unless we hold also that Europe is "genetically religious," has persisted among most American philosophers to the present time.

[53] E. L. & A. L. Frothingham: *Philosophy as Absolute Science Founded on the Universal Laws of Being.* Boston, Walker, 1864, vol. I, p. 5.

But, maintained the Frothinghams, the Hindoos are "a partial and imperfect race . . . destitute of rationality." [54] The trouble with the Hindus is that they are:

(1) isolated from other nations,
(2) stationary and unimprovable,
(3) divided into castes—each caste having its own virtues instead of all attempting to unite virtue into one people,
(4) contemplative—"an internal-intellectual sphere of thought,"
(5) ascetic, with the highest condition conceived as annihilation,
(6) unable to distinguish between gods and men,
(7) and finally, confounding the material with the spiritual, and hence naturalistics.[55]

The reason that the Transcendentalists feel such kinship with Hinduism is that both are victims of naturalism, according to the Frothinghams, especially in "the final absorption of all individuals into one original Cause." [56] The appearance of internalism in contemplation and asceticism, however, "is not a real self-conscious condition [in Hegel's sense], but only represents that internal contemplation in the consciousness which is realized in transcendentalism." [57] Also Hindu naturalism is seen in the avoidance of the sacrifice of animal life, and also in that "a great proportion of their writings is materialistic or atheistic which all include the grossest kind of pantheism and fatalism." [58] It must be observed, furthermore, that the passive state of the subject in Hinduism, the Frothinghams claimed,

is always the first step to the realization of a receptive somnambulic or entraced condition; and we therefore find that the Hindoos and also the Gypsy tribes, which belong to the same race, have always extensively practiced the art of somnambulism and necromancy.[59]

The Frothinghams having dispensed with [following Hegel] most Asian philosophy, concluded that "we have now shown that the

[54] *Ibid.*
[55] *Ibid.*, p. 6.
[56] *Ibid.*, p. 7.
[57] *Ibid.*
[58] *Ibid.*
[59] *Ibid.*, p. 8.

development of Philosophy must be confined to the Caucasian race." [60]

Of the famous American philosophers to be encouraged by Harris and Brokmeyer, such as Peirce, Royce, James and Dewey, only Royce showed any zeal for Indian thought, although, as we shall see, James by no means failed to express interest.

The St. Louis School encouraged deliberate colonization in such cities as Chicago, Milwaukee, Cincinnati, and Denver,[61] but it was only in the Chicago area that real fruit was born for Indian thought through the efforts of Edward C. Hegeler (1835–1910), Paul Carus (1852–1919), and Edward L. Schaub (1881–1953). Hegeler founded *The Monist* in 1888, Carus edited it from 1888 until 1919 at which time Schaub, a professor of philosophy at Northwestern University for many years, took over the editing until its publication was suspended in 1936. It was revived under the editorship of Eugene Freeman in 1962. Freeman, another professor of philosophy, first at Illinois Institute of Technology, and later at San Jose State College, has shown more than casual interest in Indian thought.[62]

VII

Paul Carus was deeply influenced by his mathematics teacher in the Gymnasium at Stettin. This was Hermann Grassmann, not only an important nineteenth century mathematician, but a devotee of Vedic literature, a translator of the Rig Veda, and the author of *Wörterbuch zum Rig-Veda* (Leipzig, 1873).[63] Carus came to the notice of Hegeler and subsequently married Hegeler's daughter, Mary. What first struck Hegeler was Carus' *Monism and Meliorism* (1885). Carus was invited to edit *The Open Court* as its second editor. Benjamin Franklin Underwood, its first editor, resigned its editorship after one year, being in some disagreement with Hegeler's interpretation of metaphysical monism and its meaning for religion. Underwood conceived the name, *The Open Court*, since that expressed exactly his view that the journal

[60] *Ibid.,* p. 11.

[61] Harvey Gates Townsend: *Philosophical Ideas in the United States.* New York, American Book, 1934, p. 116.

[62] Freeman's son, James, has studied village anthropology in India.

[63] The Preface was written in Stettin, August 10, 1872.

should include a wide sampling of opinions on philosophical and scientific topics.[64]

Hegeler wished to develop a religious perspective that would include current scientific thought, whereas Underwood had difficulty in seeing the relevance of scientific thought to religion, particularly that of the engineers. Carus was more sympathetic to Hegeler's views although he was doubtless carried in Oriental directions that Hegeler had not foreseen. *The Open Court* was devoted to the religion of science and *The Monist* to the philosophy of science as Hegeler, Carus, and Mary Carus conceived it. After Carus' death in 1919, his wife Mary carried on as editor until her death in 1936. The journal was revived by their daughter, M. Elisabeth, in 1961 under the editorship of Eugene Freeman.

Carus proved to be a devotee of Buddhism and noted its parallelism with Christianity. Buddhism, he said, was a positive creed:

> Buddha's doctrine is no negativism. An investigation of the nature of man's soul shows that while there is no atman or ego-entity, the very being of man consists in his karma, and his karma remains untouched by death. . . . Thus, by denying the existence of that which appears to be our soul and for the destruction of which in death we tremble, Buddha actually opens (as he expresses it himself) the door of immortality to mankind; and here lies the corner-stone of his ethics and also of the comfort as well as the enthusiasm which his religion imparts.[65]

Carus wishes to point out what truths Buddhism and Christianity share, rather than defend the exclusive rightness of Christianity:

> "There are many Christians," Carus says, "who assume that Christianity alone is in the possession of truth and that man could not, in the natural way of his moral evolution have obtained that nobler conception of life which enjoins the practice of universal good-will towards both friends and enemies. This narrow view of Christianity is refuted by the mere existence of Buddhism." [66]

To make sure that his Christian readers do not mistakenly take Carus himself for a Buddhist rather than a Christian, or at least one who preferred Buddhism over Christianity, he writes:

[64] See William Hay: Paul Carus: A Case-Study of philosophy on the frontier. *History Ideas*, XVIII, 4, 1956, pp. 502–5.

[65] Paul Carus: *The Gospel of Buddha According to Old Records.* Chicago, Open Ct., 1921 [copyright 1894], p. viii.

[66] *Ibid.,* p. ix.

> Let us hope that this Gospel of Buddha will serve both Buddhists and
> Christians as a help to penetrate further into the spirit of their faith,
> so as to see its full breadth and depth.[67]

This handsome volume which appeared in its deluxe edition in
1915 includes "Prince Siddhārtha Becomes Buddha," "The Foun-
dation of the Kingdom of Righteousness," "Consolidation of the
Buddha's Religion," "The Teacher," "Parables and Stories," and
"The Last Days." Carus himself tells us in the Preface that the
book has had a fine reception throughout the Buddhist world,
indeed it has been translated into Japanese by Teitaro Suzuki
[D. T. Suzuki] and also into Chinese, German, French, Spanish,
Dutch and saw prospects of translation into Urdu, Russian,
Czech, Italian, and Siamese. Proper Christians would be receptive
to Buddhism if it fulfilled its true role, Carus believed, as "the
religion of love made easy." [68] Mutual inspiration should animate
both Buddhists and Christians. In this work Carus' selections are
taken from many sources, some of which are Buddhaghoṣa's
Parables, The Jataka, The Dhammapada, The Questions of King
Milinda, and the Visuddhi-Magga. Translations are by H. C.
Warren, G. Max Müller, H. Oldenberg, T. W. Rhys Davids, and
H. Jacobi.

Carus, in *Fundamental Problems* [69] wrote a chapter on "The
Idea of Absolute Existence" under which heading the first section
is called "The Veil of Maya." To make this section meaningful
Carus explains that:

> The view that natural processes are not actual realities, but mere
> shadows of invisible existences behind them has been revived often
> since, and must be considered even to-day as the philosophy of our
> time . . .[70]

Such a view, which seemed so timely in the context of Machian
immaterialism, today may strike us as a major misstep taken by
the philosophy of science in the nineteenth century. Neither
Peirce nor James ever put the issue more succinctly. Carus, in

[67] *Ibid.*, p. xi.

[68] *Ibid.*, p. xiv.

[69] The rest of the title is *The Method of Philosophy as a Systematic Arrangement
of Knowledge*. Chicago, Open Ct., 1903.

[70] Carus, *Fundamental Problems* . . . , p. 135.

another section of the same work, compares Buddhism with Christianity, a favorite pastime of his. Here he claims that,

> Christ, as well as Buddha, represents a reaction against pessimism. It was the start of a new faith, a new hope, a new religion, a religion that should hear the features of meliorism.[71]

Concerning Carus' spiritualism or immaterialism, his viewpoint is expressed in his answer to Col. Paul R. Shipman: [72]

> There is no sense in calling consciousness and will either material or immaterial. Neither consciousness nor will has anything to do with matter; both are non-material.[73]

Relevant to this argument, Carus says that "Thinking is a physiological process," but thought is not material, otherwise we could bottle it.[74] Pursuing this, Carus quotes with approval Hermann Lotze's "witty" retort to Carl Vogt's statement that,

> Thought stands in the same relation to the brain as gall to the liver and urine to the kidneys.[75]

Perhaps one is no longer in doubt as to Lotze's rightful position in the twentieth century when he reads that Lotze's retort to this is that "he had not noticed thought to be so unpoetical."

In dealing with the problem of God, Carus first attacks agnosticism "as bankruptcy of thought . . . the weakest but also the most injurious philosophy." [76] Even atheism is more correct in that it attacks the myths and allegories that surround theism. In defending Buddhism, despite its atheism, Carus points out that there is "a remarkable coincidence between theism and atheism." [77] This we may see in analyzing the Lord's Prayer, which consists of "self-exhortations, of vows" rather than prayer in the usual orthodox Christian sense. "Buddhism," Carus notes, "commonly regarded as an atheistic religion, rejects prayer as an irreligious practice and replaces prayers by vows." [78] Lest the reader be left

---

[71] *Ibid.,* p. 213.
[72] An American materialist who held that "Mind is material."
[73] Carus, *Fundamental Problems* . . . , p. 351.
[74] *Ibid.,* p. 352.
[75] *Ibid.,* p. 352.
[76] Carus: *God.* Chicago, Open Ct., 1908, p. 4.
[77] Carus: *God,* p. 16.
[78] *Ibid.,* p. 16.

Paul Carus (courtesy of Eugene Freeman).

without knowing what Carus finally concludes to be a responsible conception of God, I quote the last sentence in his book of that title:

> The God-conception which I deem true might be called nomotheism or cosmotheism, or also monotheism, according to definition; but I object to deism, pantheism, and atheism.[79]

William Hay finds Carus' view not unlike that of Whitehead,[80] particularly when Carus wishes to escape the consequences of pantheism. According to Carus,

> If you could annihilate matter and energy there would be left, as an intrinsic reality from which neither existence nor non-existence could escape, the eternal laws of form, which by philosophers have been formulated in what is termed the purely formal sciences, viz., logic, arithmetic, geometry, pure mechanics, and pure natural science.[81]

These laws, according to Carus are "as omnipresent and eternal as God himself" and hence "part and parcel" of God.[82] But God and nature are different, for God is the "omnipresent law" and not the totality of corporeal things. As Hay points out, this and other passages in Carus remind us of Whitehead;[83] in his view of deity, in his dependence on the eternal objects, in the omnipresence of subjectivity, and in dependence upon the correspondence theory of truth. One remotely possible clue to the similarities, besides what appears to be chance, is that just as Hermann Grassmann was Carus' teacher, so he was the inspiration for Whitehead's *Universal Algebra*.[84]

Carus' view is that the essence of religion lies in its practical application of a world-conception motivated by religious sentiment. The basic laws of morality are based on the nature of things "and constitute an intrinsic part of the world order."[85] His extensive writing in the field of Indian philosophy and religion as well as his exegesis of Indian art are shown in the titles of his

[79] *Ibid.,* p. 239.
[80] Hay, Paul Carus: A Case-Study . . . , pp. 506–7.
[81] Carus: *God,* p. 42.
[82] *Ibid.,* p. 44.
[83] Hay, Paul Carus: A Case-Study . . . , pp. 506–8.
[84] *Ibid.,* p. 506.
[85] Carus: *God,* pp. 49–50.

works: *The Dharma, The Gospel of Buddha, Buddhism and its Christian Critics, Portfolio of Buddhist Art, Stories of Buddhism, Amitabha.* In addition to these volumes Carus wrote more than seven editorial articles on Hinduism and thirty-nine on Buddhism between 1887 and 1909 in *The Open Court* and *The Monist.*

With so many auspicious developments in the appreciation of Indian philosophy and religion, the stage was set for actual missionary work among the heathen Americans. It was not long to appear, first surreptitiously in an indigenous American religion, Christian Science; second in the growth of theosophy; and third in the founding of the Ramakrishna-Vivekananda Centres.

VIII

Theosophy in America worked contemporaneously with St. Louis philosophy but independent of it. Founded by a Russian noblewoman and a Northern Colonel of the Civil War, its inception lay with the arrival of Mme. H. P. Blavatsky in New York from Tibet in 1873. Certain monks, she announced, had filled her with philosophy. Presumably her masters were "liberal Buddhists and Hindus, united no doubt by a spirit of compromise." [86] Tindall has succinctly sought out the kernel of theosophy as:

> a mixture of Buddhism and Hinduism, including reincarnation, karma, and nirvana.[87] Like yoga, which it loosely embraces, theosophy is a method of introducing the particular soul to what Mme. Blavatsky called Anima Mundi.[88]

[86] William York Tindall, Transcendentalism in contemporary literature. In Arthur E. Christy (Ed.) : *The Asian Legacy in American Life.* New York, John Day, 1945, p. 176.

[87] That theosophy was in the air may be deduced from an entry in the *Journal* of Edward Bellamy (1850–1898) dated December 1871. Bellamy says: "Sometimes, feeling the burden and continual harassment of existence, I grow bitterly at odds with my Maker for ever calling me forth from nothingness. Only the feeling of the utter bitter impotence of my plaint restrains me from desperate blasphemy. Nirvana, Nirvana, there is no other haven for the weary soul, and even there one would not be secure. The omnipotent summons of the creating God could always wake it from grateful slumber, baby oblivion, once again to a new morning of life." Arthur E. Morgan: *The Philosophy of Edward Bellamy.* New York, Kings' Crown Press, 1945, p. 79.

[88] Tindall: p. 176. For a more detailed explanation of a theosophy see Arthur E. Ewing, Chap. XII.

Helena Petrovna Hahn Blavatsky (1831–1891) was born in Russia, lived in a Himalaya ashram for seven years, moved to New York and became a naturalized American citizen.

Not long after her arrival in New York she established a theosophical club, one of whose ardent members was Col. Henry Steele Olcott (1832–1907) who had turned to law after mustering out of the Union Army. He was educated at the College of the City of New York and Columbia University. After considerable study of Buddhism he formed with Blavatsky the Buddhist Theosophical Society in New York around 1875–1876 and began the *Theosophist* in 1879. Olcott wished to establish a nucleus of the universal brotherhood of humanity, to promote the study of comparative religion and philosophy, and to make a systematic investigation into the mystical potencies of life and matter. Today this last investigation is usually called occultism. Although like Blavatsky discontented with "civilization," Olcott did not try to destroy rationalism or rationality, evidently held in check by both his knowledge of the law and perhaps even some feature of military life.

Spiritualism in the United States was and is an attack on the pretensions of Christianity, particularly as it is embodied in clericalism. Its first and main target remains Roman Catholicism with the more formalized sects of Protestantism chosen as its alternative. Catholicism, which has remained unchallenged as the heresy-hunter of diabolism (spiritualism), is of particular significance because while posing as a guardian against paganism, it has always incorporated it within its own ecclesiastical body at the moment that it denies this act, according to Blavatsky. It does so in ritual, art, and festival. While attacking such notions as phallism in Indian religion, it has never hesitated in candle, cross, and spire to use its biologically symbolic significance for precisely those purposes for which it inveighs against Hinduism. Spiritualism appeared after the way had been made smooth by Transcendentalism and other religio-social views and has some tie with Christian Science. These views may be seen today as part of a growing development of cosmopolitanism and internationalism appearing with the expansion of industrial and monopoly capitalism. Christianity had already been weakened sufficiently by the

1870's so that spiritualism could appear quite openly. Its connection with the social dissatisfaction of the poor white-collar class and quietly rebellious middle class with a certain intellectual curiosity has received little sociological attention.

Olcott and Blavatsky went to India in 1878. Two years later they went to Ceylon where both of them embraced Buddhism in Balapitya, a small fishing village in the southern part of the island about fifty miles from Colombo in a place not far from the present national elephant preserve. Olcott then founded the Colombo Branch of the Buddhist Theosophical Society with the help of local Buddhist leaders. Before Olcott went to Ceylon there were only four Buddhist schools in that country. Most of the children attending school were enrolled in Christian ones. Four hundred schools were founded by the Buddhist Theosophical Society and administered by that Society until the Ceylon Government took them over in 1961. In a memorial account given of Olcott in the *New York Times* it is noted that:

> Newspapers throughout Ceylon made special reference to Colonel Olcott today. One newspaper article recalled that when the Colonel came to Ceylon he saw that Buddhism was on the wane. Noting that Buddhist children went to Christian Schools, his first act was to see that Buddhists knew something of their own religion. So he composed a Buddhist catechism. This was translated into Sinhalese, the language of a majority of the community in Ceylon.[89]

Some of the works of Olcott besides the Buddhist catechism, which unfortunately are not dated, in The Adyar Pamphlets series include *The Life of Buddha and its Lessons, Primer of Buddhism, The Spirit of Zoroastrianism, Theosophy, Religion and Occult Science* (1885), and *People from the Other World* (1875). He traveled widely in both Asia and Europe, dying at his home in Adyar, a suburb of Madras, where the head office of the Theosophical Society is situated. It was Annie Besant, one of the founders of the Indian National Congress and president of the society in 1906, who provided theosophy with a systematic presentation of its thought, blending Hindu and Buddhist metaphysics with a Christian moral outlook.[90] Col. Olcott with Annie Besant

[89] "American Sponsor of Buddhism Honored at Memorials in Ceylon" (February 18, 1962). I have used this *Buddhist Catechism* in its 33rd ed. in my classes.

[90] See Clifton E. Olmstead, p. 122. Annie Besant replaced Blavatsky as a leader of the Theosophical Society upon the latter's death.

founded Central Hindu College at Benares (now Varanasi).

Contrary to the mysticized title, *Isis Unveiled a Master Key to the Mysteries of Ancient and Modern Science and Theology* [91] by Mme. Blavatsky could well be placed among the volumes of free thought instead of the occult. It might well be reentitled: *The Horrors of Christianity Unveiled and the Excellences of Hinduism Praised,* for in Volume II an attack is made on the "worldliness and hypocrisy" of that venerable creed in a barrage of statistics worthy of Joseph McCabe or J. M. Robertson. The views of the "glorious example of that Prophet of Nazareth, by whose mouth the spirit of truth spake loudly to humanity," [92] are upheld as desirable and worthy of emulation. On the other hand, the views of the Christian clergy, particularly Roman Catholic, are excoriated as being inhumane and fraudulent. She claims [in 1877] that:

> In the United States of America, sixty thousand (60,428) men are paid salaries to teach the Science of God and His relations to His creatures.[93]

Of these, over 5,000 are Roman Catholic and the remainder,

> local and travelling ministers, representing fifteen different denominations, each contradicting the other upon more or less vital theological questions . . . [instructing] in their respective doctrines, thirty-three million . . . other persons.[94]

Blavatsky claims that of Christian communicants there are three main groups: materialists, spiritualists, and Christians proper. Of these, "the materialists and spiritualists make common cause against the hierarchical pretension of the clergy." [95] Preparing her readers for the new spiritualism that she will alert them to, she continues her attack:

> Among Christians there is nothing but dissension. Their various churches represent every degree of religious belief, from the omnivorous credulity of blind faith to a condescending and high-toned defer-

91 New York, J. W. Bouton, 1877.
92 *Isis Unveiled,* p. iii.
93 *Ibid.,* p. 1.
94 *Ibid.*
95 *Ibid.,* p. 3.

COL. HENRY STEEL OLCOTT IN 1883
Originally published in *The Theosophist,* Vol. LIII, August, 1932

Col. Henry Steel Olcott (courtesy of The Theosophist).

ence to the Deity which thinly masks an evident conviction of their own deific wisdom.[96]

We could continue in this vein for hundreds of pages, but the point has already been sufficiently made.[97] To what end does Mme. Blavatsky wish to lead us? She says:

> Our task will have been ill-performed if the preceding chapters have not demonstrated that Judaism, earlier and later Gnosticism, Christianity, and even Christian Masonry, have all been erected upon identical cosmical myths, symbols, and allegories, whose full comprehension is possible only to those who have inherited the key from their inventors.[98]

What can help us out of our misery is to follow two sources, Blavatsky says: the Vedas and the *Kabala*. Thereupon follow such notions as that the Mosaic Laws are borrowed from Manu, that Egypt owes its civilization to India, that the Christians pilfered a great deal from the Buddhists and such like marvels. Parallels of particular verses of the Hindu scriptures with Jewish and Christian are also shown. Some of them are remarkably similar, particularly because of the translation chosen, yet the evidence that they are borrowed is either slim or nonexistent.[99] She concludes that:

> Pre-Vedic Brahmanism and Buddhism are the double source from which all religion sprung; Nirvana is the ocean to which all tend.[100]

At this time, too, the Boston-born archaeologist, Arthur Lincoln Frothingham (1859–1923), was working in certain areas of the *Kabala,* Babylonian, and early Hindu books. Having received his early education at the Academy of the Christian Brothers in Rome between 1868 and 1873, he later took special courses in Oriental languages at the Catholic Seminary of Saint Apollonaire and the Royal University of Rome. He took the M.A. and the Ph.D. at the University of Leipzig. From 1887 to 1898 he was professor of archaeology and history of art and from 1898 to 1901

---

[96] *Ibid.*, p. 4.

[97] The British Society for Psychical Research is said to have "reported adversely on her pretensions" in 1884. Presumably these reports were concerned with her occult rather than her sociological opinions.

[98] Blavatsky: *Isis Unveiled,* p. 405.

[99] *Ibid.*, p. 556.

[100] *Ibid.*, p. 639.

professor of ancient history and archaeology, both at Princeton. In 1885 he founded the *American Journal of Archaeology* and was its editor from 1885 to 1896.

With Ephraim L. Frothingham, he wrote *Christian Philosophy* [101] in two slim volumes. In the first volume is one of the rare if not unique historical studies of nihilism ever produced in the United States. Entitled "History of Pannihilism" it contains a survey of the view "that the dualistic universe of Becoming Existence is the self-evolution and the self-dissolution of the Divinity." [102] This universe culminates in man who is the actual Deity, a Deity who must return into the abyss of annihilation.

After discussion of the Chinese view as that which regards (with the entire Mongolian race) "pure Nothing as the supreme, the absolute, God and believes the Void and Nothing [*śūnya*] as the principle, source, and final end of all things," [103] Frothingham briefly discusses Hindu philosophy as it relates to nihilism.

At the center of Hindu philosophy is the destroying, dissolving "nihility." According to him

> In both Brahmism and Buddhism, negation, diversity, unconsciousness passivity and annihilation constitute origin and final end: and between these extremes of origin and end, the middle state is that of becoming or transmutation and transmigration—which is Māyā, the Illusion of existence.[104]

For further consideration he quotes the Karl Blind translation of Ṛg-Veda X, 11 which begins "Nothing was then . . ." and ends with "Then, first, from the Nothingness enveloped in empty gloom, Desire arose, which was the first germ of mind." [105] Finally he considers the history of the problem from the Egyptian *Book of the Dead,* the Cuthah creation-tablet, the *Kabala,* Hesiod, Leukippos, through Christian nihilism to German nihilism with the culmination of these streams in Herbert Spencer. One's mouth waters for more details and especially for a fuller account of Indian nihilism, particularly that to be found in Śaivism, but evidently,

---

[101] Baltimore, Arthur L. Frothingham, 1888.

[102] *Ibid.,* I, 46.

[103] *Ibid.,* I, 47. Perhaps this is a reference to *śūnya* "the Void," which is common in Mahāyāna Buddhism.

[104] Frothingham cites the *Laws of Manu,* Ch. I, 57.

[105] *Christian Philosophy,* I, 48. This is an incorrect reference. It could be an inexact rendering of RV 10, 129.

Frothingham lacked the necessary translations and commentaries, many of which did not appear until the twentieth century.

As Americans developed their own graduate schools, beginning at Johns Hopkins in 1876, a demand for Indian studies in philosophy and literature increased far beyond the hopes of Edward Elbridge Salisbury (1814–1901), who had been appointed professor of Sanskrit and Arabic at Yale University in 1841. Indian languages had to be taught before scholarly work in Indian philosophy could progress. The basis of the study of Indian philosophy in the universities was laid by Salisbury; William Dwight Whitney (1827–1894), who occupied the first separate chair of Sanskrit in the United States, at Yale; John Avery (1837–1887), who taught at Grinnell and Bowdoin; Charles Rockwell Lanman (1850–1941), who taught Sanskrit first at Johns Hopkins and then at Harvard; and Henry Clarke Warren (1854–1899), another Harvard philologist who was the first American scholar to gain distinction in Pāli. But before giving further detail of academic advances in Indian studies, let us turn to theological activities tinged with or dominated by Indian speculation in religion.

During the period we have considered, from Thoreau to Carus, the United States underwent its greatest changes and upheavals, together even outweighing the impact of the Revolution of 1776. It was an epoch that saw the greatest Westward movement in history, Abolition and the Civil War, expansionism and the Mexican War, the development of the railroad system, the beginning of unionism in labor, and the vast immigration that grew from 7,912 in 1824 to 369,980 in 1850. Interest in Indian philosophy moved West with the immigration, its rural characteristics praised as the railroads disrupted the countryside. It was used in support of the anti-Catholicism that grew as Irish, German, and Italian immigrants poured into the country to provide cheap labor for the hungry American capitalists. For the few sensitive to the disruption of community life and the general welfare that hung by a thread in the face of individualistic, egoistic competition, it reminded Americans of a life where there were other important considerations to be thought of. Men must cooperate as well as compete; they must contemplate as well as produce; they must have an ethical base as well as mere drive for worldly success.

Chapter IV

FOUNDING OF THE RAMAKRISHNA-
VIVEKANANDA CENTERS
AND MISCELLANEOUS INFLUENCES
BEFORE 1900

I

A<small>N</small> UNPUBLICIZED influence of Indian philosophy on one mode of American idealistic thought is that upon Mary Baker Eddy, generally conceded to be the founder of Christian Science. In her bible, *Science and Health,* in the twenty-fourth edition there was a chapter, now suppressed, which allegedly began with four Vedāntic quotations or paraphrases of them. In the same chapter Mrs. Eddy quoted the *Bhagavadgītā* from the Wilkins translation published in London in 1785 and in New York in 1867. These quotations were later excised from *Science and Health.*[1] Some quotations from *Science and Health* which suffice to show the impact of Vedānta upon Mrs. Eddy are:

> Me or I. The Divine principle. The Spirit, the soul . . . Eternal Mind. There is only one ME or US, only one Principle or Mind, which govern all things . . . Everything reflects or refracts in God's creation one unique Mind; and everything which does not reflect this unique mind is false and a cheat . . . God. The great I AM . . . Principle, spirit, soul, Life, Truth, love, all substance, intelligence.[2]

There are also striking analogies between Indian thought in the Mind-Cure of Hariot W. Dresser, Henry Wood, and R. W. Trine which date after the death of Vivekananda.[3]

[1] Romain Rolland quoting Madeline R. Harding in the *Prabuddha Bharata Review,* March 1928, *Prophets of the New India,* p. 271 n.

[2] Quoted by Rolland, *Ibid.,* p. 271 n.

[3] A friend of the writer's for thirty-five years, whose late wife was a Christian Science Practitioner and chiropractor, used the work of Trine and Troward with →

70

II

It was in March, 1892 that Vivekananda (1862–1902) discussed problems of the spiritual life with Robert Ingersoll, who made a funeral oration at the grave of Walt Whitman on that day. We have no record of what was said, but let us hope that it did them both credit. It is not unfitting that Whitman should find Vivekananda at his grave, for it was Emerson's quip when he first read it that "Leaves of Grass seem to be a mixture of the Bhagavadgita and the *New York Herald.*" [4] Romain Rolland's assessment here of Walt Whitman's potentiality to receive the words of Vivekananda are in discord with Walter B. Pitkin's assessment of the poet in *A Short Introduction to the History of Human Stupidity:* [5]

> I can see clearly what Vivekananda would have disliked about Whitman—the ridiculous mixture of the *New York Herald* and the Bhagavadgita, which awoke the fine smile of Emerson: his metaphysical journalism, his small shopkeeper's wisdom, picked up from dictionaries —his eccentric affectation of a bearded Narcissus, his colossal complacency with regard to himself and his people—his democratic Americanism, with its childish vanity and explosive vulgarity ever seeking the limelight.[6]

III

Although some philosophers were taking Indian thought seriously, there were literary sages who were not. Ambrose Bierce (1842?–1914), the American Chamfort, novelist, journalist, and essayist had other opinions. This is seen, for example, in his definition of Brahma in his famous *The Devil's Dictionary:*

> *Brahma,* n. He who created the Hindoos, who are preserved by Vishnu and destroyed by Siva—a rather neater division of labor than is found

---

Vedāntic emphases for the purposes of spiritual exercises. He combined these with an incisive economic shrewdness, and still lives happily with a second wife on a farm near Missoula, Montana, being in his middle eighties.

[4] Quoted by Rolland, p. 277.

[5] New York, Simon & Schuster, Inc., 1927.

[6] *Human Stupidity,* p. 227. Rabindranath Tagore took a different view of Whitman, whom he preferred to Emerson: "Whitman gives me pictures—pictures. Through his work I know your country and can catch its heartbeat." Bailey Millard: Rabindranath Tagore Discovers America. *The Bookman,* XLIV (September 1916–February 1917), p. 248. Perhaps the heartbeat that Tagore found is not totally inconsistent with Pitkin's assessment.

among the deities of some other nations. The Abracadabranese, for example, are created by Sin, maintained by Theft and destroyed by Folly. The priests of Brahman, like those of the Abracadabranese, are holy and learned men who are never naughty.

> O Brahma, thou rare old Divinity,
> First Person of the Hindoo Trinity,
> You sit there so calm and securely,
> With feet folded up so demurely—
> You're the First Person Singular, surely.[7]
>
> Polydore Smith

Although Bierce, the keenest stable cleaner to appear on the American scene since Leif Erickson's discovery of it, had many other comments relevant to our theme; let two more examples suffice:

> *Nirvana*, n. In the Buddhist religion, a state of pleasurable annihilation awarded to the wise, particularly to those wise enough to understand it.[8]

For the amusement of Indian readers, I should like to quote Bierce's definition of

> *Occident,* n. The part of the world lying west (or east) of the Orient. It is largely inhabited by Christians, a powerful subtribe of the Hypocrites, whose principal industries are murder and cheating, which they are pleased to call "war" and "commerce."

Yet not satisfied with this volley he adds:

> These, also, are the principal industries of the Orient.[9]

Many Americans have used Indian thought to bolster their own, others to complement their knowledge sufficiently to give it an air of universality, and still others, such as Ambrose Bierce, to use it as a knife in cutting out notions that are falsely held to be those of all mankind. In attacking the notion that all of us desire life everlasting, Bierce refers to the hope of the Buddhists that just

---

[7] Ambrose Bierce: *The Devil's Dictionary*. Cleveland, World, 1942, p. 41.

[8] Bierce: *The Devil's Dictionary*, p. 228.

[9] *Ibid.*, p. 234.

the opposite obtains.[10] More frequently, however, as a onetime Californian, he prefers to contrast Western superstition to Chinese good sense, a return of early eighteenth century romanticism. Mark Twain in *Crossing the Equator* also pokes some good natured fun at meeting "God" in Bombay, who turns out to be a kindly Vedāntist. Then there are others, like John Cage, who wish to moralize without moralizing. He tells the following story:

> Two monks came to a stream. One was Hindu, the other Zen. The Indian began to cross the stream by walking on the surface of the water. The Japanese became excited and called to him to come back. "What's the matter," the Indian said. The Zen monk said, "That's not the way to cross the stream. Follow me." He led him to a place where the water was shallow and they waded across.[11]

I have inserted these comments of Bierce for two reasons: first, to indicate an attitude of some Americans towards Indian thought; and second, to acquaint the Indian reader with Bierce, since he is still too little known even within the United States.

IV

The United States recognized in some official way the existence of India, for the first time, at the Columbian Exposition opened in Chicago in 1893. Architecturally speaking, according to Lewis Mumford:

> Lacking any genuine unity of ideas and purposes—for Root had initially conceived of a variegated *oriental setting* [12]—the architect of the exposition had achieved the effects of unity by subordinating their work to an established precedent.[13]

At this auspicious gathering the World's Parliament of Religions [14] was convened with the Columbian Exposition. Not

---

[10] Bierce: Immortality, *The Shadow on the Dial and other Essays.* San Francisco, A. M. Robertson, 1909, p. 161.

[11] Cage: *A Year from Monday.* Middletown, Connecticut, Wesleyan U. P., 1967, p. 135.

[12] Emphasis added.

[13] Mumford: *Sticks and Stones . . . ,* p. 127

[14] Immediately before, and with acceleration after, the World's Parliament of Religion, Indian philosophy and life came under increasing scrutiny by such Ameri- →

only was W. T. Harris present, but as we might expect, Paul Carus. Also present at the Parliament was a youngish philosopher by the name of William Ernest Hocking who later became famous for his *The Meaning of God in Human Experience* (1912). Hocking's interest in Indian philosophy was mightily stimulated by the meetings he had with Swami Vivekananda. India was represented not only by Vivekananda, but also Protap Chunder Mozoomdar, Manilal N. Dividedi, B. B. Nagarkar, Virchand A. Ghandi [*sic*], S. Parthasarathy Aiyanger, and Ervad Sherizriji Dadabhai Bharucha.[15]

Swami Vivekananda founded the first Vedanta Society in the United States in 1894, basing it upon the teachings of Sri Rama-krishna (d. 1886). These teachings, in turn, were influenced by those of Keshab Chandra Sen, one of the leaders of the Brahmō Samaj Hindu reform society. A short time before the Parliament was to be held in Chicago, Vivekananda caught wind of it in Madras. Seeing an opportunity to spread the faith as well as take an informative trip to America, he excitedly remarked,

> The time has come for the Hinduism of the Rishis to become dynamic. . . . Shall we remain passive or shall we become aggressive, as in the days of old, preaching unto the nations the glory of the Dharma? [16]

Vivekananda did attend the Parliament at Chicago, and as one can easily see by reading the two volumes commemorating the event, he made his presence felt. Christopher Isherwood records that Vivekananda arrived in Chicago early. His funds vanished, and he lost the address of the friends who were to see to his stay. So he spent the night sleeping in a box in the freight yards. The next morning he sat down on the sidewalk in a fashionable

---

can journals as *Asia, Athenaeum, Century, Contemporary Review, Fortune, Forum, Harper's Monthly Magazine, The Nation, Outlook,* and *Review of Reviews.* Topics varied from literature to Brahmō Samaj and H. C. Sen's reforms of Hinduism. See Leidecker: Oriental philosophy in America. In Ralph B. Winn (Ed.) *American Philosophy,* New York, Philosophical Lib. 1955.

   [15] John Henry Barrows (Ed.) : *The World's Parliament of Religion,* 2 vols. Chicago, Parliament, 1893.

   [16] Quoted by Wendell M. Thomas: *Hinduism Invades America.* New York, The Beacon Press, Inc., 1930, p. 72. This is one of the earliest and most brilliant instances of grantsmanship known to me.

district "resigned to the will of God." It happened that a door opened and a well-dressed lady appeared. "Are you, sir, a delegate to the Parliament of Religions?" she asked. Invited to have breakfast, his difficulties were solved in Chicago.[17] Once asked, "Are you never serious, Swami?" He answered "Oh, yes. When I have a belly-ache." [18] During the following year he founded the first Indian religious center, still extant in New York, with branches at Chicago, San Francisco, and Los Angeles. It has had centers in Pittsburgh, Seattle, Boston, Santa Barbara, San Diego, Long Beach, Pasadena, Hollywood, and Portland, Oregon. Three decades after the founding of the first society in New York, Wendell Thomas, after visiting it, describes the center as follows:

> Looking around to the left, I saw in the long parlor a large bookcase containing about a thousand books, which I later discovered to be mostly the works of Western Idealists.[19]

Besides a painting of Vivekananda and a small photograph of Ramakrishna, there were flowers, burning candles, and fuming incense. As Thomas stood there, Swami Jñāneśvarānanda entered, mounted the one-step platform and with hands folded across his shining golden robe said:

> "Let us all try to meditate on our inner divine nature." Silence. Broken by the swami's resonant voice in a quaintly appealing Sanskrit chant. Then a prayer in English: "May that One who is called Siva by the Shivaites, Visnu by the Visnuvites, Brahman by the Vedantins . . . the Heavenly Father by the Christians, inspire our hearts with love for all mankind. Peace! Peace! Peace!" [20]

Between 1894 and 1929 there were seventeen Ramakrishna swamis in the United States, with never more than eight at a time, sent out from the Matha at Belur, Bengal. The Matha was founded in 1886, the year of the death of Ramakrishna. By 1960 there were 27,500 avowed followers of Hinduism in North Amer-

---

[17] Christopher Isherwood: *Vedanta for the Western World.* New York, Viking, 1962, p. 23.
[18] *Ibid.,* p. 27.
[19] Thomas, p. 96.
[20] *Ibid.,* pp. 96–97.

ica.[21] Over the years since the 1890's some of the Americans who became devotees of this Indian religious philosophy include Sarah J. Farmer, who gave her fortune for the study of Oriental religions at Greenacre Inn; Mrs. Ole Bull, wife of the famous violinist, who bequeathed several hundred thousand dollars to the Vedanta Centre; Luther Burbank, the botanist; Madame Galli-Curci, the operatic singer; Edward B. Davis, Texas oil magnate; and Yehudi Menuhin, the famous violinist.

While Americans became more pragmatic and materialistic in the nontechnical meaning of these words, a small but vocal minority used Indian philosophy and religion to beat back the tides with spiritual whisk brooms. There was the flowering of Christian Science with its Indian inspiration. There were the Indian Vedānta missionaries who came to save the American from his grosser nature. And finally, there were the American liberal theologians who foresaw the need of interfaith ecumenism even if it meant borrowing help from the Hindus and Buddhists. The fruits of these influences were not immediately realizable, but they did contribute to awareness that competitive secularism had its definite and frightening limitations.

---

[21] According to Harry Hansen (Ed.) *World Almanac*, New York, *New York World-Telegram and The Sun*, 1962, p. 719. Thomas claims that in 1906 there were 340 members, 190 in 1916, and 200 members in 1926. Of these in 1926, two-fifths were unmarried; three-fourths were women; ages ran from 35 to 70 with an average age of 48. Thomas, p. 116. In the same almanac Buddhists numbered 165,000 in North America, many of whom were Far Easterners by birth. In the 1964 *World Almanac* eleven Vedanta Centers are listed under "Vandanta," credited with a membership of only 1,000. This astonishing drop in membership must be interpreted as either (1) a failure of the Vedanta Centers to report membership, or (2) an alarming drop in Vedantic communicants, or (3) a typographical error in the *Almanac*. Also in the 1964 *Almanac*, the Buddhists are credited with 60,000 members in fifty-five churches. Bishop Shinshō Hanayama of the Buddhist Church of North America claims 250,000 Buddhists, most of them of Far Eastern parentage. (Letter to the author, San Francisco, in 1964). By the 1965 *Almanac* there were 100,000 Buddhists and 1,000 Vedantists. The figures for the 1966 *Almanac* show 109,965 Buddhists. This increase may well be the result of my inquiry of the Bishop in 1964. By 1968 the same almanac shows 100,000 Buddhists and 1,000 Vedantists.

Chapter V

INDIAN THOUGHT IN THE GOLDEN AGE
OF PHILOSOPHY AT HARVARD

I

FROM 1885 TO 1915 no American institution of higher learning showed anything like the interest in Indian thought evinced by Harvard University. The most venerated philosopher there was William James (1842–1910) who found much of the Indian thought to be uncongenial. That he was not ignorant of it is shown in a host of citations, particularly in his *Varieties of Religious Experience* (1902), and also in *Pragmatism* (1907). He refers to Swami Vivekananda's London Lectures of 1897, to Swami Ramakrishna's maxims found in F. Max Müller's *Ramakrishna, His Life and Sayings* (1899), admitting that:

> I am ignorant of Buddhism and speak under correction, and merely in order the better to describe my general point of view; as I apprehend the Buddhistic doctrine of Karma, I agree *in principle* with that.[1]

With his sensitive doctrinal nose lowered in the pragmatic corn stubble of the pheasant hunt, James goes on to discover in Buddhism a kind of ally to the activism he espouses against the block universe:

[1] Emphasis added. William James: *The Varieties of Religious Experience*. The Gifford Lectures in 1901–1902. New York, The Modern Library, n.d., p. 512 An American philosopher tells of an encounter with Soviet philosophers during the summer of 1963 at which time they agreed "in principle" to discuss philosophy with the American philosophers attending the XIII International Congress of Philosophy at Mexico City in September, 1963. The American's response was that this was like agreeing in principle to visting a friend's apartment. Either one did it or not, *principle* having little noticeable effect! The Soviet philosophers did subsequently meet with the Americans in Mexico City.

. . . for Buddhism as I interpret it, and for religion generally so far as
it remains unweakened by transcendentalistic metaphysics, the word
"judgment" here means no bare academic verdict or platonic appreciation as it means in Vedantic or modern absolutist systems; it carries
on the contrary, *execution* with it, is *in rebus* as well as *post rem,*
and operates "causally" as partial factor in the total fact.[2]

The Indian thought that James knew about was of interest to
him, but he did not necessarily find it agreeable. As a matter of
fact it was not harmonious with the views held by most Americans
dedicated to causes, commitment, and attachment. As Dickinson
S. Miller said of James, the quality he emphasized was "Not
detachment, but attachment . . ."[3] So much of Indian thought
would have appeared to him as detached, that it is no wonder that
except for his writing on the variety of religious experience, he
had little use for its apparent supineness and lack of "coming to
grips" with everyday living. Yet it can be seen to have appealed to
American types who were likely to withdraw from social action—
such as George Santayana of whom James says in a letter to
George Herbert Palmer "Bah! Give me Walt Whitman and
Browning ten times over."[4] And yet, Whitman himself invoked
the Indian muses. Perhaps he was less tough-minded than James
thought him to be. Nevertheless, James was tender-minded himself in assessing the values of the religious experience and in this
sense, Indian philosophy was valuable insofar as it could be useful
in curing sick souls. Human unhappiness of which James was
acutely aware in a highly personal sense, dictated to him the need
to accept as plausibly useful any outlook that could help those
incurable by admonitions of "be healthy-minded!" This may well
have led James to the belief that Buddhism was not without its
uses—especially in the climate congenial to its development. It
would fit his holding that "as a practical problem for the individual, the religion he stands by must be the one which he finds best
for *him,*" even though there might be better religions for someone
else.

It is likely that James was again led to consider Indian philoso-

2 *Ibid.*, p. 512.
3 R. B. Perry, p. 248.
4 *Ibid.*, p. 251.

phy when he reread Emerson in 1902 while lying in bed recovering from an illness. In 1903–04 he wrote "Does Consciousness Exist," [5] the first essay in his *Essays in Radical Empiricism.* Certainly there is reason to believe that his reading in Buddhism made some impression on his thinking here and that his conversations and correspondence with C. R. Lanman, professor of Sanskrit at Harvard, were not without effect. Another influence in no way uncongenial to Indian thought as it was known around 1900 was the panpsychism of his friend Charles A. Strong. A significant note from John Dewey in a letter to James in 1903 reveals Dewey's reaction to James' pluralism: "Did you ever read Lloyd's *Dynamic Idealism?* [6] I can't see much difference between his monism and your pluralism . . ." [7] In 1907 James wrote to Strong in praise of Fechner's *Zend-Avesta,* devoting a chapter in his *A Pluralistic Universe* to expounding it. [8] Panpsychism was much on his mind. As Perry expresses it:

> Residual existence may consist in experience of infra-human minds, everything which is not for man or some higher subjects being conceived as "for itself." This is panpsychism, which James was repeatedly on the verge of accepting, which he constantly praised, but to which he never gave his explicit and unreserved assent.[9]

Two of the last papers James was to write were entitled: "Suggestions about Mysticism" (1910) and "A Pluralistic Mystic" (1910) which was an exposition of the philosophy of his friend Benjamin Paul Blood. Advanced here was the notion, as Perry so well put it, that James "was much more afraid of thinness than he was of inconsistency." [10] James would rather be considered lacking in

[5] "I once asked Dr. [Oliver Wendell] Holmes towards the end of his life, the question, 'What is man?' He answered without hesitation, 'A Series of states of consciousness.' " William Sturgis Bigelow: *Buddhism and Immortality.* Boston, Houghton, 1908, pp. 13–14.

[6] Alfred Henry Lloyd (1864–1927), brought to the University of Michigan by John Dewey, asked "What is thought in its simplest nature but the use of consciousness for some act of adjustment?" *Dynamic Idealism.* New York, A. C. McClurg, 1898, p. 19.

[7] Perry, p. 306.

[8] *Ibid.,* p. 331.

[9] *Ibid.,* p. 333.

[10] *Ibid.,* p. 357.

tough-mindedness than in broad-mindedness although we know
that certain "blind spots" of his seemed to center on absolutisms
of various kinds and the sort of philosophy that he believed Hegel
was propounding. Denton Snider and W. T. Harris were among
the few American philosophers who found James narrow-minded,
largely because of his unflattering remarks about Hegel's absolute
idealism. They were justified in their complaint although one can
easily feel sympathy for James in his assessment of the symphonic
and perhaps grotesque monumentality that an American pragma-
tist would find irritating. I believe that part of the indifference of
many Americans to Indian thought has been the very qualities
that made German idealism suspect of secret vices of cognition:
vast expanses of *Grund,* eternal peering into galaxies of supposed
interrelations, sweeping generalizations about past, present, and
future, cavalier disregard of the facts right-here-in-the-hand, tor-
rential moral assessments, prophetic thundering with little more
basis perhaps than imbalance of the bowels—in short to American farmer and woodsmen eyes philosophizing without the re-
straints of common-sense, empiricism, and practical everyday experience. The similarity between the German and Indian
idealistic metaphysical luxuriousness has been many times remarked.

Yet James was willing to go along with what the Indians had to
say on a number of topics, especially when he was on his nonlogi-
cal holidays. Perry claims that:

> In the Hibbert Lectures of 1908 James solemnly and publicly re-
> nounced logic. It is true that there is some question as to the precise
> scope of this renunciation, since he repeatedly referred to the logic
> which he renounced as the "intellectualistic logic" or the "logic of
> identity," as though there might be some better logic to which he
> remained faithful. It is also true that at the very times when he was
> resolving to renounce logic he was engaged in mental operations of
> extreme rigor bearing a remarkable resemblance to what other people
> called logic.[11]

This mood never persisted for James long enough to make him
swallow any absolutistic view. Healthy strenuousness, he felt,

[11] *Ibid.,* p. 368.

required the postulates of pluralism. Perhaps he regarded Indian thought as of some value to sick souls, souls in need of quietude and passive acceptance while the mindbody is manufacturing antibodies. But the polarity of James is shown in his reference to *neti, neti* [the not this, the not that] so prominent in Brahmanical thought. James says of this negative doctrine of ascription that the Indians'

> Very denial of every adjective you may propose as applicable to the ultimate truth for these Indian philosophers . . . is a denial made on behalf of a deeper yes.[12]

So it may be said of James that he was both attracted and repelled by Indian thought. Despite this attitude alternating between watchful waiting and judicious retreat he encouraged his younger colleagues, such as James Haughton Woods, to study Indian philosophy.

II

Most knowledgeable in Indian philosophy in James' generation at Harvard was Charles Rockwell Lanman (1850–1941) who had studied Sanskrit under Whitney at Yale and then repaired to Berlin and Tübingen to study with Weber and Roth. He also studied comparative grammar with Curtius [13] and Leskien at Leipzig from 1873 to 1876. Lanman taught Sanskrit at Johns Hopkins University,[14] then went to Harvard in 1880 to teach until his retirement. One of his most notable achievements was to bring back from India 500 manuscripts in Sanskrit and Prakrit. Lanman became the founding editor of the *Harvard Oriental Series* which published mostly books on Indian philosophy, religion, and literature. He published his *Sanskrit Reader* in 1884. It is still being

---

[12] William James: *The Varieties of Religious Experience*, p. 512.

[13] Bliss Perry: in *And Gladly Teach*. Boston, Houghton, 1935, tells the following of Ernst Curtius: "One evening [Mommsen] and Curtius were talking about health and habits of work. Mommsen was then in his seventieth year, and Curtius was seventy-two. It appeared that both men rose at five, took dumbbell exercises, a cold sponge bath and a cup of coffee, and were at their desks before six. . . . I have had colleagues at Harvard who rose just in time for their ten o'clock lecture." p. 100.

[14] Lanman was appointed in 1878 by President D. C. Gilman, who was a member of the American Oriental Society.

used today in Sanskrit classes in the United States. Lanman, although respectful of what made sense to him in Indian thought,
says in the *Reader* that the Brāhmanas are "puerile, arid, inane." [15]
Max Müller referred to the same texts as "simply twaddle." [16]

Lanman is concerned with the *Beginnings of Hindu Pantheism*
(1890) [17] because it is a central development "of a most wonder-
ful period in the history of India," when the life-loving Vedic
Aryans are learning to become quietistic, pessimistic Hindus.[18] He
treats this episode of Indian thought with the idealistic touch,
explaining events in terms of "national temper." Yet this account
is not without considerable merit. He closes his description and
analysis by quoting Emerson's famous lines giving the significance, as he the Concordian thought, of the Bhagavadgītā: "If the
red slayer thinks he slays . . ." and so forth.[19]

III

James' colleague at Harvard and dialectical alter ego, Josiah
Royce (1855–1916), found Indian philosophy to substantiate his
monistic views. Royce first became enamored of Indian thought
through Lanman, who introduced Royce to the Upanisads.[20]
Royce, originally a Californian whose mother wrote about her life
there, was personally aware of Asia because of the Chinese population in that state. His interest in Japanese thought was also considerable.[21] He was, I believe, the first American philosopher to mention the code of *Bushidō*,[22] yet he seemed more taken with Indian

[15] *Sanskrit Reader*. Cambridge, Harvard, 1947, p. 357.

[16] See A. K. Coomaraswamy: Primitive Mentality, *Quar. Mythic Soc.*, 31:5 n.

[17] Charles Lanman: *The Beginnings of Hindu Pantheism*. Cambridge, Charles W.
Sever, 1890.

[18] *Ibid.*, p. 7.

[19] Or its Concord variation recited by Emerson's son, "If the gray tom-cat thinks
he sings," in Edward Waldo Emerson, *Emerson in Concord*. Boston, Houghton,
1889, p. 162.

[20] Lanman moved to Harvard around 1885, at which time he was replaced at
Johns Hopkins by Maurice Bloomfield.

[21] Josiah Royce: *The Philosophy of Loyalty*. New York, Macmillan, 1930 [1908],
pp. 72–73. In it he writes: "The Japanese won much admiration from all of us by
the absolute loyalty to their own national cause which they displayed during the
war," concerning the Russo-Japanese engagements.

[22] Royce, *William James and Other Essays on the Philosophy of Life*. New York,
Macmillan, 1911, p. 80. "Hereupon we turned for information to our various →

conceptions. Royce's interest in Indian thought was also heightened by his affection for Schopenhauer. In discussing the significance of the human personality he says:

> Here one sees, is the Hindoo way of getting at the substance. It is also
> Schopenhauer's way. Look for the substance within, in your own
> nature. You will not see it without. It is the life of your own life, the
> soul of your own soul. When you find it, you will come home from the
> confusing world of sense-things to the heart and essence of the world,
> to the reality. That art Thou.[23]

By 1892 Royce was presumably hooked by that Indian thought emphasizing idealistic monism, precisely the part rejected by James. His two main concerns were the Indian philosophy represented by the Upaniṣads and the Indian religion found in Hīnayāna Buddhism.[24] One of his estimates of Indian thought is given at the time of his writing of *Studies of Good and Evil,* as follows:

> The Hindoo, as a philosopher, has always been a keen critic of human
> illusions, but since it chanced, by some accident of race-development,
> that the Hindoo, from an earlier period of his evolution, did not love
> life, Hindoo philosophy, extensive as are its literary monuments, is in
> essential doctrine always very brief and unfruitful. Life for the Hindoo
> is an ill; one philosophizes to seek salvation.[25]

Royce's concern with Hinduism waned after 1900, whereas his desire to understand Buddhism increased as we approached the First World War. Presumably he was most stimulated in this

---

authorities upon things Japanese, and came to know something of that old moral code Bushido which Nitobe in his little book has called *The Soul of Japan.* Well, whatever our other views regarding Japanese life and policy, the United States was having trouble with the Japanese in Manchuria, I think that we have now come to see that the ideal of Bushido, the ancient Japanese type of loyalty, despite the barbarous life of feuds and of bloodshed in which it first was born . . . [arose from] Chinese sages, as well as Buddhistic traditions, influenced his views of the cultivation of this interior self-possession and serenity of soul." Royce: *The Philosophy of Loyalty,* pp. 72–73. An interesting postscript from Tenney Frank (Ed.) : *An Economic Survey of Rome.* Baltimore, Johns Hopkins, 1938, vol. IV, p. 5, is "Those who remained loyal to Carthage until the end were sold into slavery."

[23] Royce: *Spirit of Modern Philosophy.* Boston, Houghton, 1899, p. 255.

[24] Kurt Leidecker, *Josiah Royce and Indian Thought.* New York, Kailas Press, 1931, pp. 7–9.

[25] Royce: *Studies in Good and Evil.* New York, Appleton, 1898, p. 353.

direction by reading Schopenhauer.[26] Royce's attachment to
Buddhism depends upon his belief not only that it was Christianity's greatest rival, but also that it was concerned with the recipro-
cal relations between metaphysical and moral problems. Furthermore, the Buddha was loyal in that basic sense of loyalty, as loyal
to the community and not simply to himself.[27] This struck Royce
as splendidly anticipatory of his own view of loyalty.

Whereas Santayana used Sāṁkhya to bolster up the sense of the
natural in Indian thought, Royce used it as a stick to beat the
wily nag of realism. For as he points out:

> The world of the realist is full of chasms; all elements are in greater or
> less isolation; unity becomes mysterious and, if dispensed with, will
> still leave the problem of the linkage in knowledge which the realist
> must assume but cannot satisfactorily solve.[28]

The greatest weakness of realism is its dualism.[29] The soul is
absolutely immaterial for Sāṁkhya while objects are known outside one's own ideas. Ultimately, Royce believed that:

> Salvation, for the Sankhya philosophy, depends upon coming to know
> precisely this utter independence of the true soul and the material
> world. In fact the soul is not only separated by a chasm from matter; it
> is even really unaffected by matter. What seem to be affections of the
> soul are, according to the Sankhya psycho-physical theory, material
> states, which merely appear to be in the soul, as, according to a favorite
> Sankhya similitude, the red Hibiscus flower is reflected in a crystal that
> all the while remains inwardly unaltered by the presence of the flower.
> The result is a theory of a sort of psycho-physical parallelism, founded,
> to be sure, according to the Sankhya, upon an illusion.[30]

Aside from contending that Sāṁkhya makes no such assertion regarding illusion, it must be admitted that at the time Royce was

[26] Leidecker: *Josiah Royce and Indian Thought,* p. 19.

[27] *Ibid.,* p. 20 f.

[28] See Leidecker's admirable synopsis of Royce's analysis of the weakness of
realism in *Josiah Royce and Indian Thought,* pp. 14–15.

[29] Like most other American philosophers of his day Royce never even conceived
that monistic materialism was a serious contender for a rung on the ladder of
realism. From Thomas Cooper to Santayana no one gave it a moment's expressed
thought. It was almost as if American philosophy was contemporaneous with an
evolutionary Neoplatonism, or had never stepped beyond Scotch Realism.

[30] Royce: *The World and the Individual,* New York, Macmillan, 1904, p. 103.

writing the easily-obtainable literature on Sāṁkhya was extremely limited, and within that boundary the interpretations were likely to favor its union with Yoga, thus making it a clearly orthodox philosophy from the Vedāntic point of view. Early and Middle Sāṁkhya were conveniently overlooked in the same way that most American parsons overlooked discrepancies in the Old and New Testament before Col. Robert Ingersoll's volatile appearances on the lecture platform.

Royce's most sustained single writing on Indian thought is to be found in his major work, *The World and the Individual.* I shall quote several longer passages to indicate his outlook here:

> What is, is at all events somehow One. This thought came early to the Hindoo religious mind. For the sake of its illustration and defense, the thinkers of the Upanishads seize, at first, upon every legend, upon every popular interpretation of nature, which may serve to make the sense of this unity living in the reader's or hearer's mind. For the writers of the greater Upanishads, this unity of Being is not so much a matter of argument as it is an object of intuition. . . . But, as we saw . . . a metaphysical realist also can attempt, however inconsistently, to call all Being One. In this case there would result such a doctrine as that of the Eleatic school.[31]

One scarcely need take seriously Royce's view here of the metaphysical realist since at least one perspective of realism quite consistently holds all being to be one—namely materialism. Royce's brand of idealism was not such as to find a thoroughly congenial ally in Vedānta either, although, as Richard Hocking has shown, Royce had conducted "his own studies of the schools of the Vedānta [recognizing] the mystic and the realist as dialectical companions, each requiring the other." [32] The trouble with the realist is that he is essentially a dualist, said Royce. This outcome of realism, Royce believed, was seen by the Hindu who,

> was early aware of the danger threatening every monistic interpretation of the Real. He undertook to escape the danger by a device which

[31] *Ibid.,* vol. I, 156–157.
[32] William E. Hocking: Process and Analysis in the Philosophy of Royce. In Grover Smith (Ed.) : *Josiah Royce's Seminar 1913–1914,* as recorded in the notebooks of Harry T. Costello. New Brunswick, Rutgers, 1963, p. xxiii.

in the Upanishads appear so constantly, and with such directness of expression, as to constitute a sort of axiom, to which the thinker constantly appeals. The Hindoo seer of the period of the Upanishads is keenly and reflectively self-conscious.[33]

The thinking process of this seer, Royce continues,

is constantly before him. He cannot view any reality as merely inde-pendent of the idea that knows it, because he has a strong sense that he himself is feeling, beholding, thinking, this reality, which he therefore views as an object meant by himself, and so as having no meaning apart from his point of view.[34]

An axiom of European idealists, said Royce, is often stated in the form:

No object without a subject, is therefore always, in one shape or another, upon the Hindoo's lips. He states it less technically, but he holds it all the more intuitively. *The world is One—why? Because I feel it as one. What then is its oneness?* And who am I? I am Brahman; I myself, in my inmost heart, in my Soul, am the world-principle, the All.[35]

According to Royce, carrying the analysis of Hindu idealism further, "the Hindoo's Monism becomes at once a subjective idealism," a shrewd score which might be developed into a highly controversial monograph. The Hindu is led from monism to a "series of reflections upon the mystery of the Self." [36] Mere episte-mological idealism is led then to metaphysical idealism through a series of steps shown in the Chandogya Upanishad III, 14,[37] according to Royce. These steps are:

(1) Realization that the universe is Brahman.
(2) Everything is infinite One.
(3) The spirit within my heart is greater than the universe.
(4) The spirit within my heart is Brahman.

[33] Royce, *The World and the Individual,* vol. I, pp. 157–158.
[34] *Ibid.*
[35] *Ibid.*
[36] *Ibid.*
[37] Translated for Royce by C. R. Lanman.

Royce then quoted from the passages that deal with the opinions of Uddalaka. Royce admitted that the viewpoint of Uddalaka begins on a realistic note:

> The Beginning of the argument . . . appears, from one side, realistic. The World, says Uddalaka, is, and is one. The disciple is to note this fact and to bring it home to himself by frequent empirical illustrations taken from outer nature. Then he is to observe that he, too, in so far as he is at all real, is for this very reason one with the world principle.[38]

This teaching, said Royce, seems still to be realism,

> only now a realism that has become reflective, recognizing the observer of the reality as also a real being, and therefore asserting of him, as knower, whatever one also asserts of the Being that he knows. But suddenly, even as one speaks, one becomes aware that. . . . one never really has observed it as an external world at all.[39]

One finally becomes aware, Royce said, that:

> Through this very identification of the essence of the knower and of the object known, the innermost reality of the world has itself become transformed. It is no longer a world independent of knowledge.[40]

Royce then quoted Uddalaka, but the passage quoted shows no such trend at all, and it remains at variance with the recent interpretation of Walter Ruben who maintains that Uddalaka remains a realist while Yājñavalkya carries on the idealistic note that surprises Royce.[41] What Royce had noticed, interestingly enough, is an interpolation by some later idealist (Brahmin) who cannot abide the pleasant naturalism which must have "contaminated" many people in those golden days. Nevertheless it is worthy of mention that Royce, despite his strong idealistic proclivities, can find evidences of realism tucked away in what was held in his day, at least, to be a bastion of idealism—the Upaniṣads. His sharp eye is

---

[38] Royce, *The World and the Individual,* vol. I, p. 160.
[39] *Ibid.*
[40] *Ibid.*
[41] See Ruben, *Geschichte der Indischen Philosophie* Berlin, Deutscher Verlag der Wissenschaoften, 1954, pp. 83–86.

Josiah Royce

focused on the least sign of unorthodoxy in the idealistic life of the spirit.

In discussing the Sāṁkhya viewpoint, Royce immediately pointed out that it is a dualism. The soul is absolutely immaterial for Sāṁkhya while objects are known outside one's own ideas. Ultimately, Royce believed that,

> Salvation, for the Sankhya philosophy, depends upon coming to know precisely this utter independence of the true soul and the material.[42]

Royce's alert mind not only recognized the major interpretative difficulty in the Chandogya Upaniṣad but he also noticed, always scenting dialectical aberrations, that all was not well in Buddhism in so far as consistency in ethics was concerned. He noticed that:

> Buddhism, as we know, is a religion wholly founded on self-denial, and it counsels austere self-extinction. And yet by a strange freak of moral dialectics, it is Buddhism that has given us some of the best expression of the Titanic individualism.[43]

He then quotes from the Sutta Nipata (from the *Sacred Books of the East*, X, part II, p. 6 ff.) to adequately prove his point.

It would not be far from the truth to say that Royce was the favorite American philosopher of Indian academic philosophers of the last generation. When I visited Professor N. G. Damle (1893–   ) in Poona in January 1967, he grew enthusiastic about Royce and what reading him had meant to his own philosophical development. Part of this may be attributed to the encouragement of his uncle, R. D. Ranade (1886–1955?) of Allahabad, who believed that

> "Śaṁkara's Absolute Consciousness, Bradley's Absolute Experience and Royce's Absolute Person differ, if at all, only in names. . . . The great difference between Royce and Śaṁkara is that while the former says that the soul comes into existence in time, Śaṁkara says that, seen from one point of view it is eternal, while seen from another and higher, it is merely appearance as compared with the absoluteness of the Absolute, which is Bradley's position." [44]

[42] Royce, *The World and the Individual*, I, 102.
[43] Royce, *The Religious Aspect of Philosophy*. Boston, Houghton, 1891 [1885], p. 207.
[44] Ranade, The evolution of my own thought. In S. Radhakrishnon and J. H. Muirhead (Ed.) : *Contemporary Indian Philosophy*, rev. 2nd and enlarged ed. London, Allen & Unwin, 1952, pp. 544–45.

Had Royce spent more of his efforts studying Indian metaphysics and ethics we doubtless would have had a rich monograph from his fluent pen. As it happened we must be satisfied with what he did write and with the stimulation he imparted to such students as Woods and Hocking.

IV

A year older than Royce was Henry Clarke Warren (1854–1899) who was educated at Harvard and Johns Hopkins. He was the first American scholar to gain distinction in Pāli, although he of course knew Sanskrit as well. Originator of the *Harvard Oriental Series* in 1891, he is most famous for his *Buddhism in Translations* (1896) which is a felicitious group of selections enjoying a steady sale among American readers for more than sixty years. A remarkable feature of this book is that it was "done wholly in America" based mostly on printed texts with the addition of Pāli manuscripts found in the Brown University library. Warren's allegiance to Pāli followed his discovery that whereas "Sanskrit literature is a chaos, Pali, a cosmos." [45] Hindu chronology seemed nonexistent, a complaint voiced not only by Hegel but by Whitney, and the authors of texts could scarcely be identified with any degree of accuracy. Of special interest is the short but meaty ten-page appendix explaining the five groups, eighty-nine consciousnesses, and *karma* in its relation to consciousness (pp. 487–96). His translation of Buddhaghoṣṣa's *Visuddhimagga* was not completed before he died.[46]

Warren was a sickly boy as the result of a fall in early childhood. At Harvard he was close to Professor George Herbert Palmer of the philosophy department who helped him in his passion for the history of philosophy. He was a good student of Plato and Kant, according to Lanman. But he also worked in botany, in chemistry, and maintained special interest in his aquarium for most of his life. He read Oriental studies in Sanskrit, Pāli, French, German, Dutch, Spanish, and Russian.

---

[45] Harvard Oriental Series, III, ed. C. R. Lanman. Cambridge, Harvard, 1909, p. xix.

[46] It had been worked on by four Harvard Sanskritists and two Asians by the time it appeared.

Warren studied Sanskrit with Greenough [47] at Harvard, then under Lanman and Maurice Bloomfield at Johns Hopkins. Later he also studied in England with Rhys Davids, the Buddhist scholar. Warren was a donor of the Harvard Oriental Series, Royal Asiatic Society, and the Harvard Semitic Museum. Shortly before Warren's lamentably early death, Lanman relates, a friend sent Warren some brandied peaches and received this response: "I can't eat your peaches, but I appreciate the *spirit* in which they are sent." [48]

He stood at his desk with two crutches under his arms to take the weight off his spinal column, later he worked on his knees at a chair. About this he said, when it was commented upon by his friends that the knees of his trousers were getting hard use, Warren replied: "Ah, but when Saint Peter sees these knees, he'll say, 'Pass right in, sir, pass right in.' " [49]

V

James Haughton Woods (1864–1935) studied Sanskrit under Lanman and Indian philosophy with Deussen at Berlin. He took his B.A. at Harvard University, studied at Oxford University and the University of Strasbourg, where he received his doctorate. He also studied at The Episcopal Theological School which increased his interest in comparative religion. He first went to India in 1902–04, stopping to study with Jacobi on the way, and for a second time in 1907. Woods died in Japan in 1935 while studying Tendai Buddhism. After Warren's death his great preoccupation was to finish the translation of the *Visuddhimagga* after Lanman and Kosambi initially tried to complete it. Woods continued with Kosambi and later with Bapat, but it was not completed in his lifetime either and was next committed to the hands of Walter Clark. Upon his death it was taken over by Daniel H. H. Ingalls. When it finally appears it will be one of the great involuntary composite translations of recent times.

---

[47] James Bradstreet Greenough (1833–1901), professor of Latin from 1874–1901 and editor of classical texts.

[48] Lanman: A brief memorial. In H. C. Warren: *Buddhism in Translations,* Abridged Issue, 1922, p. 380.

[49] *Ibid.*

Besides the works of other American Sanskritists on Indian philosophy, Woods' works were among the first to be written by an American scholar. His *The Yoga System of Patanjali* appeared in the *Harvard Oriental Series* in 1914, one of the first systematic scholarly works in America on Indian philosophy. As a professor at Harvard University, Woods was to influence several of his students to pursue various aspects of Indian thought, including William Ernest Hocking, William Savery, James Bissett Pratt, and Daniel S. Robinson.

Woods began teaching at Harvard around 1890, first in the department of history and then in that of philosophy. His advanced interest in Indian thought was encouraged by William James "who prophesied that it was a subject which was to grow in interest to philosophers in the years to come." [50] As chairman of the philosophy department, Woods brought Chinese, Indian, and Japanese scholars to Harvard.

The importance of Woods' *The Yoga System of Patanjali* (1914) rests on the fact that it is the first technical and scholarly work on Indian philosophy written by an American professor of philosophy. It is a model of thoroughness and excellence in its 381 pages. Included, besides a complete bibliography of the subject beginning with 1834 and terminating in 1912, is an index of quotations in the commentary, an index of and in the *Tattva-Vaiçāradī,* and an index of words in the sūtras themselves. The work also begins with an analytical summary of the Yoga-sūtras, goes on to give the bare translation of them, followed by a greatly detailed commentary of the four books called the *Yoga-Bhāshya* attributed to Veda-Vyāsa and the explanation called the *Tattva-Vaiçāradī* of Vāchaspatimiçra. Stylistically the work leaves something to be desired because so many words are inserted in brackets and parentheses, of which some are Sanskrit and some English. Nevertheless this style was indispensable for the sake of accuracy and represents the necessary caution required in a pioneer work of its kind. Later writers could then feel at liberty to write a more popular account of the yoga philosophy.

Woods was editor of the *Papañca-Sūdanī* (1923) for the Pali

---

[50] *Letter* from Mrs. James H. Woods, Wellesley, Mass. (January 4, 1962).

Text Society, translated Deussen's *Outline of the Vedanta* (1906), and wrote two books on comparative religion: *Values of Religious Facts* (1900) and *Practice and Science of Religion* (1906). His *The Gem's Ray* (*Maṇi-prabhā*) appeared in 1915. From 1916 to 1918 he was visiting professor in France and again in 1928.

VI

The year before Woods' study of Yoga was published, Crawford Howell Toy (1836–1919) wrote one of the pioneer American works in comparative religion. A graduate of the University of Virginia and the Southern Baptist Theological Seminary at Greenville, South Carolina, he was Hancock Professor of Hebrew and Oriental Languages at Harvard University from 1880 to 1909. He wrote *Introduction to the History of Religions*[51] in which he discusses many aspects of Hinduism, Jainism, and Buddhism. One section in his broad account stands out: that on monachism, where he states:

> The birthplace of monachism proper was India. In the Brahmanic scheme the highest sanctity and most brilliant prospects[52] attached to a man who forsook the life of men and devoted himself to solitary meditation in the forest. . . . The organization into communities was made by Buddha and, contemporaneously, by Mahavira, the founder of Jainism. It is the organization that has made the institution a power in religious history.[53]

VII

At this time William Ernest Hocking (1873–1966) was already aware of Indian thought, long before being appointed at Harvard, having attended the Parliament of Religions in Chicago in 1893. Here Hocking was particularly struck by Swami Vivekananda's moving phrase, "Sinners! It is a sin to call men sinners."[54]

[51] New York, Ginn, 1913.

[52] Perhaps a malapropism in that "prospects" could only with straining be attached to such a negative and nihilistic role. It is fascinating to note the ingression of commercial and mining terms into the terminology of other philosophers of this day, particularly William James.

[53] Toy, *Introduction to the History of Religions,* pp. 553–554.

[54] *Letter* from William Ernest Hocking, Madison, New Hampshire, (May 6, 1962).

Hocking's own vivid account reveals how he was initiated into the circle of Indianophiles.

> I had done some reading in the translations [of Indian literature] available at Harvard and some of the writings of George Foote [*sic*] Moore. It happened that Moore was just at that time (1904) leaving Andover to come to Harvard, and Andover Theological School was in straits. Whom could they get to take Moore's place? They consulted George Herbert Palmer [55] who told them they could not fill that place. He suggested a wild alternative: "Get a young fellow interested in the subject: give him three hours a week to teach (instead of 15), and let him spend his days in the great library built up by Moore in Andover, and *work up the subject* with his class." The staff at Andover accepted the suggestion, if Palmer could suggest a "young fellow." Palmer nominated me. I was in a considerable doubt; and consulted Jim Woods,[56] recently back from two years in India. Woods proposed a course of reading for me, and encouraged me to go ahead,—which I did, with trepidation.[57]

Hocking became, some twenty-seven years later, chairman of the "Commission of Appraisal" of the Laymen's Inquiry, and as such visited India, China, and Japan in 1931, an experience which made Indian thought more vivid for him.

Hocking's philosophical position has been called "individualistic idealism," yet if one judges his opinions over the years this seems excessively restrictive, for Hocking has been highly involved in showing the influence of the social life of man upon his personal philosophy. His view is a religious view of life and it is in this perspective that Hocking finds Indian viewpoints interesting. "Mighty religion and mighty strokes of speculation have always gone together," [58] he said. Yet man cannot have as his aim a man-centered goal, but rather must focus on the "Most Real, beyond his will." [59] Reality is one, Hocking opined; it is good

---

[55] The genial earth of the Harvard philosophy department about whom the planets sailed: James, Royce, Münsterberg, Santayana, of whom the latter acidly remarked: his "method was Hegelian adapted to a Sunday School." Santayana, *Persons and Places*. New York, Scribner, 1944, p. 246.

[56] James Haughton Woods.

[57] *Letter* from William Ernest Hocking, Madison, New Hampshire (May 6, 1962).

[58] Hocking: *The Meaning of God in Human Experience*. New Haven, Yale, 1934, p. 59.

[59] *The Meaning of God in Human Experience*, p. 152.

rather than evil; and at its highest level it, as God, is an intimate and infallible associate of man. Through this God human peace of mind is achieved. Without God the universe is without meaning. Yet each man by a mystical understanding lives by his own vision, and it is in this sense that Hocking's idealism is "individualistic."

With Hocking, as with Royce, Indian philosophical and religious insights are not incorporated into his thinking so much as they are seen as corroborations of his own insights. As he said fifteen years after his "trepidation" at Andover:

> My own view is that conscience stands outside the instinctive life of man, not as something separate, but as an *awareness of the success or failure of that life* in maintaining its status and its growth. It is a safeguard of the power at any time achieved . . . What conscience recognizes is that certain behavior increases our hold on reality while certain other behavior diminishes that hold, constitutes what the old Southern Buddhists called an *asava,* a leak.[60]

Hocking's approach to Indian thought was more confident than James'. He wrote as if he were at ease with it:

> The most widely influential of religions, Buddhism, must by its own logic regard itself a failure in so far as it tends in any way to make the present existence, whether personal, social or political, more attractive. And Buddhism is not alone in this deprecation of things present.[61]

This is a fault that was later to be echoed by Santayana for Santayana had taken on more of American pragmatic optimism than he probably would have liked to admit.

Hocking criticized the emptying of individuality out of the religious or philosophical experience of Buddhism as follows:

> Buddhism . . . more completely [than Vedānta] . . . subtly defines the goal of all passion as a passionless transparency of seeing. It attacks the self-element in all desire, demanding that the individual organism shall become the instrument of a perfect universality of indifference, to which neither existence nor yet non-existence shall appear as an object of strife. For even in the determined rejection of existence by the

[60] Hocking, *Human Nature and Its Remaking.* New Haven, Yale, 1919, p. 99.
[61] Hocking, *The Meaning of God . . . ,* p. 6.

Brahmanic ideal a love for being lies concealed. It is evident nevertheless that this position is attractive to the Buddhist because of the
initiation which it represents into the very moving principles of the
cosmos; the love of power has not disappeared into something else, but
has taken the form of an aspiration for metaphysical *status* with all the
power over one's own destiny (and over other men's minds) therein
implied.[62]

Vedānta is at fault, according to Hocking, because it "empties all
passion into the will to know." [63] The power of knowledge is that
I (every particular being) am Brahman. "This is the power that
can strike off the chains of reincarnation; in it all lesser powers
are believed to be included." [64] Hocking is here valiantly trying to
make sense out of the union of the individual to society through
the particular relationship of religion—which he takes to be the
fundamental relation. Evidently the Vedānta and Buddhism are
not helpful in the last analysis because they allow the individual
to disappear into the vortex of the loss of individuality, in Brahman, in "a perfect universality of indifference," as he puts it.
Hocking's dead seriousness with regard to *the* fundamental question, the question of religion, is well shown in a paper he delivered at the Sixth International Congress of Philosophy in September of 1926. He here recounts that,

A Hindu scholar, who was recently pointing out to a group of students
certain differences between Oriental and Western thought, was asked
whether the mystical trait in Hindu metaphysics might not be due to
the enervating influence of a hot climate. There was a slightly delayed
response and a certain added vigor in the reply: "In so far as mysticism
is true, it is true in all countries, even in America!" What was the
meaning of that prompt repudiation of a simple and banal psychological theorem? Why does the innocent suggestion that *your* doctrine may
be a function of the climate become so outrageous when it is my
doctrine that is so explained? [65]

[62] Hocking: *Human Nature and Its Remaking*. New Haven, Yale, 1918, p. 334.
[63] *Ibid.*, p. 333.
[64] *Ibid.*, p. 334.
[65] Hocking: Mind and Near-Mind. In Edgar S. Brightman (Ed.) : *Proceedings of
the Sixth International Congress of Philosophy*, New York, Longmans, Green, 1927,
p. 205.

According to his son Richard, Hocking was still meditating on the Hindu and Buddhist scriptures at the age of ninety-three, always eager to demonstrate their relevance for today.

VIII

Another Indianophile professor at Harvard was William Sturgis Bigelow (1850–1926), one of the first Americans to publish a monograph on any aspect of Buddhism. The only medical practitioner to be mentioned in our account besides Oliver Wendell Holmes, Sr., Bigelow took his A.B. and M.D. at Harvard. Although he gave the Ingersoll Lecture on Buddhist doctrine as early as 1908, it is obvious that he was more interested in Japanese Buddhism than Indian. Attesting to this besides his lecture itself is his being awarded a Commandership of the Imperial Order of the Rising Sun. His lecture was primarily on Tendai and Shingon Buddhism, but Indian Buddhism forms its background.

According to Bigelow, consciousness, as viewed by these two sects and not in conflict with Hīnayāna Buddhism, is first of all conditioned "mechanically" by outside material events, second, only by the will, and third, by dreaming. Space-time relations which condition matter are summed up in separateness, whereas conscious is summed up in unity. Deeper than either is the will which is not passion or objective but "essentially and necessarily active." "Will is the assertion of a form of consciousness from the center outward." [66] Furthermore, consciousness has no dimension, so that "the self is co-extensive with the universe." [67] With this introduction, Bigelow was prepared to explain Buddhism. He said:

> If a man consists of states of consciousness, as the Buddhist doctrine affirms, then so far as any of them ceases, the man ceases.[68]

Character, Bigelow claimed, consists of the sum of habitual reflexes. "Where does it come from? From the parents?" While in the West we say it comes from heredity, "in the East it is regarded as an illustration of rebirth or reincarnation." [69]

Bigelow then tied this up with evolutionary doctrine:

[66] Bigelow, *Buddhism and Immortality*, p. 40.
[67] *Ibid.*, p. 43.
[68] *Ibid.*, p. 48.
[69] *Ibid.*, p. 50.

The difference in things [and men], therefore is how much they realize of . . . universal consciousness. The process of evolution is the process of increase of the amount realized. The only thing that prevents a man from realizing the whole of it is the accumulated habit of thinking in terms of the self, that is, of the material self. It was not the fault of our struggling predecessors on this planet that they thought in these terms. Natural selection took care of that. They had to, or die.[70]

Growth toward universal consciousness is achieved in Japanese Buddhism, Bigelow thought, by two methods: First, by exterior and second by interior ones. The exterior is by good deeds; the interior by direct action of the will which may dominate the habitual character. At this juncture Bigelow retold a story attributed to Emerson. One day that sage was stopped by an excited Millerite who exclaimed:

"Mr. Emerson, do you know that the world is going to be destroyed in ten days?" "Well," said Emerson, "I don't see but we shall get along just as well without it."

That is good Buddhist doctrine,[71] according to Bigelow. But one wonders if even the irascible Bishop Berkeley would go along with such improbity.[72] Man tries to reach the summit of the mountain by many roads, according to a Japanese proverb, but at the top there is always seen the same moon. "The mountain top," said Biglow,

is the apotheosis of personal existence . . . But it is not the end. Deeper than the kingdoms, and higher than the stars, is the sky that holds them all. And there alone is peace . . . That peace is NIR-VANA.[73]

Thus ends the lecture on Buddhist immortality.

IX

George Foot Moore (1851–1931) was, with Toy, one of the first theologians to include Indian philosophy and religion in his ac-

[70] *Ibid.*, pp. 60–61.
[71] *Ibid.*, pp. 66–67.
[72] *Ibid.*, pp. 74–75.
[73] *Ibid.*, pp. 74–75.

counts of general religion. He took his A.B. and M.A. at Yale University and then graduated from Union Theological Seminary. He taught first at Andover and then at Harvard after 1904. The first volume of his *History of Religions* appeared in 1913 and the second in 1919.

Moore, in his *History of Religions* has given us an account of "The Religion of the Veda," "The Great Heresies," of Buddhism and Jainism, and "The Philosophical Systems," and Hinduism. His description of Indian religion and thought seems later to have been followed and expanded by E. Washburn Hopkins.[74] In his *The Birth and Growth of Religion* (1923) Moore has some scattered references to Hinduism.

To the fact that American evolutionist philosophers were not totally unaware of India and Indian thought, John Fiske (1842–1901) attests in references to Indian culture and religion in his *Essays Historical and Literary*.[75] He refers to the Vedas, the *gandharvas*, Indra, Paṇis, and Hindu mythology in II, p. 288. He also speaks of the Pantcha [*sic*] Tantras, Aryan language and folklore as well as Max Müller. This may well be about all that an educated man with no proclivity for such knowledge might pick up in reading the daily papers and current magazines.

X

The founder with Paul Elmer More of American Neohumanism was Irving Babbitt (1865–1933), who studied Sanskrit in the same class with More. Babbitt took his A.B. and A.M. at Harvard, studied in Paris in 1891–92, taught romance languages at Williams College before taking his post as professor of French at Harvard which he held until his retirement. He also lectured at Kenyon College, Yale University, the Sorbonne, Amherst College, and Toronto University. Christy claims that the Orientalism of More and Babbitt in their Neohumanism was the first in the United States "based on sound scholarship and an acquaintance with Sanskrit and Pali." [76] The quarrels of the Neohumanists

[74] E. Washburn Hopkins: *The History of Religions*. New York, Macmillan, 1918.

[75] John Fiske: *Essays Historical and Literary*, 2 vols. New York, Macmillan, 1902.

[76] Christy: The sense of the past. In Arthur E. Christy (Ed.) : *The Asian Legacy and American Life*. New York, John Day, 1945, p. 50.

with the literary critics resulted in *Humanism and America,*
edited by Norman Foerster, and *The Critique of Humanism,*
edited by C. Harley Grattan. Younger critics, Christy says,

> probably would have raised no voice in protest if the Neo-Humanists
> had been satisfied with the role of antiquarians crying "Mahabharata"
> from rooftops. But they rose in defense of modernism against the
> erudite attacks of the academicians and characterized their utterances
> as "Mahabracadabra." [77]

Christy interprets the clash as one between an essentially Hindu
sense of human values and a civilization hell-bent for the economic debacle of 1929.[78]

Babbitt's only book to deal almost exclusively with Indian
thought was his *The Dhammapada* [79] which contained an "Essay
on Buddha and the Occident." He translated the former from the
Pāli. Walter E. Clark helped with the completion of the posthu-
mous volume as did Dora D. Babbitt. She stated in the editor's
prefatory note that this work was "the fruit of Irving Babbitt's
whole life's devotion to the study of Buddhism." The translation
is surely the finest in the English language, revealing Babbitt's
years of devotion to style.

Babbitt, who fought romanticism, also found what he believed
to be its American manifestation: the industrial and utilitarian
view of life. Europe, in order to escape the industrial and utilitarian view of life, turned to the East.[80] But the East had already
become sullied by the West. "Japan in particular has been dispos-
ing of her Buddhas as curios and turning her attention to
battleships." [81] In the authentic teachings of the Buddha, nevertheless, the best of the West is preserved without Western theological and metaphysical complications. Furthermore, Babbitt said,
the Buddha "was more prone to humor than most religious
teachers," [82] perhaps concomitant with his absence of casuistical
and obscurantist propensities. Babbitt the stylist could not let the

[77] *Ibid.,* p. 50.
[78] *Ibid.*
[79] Irving Babbitt: *The Dhammapada.* New York, Oxford, 1936.
[80] Babbitt, *The Dhammapada,* p. 67.
[81] *Ibid.,* p. 68.
[82] *Ibid.,* p. 71.

Buddhist literature pass without a few remarks. First of all he pointed out the "damnable iteration." This he explained away as a mnemonic device. Also the aphoristic gifts of the Buddha were not quite up to those of Jesus Christ, he thought.[83] The Buddha was humble, said Babbitt, but he was not modest as his claims outdo even those of the Christ. Indeed, his whole essay is one of the most sensible and refreshing that one could read in any of the mountain of Buddhist exegesis.

Babbitt claimed that whereas Western philosophy had been "from the time of Locke . . . a long debauch of epistemology"[84] it had not resulted in the answer to Kant's second question—What must I do? Buddhism, on the other hand is a path[85] philosophy, Babbitt asserted. One must not only *know* the Four Noble Truths but act on them. Hence, it is a voluntaristic philosophy. Babbitt illuminated much more, but we shall pass on after quoting his closing remarks in this book.

> The meditation of the Buddhist involves like that of the Christian the exercise of transcendent will. . . . Persons of the "positivistic" and critical temper who yet perceive the importance of meditation may incline here as elsewhere to put less emphasis on the doctrinal divergence of Christianity and Buddhism than on their psychological agreement.[86]

According to Irving Babbitt,

> The chief obstacle to a better understanding between East and West in particular is a certain type of occidental who is wont to assume almost unconsciously that the East has everything to learn from the West and little or nothing to give in return.[87]

Romantic Orientalism, according to Babbitt, consists of "Picturesque surfaces," is the locus of "the bower of dreams," a kind of "subrational spontaneity and in Schopenhauer the Buddha is

[83] *Ibid.*, p. 73.

[84] *Ibid.*, p. 73.

[85] A notion later to become a central view of Karl Potter in his *Presuppositions of India's Philosophies*.

[86] Babbitt, *The Dhammapada*, p. 121.

[87] Babbitt: Romanticism and the Orient. In *On Being Creative and Other Essays*. Boston, Houghton, 1932, p. 235.

converted into a heavy-eyed, pessimistic dreamer" whereas he was "one of the most alert and vigorous figures of whom we have historical record." [88]

The world of Harvard reached out to Eastern civilization during this period just as the world of Tokyo University leaned eagerly westward. Harvard's influence was to extend Indian philosophy to Los Angeles, San Francisco, and Seattle where another influx, from China and Japan, was already changing American urbanites on the Pacific Coast.

Another sometime Harvard professor, George Santayana, whose concern for Indian philosophy was kindled during these years, will be treated in the next chapter. His attention was to be focused on Indian philosophy from the time Royce began writing about it until the 1950's, much of which time he lived in Europe as a man of letters in England, Spain, and Italy.

[88] Babbitt, Romanticism and the Orient. In *On Being Creative*, pp. 241–243. A view held later by Edwin A. Burtt of Cornell University.

Chapter VI

SANTAYANA AND INDIAN PHILOSOPHY
1900–1950

I

No american has given higher praise to Indian classical philosophy than George Santayana (1863–1952). He observed, not long after the First World War, that:

> The first philosophers, the original observers of life and nature, were the best; and I think only the Indians and the Greek naturalists, together with Spinoza, have been right on the chief issue, the relation of man and of his spirit to the universe.[1]

Ever since he had listened to the lectures of Paul Deussen in the 1880's Santayana was aware of Indian thought. Although the technical or comparative aspects little concerned him at first, he was keenly concerned to include Indian thought in his overall view of the thought and metaphysics of mankind. Although he made relatively few references to Indian thought until after World War I, from that time onwards his writings increasingly related directly to it, or alluded to it, almost as if he felt that he should continue a tradition begun by Emerson and continued by Royce. Making no claim to constructing a universal philosophy, Santayana continued until his death to search for parallels and differences in Indian philosophy which gave him the requisite outings from the constricted European and American dialogue.

Santayana was in a sense a metaphysical son of Pierre Gassendi (1592–1655). Both attempted to combine materialism with spirit-

---

[1] Santayana: *Scepticism and Animal Faith*. New York, Scribner, 1923, p. viii.

103

ualism. On the dancing bed of atoms they constructed systems which refused to clip the chord of spiritual testimony or transcendentalism. They also refused to separate their focus of interest from their Christian tradition. Santayana, an avowed materialist, shamelessly used Christian tradition and Hinduism as well in order to interpret the cosmic as well as the human world.

With Emerson, Santayana appreciated much of the novel metaphysics and poetry of Indian thought. Like Emerson he was largely casual toward if not oblivious of its epistemological subtileness. But where he parted company most with Emerson was in maintaining as late as 1949, at the age of eighty-five, that:

> I follow the Indians in their Brahman Spirit, in its essence, but of course not in its absolute status as the root of all things. It is the root, in an animal psyche, of the *universe of appearances,* but the real universe, with its movement and competion [*sic*] must first have produced the psyche with its interests and powers. . . .[2]

Such was his note from the materialist clarinet. Of Santayana as of Emerson it could not be said that he was parochial. Yet where Santayana took the real universe to be the flux of materiality, Emerson took it to be the spiritual root. When contemplating the philosophy of William James he put James in an Indian materialistic context. For he held that for James:

> "Experience" would turn into a cosmic dance [of Śiva?] of absolute entities created and destroyed *in vacuo* according to universal laws, or perhaps by chance.[3]

In what sense Santayana meant to take the Brahman Spirit *in its essence* without also taking it *in its absolute status* requires conjecture, than which nothing is more pleasing to philosophers who have not lost their sense of professional dignity.

Is it surprising that Santayana's interpretation of Indian spirit-

[2] Daniel Cory: *Santayana: The Later Years.* New York, Braziller, 1963, p. 291. Santayana later held that "Where we find Spirit fully expressed is in Indian and Platonic Philosophy . . ." In John Lachs (Ed.) : *Animal Faith and Spiritual Life.* New York, Appleton, 1967, p. 284.

[3] Santayana: *Character and Opinion in the United States.* New York, Scribner, 1921 [1920], p. 72.

ualism was subtler and keener attuned to the Christian tradition than Emerson's? Yet Emerson may be closer to Indian intentions as Santayana demonstrates in the following passage:

> In calling existence an illusion, the Indian sages meant that it is fugitive and treacherous; the images and persons that diversify it are unsubstantial, and myself the most shifting and unsubstantial of all . . . life is an illusion if we trust it, but is is a truth if we do not trust it; and this discovery is perhaps better symbolized by the cross than by the Indian doctrine of illusion [*māyā*].[4]

One might contend that nothing more inappropriate could be juxtaposed than the symbol of the cross on the one hand and the doctrine of *māyā* on the other. Perhaps the meaning Santayana intended to convey is best left uninterpreted. Late in life Santayana approached the Indian perspective of existence again. He said of it:

> Ontologically the place and character which I assign to existence are the same assigned to it, if we may trust reports, by the orthodox doctrines of India. Pure Being, or Brahma, since it is eternal and undivided, is an essence, not a substance or existence. This essence has infinite potential manifestations, each a different essence containing pure Being, and all together forming the realm of essence.[5]

It can be seen that by this time Santayana feels called upon to make the distinction between the "orthodox": as opposed to the "unorthodox," that which denies the eternal validity of the Vedas.

II

Of the Indian doctrines that Santayana discussed throughout his writing, the following are the most important, in order of their importance: being, spirit, *māyā*, transmigration, *karma*, transcendentalism, mysticism, and deep sleep. It is instructive to compare his reactions to those of Emerson with which Santayana was probably familiar. Both Americans showed a certain respect for transcendentalism, despite Santayana's revulsion when it took

---

[4] Santayana: *Soliloquies in England.* London, Constable, 1922, p. 93.
[5] Santayana: *The Idler and His Works, and Other Essays,* Daniel Cory (Ed.). New York, Braziller, 1957, p. 116.

certain German forms. They both believed that the notion of *māyā* adds a dimension to Western thought. They thought that there might be something to *karma,* yet they both rejected transmigration as contrary to their respective reality-principles or to the American spirit that is full of pragmatic hopefulness for the future. Indian "spirit" they could tolerate, with Emerson reading into it more transcendentalism and Santayana more animality. Neither of them had anything against "deep sleep," a posture not surprising in philosophers. It is curious that both Emerson and Santayana were accused of playing around with foreign ideas of a peculiarly dangerous and noxious kind when they considered such Indian conceptions. Erwin Edman, whom Santayana in his last years claimed to have tried to make him out a fascist,[6] felt that Santayana was at once "an unamalgamated compound, of Aristotle and the Hindus in metaphysics," [7] a Platonic materialist and a devotee of Lucretius and Sāṁkhya. Charles S. Peirce, seventy-five years earlier, also referred slightingly to this Indian interest of Emerson's.

In Sāṁkhya Santayana found the most congenial Indian philosophy, a naturalistic *darśana* that he found worthy of the pre-Socratics. Put in the briefest possible terms, this Indian philosophy holds that the universe is constructed out of material substances by an immaterial principle. This dualism would not have received Santayana's approbation, but what did was the emphasis this system put upon the development of the cosmos in a natural and systematic way once the immaterial had set it in motion. It was the Hindu parallel to Western deism. Emerson knew little of Sāṁkhya but if he had known more it is easy to conjecture that he might have found a good deal of it congenial to his own views of nature. For Santayana it dispensed with the more florid features of Indian transcendentalism.[8]

---

[6] Santayana's detached attitude and downright political ignorance during World War II plus his love of Rome led him to express opinions that occasionally brand him as not only conservative but perhaps even reactionary.

[7] Paul Schilpp (Ed.): *The Philosophy of George Santayana.* Evanston, Northwestern U., 1940, p. 295.

[8] By the middle of the 1950's George P. Conger (1884–1960), professor of philosophy and chairman of the department of philosophy at the University of Minnesota, who taught Indian philosophy there, tried with no great success to revive interest in Sāṁkhya.

Just as the first academic teacher of philosophy in the Americas was born in Spain,[9] so was the most genuinely receptive to the totality of Indian philosophy, George Santayana. Until very recently in the United States, only Emerson and Santayana among philosophers incorporated Indian philosophy into the weft of their prehensions and writings.[10] Santayana, however, as a technically-trained philosopher, knew considerably more about Indian thought than did Emerson. Equally important, he also sensed the cultural and physical outlook of the Indians more completely than Emerson who had not been brought up under the pervasive sway of the newly-developing behavioral sciences. Emerson's touch was not as knowledgeable and tended to be more superficial, although it is not unlikely that Santayana, usually partial to Emerson, would himself have denied this. Santayana knew, furthermore, about Buddhism, whereas Emerson was almost completely ignorant of it, not really knowing the crucial differences between it and Hinduism.

III

Santayana's view of Indian thought shifted from his writing of *The Realm of Essence* (1927) where he said, "As for me, I frankly cleave to the Greeks and not to the Indians, and I aspire to be a rational animal rather than a pure spirit." [11] But by the time he was writing his first general confessions for Paul Schilpp's Library of Living Philosophers (1930–39) he said that "There is no opposition in my mind between materialism and a Platonic or Indian discipline of the spirit." [12] If this is interpreted in the general framework of his naturalism, his position was now more sympathetic to some interpretation of Indian spiritualism. In the same volume (1940) he also said "I no longer tend to identify rational life with any single Kultur, such as the Greek." [13] For him this is a radical step. His philosophical carpet is Greek and Christian for half a century and then gradually the threads of the Vedas and Sāṁkhya are woven in. This should not be understood in terms

[9] He was Fray Alonso de la Veracruz (1504–1584), the first professor of philosophy at the University of Mexico.

[10] Several Sanskritists like E. Washburn Hopkins of Yale did too.

[11] Quoted by Irwin Edman in *The Philosophy of George Santayana,* p. 65.

[12] *Ibid.,* p. 13.

[13] *Ibid.,* p. 560.

George Santayana

of a mountain of material written by Santayana but in terms of his casual comments as he writes about other things. For Indian philosophy is paid a high compliment by being incorporated into not only his scholarly writing but also into his more intimate creations, his sonnets.

Noteworthy in this respect is his Sonnet XXIII:

'Tis love that moveth the
celestial spheres
In endless yearning for the
Changeless One.[14]

Here the "Changeless One" could be Brahman, or a reification of a notion from Parmenides. In Sonnet XXIX he says "To me the faiths of old are daily bread" [15] by which he might have meant to include the Vedic as well as the Greek and Jewish. But I have looked in vain for a reference to Indian thought in his single novel, *The Last Puritan* (1936) for the perhaps obvious reason that the puritan was not likely to be encumbered with the paganism of Indian philosophy and religion even though he was willing to travel to India to convert the Hindu to his own.

IV

Turning now to the qualities of Indian philosophy that Santayana most approved, I hypothesize that the single most attractive feature for him was its translatability into his own theory of essence. This he conceived to be its doctrine of pure being. Inti-

---

[14] Santayana: *Poems*. New York, Scribner, 1923, p. 26. Professor Luis A. Baralt of Southern Illinois University has suggested that Santayana here may well be referring to a Neoplatonic theme. A moving instance of this, and one with which Santayana may have been familiar, is Luis de León's (1527–1591) "Ode to Francisco Salinas" [a blind musician] which begins,

El aire se serena
y viste de hermosura y luz no usada,
Salinas, cuando suena
la música extremada
por vuestra sabia mano gobernada.
A cuyo son divino
el alma, que en olvido está sumida,
torno a cobrar el tino
y memoria perdida
de su origen primera esclarecida.

Baralt translates this as: "When the consummate music of your lute, governed by your skillful hand, resounds, Salinas, the air becomes serene, bedecked in splendor and rarest light. The soul, hearing the strains divine—stirred from its deep oblivion—regains its aim and the lost memory of its primordial exalted origin."

[15] *Ibid.*

mately associated with essence is his doctrine of spirit which is truly remarkable for its Hegelian ability to incorporate within itself widely divergent conceptions peculiarly embarrassing to materialists and naturalists who wish to disown him at this point. According to Morris Grossman,

> Many fragments wrestle with the difficulties, with the relationship of spirit to comparable Indian categories, and particularly with the problem whether or not to attribute existence to spirit.[16]

In one of his last essays Santayana says: "Ancient philosophy was a great aid to me in extricating my meaning from my words: the more I retreated in time, and the farther east I looked, the more I discovered my own profound and primitive convictions." [17]

What is it in Santayana that finds kinship in Indian doctrines of being and spirit? According to Paul Schilpp it is that:

> The Indians and mystics [and George Santayana] are inspired people, and their language does not always bear critical examination.[18]

But even if we assume that Santayana is inspired, there is nothing to prevent us from discovering what inspired him in Indian metaphysics. There can be no doubt that their outlook on pure being struck him most forcibly:

> The institution of an infinite pregnancy in pure Being came to the Indians as to so many mystics, because in them dialectic was not mere dialectic, but part of a spiritual discipline leading to the highest sublimations of character and experience.[19]

"Excellent too," he says, "is the insight that the aim of spirit is not to know, say, the truth, but to be or live after its own nature." [20]

Although Santayana appreciates the grace of Vedānta and its doctrine of pure being, he claims that,

---

[16] Morris Grossman: A Glimpse of some unpublished Santayana manuscripts. *J. Philo.*, LXI, 1, 1964, p. 67.

[17] Santayana, *The Idler and His Works*, p. 7.

[18] Schilpp, p. 396.

[19] Pure Being. In Lachs, *Animal Faith and Spiritual Life*, p. 139.

[20] "Spirit in Indian Philosophy," *Ibid.*, p. 303.

> At the threshold of natural philosophy, the Vedanta system must yield to the Samkhya; and this the Indians seem to have admitted by regarding the two systems as orthodox and compatible. It might be well if in the West we could take a hint from this comprehensiveness.[21]

In the West this might be equivalent to scholasticism giving way gracefully to Locke, which has not yet happened. Again of pure being, Santayana says:

> At the other pole of reflection, on the contrary, as among the Indians or the Eleatics, the most real of things might seem to be pure Being, or the realm of essence, excluding change and existence there is essential privation.[22]

If this is true, that pure being lacks change and existence in Indian thought, then they must be rejected from the viewpoint of one clinging to pure being. But Santayana cannot accept this change-less and existenceless being. What we learn from him is that we must add the dynamic quality provided by the agency of *puruṣa* in Sāṃkhya [23] as representative of the natural philosophy that provides animal existence and hence ineradicable root of even the contemplation of pure being.

From the Indians we learn about the birth of spirit itself in examining the claims of deep sleep. According to Santayana:

> When the Indians tell us that in deep sleep we return to Brahman, we may say that from the point of view of spirit they are describing the birth of spirit itself, representing the absence of consciousness as consciousness in a perfectly placid, equable, infinitely, potential equilibrium.[24]

In another passage he makes further reference to this state:

> But the dialectics of the spiritual life, while not in the least incompatible with . . . monarchical theism, has a first or ultimate object of quite

---

[21] Santayana: *Realms of Being.* New York, Scribner, 1942, p. 211.

[22] Santayana, *Realms of Being*, p. 650.

[23] According to Santayana in the essay, "Spirit in Indian Philosophy," *Animal Faith and Spiritual Life,* p. 304, Sāṃkhya also has something to say about salvation, "the withdrawal of the spirit within itself is really, as the Sankhya teaches the salvation to be hoped for . . ."

[24] Santayana, *Realms of Being*, p. 414.

another kind. This subsists in the minds of Jewish and Christian mystics side by side with their positivistic faith and in the Indian tends to predominate. They tell us, for instance, that in deep sleep a man may be identified with Brahma, but only passively because (having still a body) he can awake and revert to his habitual imaginations: had he become identical with Brahman in fact, or by a positive insight, like the sage who has annulled all his illusions by viewing them together and seeing them to be all illusions, he could never again descend to distinct imagination or divided existence. In a word, *there is no way down from heaven to earth, from Being to existence.*[25]

Santayana is not only perfectly willing to examine the claims of Indian philosophy in the realm of being and spirit, but goes out of his way to make them sensible in his own transcendent naturalism. But he regretfully returns to his dynamic view which is harmonious with the realm of natural philosophy. Yet he must be given credit for having attempted to make sense out of even what at first or last look appears to be so farfetched that no other Western naturalist has been equal to the task. One might hold that even he is not equal to it, but he has made a valiant effort that lifts him high above the rigidity or perhaps good sense of most American philosophers.

V

Turning now to the power of *māyā*, we find that Santayana regrets anything that obscures what is gently or precipitously given in the light of natural reason. For, he says,

Transcendentalists are . . . driven, like Parmenides and the Vedanta philosophy, to withdraw into a dark interior yet omnipresent principle, the unfathomable force that sets all this illusion going, and at the same time rebukes and annuls that illusion.[23]

Yet, does not Santayana himself import transcendentalism into his own philosophy when he gets carried away by explaining the true significance of poetry and religion? Does he make clear where poetry ends and philosophy begins, where religion begins and

[25] Santayana, *The Idler and His Works and Other Essays*, pp. 122–123.
[26] Santayana, *Scepticism and Animal Faith*, p. 61.

philosophy leaves off? Where does he distinguish between what is rational and what is illusory, the flesh and the spirit? He is a dualist seeking monism. When he finds monism he finds it intolerable so flees back to dualism and this is why he cannot cut the umbilicus of transcendentalism, of tradition, of religion, or of illusion. He must keep all of them, and he does this by dividing the universe of discourse into two realms: one is the natural world which contains everything that there is, almost; the other is the world of as-if which is really in the natural world, almost. Santayana's greatness lies in this—that he wishes to include all human experience in natural experience. His weakness is that he cannot separate human experiences into natural types. And in this he is as irritating as Kant. Part of his strong negative reaction to German philosophy is that the Germans will not do what he himself will not do. They will not come down to earth.

Indian proclivities to "divine" repose and the suspension of life find agreeable echoes in Santayana, but the final longing to find peace in a primeval substance can only mean the defeat of actuality by potentiality, he thought. He says of this that "The peace of the sea is treacherous, and potentiality is not an ideal, but a blind commitment." Here again Emerson and Santayana can easily agree, for whatever else either of them is, he is an American activist who will be satisfied with nothing but an ongoing enterprise despite Santayana's gloomy pronunciamentos on the Protestant *Weltanschauung* in *Soliloquies in England and Later Soliloquies* (1922). If Santayana and Emerson are Platonists, they have endowed the eternal objects with batteries at least.

Despite his attempted allegiance to what is most sane in the Greek tradition, Santayana is as much taken by the intellectual prodigies as by the Indian metaphysical subtlety. This flight from boredom has affected other students of Indian thought. According to Santayana:

> The Indians, who deny the existence of the world, have a keen sense for its infinity and its variegated colours; they play with the monstrous and miraculous in the grand manner, as in the Arabian Nights.[27]

[27] *Ibid.,* p. 67.

Santayana is of course wrong when he says the Indians deny the existence of the world. Some of them do but most no more deny it than he denies the existence of essences.

During the Second World War, Santayana found that the Indian outlook even served a useful purpose: "I am reading the *Upanishads,* St. Augustine's *Confessions,* and Spinoza's *Politics* to take the bad taste out of my mouth." [28] Doubtless part of his feeling of kinship with Indian philosophy, which seemed to grow rather than diminish over the later years, was the result of his feeling like that of the old German spinster whom he quotes as singing nothing "at the piano save '*Wie dumn sind die Leute-von Heute!*'" [29] At this time also he voiced a typically romantic hope that somewhere mechanization and industrialization might cease, at least in the East. Perhaps it was too late, even there! He opined,

> Yet if, for instance India should now attempt to restore human life to its ancient simplicity, and to renounce industrialism, it might easily be overrun and subjugated by the iron hand of some neighbor less devoted to spiritual goods: or if they were left alone materially, they might subsist unregarded, as ancient life actually subsists today in the West in a few monasteries and sacred preserves surviving by insulation.[30]

Santayana also reveals the commonly held American view that India is or has been rather exclusively devoted to spiritual goods, a view nurtured by Vivekananda, Rabindranath Tagore and A. K. Coomaraswamy when giving American lectures idealizing India. Nothing could have dashed cold water on this view of Santayana's so fast as a prolonged visit to India as it was emerging from its colonial status.

VI

Surrounded by the quiet of his Roman convent, Santayana takes a dim view of transmigration. Although Emerson was not able to appreciate this effulgent flower of the Indian garden

[28] Daniel Cory, *Santayana: The Later Years,* p. 196.
[29] *Ibid.,* p. 271.
[30] Santayana, *The Idler and His Works,* pp. 36–37.

either, he was more circumspect in criticizing it. But Santayana says:

> Life is the form or order that all suitable substances conspire to compose when any seed develops into an ordinary body. This form is hereditary; and the psyche is a name for the natural magic that keeps each individual true to his species, and predetermines his normal organs, habits and passions. Hence the absurdity of transmigration; as if functions could migrate from one organ to another, so that the eye should hear and the ear should see, or as if music, which is the soul of the lyre, could migrate into an axe, or the power of cutting from the axe into the lyre.[31]

Twenty years earlier, in 1922, Santayana quipped, in one of his most gallic masterpieces that,

> If to be saved were merely to cease, we should all be saved by a little waiting; and I say this advisedly, without forgetting that the Indians threaten us with reincarnation.[32]

Santayana is clearly disappointed in the loss of naturalistic and Lucretian nerve that impelled first the Hindus, and then the Buddhists, to call upon transmigration to solve major metaphysical and ethical problems. In *Scepticism and Animal Faith* (1923) he says:

> The Indians were poets and mystics; and while they could easily throw off the conventions of vulgar reason, it was often only to surrender themselves to other conventions, far more misleading to a free spirit, such as the doctrine of transmigration of souls; and when, as in Buddhism, they almost vanquished that illusion, together with every other, their emasculated intellect had nothing to put in its place.[33]

Certainly Santayana believed that the Indians had had veridical insights unique in the history of thought. Yet he could not forbear to criticize Indian antinaturalism and Indian transcendentalism which gave it the appearance of a Disneyland engineered in

---

[31] Santayana: *The Idea of Christ in the Gospels.* New York, Scribner, 1946, p. 224.

[32] Santayana, *Soliloquies in England*, p. 93. The double relief Santayana must have felt at leaving both Harvard and New England makes this one of his most irrepressible works.

[33] Santayana, *Scepticism and Animal Faith,* pp. 305–6.

Banaras. An exception would be the sort of transcendentalism he approved such as that dealing with essence. Some doctrines of the Indians are, he thought,

> unmanly, held by saints and gymnosophists, who were so frenzied by their own more monstrous imaginations, that they became incapable of conceiving a happy life.[34]

Existence itself is questioned by the Indians, Santayana noted:

> No doubt, existence compels [man] to wish to keep it, because it is essentially a propulsive movement, but this wish in itself is so far from a good that the most venerable of philosophies, the Indian, regards it as the source of all evil.[35]

The Hindus are like the Neoplatonists in their outlook, said Santayana, for they show a generosity of spirit towards most other views. He contended that,

> The Neo-Platonist tended to regard as orthodox all philosophies that accepted Homer, such as the Hindus . . . accepted the Vedas, however different they might be technically; only the atheists, i.e., the Epicureans and the Christians were tabooed.[36]

In praising Lucretius, his favorite philosophical poet, Santayana also criticized the Indian mystic whom he called a "despiser of understanding." But not all Indians were mystics. Not only did Lucretius "dominate, foretell, and transform this changing show with a virile, practical intelligence" but so did the Indian materialists called Lokayātikas. Had Santayana been familiar with the material available in Roman libraries by Giuseppi Tucci [37] and Angelo Maria Pizzagalli [38] he would have discovered an atomism congenial to Lucretius and an attack on superstition more than equal to the Roman poet.

---

[34] Santayana, *Obiter Scripta.* Justus Buchler and Benjamin Schwartz (Ed.). New York, Scribner, 1936, p. 9.

[35] Santayana, *Dominations and Powers.* London, Constable, 1952, p. 333.

[36] Santayana, *Obiter Scripta,* p. 79.

[37] See his Linee di una storia del materialism indiano, *Atti della Reale.* Accademia Nacionale dei Lincei (Roma), Serie Sesta, vol. II (1926).

[38] See his Nastika Carvaka e Lokayatika, *Annali Della R. Scuola Normale.* Pisa, XXI (1908).

In 1949, three years before he died, Santayana wrote from Rome to Daniel Cory that:

> I also have two books of Indian philosophy to restore my tone, sent me by Swami Nikhilananda,[39] who visited me here recently and was very sympathetic. I follow the Indians in their Brahman Spirit, in its essence, but of course not in its absolute-status as the root of all things.[40]

VII

Whereas Santayana was most intrigued by the metaphysics of Hinduism, he focused on the ethics of Buddhism. His sharp reaction against *karma* and transmigration he early showed in *Reason in Science* (1906) . He said of *karma* that:

> In the doctrine of karma . . . experience of retribution is ideally extended and made precise. Acts, daily experience teaches us, form habits; habits constitute character, and each man's character, as Heraclitus said, is his guardian deity, the artisian of his fate.[41]

Certainly one of the parameters of predicting Santayana's reaction to Indian doctrine is to know if he can find a precedent for it in the early Greeks whom he normally uses as a standard for what is to be allowed serious consideration. But to continue with his reaction to Buddhist *karma*. He said:

> Buddhism had its mission of salvation; but to express this mission to its proselytes it was obliged to borrow the language of the fantastic metaphysics which had preceded it in India. The machinery of transmigration had to serve as a scaffolding to raise the monument of mercy, purity, and spirituality. But this fabulous background given to life was really inconsistent with what was best in the new morality of [Buddhism].[42]

Then Santayana made the kind of shrewd observation that made him beloved among his Harvard colleagues:

[39] For many years head of the Ramakrishna-Vivekananda Center in New York City and later in Boston.

[40] Cory, *Santayana: The Later Years*, p. 291.

[41] Santayana: *Reason in Science.* New York, Scribner, 1924, p. 291.

[42] *Ibid.,* pp. 295–96.

The doctrine of karma was a hypostasis of moral responsibility; but in making responsibility dynamic and all-explaining, the theory discountenanced in advance the charitable efforts of Buddhism—the desire to instruct and save every fellow-creature.[43]

In elaborating upon this failure in Buddhism, Santayana adds:

Therefore the empirical fact that we can help one another remains in Buddhism (as in any retributive scheme) only by a serious inconsistency; and since this fact is the sanction of whatever moral efficacy can be attributed to Buddhism, in sobering, teaching, and saving mankind, anything inconsistent with it is fundamentally repugnant to the whole system. Yet on that repugnant and destructive dogma of karma Buddhism was condemned to base its instruction. This is a heavy price paid for mythical consolations, that they invalidate the moral values they are intended to emphasize.[44]

This significent critique is appropriate for any nonrational, antiscientific metaphysic. It is worthy of being etched into precious metal and hung over the entrance to the Temple of the Tooth in Kandy, the most sacred Buddhist temple in Ceylon.

Of all American philosophers, the one who wrote most originally and sensitively about Jesus Christ was the atheist George Santayana. There is an Indian precedent for this. In some circles in India it is said that the man who denies God is closer to Him than one who affirms Him. The first feels more compassion for the human race than the second who is more authoritarian and cruel. In comparing Jesus with the Buddha, as Santayana liked to do, following a good Emersonian tradition of the uses of great men, he said:

The other side or level of Christ's teaching is more like the Buddha's, and strikes at the root of self-will, illusion, and passion within the soul. In Christ's spiritual discipline, as in Buddha's there is nothing superstitious or terrified. He comes eating and drinking, lives familiarly among sinful men, and what is more, and not found in Buddha, exercises a personal magic, a direct ascendancy of secret love, over those whom he chooses, such that when he says, *Follow me,* the cross that is to be taken seems light and the death to be suffered seems sweet.[45]

[43] *Ibid.,* p. 296.
[44] *Ibid.,* pp. 296–97.
[45] Santayana, *The Idea of Christ in the Gospels,* p. 109.

But whereas the Buddha and Christ are basically humanistic for Santayana, it must be admitted that,

> To transcend humanity is no new ambition; that has always been the effect of Indian and Christian religious discipline and of Stoic philosophy.[46]

So long as this is the spearhead of Indian thought, it can never gain the wholehearted allegiance of the naturalistic George Santayana. So long as metaphysics and religion are metaphorical and aesthetic instruments to enhance the natural life or the natural life of reason, then they are worthy of gratitude, but when they make a mockery of life and become life-denying, then they must be rejected by manly philosophers. This is the summation of Santayana's sixty years of reflection on Indian philosophy. No other American philosopher up to his time was able to appreciate the good in it and to reveal the false in it in the same lucid way.

From Santayana we turn to various philosophers and writers such as Edgar Saltus and A. K. Coomaraswamy who were to influence American thinkers in aesthetics, metaphysics, and morals. Their concern with Indian thought accelerated also the general public's awareness of certain key outlooks that became quite common in the United States.

[46] Santayana: *Egotism in German Philosophy*. London, J. M. Dent, n.d. [ca. 1918].

Chapter VII

EXTENSION OF INDIAN THOUGHT IN THE WORLD OF LETTERS AND PHILOSOPHY

EDGAR SALTUS (1858–1921) was a disciple of Schopenhauer, a free-lance writer in New York who was educated at the Sorbonne and Columbia University. He wrote two philosophical works: *The Philosophy of Disenchantment* (1885) and *Anatomy of Negation* (1887). After his fling at the philosophy of pessimism in his late twenties he settled down to write a variety of papers and books over his largely journalistic career. Saltus claimed in 1885 that,

> As a creed, the birthplace of pessimism is to be sought on the banks of the Ganges, or far back in the flower-lands of Nepaul, where the initiate, with every desire lulled, awaits Nirvana, and murmurs only, "Life is evil . . ." . . . To the Brahmin, while there is always the hope of absorption in the Universal Spirit, life meanwhile is a regrettable accident. But in Buddhism, which is perhaps the most naive and yet the most sublime of all religions, and which through its very combination of simplicity and grandeur appeals to a larger number of adherents than any other, pessimism is the beginning, as it is the end. . . . In brief, then, life to the Christian is a probation, to the Brahmin a burden, to the Buddhist a dream, and to the pessimist a nightmare.[1]

---

[1] Edgar Saltus: *The Philosophy of Disenchantment*. New York, Belford Company, 1885, pp. 33–5. According to John Bates Clark (1847–1938), considered by some to be the United States' leading economic theorist, capital "lives, as it were, by transmigration." *Distribution of Wealth*. New York, Macmillan, 1899, p. 120.

But Saltus was more concerned with spreading the doctrines of Schopenhauer than those of Indian thought. His knowledge of Hinduism seems very slight, yet he could not entirely eschew it as a disciple of Schopenhauer, as when he says:

> According to Schopenhauer, art should be strictly impersonal, and contemplation as calm as a foretaste of Nirvana, in which the individual is effaced and only the pure knowing subject subsists.[2]

One catches in John Dewey's (1859–1952) letters from Tokyo, written in 1919, a hint of the disapproval he felt for the Hindu swamis whom he doubtless associated with Indian philosophy and the fakirs he had met in New York City. He contrasts the figure of Shaku, at that time head of the Zen Sect at Kamakura with the swamis in the following way:

> His personality is that of a scholarly type, rather ascetic, not over refined, but not in the least sleek like some of our Hindu swamis, and very charming.[3]

It is curious to note that Shaku immediately reminds Dewey of Royce, but,

> He was more modern than Royce in one respect; he said God is the moral ideal in man and as man develops the divine principle does also.[4]

Although Dewey may not have scorned other cultures and other peoples bereft of the unmixed blessings of technology, he is a kind of technological if not technocratic elitist, nowhere better illustrated than in an article in the *New Republic* in 1927. He is here defending the natural sciences against those he wrongly believes undervalue it. He says:

> And no matter how much one may draw upon contrasting phases of life, Greek, Indian with Mr. Santayana, or the Golden Day of Emer-

2 *Ibid.*, p. 95.

3 John Dewey and Alice Chipman Dewey: *Letters from China and Japan,* Evelyn Dewey (Ed.). London, J. M. Dent, 1920, p. 49.

4 *Ibid.* This notion of God is also curiously anticipatory of the view of Whitehead in *Process and Reality,* to be published ten years later, in 1930.

son, Thoreau, and Whitman with Mr. Mumford . . . without an
understanding of natural science and technology . . . criticism is . . .
"transcendent" and ultimately of one's own private conceit.[5]

Here Dewey is responding to an attack on the narrowness of
pragmatism (instrumentalism) by Lewis Mumford, America's
leading defender of a rich aesthetic texture for living even if this
might call some halt to the escalation of commodities.

Not long before his death, Dewey wrote a short article on the
value of philosophical synthesis for the first issue of *Philosophy
East and West,*[6] in which he warns us against thinking that because there are political blocs there are also cultural blocs, and
indeed that there is such a thing as East and West that have to be
synthesized. Says Dewey, "the point is that none of these elements
[of culture]—in the East or the West—is in isolation. They are all
interwoven in a vast variety of ways in the historico-cultural
process."[7] A valuable task that the new journal can perform,
Dewey believes, is to "keep the idea open and working that there
are *specific* philosophical relationships to be explored" for "contributing most fruitfully and dynamically to the enlightenment
and betterment of the human estate."[8] This fine statement by
Dewey makes us wish that he had spent more time in the larger
area of world philosophy and relatively less in restating educa-
tional views that in time became platitudinous. It might be responded that, even as one professor has said in recommending
tactics by which to deal with a college dean: "You have to keep
pounding it into his head until he can see no alternative." Dewey
must have felt that it took a great deal of pounding to make
educators see his views.

American Indianophiles found in Ananda K. Coomaraswamy
(1863–1947) a mountain of inspiration and information about
Indian thought and art, raising the standard of Indian scholarship to an unprecedented aesthetic height still unequalled. He
was born the son of Sir Mutu Coomaraswamy, the first Hindu to

[5] Dewey, *New Republic*, XLIX, 1927, pp. 88–89.
[6] I, 1, 1951, p. 3.
[7] *Philos East West,* I, 1, 1951, p. 3.
[8] *Ibid.*

be called to the English Bar,[9] and Elizabeth Clay Beeby of Kent. He attended Wycliffe College, took his B.Sc. in geology and botany at the University of London. In 1903 he became a Fellow of University College and as director of the Mineralogical Survey in Ceylon (1903–1906) discovered thorianite. After receiving his doctorate at the University of London he founded and accelerated the growth of the Ceylon Social Reform Society. His professional work in Indian art and Indian philosophy began around 1910 although he had been working fitfully in the field previous to that time. He was appointed keeper of Indian art at the Museum of Fine Arts, Boston, in 1917 and remained in the United States for the next thirty years.

Coomaraswamy was one of the few Indologists treated in this volume who was born abroad. In many ways he was the most knowledgeable scholar in all phases of Indian culture to have lived and worked in the United States. I do not mean to underestimate the work of such giants as Whitney who must be considered as a great Indologist, yet if we consider that from 1900 to 1950 Coomaraswamy had produced 572 scholarly and artistic contributions to his profession one must be very cynical not to be impressed. If we also take into account the high performance achieved in these it is difficult to restrain one's admiration. Few of his books and articles fail to contain some philosophical content or reference to the philosophical foundations of Indian thought, although most are contributions to art history and aesthetics. No writer on art in the United States has insisted with the same passion that art is based on civilization and civilization is based upon philosophical ground. He was thought to be totally reactionary by some philosophers who did not trouble to understand him. When he says that

> The bases of modern civilization are to such a degree rotten to the core that it has been forgotten even by the learned that man ever attempted to live otherwise than by bread alone,[10]

one feels Lewis Mumford's antipragmatic spleen to be rather mild. The experts of American education he says are "even more

---

[9] There were others who went even though not called!

[10] Coomaraswamy: Am I my brother's keeper? *Asia,* March 1943, p. 3.

nefarious than your traffic in arms." [11] He continues by pointing out that what the English did to the Irish and Indians is what Middletown U.S.A. is doing to "savages" and others unable to protect themselves in the rest of its sphere of influence.

> Let us make it clear that . . . where production is really for *use,* and not only for profit, the workman is still naturally inclined to do his work faithfully.[12]

What throws off the unwary reader of these and hundreds of other prophetic lines is that Coomaraswamy hedges them around with quotations from Indian scripture, Plato, St. Bonaventura and others believed to be harbingers of musty views. It proves almost irreparably difficult when he quotes not only the Sanskrit, Pāli, Latin, Greek, but also German, French, and Russian. Mrs. Alfred North Whitehead once confided to me that "he is *such* a strange man." When I said that I believed him to be an imposing thinker, she looked at her husband with a little knowing smile and let the subject drop. Those who could agree with his jeremiads against the established lack-of-order would be repelled by his constant references to religious ultimates.

In his "Paths that lead to the Same Summit" [13] he embarked on a favorite theme that the truth should be taught and begins by pointing out the insipidity of tolerance, which originally meant "to endure," "to put up with." It "is a merely negative virtue" while it "allows us to pity those who differ from ourselves, and are consequently to be pitied!" [14] As Professor James Marshall Plumer [15] has said, "the surest way to betray our Chinese allies is to sell, give or lend-lease them our [American] standard of living." [16] We do not need to bring others up to our standard, according to Coomaraswamy, because,

[11] *Ibid.,* p. 2.

[12] *Ibid.*

[13] *Motive.* Nashville, Board of Education of the Methodist Church, May 1944, p. 29.

[14] *Ibid.*

[15] Late Professor of Oriental Art at the University of Michigan.

[16] He said this before the Chinese People's Republic was founded in 1949. *Ibid.,* p. 31.

As a German theologian has said, "the formation of humanity (*Men-schheitsbildung*) is a unitary whole, and its various cultures are the dialects of one and the same language of the spirit." [17]

One wonders whether Coomaraswamy picked up this idealistic historicism in the East or in the West. With such a view there can be no doubt that Coomaraswamy goes beyond most Indologists by holding that not only Indians but more "primitive" people have something to offer the United States. Indeed man as a man, not as an Indian, Englishman, or American, has discovered truths that are worthy of enshrining.

One of Coomaraswamy's finest essays is entitled "The Intellectual Operation in Indian Art," [18] in which he shows how philosophy plays an integral part in the creation of beautiful objects. The preparation of the Buddhist artist is here shown in considerable detail and then compared with Plotinus on the creation of objects of art. The upshot is that the artist cannot work *in vacuo*; [19] that he works not only with his senses but with his intellect. When we speak of formless art we are not speaking of art because what is lacking is an essential ingredient, namely "an intrinsic logic." [20]

One of Coomaraswamy's most interesting contributions to philosophy is to be found in his "Recollection, Indian and Platonic and On the One and Only Transmigrant." [21] As stated in the *Chandogya Upaniṣad* 7.26.1 " 'Memory is from the Self or Spirit' (*ātmatah smarah*) ." [22] The Self never remembers anything because he never forgets. Divinity intuits Greatness in clairvoyant-sleep (*svapne = dhyāna*) . In Buddhism certain people are designated as birth-rememberers (*jātissarā*) . When we remember, on this view, it is milking an innate prescience (*prajñāna-pronoia*) . When our

---

[17] "Paths that Lead . . . ," p. 311.

[18] *J. Indian Soc Orient Art*, June 1935.

[19] The present Western School of mannerism (not in the sense used by Arnold Hauser, see his *Mannerism*, 2 vols. London, Routledge & Kegan Paul, 1965, p. 3) , was of course held in supreme contempt by Coomaraswamy! "Most of these people do not know even the rudiments of drawing and design," he once stated in Boston,

[20] Supplement to the *J Amer Orient Soc*, 3, 1944.

[21] *Ibid.*

[22] *Ibid.*, p. 3.

memory fails, "The Gods fall from heaven."²³ Coomaraswamy then compared the Indian doctrine with *Meno* 81, C.D. He also pointed out that the doctrine survives in Philo, Dante, Manasseh ben Israel (seventeenth century), Meister Eckhart, and Blake, where he asks "Is the Holy Ghost any other than an intellectual fountain?"²⁴ Generally unknown in the United States, except among Orientalists, Coomaraswamy time and again reveals himself as one of the great historians of our time. He continued to show this power in "On the One and Only Transmigrant."²⁵

Coomaraswamy's partially reactionary political doctrine is rooted in his consistent focus on the creation of art works. In a competitive money society, as he called it, dominated by trade, legal obligations replace the moral. His outlook on alienation is exemplified in his quoting Milton Mayer's judgment "The economic slavery of Detroit may be constrasted not entirely favorably, with the medieval serfdom in which the serf could not be deprived of his tools."²⁶ Coomaraswamy's own comment is no less trenchant:

> Trade today—the word itself means "tread" or a way of life, whether of priests, kings, or cooks—is always in some way thought of as a form of exploitation, and it is as such that it is fostered by imperialistic governments; the modern advertisement, the people's hope, makes us take it and like it, blinds us to the fact that, as Albert Schweitzer says, "when trade is good, permanent famine reigns in the Ogawe region."²⁷

It would appear that Coomaraswamy did not believe that capitalism can move forward but must return to a caste system and monarchy where "make" and "make sacred" were the proper outlook. The real solution which he claimed that no one dares to propose is not a change but a change of heart.²⁸ Since this book is not the ideal medium in which to develop a social theory, suffice it to say that Coomaraswamy in his approach to certain modern

---

²³ *Ibid.*, p. 7.
²⁴ *Ibid.*, p. 18.
²⁵ *Ibid.*, p. 19.
²⁶ Coomaraswamy: *Indian Culture and English Influence.* New York, Orientalia, 1946, p. 39.
²⁷ *Ibid.*
²⁸ *Ibid.*, p. 40.

problems sided with Gandhi and Sri Aurobindo. No one doubts that he has put his finger on a disease. The question is whether in the light of historical analysis he has discovered a cure in a return to a medieval paradise. The statement of the problem as he sees it, stems from "an opposition of the traditional or ordinary way of life that survives in the East [1946] to the modern and irregular way of life that now prevails in the West." [29] The men who understand the problem in the West are three in number according to Coomaraswamy: René Guenon, Frithiof Schuon, and Marco Pallis, all admirable Oriental scholars in the transcendentalistic tradition. Thus he showed his belief that "politics and economics, although they cannot be ignored, are the most external and the least part of our problem." [30] When we get to economics Coomaraswamy is the spiritualistic Brahmin who does not have to consider such secondary matters. It is partly attributable to this firmly held position that he is so generally ignored by secular thinkers in the West. His ideal which made him the object of Alfred North Whitehead's tolerant quizzicalness was the feudal system which prevailed in India in the sixth century A.D. The chain of personal loyalty bound retainer to chief, tenant to lord, and baron to *rāja* or *mahārāja*. What was needed for this tightly knit organization was personal devotion *(bhakti)*. And this *bhakti* did not appear in Indian history until the rise of the great centralized personal empires. As late as the thirteenth century Marco Polo reported that the lords *(seigneurs)* cast themselves upon the king's funeral pyre. D. D. Kosambi concludes his analysis of the philosophy of the *gītā* (and to an important measure that of Coomaraswamy), the feudal philosophy of India, by saying that it "is based in the final analysis upon the inability to satisfy more than the barest material needs of a large number." [31]

Immediately following World War I a number of societies came into prominence having as their aim the improvement of Indian-American understanding. The Hindustan Association of America began a bimonthly *Oriental Magazine* in 1922. Out of

[29] The Religious Basis of the Forms of Indian Society. *East and West*, p. 43.
[30] *Ibid*.
[31] Kosambi, p. 41.

this association the India Society developed, founded in 1924 and incorporated in 1925. Its honorary president was A. K. Coomaraswamy, its president J. T. Sunderland, D. D., with an advisory council including Upton Close, Sidney L. Gulick, Jane Addams, Ruth St. Denis, and Heywood Broun. Its sponsors included such luminaries as Professor Edwin R. A. Seligman, Oswald Garrison Villard, Professor William R. Shepherd, John Dewey, Alfred W. Martin, and Rev. Dr. John Haynes Holmes. Lecturers included Coomaraswamy, Mme. Sarojini Naidu, S. Radhakrishnan, Surendranath Dasgupta,[32] Pandit Jagadish Chandra Chatterji, Dhan Gopal Mukerji, and Dr. Jagadisan M. Kumarappa. Radhakrishnan delivered the Haskell Lectures at the University of Chicago in 1926 and then visited Cornell University. Surendranath Dasgupta delivered the Harris Lecture at Northwestern University the same year. Previously, of course, Vivekananda had made two visits to the United States and from 1910 onwards Rabindranath Tagore visited a half dozen times. The first Hindu students to study in the United States arrived in California in 1901, six more came in 1904, and by 1908 there were seventeen of them.

Rev. John Haynes Holmes allowed Kedar Nath Das Gupta to use his new Community Church to put on a play called *Buddha,* taken from Edwin Arnold's *Light of Asia* and William Norman Guthrie and Rabbi Stephen Wise also put their houses of worship at the disposal of K. N. Das Gupta.[33]

The International School of Vedic and Allied Research had as its director Pandit Jagadish Chandra Chatterji and as secretary Dr. George C. O. Haas, an American Sanskritist. The executive council of the American section included John Dewey, John H. Finley, Stephen P. Duggan, Paul Munroe, William Ernest Hocking, and its president of council, Charles Rockwell Lanman. The International School of Vedic and Allied Research had several special departments such as the Department of Education Exchange and Relations. Hindu students would come to the West and Western students would go to Banaras, Peking, Cairo and so

---

[32] India's greatest historian of philosophy, author of the *History of Indian Philosophy,* 5 vols. (1922–1955) .

[33] Thomas, p. 189.

on. Another department was for archaeology. Many of the proposals to be realized in the School were advanced by Lanman in his presidential address before the American Oriental Society in 1920. According to Lanman in that address:

> The business of us Orientalists is something that is in vital relation with urgent practical and political needs. The work calls for co-operation, and above all things else, for co-operation in a spirit of mutual sympathy and teachableness. . . . India with her great learning is eager to adopt modern methods to make that learning available to her own sons and to us, and is ready to join hands with us of the West in order to make her spiritual heritage enrich our too hurried life.

The New Orient Society of America operated out of Illinois where it was incorporated in 1930 as a non-profit organization. Its aim was to further cultural relations between the Orient and the Occident, not only by bringing together individuals with mutual interests but also by publishing work of benefit to those concerned with Oriental-Occidental relations. Some of the individuals involved in these affairs were Albert H. Lybyer of the University of Illinois, Halford L. Hoskins of Tufts College, Henry Field, and Arthur W. Hummel and Albert T. Olmstead of Chicago.[34]

Beginning with James Bissett Pratt (1875–1944) we encounter a series of American philosophers who not only were interested in Indian thought, but who also visited India to study the customs and culture of the country first-hand. Pratt received his A.B. from Williams College and his A.M. and Ph.D. from Harvard. He at first taught Latin at a preparatory school and from 1905 was a professor at Williams College. He made three trips to Asia, all of which landed him in India: he was in India in 1913–14; in 1923–24, and at this time he visited all the major Buddhist countries in preparation for his *Pilgrimage;* and again in 1931–32. He was president of the American Philosophical Association during his later years.

Pratt said to his wife in April, 1913:

---

[34] In the opinion of W. Norman Brown, President of the American Institute of Indian Studies, none of these societies amounted to much although they got many important people to lend their names to their activities.

> Let us take a little walk [as] I have decided that I feel a little stale having taught these [Indian] religions ten years or thereabouts—we shall go to India and see them practiced.[35]

Ten years later, after having visited India and having taught comparative religion at Williams College during the years after his return from India, Pratt again went to Asia with his wife and two children to study Buddhism in detail during a sabbatical in 1923–24. The result was his invaluable study, *The Pilgrimage of Buddhism* (1928). During his third sabbatical in 1932–33, Pratt again visited India, this time giving weekly lectures on Buddhism at Shantiniketan at the behest of his friend Rabindranath Tagore.[36]

Pratt's point of departure was the sickness of the West. The social disease of the West is its complacency,[37] avoirdupois, harlotry,[38] open immorality, depraved tastes, and public indecencies such as erotic or suggestive plays. To prove his point, Pratt quoted: "A traveled Indian gentleman who said . . . 'No Indian prostitute would have anything to do with such public obscenities as any one may see in the suburbs in Chicago.' " [39] In contrast to the vices of America, Pratt found in India a kind of simplicity, a quietness, an innate modesty, lack of self-obtrusiveness, interest in the inner world,[40] and a charming lack of self-consciousness.[41] The cause of our being called materialistic in the West is the

---

[35] *Letter* from Mrs. James Bissett to the author, Williamstown, Mass. (June 11, 1962).

[36] *Ibid.*

[37] Pratt held that curricula of colleges indicated the principle of *"Nothing East of Suez."* Study of Indian Philosophy. In Isherwood (Ed.) : *Vedanta for Modern Man.* New York, Harper, 1951, p. 25.

[38] James Pratt: *India and Its Faiths: A Traveler's Record.* Boston, Houghton, 1915.

[39] *Ibid.,* p. 464 n. Why Pratt must mention Chicago when he is so close to Boston is a piece of curiosa. The cruel hypocrisy of the Indian upper classes is of a piece with those in the United States, although it might appear to the casual observer that there is some basic difference. My own information is such that I was somewhat startled to find fathers regularly pimping for early teenage daughters in India, which of course reflects less on morality than economics. That this is not done in front of the major temples, but rather by the rickshaw middleman who served as pimp, should have startled Pratt as much as events in Chicago.

[40] Katherine Mayo's account of this is still worth reading. See *Mother India.*

[41] Pratt, *India and Its Faiths: . . . ,* pp. 466, 468.

result of "The self-consciousness . . . and its self-assertiveness." [42]
Of the East, Pratt said:

> [It] has always known exactly what it most supremely desired, and in
> the pursuit of its ideal it has never been afraid of poverty or of any-
> thing else. Bodily comforts it has despised, and bodily suffering it has
> even welcomed if by such means the soul might profit.[43]

The greatest thing about India is that it has not lost the vision of
the eternal Pratt claimed.[44] He enthusiastically declared also that:

> The culture of the soul has been, and is still, the one great ideal of
> India. Conquest, government, money-making, pleasure, the things that
> have occupied the chief attention of the West, have been for India of
> very secondary importance.[45]

Of all American philosophers who became enamored of Indian
thought only Pratt became expert in the cults of Indian religion,
especially Buddhism. By 1920 his fascination had already led him
to advanced study of "Objective and Subjective Worship." [46]
Much of his study of the religious consciousness was of worship in
all of its ramifications. He constantly compared the Indian practice with the Christian. His *magnum opus, The Pilgrimage of
Buddhism* (1928), is one of the most complete and elegant works
of its kind in any language. It includes accounts of that religion in
India, Ceylon, Burma, Siam, and Cambodia—all but India—
Hīnayāna strongholds in Pratt's day. This account takes up 188
pages. The remainder of the book is concerned with Mahāyāna,
another 500 pages, except for the summary chapters which dealt
with the present conditions of Buddhism, its unity and "Buddhism and Christianity."

Pratt pointed out that the basic inner conflict that devoted

---

[42] *Ibid.,* p. 469.
[43] *Ibid.,* p. 470.
[44] *Ibid.,* p. 473.
[45] *Ibid.,* p. 471.
[46] Pratt: *The Religious Consciousness, A Psychological Study.* New York, Macmillan
1930 [1920].

Buddhists must face is to reconcile a "composed mind" while one is "shaken with compassion." He said of this conflict:

> So far as I am aware this . . . is never faced by Buddhist books as a matter of theory; and the result is that each Buddhist is left to fight it out for himself.[47]

Reconciliation is difficult, yet "Pleasure is not compatible with sorrow, but joy and the Great Peace may be." [48] Pratt traced, after his statement of the original views of Buddhism, its growth in India in a felicitious and scholarly fashion.

Turning to Greater India, Pratt claimed that:

> The Buddha, in short, for the orthodox Hinayana, whether in Siam, Burma, Ceylon, or Cambodia, belong now to the world of the ideal rather than to the actual. On this point Buddhism is a kind of Asiatic Platonism. To make use of a distinction common in the philosophical language of our day, the Buddha is subsistent but not existent.[49]

A point made by Pratt, although seldom stressed concerning Buddhism is as follows:

> The Buddha [in Siam] is in Nibban [nirvāna]. He is not conscious . . . But he is not dead. Between being dead and being in Nibban there is a great difference. When a man is dead the element of desire still remains. Hence death brings birth again.[50]

Pratt's exegesis is generally delightful in its wit, good sense, and use of Western parallels to make a point clear. There is little doubt that *The Pilgrimage* taken as a whole is the best account of Buddhism written by any American.

An American philologist born abroad was an Austrian by birth, Maurice Bloomfield (1885–1928). Beginning as a student at the University of Chicago, he went also to Johns Hopkins, Berlin, and Leipzig. He was professor of Sanskrit at Johns Hop-

---

[47] *Ibid.*, pp. 93–94.

[48] Pratt, *The Pilgrimage of Buddhism and a Buddhist Pilgrimage*. New York, Macmillan, 1928, p. 94.

[49] *Ibid.*, p. 167.

[50] *Ibid.*, p. 172.

kins University from 1881 until his retirement. His book writing
began with the *Atharva Veda* (1899) and continued with *Prole-
gomena to the Atharva Veda, The Religion of the Veda* (1908),
Vedic Concordance (1906), *Rig-Veda Repetitions* (1916), *Stories
of the Jaina Savior Pārçvanātha*, perhaps the first monograph by
an American scholar on Jainism. Bloomfield is probably best
known for his translation from the *Atharva Veda* for the *Sacred
Books of the East*. He reproduced, with Richard Garbe of Tübingen, the only manuscript then known of the Kashmirian Veda.

Many American Sanskritists have been fine stylists, but few are
superior to Bloomfield in his felicity of phrase, choice of examples, humor, sympathy for the reader and American idiom. In his
"Brahmanical Riddles and the Origin of Theosophy" he is certainly at one of his better, which is to say, superb, moments.
Although born in Austria, like Santayana he mastered his second
language.

Bloomfield points out that in the Vedas and Upaniṣads "we see
the whole stuff of religions: nature, myth, ritual, liturgy, human
psychology, theosophy; they are present themselves as a mystery fit
for the riddle, and they are handled often in a very fresh and
original way." [51] The *Atharva Veda*, says Bloomfield, asks the
riddle: "In that which lies stretched out there is hidden that
which stands: what is it?" Answer: "The foot in the shoe." [52] How
did the nursery-charade get into this serious book? How did this
fossil become here embedded? By some "accidental" tie. Yet after
sufficient generations, Bloomfield claims, it achieved a sanctity by
virtue of its location despite its "social justification." The sacrifice
in its social character is responsible for this as well as for the
theosophical riddles. The Rig-Veda I, 164, is the *piéce de resistance* of such riddles, many of which have philosophical import. It
goes like this:

Of this gray Hotar priest the middle brother is of the rock the third
brother carries ghee on his back. Here have I seen the householder that
has seven sons.

[51] Howard J. Rogers (Ed.) : *International Congress of Arts and Science*. London,
Univ. Alliance, 1906, IV, 484.
[52] Bloomfield in *International Congress of Arts and Science*, p. 484.

What is it?

It is the god Agni, Fire in three important aspects.[53] These three are the sun, lightning, and the earthly fire upon which the oblation of ghee is poured.

Such riddles, according to Bloomfield, recommend two points for theosophical development: (1) they are attempts to approach the mysteries of existence, despite "excogitating sacrifice after sacrifice, and hair-splitting definitions and explanations of senseless ritualistic practices;" [54] and (2) they are also indications of the sudden rise of Hindu theosophists to "lofty speculation." The latter came about by "shutting down on the ritual" possibly by the Brahmians themselves. But if there is any lesson to be learned from it, it is that generally such changes are the combined efforts of the more vigorous intellects.[55]

Another Sanskritist, but more philosophical-directed than Bloomfield, was Edward Washburn Hopkins (1857–1932). After receiving his Ph.D. at Leipzig he taught at Yale University where he was professor of Greek and Sanskrit language and literature and comparative philology from 1895 to 1926. He was editor of the *Journal of the American Oriental Society* from 1897 to 1907 and was twice president, as was Lanman before him, of that society. When Whitney died, the Yale chair was given to Hopkins. He wrote a number of important books including *Caste in Ancient India* (1881), Chapters on the Indian Epic for the *Cambridge History of India,* Vol. I, *Religions of India* (1895), *The Great Epic of India* (1901), *Epic Mythology* (1915), *Ethics of India* (1924), and *Legends of India* (1928).

Hopkins' *Ethics of India* remains the only work of its kind in

[53] *Ibid.,* p. 488.

[54] *Ibid.,* p. 489–90. Since Bloomfield's day we have learned somewhat more about ritual. According to Roger Garaudy, "Ritual is a first technology just as myth is first science . . . ritual and myth release thought from brute perception by distinguishing that which is from that which causes to be and that which must act in order to control things." From *Anathema to Dialogue,* Luke O'Neill, trans. New York, Vintage Books, 1968, pp. 76–7.

[55] *Ibid.,* p. 492. An interesting sidelight of the discussion was Bloomfield's witty rebuke to the anti-Brahminical passion of the famous German Indologist Richard Garbe, Garbe frequently attempting to demonstrate that brahmins are knaves. Perhaps this argument proved to be a draw. But the military and kingly caste may have been responsible for advances toward a monism away from ritualism.

the American philosophical literature. Its last chapter, called "Pro and Contra" presents a critical and comparative study of popular Indian and American ethics. Of his study he says:

> There can be no harm in standing off at a safe distance and calling closer attention to any object of virtue that is to be admired there, even if we decide not to import it for our own use.[56]

Hopkins demonstrated a positive liking for the doctrine of *ahimsā*, indeed is one of the few American Indologists who has bothered to write about it at all. Says Hopkins:

> There is in India, a doctrine called non-injury, which in some regards transcends any ethical teaching to be found in Christianity as known in America. It is the gentle doctrine of harmlessness. . . . This is not a teaching of Christianity, though it has been engrafted upon it and finds expression to a small degree in the Society for the Prevention of Cruelty to Animals.[57]

Hopkins felt so strongly in favor of "harmlessness" that he attacked the educationally sancitified zoo concept as he shows clearly in a footnote:

> To keep tigers and lions for life in a close confinement is a moral offence not justified by the "education value" of the pitiable exhibition.[58]

According to Hopkins it is in the total scope of noninjury that the Indian code is superior to ours for it includes people, beasts, birds, trees and flowers.

Hopkins epitomized the spiritual struggle of the Indian people from naïveté to maturity in a lengthy but admirable passage:

> The naive belief that the gods in the sky are watching to see whether man worships them correctly and is "straight" in conduct as the gods are straight and true, the feeling that wrongdoing is sinful because it is not in accord with the ways and wish of the gods, the temporary chaos

---

[56] Hopkins: *Ethics of India.* New Haven, Yale, 1924, p. 227.

[57] *Ibid.,* p. 227.

[58] *Ibid.,* p. 230 n.

resulting from the conviction that the gods can be overcome by magical means and that the gods after all are only forms of One God . . . representing all life . . . spiritual life, and that all besides pure sinless spirit (soul) is of no importance or even is a mere illusion of the senses, the firm conviction that the emancipation of the soul is based on a cleansing process, which frees it from sin the sudden irruption of materialism, which denies God and yet holds that to free oneself from all ill one must free himself first from all evil; the gradual weakening of this materialism with the belief that the Great Master is himself a divine exemplar of virtue and that to be like him, to imitate him in ethical conduct and devotion to man, in sympathy and in self-sacrifice, is the only way to reach lasting happiness; the endowment of the All-soul with ethical qualities, after the denial that it has any qualities at all, first by identifying Righteousness with God and then by making ethical conduct a part of the knowledge through which man may become divine; the final effort to free oneself from all sin by casting oneself before God and trusting in his grace to accept the suppliant and forgive what sins still burden him; the ever growing insistence upon gentleness and compassion as marks of the truly virtuous; the belief that religion itself is based upon ethics; the realization that men are all brothers, no matter what their social rank, and that it is better to be a virtuous slave than an immoral master; the perpetual endeavor to find a synthesis of religion and morality, ending in the conviction that morality and sympathetic kindness are essential elements of religion itself—this record of a people's spiritual and ethical development, in its greatness and in its weakness, in its backsliding and in its irresistible advance, is one of extraordinary and poignant interest.[59]

Besides working on Indian ethics, Hopkins wrote the first and most definitive American account of Indian epic philosophy.[60] He divided the great period into (1) Vedism or orthodox Brahminism, (2) ātmanism, which he characterized as "an idealistic interpretation of life," [61] (3) Sāṁkhya, (4) Yoga, (5) Bhāgavata (sectarian Yoga), and (6) Vedānta or Illusionism-idealism. His account includes the heretical views of the materialists and naturalists, Nyāya, Vaiçesika, and Kapila. His description of the development of Sāṁkhya is short but greatly compressed as are the details of "Pañçacika." Hopkins allowed the systems to speak for themselves with a minimum of exegesis and philosophical critique.

[59] *Ibid.*, pp. 256–7.
[60] Hopkins: *The Great Epic of India.* New Haven, Yale, 1920.
[61] *Ibid.*, p. 161.

The organization of his account is different from the usual approach in the later decades of the nineteenth century and not without originality. Not for another sixty years did an American attempt such a broad treatment of Indian philosophy.

In *The Origin and Evolution of Religion* (1923) Hopkins discusses at some length "The Hindu Trinity," "The Buddhist Trinity," and "Religion and Philosophy." Much of what appears in this book would now fall under the rubric of mythology. In *The History of Religions* (1918) he discusses "Religions of India from the Vedas to Buddhism," "Buddhism in India," and "Hindu Sectarian Religions." The last is a highly compressed account packed with allusions and references. We turn now from the academician Hopkins to a philosopher-journalist, Paul Elmer More.

More (1864–1937) was one of the founders of American Neohumanism along with Irving Babbitt. He took his B.A. and M.A. at Washington University in St. Louis and then took an M.A. at Harvard where he met Babbitt in a Sanskrit class. After serving as an assistant in Sanskrit he taught Sanskrit and classical literature at Harvard from 1895 to 1897, at which time he retreated for two years to Shelburne, New Hampshire, where he began writing his Shelburne Essays. He was literary editor of *Independent* (1901–03), the New York *Evening Post* (1903–09) and *The Nation* [62] (1909–14). He wrote a *Century of Indian Epigrams* after the Shelburne Essays which appeared in eleven volumes from 1904 onwards.

"More held that modern Christianity had less to offer than the mysticism of ancient Hinduism," [63] and in his "The Forest Philosophy of India" [64] he combined the outlook of a Sanskritist with a journalistic *joie de vivre* which gave all of his writing a spirited appearance. One of his students, Whitney J. Oates, at present a professor of classics at Princeton University, said of him that:

[62] More feared that after he resigned this post "Villard's influence will cheapen *The Nation* and deprive it of its unique quality." Barrows Dunham: Paul Elmer More, *The Massachusetts Review*. (Winter, 1966.)

[63] Irving Dilliard: Philosopher With a Pen That Stabbed. *St. Louis Post-Dispatch,* December 30, 1964.

[64] It appeared in More's *Shelburne Essays,* Sixth Series. New York, Putman, 1909.

Not only were his colleagues stimulated—not to say irritated—by this Socratic gadfly, but also numberless students benefited by an intellectual association which none of them will ever forget.[65]

More was asked in 1906 to write a review of Paul Deussen's *The Philosophy of the Upanishads*, translated from the German in 1906, for the *Atlantic Monthly*. More characteristically attacked Deussen's approach as being too intellectualistic and too close to the lecture room. He held that:

To grasp the force of these books we must go back to the time of the Vedas and store our memory with those earliest hymns of the Aryan race.[66]

He thought, furthermore, that we must be on guard against *Gefühlsphilosophie,* that romantic accompaniment to German metaphysics. Nothing could be farther from the virile faith of the ancient Hindus.[67] After all, our interpretations of the philosophy of ancient India come from the same romanticism that "dissolved the philosophy of J. J. Rousseau into a cloud of mystifying words." [68] Higher religion, "Ritschlianism," has come down to us from Fichte, Schelling, and Schleiermacher. The *Ich* of Fichte is not the *Ātman;* it is a mummery of egotism, part of the romantic magnification of the ego to be found in emotional self-containment and self-contemplation. This is not the Vedāntic self-restraint and discipline of knowledge, says More. Deussen must here be fingered as having led us astray. There seems to be little doubt that the attack by More on Deussen and later that by Santayana and Dewey on German philosophy were part of the tendency around World War I for some American intellectuals to display Germanophobia through the medium of philosophy.[69] More also

[65] Dilliard, *op. cit.*

[66] *Ibid.,* p. 4.

[67] *Shelburne Essays,* Sixth Series, p. 35.

[68] *Ibid.,* p. 36 n.

[69] Philosophy as counter-ideology during the First World War has been considered in a more literary form by George Baos, the Johns Hopkins philosopher and Carus Lecturer, in his novel *Never Go Back.* New York, Harper, 1928. It again became apparent after World War II in the East-West Philosophers' Conferences since philosophers from behind the so-called Iron Curtain were not invited to come and when invited, as in 1969, were unable.

felt, justifiably, I believe, that certain publications of modern Hindus in the Vedanta Society and elsewhere only served to increase the confusion of modern Indological research.

Probably the first American classroom philosopher to do a doctoral dissertation on Indian philosophy in the United States was Ethel May Kitch (1884–1941) at the University of Chicago in 1914. It was titled "The Origin of Subjectivity in Hindu Thought." [70] In the "Forward" she extended her appreciation to George Herbert Mead and Walter Eugene Clark for directing the thesis. More, she thanked Simon Frazer MacLennan of Oberlin College for suggesting investigation into this topic. Chapter I is an account of Vedism, Chapter II considers the transition from Vedism to Brahmanism, Chapter II discusses the theory of sacrifice, Chapter IV deals with philosophical Brahmanism, Chapter V with the Buddha and other religious revolts associated with such founders, and finally, Chapter VI with orthodox developments.

Kitch considered Vedism a period of objectivity. Subjectivity began as the warrior's position was usurped by the priest. In Buddhism subjectivity became more complete. With them and the Vedāntists "only the unknown and universal self . . . is real." [71] She summarized in a way that must have pleased G. H. Mead and other social philosophers at Chicago. She wrote,

> Every great wave in Hindu thought has been coincident with a freer political life and with a centralization of government. The union of native tribes occurred at approximately the same time as the development of the Upanishad theory.[72]

Kitch claimed of the Mahābhārata that it showed a period which ended in the supremacy of one tribe:

> Buddhism and other heretical tendencies can be associated with the great Maurya dynasties of the third and fourth centuries B.C., while the rise of the more enlightened phases of Hinduism and the Renaissance

---

[70] Published as Number 7 of Philosophical Studies in the Department of Philosophy. Chicago, U. of Chicago, 1917.

[71] Kitch, *The Origin of Subjectivity in Hindu Thought*, p. 78.

[72] *Ibid.*, p. 78. W. Norman Brown considers this generalization to be "quesionable."

is associated with the great Gupta powers of the fourth and fifth centuries A.D.[73]

As the eastern kings gave patronage to the Brahmins in the development of science and literature, it may be seen, according to Kitch, that viability was coming from a class and portion of the country still free. But as it met entrenched Brahmanism their purposes were thwarted and distracted. Finally, the "Self turned within to find in its own capacity for being all that was real and eternal." [74] Concluding, she held that:

> Hence Indian thought must always be subjective as long as the caste system and its counterpart, an unknowable pantheism, can control the social life.[75]

Although it was not unusual between 1900 and 1950 for Americans to blame nearly everything wrong with India on the caste system, and despite the British encouragement of this explanatory shibboleth, behavioral scientists today do not take such a simplistic view of the major troubles in Indian thought. With the analytic tools provided her by G. H. Mead, this was as far as her analysis could take her. Yet, it was still an augury of a growing interest in social interpretation and social philosophy that reached its first peak in the United States in the 1930's, but which was again to appear, nearly as strong in the late 1950's after the abatement of right-wing patriotism personified by Senator Joseph McCarthy.

The first American academic philosopher to incorporate Asiatic systems of ethics into a monograph on ethics for classroom use was [Isaac] Woodbridge Riley (1869–1933) in his *Men and Morals* [76] which appeared in 1929. In it he dealt with Buddhism and Confucianism. We are concerned here with only the former.

---

[73] *Ibid.*, p. 79. W. Norman Brown believes that this is "perhaps" true, but not probable.

[74] *Ibid.*, p. 79.

[75] *Ibid.*

[76] Reissued, New York, Ungar, 1960.

Riley took his A.B., M.A. and Ph.D. from Yale University. He taught at New York University, the University of New Brunswick and Johns Hopkins; lectured at the Sorbonne in 1920; and taught at Vassar College from 1908 to 1933.

Riley began by contrasting Buddhist *karma,* or "the natural law of the spiritual world" with Western thoughts on responsibility. Blame cannot be put on destiny as in the Homeric age, nor upon original sin as in the Christian era, for the individual is responsible for his own fate. When he reaches the stage free of illusion, Riley said, "the debt is paid, the mortgage lifted, the account cleared." [77] This metaphor is particularly apt on the eve of the Great American Depression. Continuing, he held that even though this may be a mercantile way of looking at it, "Buddhism appears to be built upon a veritable system of double-entry bookkeeping." [78]

> Yet, while the account is checked up at every turn, many an extension of time is allowed; there are countless lives in which expiation may be made, but in the end full payment must be rendered.[79]

How does the Western [American?] mind react to such a hypothesis?

> It is as cold-blooded as banking. It does not appeal to those who would have recourse to some outside benefactor who is expected to erase the record by an act of forgiveness.[80]

Buddhism, however, seems to be in trouble because there is no doer but only a deed Riley believed. There is no real self, but "a series of conjoined phenomena." Yet this abrogation of animism is not so different from the twentieth century Western conception of the stream of consciousness, made famous in the United States by William James.

[77] Isaac Woodbridge, Riley, *Men and Morals,* p. 104.
[78] *Ibid.*
[79] *Ibid.*
[80] *Ibid.*

> Karma, then, represents ethical energy and Karma as a process of
> causation is a self-recording process registered on the unfolding roll of
> time.[81]

This is another typical American metaphor when comfortable
households maintained the roller or player piano. How is the
psychology of no-soul to be explained to the followers of Aristotle
who believed that without a soul there would be no free will?
Riley answered by asserting that,

> It is the task of the wise man to learn . . . [that] his reality does not
> consist so much in his personal identity in this little span of life, as in
> the sense of union with all that was, is, and shall be. In short, this life
> is but one in an endless series of past existences. . . .[82]

It is of interest to note that of two references cited by Riley in
this section on Buddhism, one is to *The Sacred Books of the East*
and the other to E. W. Hopkins' *Ethics of India* which had
recently appeared. Despite Riley's inclusion of Buddhistic ethics
in this volume, it is still today an uncommon practice. With the
growth of positivistic and analytic ethics, beginning in the 1930's
with the influence of G. E. Moore and A. J. Ayer, there was little
room for Indian or Buddhist ethics or any constructive ethics
except among the smaller and less renowned denominational
colleges and universities. Constructive and substantive ethics
nearly vanished into what appeared to have been an imperial
evanescence. It still lay largely in the writings of theologians and
religionists, an ironical development in that Buddhism was atheistic in character. But even these, the irrational tendencies of German neoorthodoxy and existentialism, seemed to have nearly
carried the day as against Buddhism except in its most irrational
form in Zen.

From the end of the nineteenth century to the beginning of the
Great Depression, Indian philosophy gradually became naturalized. Theses on Indian philosophy were written and accepted for
doctoral degrees. American philosophers began traveling to India
to see for themselves the civilization which produced such marvels

[81] *Ibid.*, p. 106.
[82] *Ibid.*, p. 107.

of ethics, epistemology, and metaphysics. A dozen societies were formed promoting knowledge of India, and Indian intellectuals came to the United States to lecture on Indian philosophy, religion, poetry, and art. Coomaraswamy at Boston encouraged the foundation of the great collections of Indian art now to be found there and in New York, Philadelphia, Washington, Cleveland, Chicago, and Kansas City. It was a great period of solidification just before the onrush of specialization to appear in the next forty years.

Chapter VIII

INDIAN THOUGHT IN THE 1920's
AND 1930's

F OR TWO decades after the death of Royce there was a decline of American interest in Indian thought among philosophers. One reason for this was American concentration on Europe as a result of World War I, the realization that American destiny was primarily of Western scope, and the realization that in the Soviet Union a new civilization was trying to rise based upon a philosophy that Americans had been ignoring. However, even when American attention was led back to Asia it was to be engrossed in the partition of China and temporarily away from the Indian subcontinent. Ernest Fenellosa, Edward Sylvester Morse, Royce, and Bigelow had already anticipated this shift in focus before the First World War.

The first philosopher-theologian to make his mark after World War I was the only American Sanskritist native to India, Robert Ernest Hume (b. Ahmednagar in Bombay Presidency 1877—d. New York City 1948). He took his A.B., M.A. and Ph.D at Yale and his B.D. at Union Theological Seminary. He also attended the University of Göttingen and in 1932 received his D. Theol. from the University of Strasbourg. In 1907 he was sent to India as a missionary, but returned to the United States at the eve of the First World War and was thereafter professor of the history of religion at Union Theological Seminary (1914–43). He also taught, at various times, at Bombay, Punjab, Banaras, Aligarh, Viśva-Bhārati, Baroda, and Oxford. His most important works were *Thirteen Principal Upanishads* (1921), *The World's Living Religions* (1924), and *Treasure House of the Living Religions* (1932).

Seventy-two pages of Hume's *Thirteen Principal Upanishads* are a technical account of the Upaniṣads. They comprise a fine monograph on the subject, worthy of separate publication. The main topics discussed include "First Attempts at the Conception of a Unitary World-Ground," "The Development of the Conception of Brahma," the doctrine of illusion, "Idealism and the Conception of Pure Unity," the doctrine of *karma,* the outcome on practical life, and unity in renunciation and in yoga. Says Hume in this account,

> In a few passages the Upanishads are sublime in their conception of the Infinite and of God, but more often they are puerile and groveling in trivialities and superstitions.[1]

Despite the weaknesses of the Upaniṣads, Hume continues,

> In the main, however, there was an appreciation of idealism. This, having seen in the psychic self the essence of the whole world, and having identified it with Brahma, reacted against the realistic philosophy which had produced the concept of Brahma; and then it carried the atman, or the purely psychical, element over into the extreme of philosophical idealism.[2] It is like the simple intuition of the early Greek philosopher Xenophanes . . .[3]

Of universal frame are the following Upaniṣadic lines:

> From the unreal lead me to the real.
> From darkness lead me to light.
> From death lead me to immortality.
>   Brihad-Aranyaka 1. 3. 28

---

[1] *Thirteen Principal Upanishads,* p. 70. The Upaniṣads have always held a high place in the regard of most philosophers acquainted with them, but the most fulsome praise comes from the lips of Arthur Schopenhauer who read them in Aquetil du Perron's Latin translation of a Persian rendering. He says: "It [the Upaniṣads] is the most rewarding and the most elevating reading which (with the exception of the original text) there can possibly be in the world. It has been the solace of my life and it will be of my death." Quoted from *Parerga* 2, 185 (*Werke* 6, 427) by Hume in *The Thirteen Principal Upanishads.* Madras, Geoffrey Cumberlege, Oxford, 1941.

[2] *Ibid.,* p. 71

[3] *Ibid.*

Another work of Hume's was *The World's Living Religions* which passed through twenty-eight printings between 1924 and 1953. Its lucid account of the religious philosophies of India include chapters on Hinduism, Jainism, Buddhism, and Sikhism. In his assessment of the elements of strength and weakness of each of these in turn he reveals his own Christian bias to some extent for he still belonged to that age in the United States when it made a significant difference that he was not only a comparative religionist but also a professor of comparative religion at Union Theological Seminary.

In his *Treasure-House of Living Religion* (1932), Hume provided Americans with their most complete compendium of world religions. Included were sections on "Faith in the Perfect God," "Man and His Perfecting," "Man and His Social Relations," and a final one entitled "A Program of Joint Worship" with an arrangement as responsive readings which could serve one imagines at certain unitarian meetings. With the thoroughness which characterized his work, 190 pages were devoted to references and indices, providing the reader a permanent thesaurus and reference work for dozens of diversions and professional requirements.

Under the heading of "Giving and Helping" are quotations from Buddhism, Christianity, Confucianism, Hinduism, Islam, Judaism, Shintō, Sikhism, Taoism, and Zoroastrianism. According to Hume,

> This labor has involved scrutiny of the original languages in the case of Hebrew, Greek, Chinese, Sanskrit, Prakrit, Gurmukhi, and Avestan.[4]

These were taken from 134 documents, in sixteen oriental languages in which 106,423 pages of translation were handled. Hume's reason for putting together such a volume covering thirty centuries of wisdom he states as,

> In the hurried life of today we frequently overlook the wisdom of other lands and other ages. These selections, veritable treasures from

[4] Hume, *Treasure-House of the Living Religions.* New York, Scribner, 1932, p. viii.

rich and deep deposits of the world's religious knowledge are . . . for persons who seek information and inspiration.[5]

Two American Sanskritists were born in Nova Scotia. The first of these, Walter Eugene Clark, was born in 1881 and died in 1960. He took his A.B. M.A. and Ph.D. at Harvard after which he also studied at Berlin and Bonn in 1906–07. He advanced from instructor to professor of Sanskrit at the University of Chicago between 1908 and 1923, was called to Harvard as visiting professor in 1927 to remain as Wales Professor until his retirement. Clark's approach to philosophy was through his researches in Buddhist Sanskrit.

While in his senior year at Harvard, Clark took Sanskrit under Arthur Ryder and later also took work under Lanman. Waiting for a position to appear he then went to Berlin where he studied under Richard Pischel. He was appointed the first full-time Sanskritist at the University of Chicago in 1908 after he returned from Berlin. According to Ingalls,

> In Sanskrit he acquired a thorough knowledge of the Veda, of Epic texts, court literature,[6] philosophy, and the texts of mathematics and astronomy; in Pali he ultimately read the whole of the Hinayana Buddhist canon with all its published commentaries. He came to read these texts as rapidly as most of us read English.[7]

Clark assumed the Wales Professorship of Sanskrit at Harvard in 1928 and taught besides Sanskrit, Pāli, Tibetan, and the history and culture of India. Before retiring from Harvard in 1950 Clark was editor of the Harvard Oriental Series, was secretary of the American Academy of Arts and Sciences, and was twice president of the American Oriental Society. After retirement in California, he continued working on the *Visuddhimagga* (Path of Purity) begun in 1895 by Henry Clark Warren and continued by James H. Woods of the Harvard philosophy department with the help of

[5] *Ibid.*, p. x.

[6] Here he was an influence on Ingalls who subsequently published *An Anthology of Sanskrit Court Poetry: Vidyākāra's "Subhasitaratnakosa."* Harvard Oriental Series, vol. 44. Cambridge, Harvard, 1965.

[7] D. H Ingalls: Walter Eugene Clark, *Harvard University Gazette*, LVII, 7, 1961, p. 44.

Dharmanandi Kosambi [8] and P. V. Bapat. In 1960 Clark sent the final typescript to his former student Ingalls, by now editor of the Harvard Oriental Series which proved to be 2,500 pages, all rewritten by Clark. The edition and translation of the *Divyava-dana* he left unfinished. "It is typical of Clark that at the end of his life he completed the work of others at the expense of his own." [9]

Walter E. Clark's Ingersoll Lecture at Harvard in 1934 was entitled "Indian Conceptions of Immortality." [10] His opening words give a significant clue to the intellectual bent of this distinguished Sanskritist:

> I do not feel competent to speak positively either in defense of or in denial of immortality. So far as I can discover from observation on myself the concept of immortality plays little part in my own thought, and has had no appreciable influence on the formation of my character or on my conduct. It is hard for me to understand those to whom it is an obsession.[11]

Whether doctrines of immortality are true or false, Clark said, seems to be beyond the range of "normal intellectual experience and reasoning." Yet the Indians found the topic of such absorbing interest that perhaps we too should look into it. Indeed says Clark:

> Recently I read in a detective story the following two sentences: "Wot I say is, when yer dead, yer dead." "You don't know that, *not* until you are dead." These two simple sentences cut through the fog of much theological and philosophical argument.[12]

Clark then began to explain the doctrine of immortality by pointing out that the Cārvākas denied it. Despite their denial, the main tendency was to believe it during the three main periods in the development of Indian philosophy: the age of the Rig Veda,

---

[8] Father of the late Sanskritist, mathematician and philosopher, D. D. Kosambi of Poona.

[9] *Harvard University Gazette*, p. 45.

[10] Walter E. Clark: *The Indian Conception of Immortality*. Cambridge, Harvard, 1934.

[11] Clark, p. 3

[12] *Ibid.*, pp. 6–7.

of Brahmanism, and of Hinduism. It was during the period of Brahmanism (seventh to sixth century B.C.) that the doctrines of *karma* and transmigration developed. Contrasted to the Christian view of immortality, the Hindu belief had positive virtues which Clark summarized as follows:

> There follows as a corollary to the doctrine of transmigration that there is a continuity of life throughout the universe and that man is only a part of this general current of life, is not a privileged and special creation with a soul which is denied to lower forms of life. Man is not the centre of the universe. Man is merely a stage higher than the animals and a stage lower than the gods.[13]

Clark also holds that in India the Judaic-Christian view that man assumes "exaggerated and sentimental importance" is simply impossible.

In closing his lecture, Clark points out that:

> The fanaticism of the more extreme forms of *yoga* and of the more emotional types of *bhakti* are not very attractive to me. I cannot believe that the *summum bonum* lies in them or in such a frenzied obsession with the gaining of immortality.[14]

Franklin Edgerton (1885–1963), the only American Sanskritist to come from the American Great Plains, was a student of Maurice Bloomfield at Johns Hopkins, receiving his doctorate under Bloomfield in 1907. Between the time he graduated from Cornell and attended Johns Hopkins, Edgerton spent a year at Munich and Jena. Just as he was about to give up hope of getting one of the few positions in Sanskrit in the country, Morris Jastrow, the Semitic scholar at the University of Pennsylvania, was instrumental in founding a chair of Sanskrit at Yale University. When E. W. Hopkins retired in 1926 from Yale, Edgerton was appointed Salisbury Professor of Sanskrit and comparative philology there and made Sterling Professor in 1953.[15]

Although most of Edgerton's work was in philology and linguis-

---

[13] *Ibid.*, p. 25.

[14] *Ibid.*, p. 45.

[15] W. Norman Brown: Franklin Edgerton. *American Philosophical Society Yearbook*. Philadelphia, Am. Philos. Soc., 1965.

tics, he also published more than most American Sanskritists in the area of philosophy. He published a translation with an introduction of *The Mīmānsā Nyāya Prakāsa* (1929) with an introduction of a work by Apadeva. It was the first attempt by an American scholar to do a monograph on this school of Indian philosophy. His two-volume *The Bhagavad Gītā* appeared in 1944, an extension of a slighter and earlier work on the same subject.[16] Appearing posthumously was his *The Beginnings of Indian Philosophy* (1965).

Of this work [17] Edgerton says,

> It sums up my views on early Indian speculation, in what will certainly be, for me, their final form . . . Some of them are unconventional, not to say unorthodox.[18]

The "Introduction" is a masterful epitome of his thinking about the Rig Veda, Atharva Veda, the Upaniṣads, the Bhagavad Gītā, and the Mokṣadharma (Mahābhārata Book 12). Edgerton's interpretations may well have been unconventional when he first thought them, but today they seem less so.

What Edgerton points out immediately is that in Rig Veda times only rich men could engage in the priestly ritual. As such it was an aristocratic cult. The religion of the masses, on the other hand, is portrayed in the Atharva Veda. We can see in the early Upaniṣads the greater influence of the practices and beliefs of the masses. Then develops henotheism, monotheism and monism. Monism develops because of the "passion for identification," Edgerton maintained, staying in the best tradition of American mentalistic explanation of events.[19] Having its roots in magic, monism was the result of the desire to set cosmic forces in motion.[20] From this followed the belief that *to know* the one principle, or the prin-

---

[16] Part of this work was Edgerton's translation and introduction reissued with some modification in the Harper Torchbooks, The Cloister Library. New York, Harper, 1964.

[17] Posthumously published by Harvard University Press.

[18] *Ibid.*, p. 7.

[19] Nevertheless, Edgerton was a linguistic mechanist who felt that much "mentalistic" phraseology must be changed. See E. Adelaide Hahn: Franklin Edgerton, personal reminiscences. *J. Amer. Orient. Soc.*, 58, 1, 1965, p. 4.

[20] Edgerton, *The Beginnings of Indian Philosophy*, p. 21.

ciple of the One, would enable one to have complete control of cosmic forces. Why one wished to have control of cosmic forces is not limned by Edgerton. *Brahman* itself originally meant "holy knowledge." Later the One is connected to the empirical world and thought of as a carpenter or smith. Anthropomorphism grows in the Upaniṣads, according to Edgerton, with the notions of re-birth and *karma* soon following.[21] Edgerton's chronology has been seriously challenged by Walter Ruben, Debiprasad Chatto-padhyaya, and D. D. Kosambi, but nevertheless the interpretation is an interesting one, particularly for an American to make, as so little American writing on Indian philosophy makes any attempt to explain the roots or motives for actions and beliefs. The earliest occurrence of the word *karma* in the literature is in the Bṛhad Āraṇyaka Upaniṣad (4. 4. 4. 5M), according to Edgerton.

The way out of the rebirth impasse, Edgerton comments, was at first knowledge, with morality and devotion as ancillary. With Sāṁkhya the way to salvation is knowledge and abstention from action; for yoga, it is salvation through action. These appear during the composition of the Mahābhārata. It is also held in this work that Sāṁkhya and Yoga are one. The knowledge that one should seek, however, is no longer magical, but the truth of the universe and man. Whereas "soul" was the source of concern in the Upaniṣads, in the epic it becomes body and matter as well, leading to dualistic speculation. At this time also the notion of double-soul emerges in which there is the soul connected to body and the soul which is cosmic and imperishable. At the culmination of the vedic speculation is Vedānta which is monistic or dualistic or qualified monism. With this Edgerton concludes his philosophical and his-torical introduction and devotes the remainder of the work to se-lections which portray his analysis. It is a beautifully compressed account which should appeal to students and scholars alike, but for different reasons: to the first because it is a concise guide leading to understanding of a maze of material; to the second because it is such an admirable pedagogic as well as interpretative *tour de force*.

One of the most elegant accounts of the development of Hindu speculation was Edgerton's account by that name which makes up

---

[21] *Ibid.,* p. 29.

Chapter II in his *The Bhagavad Gita.* Of the next chapter, entitled "The Upanisads and Later Hindu Thought" similar praise may be exacted. It is perhaps amusing that Edgerton tried always to give the impression that he was not a philosopher.[22] What bothered him about the rubric "philosophy," I believe, was its connotation of vast systems of interlinked hypotheticals likely to confuse the religious and poetical issues. Perhaps this is a wrong interpretation, but that is how it struck me in 1952 and later, from reading his letters.

Leroy Schaub was born in 1881 and died in 1953. Educated at Charles City College, he took his M.A. at the State University of Iowa and the Ph.D. at Cornell University. He also attended the University of Berlin for a year in 1910. Schaub taught at Cornell University, Queen's University in Ontario, the State University of Iowa, and at Northwestern where he finished his career. He was editor of *The Monist* from 1925 to 1936, successor in that post to Paul Carus.

Schaub was invited in 1929 to lecture at Calcutta University by S. N. Dasgupta while he was visiting Shanghai. He delivered the Calcutta University Readership Lectures the same year. They were published as *Progressism: An Essay in Social Philosophy.*[23] The first lecture was entitled "Progressism: An Interpretation of Indian Philosophy in its Divergence from the Spirit of the Contemporary West." Our knowledge of his understanding of Indian thought must be largely based on these lectures, one of which, entitled "Interpretation of Indian Philosophy," is nearly comparable to those prepared by Conger, Burtt, and Northrop for the First East-West Philosophers' Conference in Hawaii in 1939. It shows considerable grasp of semipopular material on Indian culture but no sustained or exact mastery of the classics of Indian thought. His views are based on those of such philosophers as Radhakrishnan, Jivala Prasad, and S. N. Dasgupta (only the first volume of whose *A History of Indian Philosophy* (1922–1955) was available for the lectures delivered by Schaub).

Schaub in this essay gives to Indian thought more religious

[22] E. Adelaide Hahn remarks also about Edgerton's rejection of speculation in "Franklin Edgerton, Personal Reminiscences," *op. cit.,* p. 3.

[23] Calcutta, Calcutta Univ. Press, 1937.

significance than it is to receive at the hands of the newer generation who began teaching Indian thought after the Second World
War. For Schaub, Indian philosophies revealed what the "people
of Indian generally have displayed . . . an acute sense of the
infinite and a reverent devotion to the unseen." [24] These philosophers held, according to Schaub, that:

(1) being possesses a depth unfathomable by the instrumentalities of
    abstract thought,
(2) being is unknown or unknowable,
(3) being is bridged between the cognitive consciousness and the ul-
    timate.

Said Schaub, American and Indian thinkers agree in their pursuit
of the "natural and psychological orders of perceptual and introspective experience, and who are very fearful of any departures
from the leadings of modern science." [25] Compared to the American, the Indian expresses a longing for the unknown, the infinite,
the real being. Indian thought shows a "restless feeling of wonder," roused by the awesome features of physical nature in India.
This wonder is akin to what we in America think of as religious
consciousness or what Kant refers to as wonder at the starry
heavens. Schaub summed up his convictions as follows:

Indian philosophy has its orientation in the self and the world. In its
doctrine of Karma it conjoins power and goodness. Its goal is not
abstract knowledge but a characteristic type of experience. Its aims are
practical—practical however, not in the sense of enhancing man's
power over the material and social environment, or of realizing ends of
a purely or a specifically ethical sort, but in the sense of satisfying the
more ultimate need of salvation. They thus transcend the plane of
morality. . . . Its emphasis is upon being rather than upon becoming
. . . and the philosopher is inclined to a metaphysical monism which
looks beyond particulars to a whole or a totality with which they fall.[26]

As Schaub saw it, the Indian philosopher differs from the American in (1) the feeling of wonder, (2) the concept of the practical,
and (3) the value attached to abstract or intellectual
knowledge.

[24] Schaub, *Progressism,* p. 46.
[25] *Ibid.,* p. 49.
[26] *Ibid.,* pp. 52–53.

It is significant that the American philosophers of German origin like Schaub, or of German training such as Woods, or of German inspiration as in the case of the Transcendentalists, showed a special appreciation of Indian thought in the nine-teenth and twentieth century. This group included Royce, San-tayana, Carus, Woods, Savery, Haas, Leidecker and Conger, to mention just a few.

Clarence H. Hamilton (1886–   ) was educated at the Uni-versity of Chicago where he took his Ph.D. in 1914. He also attended Union Theological Seminary in 1920–21. Professor of philosophy and chairman of the department at the University of Nanking from 1914 to 1927, he also taught at the Kennedy School of Missions as professor of Eastern philosophy and since 1931 was on the faculty of the Graduate School of Theology at Oberlin College. His better known works are *Buddhism: A Religion of Infinite Compassion, A Psychological Interpretation of Mysticism,* and *Buddhism in India, Ceylon, China and Japan.*

Hamilton first became acquainted with Indian philosophy in a course in Oriental religious philosophy under George Burman Foster (1858–1918) at the University of Chicago in 1909–10. Later when Hamilton was serving as professor of philosophy and psy-chology at the University of Nanking (1914–1927) he became in-terested in Buddhist philosophy as an integral part of the history of Chinese philosophy. At that time at Nanking the Chinese schol-ars were especially interested in the idealistic system of Vasu-bandhu, encouraging Hamilton to make a detailed study of Hsuan Tsang's Chinese version of Vasubandhu's *Viṃsatika* or *Treatise in Twenty Stanzas.* Of this he made an English translation, later pub-lished in 1938 by the American Oriental Society. When he re-turned to the United States in 1927 he was called upon to lecture on Eastern religions and philosophy. He also served after this time for a number of years on committees of the American Council of Learned Societies, one of whose purposes was to promote an inter-est in the study of Asian cultures. Hamilton says that:

> I suppose my interest in Indian thought may be said to be more historical than strictly philosophic. However, I remember that in first encountering the Vedantic idea of the oneness of Atman and Brahman

I felt it was somehow congenial for, from certain lines of Christian thinking at least, I accept the conception of God as immanent in as well as transcendent to the world he had made.[27]

Hamilton has shown in his study of Wei Shih (Vijñānavāda) that he agreed with other authorities that Vijñānavāda is the highest form of Mahāyāna reflection. According to this school, "all that exists is consciousness only." The thought of the leading figure of the school was Vasubandhu (fourteenth century A.D.) who developed in four stages, a kind of paradigm for this form of mysticism. The first stage was direct realism (Sarvāstivāda), then indirect realism (Sautrāntika), followed by idealism (Vijñānavāda), and finally devotion to the ideal of salvation (Sukhāvatī). At the time Hamilton was making this study (1929) Vasubandhu had not been translated into any European language which added to the interest of Hamilton's account. The original Sanskrit text published by Sylvain Levi in 1925 was known to Hamilton who also had the Chinese text at his disposal, entitled "The Treatise of Twenty Verses on Absolute Consciousness." Wei Shih literally means "only consciousness," which Hamilton chose to translate as "absolute consciousness." He warned that it is not to be interpreted in any Western sense. According to Hamilton:

> The idealism of Vasubandhu's central proposition appears in his opening words "In the Mahayana is established the doctrine that the three worlds are consciousness only." These worlds make up the sum total of existence. The word "only" eliminates external objects but it does not banish images.[28]

But why do these have fixed places and times? Because even in dreams, counters Vasubandhu, there are fixed places and times.

> As to the fact, that the same object is common to several different consciousnesses, it may be understood by reflecting that in hell they who have committed the same crime behold the same objects of torment.[29]

---

[27] *Letter* to the author, Oberlin, Ohio (January 15, 1965).

[28] Clarence Hamilton: Buddhistic idealism in Wei Shih Er shih Lwen [lun]. In T. V. Smith and William Kelley Wright (Ed.): *Essays in Philosophy*. Chicago, Open Ct., 1929, p. 104.

[29] *Ibid.*, p. 185.

Even though these are in consciousness they still are not private possessions. Space does not permit further pursuit of this fascinating topic of which Hamilton shows himself a master of exposition.

Hamilton is the only American philosopher since William Savery to grapple with the philosophy of Nāgārjuna, the second century founder of Mādhyamika Buddhism. This record is found in his "Encounter with Reality in Buddhist Mādhyamika Philosophy." [30] Hamilton claimed that Nāgārjuna interpreted the silence of the Buddha, not as withholding secrets but as pointing out that "deliberate suspension of judgment" was the aim, since what was "secret" was "what transcends conceptual power," [31] for true wisdom is direct intuition. Nāgārjuna like Kant used the dialectic to bring out the knowledge that speculative metaphysics (*dṛṣṭi*) yields not knowledge but illusion. Having shown that each postulated position ends in contradiction he advanced his own view— the no-reality hypothesis or a standpoint of reasoned suspension of judgment. The possible circularity of this activity is not considered by Hamilton. For Nāgārjuna,

> Every envisaged entity is unreal, devoid of what is taken to be its own self-nature. Nothing mundane is finally real.[32]

If this is so, is the view of Nāgārjuna nihilistic or negativistic? According to Hamilton,

> The answer is both Yes and No; Yes, if we are thinking of the relativity of all concepts framed by finite human intelligence; No, if we are thinking of the religious encounter with reality. For it is part of Mādhyamika teaching that genuine realization of the emptiness and unreality of our phenomenal world as apprehended is at the same time awakening. Dialectical criticism is severe, but it is in the service of a higher end, what the *Ratnakūṭa Sūtra* calls "the vision of the Real" in its true form.[33]

Whereas Hegel's dialectic affirms negations when taken up into a more inclusive synthesis, Nāgārjuna's rejects all alternatives. Hamilton believed that ultimately,

[30] *J Bible Relig,* January 1958.
[31] *Ibid.,* p. 16.
[32] *J Bible Relig,* January 1958.
[33] *Ibid.,* pp. 16–17.

By stressing the relativity of every expressive concept, image or symbol, the Mādhyamika dialectic opens a wide door for every actual encounter with reality, whether in the East or West.[34]

Yet I think it is fair to add that Mādhyamika dialectic opens the door on nonrational and indeed irrational encounters to the detriment of the rational.[35] This may be best seen in the activity of Zen Buddhism, particularly of the Rinzai Sect. That this may have salutary results in painting, poetry, and gardening as opposed to its effects on philosophy and science is not to be lightly discarded.

In *Buddhism: A Religion of Infinite Compassion*, Hamilton explained the Pāli Buddhist literature as it pertains to the life of the Buddha, the early teachings of Pāli Buddhism, and then concluded his Indian section with Sanskrit Buddhist literature. The account is rounded out with Chinese, Japanese, and Tibetan Buddhist literature. Since this is a group of selections, only the introduction and framework is Hamilton's own except for a short, useful chronology of Buddhism which was, to my knowledge, the first one compiled by an American philosophical scholar.

Will Durant, born in 1885, shares with Walter B. Pitkin the distinction of having left the microcosm of American academic philosophy to make a fortune in the world of letters. Like the encyclopaedists of the eighteenth and nineteenth century, Durant has written a monumental series concerned with world culture. It is entitled "The Story of Civilization." Begun in 1935 it now comprises eight volumes.

Taking his B.A. at St. Peter's College, M.A. and Ph.D. at Columbia University, he was at first a professor of Latin and French at Seton Hall College. He then became director of the Labor Temple School in New York, instructor in philosophy at Columbia, and finally professor of philosophy at the University of California at Los Angeles in 1935. Like Santayana and Pitkin, upon achieving financial independence, he retired from teaching to devote himself to writing what pleased his fancy.

Before retiring from teaching, Durant had already become

[34] *Ibid.*, p. 32.
[35] But see also Richard Robinson's view below.

famous for his popular and insightful *The Story of Philosophy*
(1926),[36] which became the bestseller of American philosophy;
The Mansions of Philosophy (1929) ; *The Case for India* (1930) ;
and *Our Oriental Heritage* (1935) being the first volume of "The
Story of Civilization."

In this first volume comprising over a thousand pages, Durant
devoted 244 pages, or a good-sized monograph, to tell the story of
India including its early history, religion, philosophy, and hopes
for the future. He began by confessing that:

> Nothing should more deeply shame the modern student than the
> recency and inadequacy of his acquaintance with India . . . a new
> intellectual continent, to the Western mind which only yesterday
> thought civilization an exclusively European thing.[37]

Like the realist and humanitarian that he is, Durant began his account of Indian philosophy by questioning the Vedāntic interpretation of its monolithic idealistic and unrealistic growth from the
time of the Vedas to the middle Upaniṣads. This skeptical and materialist mood he traced to the early Upaniṣads and to the period
during which the Buddha grew to manhood. Throughout the rest
of Durant's account he alternated between the outlook of a Voltaire and that of the Buddha himself. He showed his encyclopaedic
reading and broad travel as he filled in the vast painting of Indian
life and culture. His account of Rabindranath Tagore rounds out
the richest account of India we have by the hand of an American
philosopher. His last note on the future of India was written during the height of American enthusiasm for India's Independence:

> It is true that even across the Himalaya barrier India has sent us such
> questionable gifts as grammar and logic, philosophy and fables, hypno-
> tism and chess, and above all, our numerals and our decimal system.
> But these are not the essence of her spirit; they are trifles compared to
> what we may learn from her in the future. . . . Perhaps, in return for
> conquest, arrogance and spoliation India will teach us the tolerance
> and gentleness of the mature mind, the quiet content of the unacquisi-

---

[36] It had sold over three million copies by 1965.
[37] Will Durant: *Our Oriental Heritage*. New York, Simon and Schuster, Inc., 1942,
p. 391.

tive soul, the calm of the understanding spirit, and a unifying, pacifying love for all living things.[38]

One may wonder where this romanticized India exists, but in the 1930's one sought for qualities in colonial India that imperialism obviously lacked. Durant wrote *The Case for India* "in a burst of youthful indignation." [39] He was moved by the poverty of the Indian people that he and his wife saw on a round-the-world tour. He was also stimulated by the lectures on India by John Haynes Holmes in the Community Church in New York.

William Norman Brown (1892–   ), another student of Bloomfield and the best known living Sanskritist in the United States, attended Hiram College, and then took his A.B. at Johns Hopkins and his Ph.D. there in 1916. He studied Sanskrit in Banaras from 1922 to 1924, was editor of the Journal of the American Oriental Society from 1926–1941, and has been president of the American Institute of Indian Studies, with headquarters at Philadelphia and Poona, since 1962. He has been professor of Sanskrit at the University of Pennsylvania since 1926, becoming emeritus in 1966.

Brown's *The Indian and Christian Miracles of Walking on the Water* [40] is a study showing the relationship between the Indian and the later Christian accounts of such miracles. Evidently such stories of walking on the water arrived in Syria from India at the time of Aṣoka (256–251 B.C.). From the methodological standpoint, Brown's technique of determining which of two or more legends genetically related is the original, is of more than passing interest. The technique depends upon the following considerations: (1) The theme must be shown to have an unequivocal, well-established place in the lore of the land posited as its home; (2) it must occur in the supposed homeland at an earlier date than elsewhere (this condition, according to Brown must be modified in illiterate areas such as Central Africa) ; (3) It must have some more apposite physical or psychological basis in the homeland than

[38] *Ibid.*, p. 633.

[39] *Letter* to the author, Los Angeles, California (September 29, 1965) .

[40] Brown: *The Indian and Christian Miracles of Walking on the Water*. Chicago, Open Ct., 1928.

in the other lands where it appears; and (4) It must be traced from the homeland to the lands of its later sojourn. These considerations are certainly useful to those engaged in comparative philosphy.

In an eschatological article entitled "The Rigvedic Equivalent for Hell," Brown digs into that mine to discover the facts about the ancient Indian recorded view of hell. Hell is downward, beneath the earth, dark, cold (being without sunlight), silent, a place of annihilation, and populated by antidivine creatures. Brown says that:

> These creatures go there because they operate with charms that are contrary to *ṛta* . . . They use charms that are *asat* "dealing with the non-existent" and conflicting with charms that deal with *sat* "the existent [being]" . . . He who speaks false charms—works black magic . . .—is slain by Soma; Agni smites him who makes the non-ṛta (*anṛta*) his god (stanza 14), the false worshipper. . . .[41]

Brown maintains that this is the crux of the discussion of Rigvedic hell: hell is "contrasted with the ordered universe." In the ordered universe is light, water, the sun, and the stars; whereas the unordered antiverse contains none of them.

Originally there was chaos dominated by Vṛtathe, a demon who had to be slain. Indra slew Vṛta, opening the cave of chaos. Then the sun and cosmic order emerged. Brown in "The Creation Myth of the Rig Veda" attempts to vivify this famous myth of creation in the following way:

> In the beginning were the Waters restrained with a shell. . . . There existed a natural force for expansion, which in its turn was personified as the god Varuna.[42]

At first the power of contracting or conservatism, Vṛta, was greater than that of liberation and growth.[43] Indra, however, coming to the creative rescue forced open the shell which released the Waters. Impregnated, they gave birth to the Sun while the Waters flowed into the "atmospheric ocean." To turn to the more philosophical

[41] Brown, *J Amer Orient Soc,* 61, pp. 78–79.
[42] *Ibid.,* p. 80.
[43] *Ibid.,* 62, pp. 97–98.

aspect of creation speculation after the earliest sections of the Rig
Veda where "each hymn merely tries to identify a remoter active
agent than any assumed in other theories," [44] Brown traces the
course of the principle of monistic development. The hymns themselves state or imply two major types of explanation. First, the animate and psychical, second, the inanimate and material, thus emphasizing the bifurcation of nature. Then in the hymn R.V. 10,
129, according to Brown, "both the will of a deity and the power
of sacrifice are ignored . . . and instead there appears the idea of a
single principle from which our entire universe is evolved." [45] This
was a "single, neuter principle." It was self-generated by inner
creative heat. Having been born it experienced desire, which desire became the seed of mind. Sages discovered this neutral principle by means of introspection.

Other efforts to explain the origin of the universe in a single
principle led to the idea of time *(kāla)* and frame *(skambha)* in
the Atharva Veda.[46] *Skambha* is of course unique in Indian cosmology, but contains something like the notion of the receptacle
in Plato's *Timaeus*. Time and frame were to be united in the idea
of a monistic *(advaita)* concept which is "neuter, mechanistic in
operation . . . [and] might also have had an oversoul *(adhyāt-
man)* component." [47] Again, this ultimately developed into the
Brahman which Coomaraswamy and others have felt was similar
to the One in Plotinus. That there are differences between the
two does not militate against their being mentioned in the same
breath.

Brown has also edited and translated *The Mahimnastava or
Praise of Shiva's Greatness* as the first publication of the American
Institute of Indian Studies from Poona in 1965. This work, little
known outside Sanskrit circles in America, is highly venerated in
Hinduism and appears to date back to the ninth to eleventh centuries. As a lyric devoted to celebrating Śiva sectarian Hinduism,
it defends monism as well as the superiority of Śiva over Brahmā
and Viṣṇu. Śiva, as conceived here, is "greater than mere godhead,"

[44] Brown: Theories of Creation in the Rig Veda, *J Amer Orient Soc*, 85, p. 27.
[45] *Ibid.*
[46] *Ibid.*, p. 28.
[47] *Ibid.*

W. Norman Brown

"is the Vedas and all else," and "transcends the pairs of opposites, which are synthesized in him." Indeed, Śiva is Creator, Preserver, Destroyer, great supreme principle, and source of the highest joy.[48] The appendix of this hymn ends on a mystical philosophical note:

> Initiation, alms, asceticism, holy bathing places, knowledge, sacrifice, and other rites are not worth a sixteenth part of recitation in praise of Śiva's greatness.[49]

[48] Brown, *The Mahimnastava*. Poona, Am. Inst. of Indian Studies, 1965, p. 4.
[49] *Ibid.*, p. 19.

Brown's treatment of Indian mythology,[50] although not directly impinging on philosophy, is important to an understanding of its origins and its thrust. The relation of Śiva to asceticism and sexual concerns bears heavily upon an understanding of Saivism and Shakta, to cite only two instances. These in turn are of significance in making sense of total Hinduism. American philosophical accounts of Indian thought are enormously attenuated and abstract; they are amateurish in the sense that they do not often come to grips with the cultural and economic bases of that thought. Psychic determinism rides high, depending largely upon earlier Indian and European accounts, themselves often of a spiritualistic type. What is missing is explanation in depth—or even explanation. What these philosophers lack can be partially supplied by the Sanskritists like Brown who have an intimate knowledge of the mythology, politics, art, and laws of India. But the Sanskritists themselves are generally lacking in critical economic information.

Others of Bloomfield's students who made contributions to the knowledge of Indian philosophy were Arthur H. Ewing (1864–1912), who wrote *The Hindu Conception of the Functions of Breath, A Study in Early Hindu Psycho-Physics;* George William Brown (1870–1932), who wrote *The Human Body in the Upanishads;* George Weston Briggs (1874–1966), the author of *Gorakhnāth and the Kānphata Yogīs;* [51] and Helen Moore Johnson (1889–1967), who translated the voluminous *Triṣaṣṭiśa-lākā-puruṣacarita* by Hemacandra in several volumes.[52] Johnson also contributed to the *Festschrift für M. Winternitz* (1933), and published "Botanical References in Hemacandra" for the University of Missouri Studies.

The best short account of Theosophy that I have found is that of Arthur H. Ewing in his work entitled *Theosophy Examined*. It contains three main parts: I, The Campaign Material of Theosophy; II, Fundamental Assumptions of Theosophy; III, The Fundamental Principles of Theosophy; and IV, Critique of Theoso-

---

[50] Brown: Varieties of Religious Mythology in India. In Samuel Kramer (Ed.): *Mythologies of the Ancient World*, Chicago, Quadrangle, 1961.

[51] Calcutta, Y.M.C.A. Publishing House, 1938/also London, Oxford 1938.

[52] In the Gaekwad's Oriental Series. Baroda, Oriental Institute, 1931.

phy. According to Ewing the three major strata of Theosophical Doctrine combine the following elements:

(1) theosophical doctrines of India and Egypt combined with Neoplatonism and Kabbala.

(2) etheric (celestial and chemical ether) material culled by Madame Blavatsky and other psychical adepts from many sources, including marvelous information about lost continents, lost races, and ordinarily invisible phenomena.

(3) an occidental strain due to the scientific and religious training of the interpreters, including misrepresented "scientific" evolution, god, man, life, and service.

The *principles* of Theosophy come from (1) above, the *assumptions* from (2) above, and the *campaign material* from (3) above. By campaign material is meant that which will appeal to the popular mind, such as (a) the fatherhood of god, (b) the brotherhood of man, and (c) life is in order to serve. Darwin is considered to have made a "Western blunder" by holding the process of life to be a "purely physical succession." What propels evolution is Ātma-Buddha or the Universal Oversoul. "The human foetus runs through forms belonging to every kingdom before attaining human shape," [53] it is maintained, by the action of the Oversoul, a view congruent with the Roman Catholic interpretation of evolution, if we change Oversoul to the Christian God.

Basic assumptions of Theosophy are:

(1) There is an all-pervading ether (*ākāśa*) filming the unconscious and conscious actions of human will and thought.

(2) Some chosen individuals have extremely delicate psychic organization allowing clairvoyance, clairaudience, thought transference, and trance.

(3) Man's nature is seven-fold, shown as follows:

  (a) body;
  (b) ethereal or astral body;
  (c) vital energies (*prāṇas*) ;
  (d) body of desire and appetite;

---

[53] Arthur Ewing: *Theosophy Examined,* new and enlarged ed. London, Christian Literature Soc., 1905, p. 4.

(e) self, spirit, *logos;*

(f) spiritual or divine soul;

(g) the thinker, the intelligence.

(4) There are 2,400 kinds of elemental essences making up the largest part of the collective thought of mankind.

(5) A luminous cloud called the "aura" surrounds human bodies to a distance of from one and one-half to two feet. An "aura" may be read to reveal dispositions, thoughts, and past histories of individuals.

(6) There is an "astral plane" into which psychically superior individuals can pass at will.

(7) Every body has an etheric double which may expel disease and may be seen, Ewing says, "oozing out of the left side of a medium."

(8) The "great adepts" enter the bliss of Brahma but return reincarnated for the good of mankind.

(9) There is nothing of historical importance in religion.

(10) Soul is independent of physical sense-organs.

(11) The wise man is unaffected by action.

(12) "The Higher Manas is 'Our Father in Heaven' to the Lower Manas and Ātma-Buddhi is 'Our Father in Heaven' to Higher Manas." [54]

Ewing's comments on these twelve propositions are historically illuminating, but we cannot tarry to consider them for we wish to turn now to the barest statement of the fundamental principles of Theosophy. They are: (1) the impersonality of the supreme being, (2) the unity of the world and god, (3) cognition as the fundamental element of self-consciousness, (4) the ecstatic character of ultimate Theosophic truth, (5) *karma* and reincarnation, and (6) the power of magic.[55] Far back in the Indian past, many of these are found in the theosophical hymns of the Atharva Veda, in some of the Upaniṣads, and in the gītā. Although the plea for service to our fellow man is a worthy ideal, according to Ewing, an examination of theosophy from its earliest inception in India shows it to be completely speculative. It has allowed "the world to degenerate into caste divisions and the enforced degradation of

[54] *Ibid.,* p. 8.
[55] *Ibid.,* p. 13.

whole classes." [56] And he quotes Syensius, a Greek who tried Neo-platonic Theosophy, as saying: "Theosophy neither finds God, nor supplies a motive to live by." [57] This by no means refutes contemporary Theosophy's claims, but it is an interesting antitestimonial. In my opinion, Ewing's weak point in his analysis is that he is defending Christianity in his analysis of Theosophy and hence falls into errors that are little different from those of Theosophy—lack of evidence, lack of rational or logical basis, and glossing over, when necessary, the black pages of Christian history in a world crying for social reform. What Ewing says about Theosophy is largely true, but what he ought to say about Christianity might often parallel what he says about Theosophy.

Ewing's long article on "The Hindu Conception of the Functions of Breath—A Study in Early Hindu Psycho-physics" composes a chapter in the history of science and by extension, the philosophy of science.[58] He himself summarizes his findings that may be reduced further to the statement that the Hindus early noticed in-and-out breathing and believed it to be related to psychical states. Is the *Vedāntasāra,* five types of breathing or winds connected with breathing are noted. These are as follows:

(1) *prāṇa* which goes forward and has the tip of the nose as its locus of activity.[59]

(2) *apāna* going downwards and has the anus as its place of activity.

(3) *vyāna,* going in all directions and having the entire body as its place of activity.

(4) *udāna* in the throat, going upward and is the departing wind at the last expiration.

(5) *samāna* producing the assimilation of food.[60]

Other references are to be found to the analysis of breath: in the *Vedānta Sūtras,* Gāudapāda's *Sāṁkhya-Sutras,* in the *Sāṁkhya-tattva Kāumudi,* and in Suśruta.[61] The functions of the breath play a vital role in yogic practices which make the navel the starting

56 *Ibid.,* p. 31.
57 *Ibid.,* p. 32.
58 *J Amer Orient Soc,* XXII, 2, 1901.
59 *Ibid.,* p. 305.
60 *J Amer Orient Soc,* p. 306.
61 A founder of early Indian medicine.

point of the system of veins as opposed to the Vedāntins who awarded this to the heart.

Helen Moore Johnson was born in 1889 and died in 1967. She attended Drury College for two years and then transferred to the University of Missouri, where she took her A.M. at the age of eighteen. She then did graduate work at Tulane University, Bryn Mawr, and the University of Wisconsin where she received the Ph.D. in 1912. At first her work was in the classics, her first publication being the translation of two fragments of Ammonius Saccas which had been included with her father's translation of the *Metaphysical Elements of Proclus* (1909).[62] She then went on to Johns Hopkins University for two years where she studied Sanskrit and was particularly interested in Jainism. Her brother, Franklin P. Johnson, claims that "she was attracted by a special feature of this religion, a high respect for animals. Throughout her life, she had strong feelings of compassion and affection for animals, and devoted much attention to their protection and well-being."[63] When she was awarded a fellowship by the American Association of University Women, she chose to go to India to study Jainism. This proved to be her principal life-work. Besides this grant, she received three others enabling her to study in India at four different times. Her other awards included the Guggenheim Fellowship, a grant from the American Philosophical Society, and a Fulbright Award.

Most of the work comprising Helen Johnson's translation of *Sixty-Three Lives*[64] consists of stories surrounding the lives of various Jaina saints. Only chapter XIII can be regarded as philosophical at all, dealing as it does with the *nirvāṇa* of Śrī Mahāvīra, founder of Jainism. His sermon at this occasion begins in the following way:

> There are four objects of existence of people in the world. Of these wealth and love are valuable in name only; in reality they are worthless. Emancipation alone is of value and dharma is the cause of it. . . . Just as a lame man may go a long way slowly, if he follows a

[62] See Thomas M. Johnson above.

[63] *Letter* to the author from Osceola, Missouri (June 10, 1968).

[64] The *Triṣaṣṭiśalākāpuruṣacarita* by Ācārya Śrī Hemacandra, 4 vols. Baroda, Oriental Institute, 1962.

path, so one even with heavy karma may attain emancipation if he practices dharma.[65]

This is reminiscent of that other encourager of the retarded, Confucius. One of Mahāvīra's imaginative predictions of the destruction of the world to last for 21,000 years because *dharma* has perished, can be compared with forecasts of calamitous events today. He says,

> The essence of dharma having perished, the people . . . will be like cattle without any laws about mother, son, et cetera. Harsh winds with much dust . . . will blow. The heavens will smoke, terrifying by day and night . . . Clouds of acid and clouds of vinegar, clouds of poison, fire and lightning will rain . . . Because of this there will be cough, asthma, gout, leprosy, dropsy, fever, headache and other serious diseases of humans. The animals will feel pain . . . There will be destruction of fields, forests, gardens, creepers, trees, and grass. . . . The earth will be reduced to ashes, resembling embers and charcoal sometimes with much dust, sometimes with thick mud. Men and women will be a cubit in height, bad-colored, harsh-spoken, afflicted with diseases, violent-tempered, hunch-backed, snub-nosed, shameless, without clothes. . . . There will be cave-dwellings . . . In each bank of the rivers there will be nine caves and those animals will come into existence only enough to preserve the species.[66]

It is curious also that man will be reduced to eating fish from the depths of the rivers since everything on the ground will have been destroyed or unfit to touch.[67] There is a more pleasant aftermath, but let us duly note the closest description of the probable effects and conclusion to atomic warfare that we possess in medieval world literature.

George William Brown (1870–1932) took his B.A. and M.A. from Hiram College and his Ph.D. at Johns Hopkins University under Maurice Bloomfield in Sanskrit, Hebrew, and Arabic. He taught at Central Christian College, went to India as a missionary of the Disciples of Christ for sixteen years, where he lived at Harda and Jubbulpore in South India. From 1917–21 he was professor of Semitic languages and missions in the College of the Bible, Tran-

[65] *Ibid.*, II, 336.
[66] *Ibid.*, II, 344–45.
[67] *Ibid.*, II, 345.

sylvania University and from 1921–27 dean of the faculty and professor of Indology at the College of Missions at Indianapolis, whereupon he went to the Kennedy School of Missions of the Hartford Seminary Foundation until his death. Brown was a founding member of the Linguistic Society of America. Most of his published scientific work was focused on the Upaniṣads and the Tulsi Das Rāmāyaṇa, and various Dravidian studies. His son W. Norman Brown, who also studied with Bloomfield, became a noted Indologist at the University of Pennsylvania and president of the American Institute of Indian Studies at Poona.

Brown's doctoral dissertation at Johns Hopkins University was published as *The Human Body in the Upanishads* (Jubbulpore, The Christian Mission Press, 1921). It will doubtless be recognized in the future more than it has been in the past as the reconstruction of Indian philosophy conjointly with Indian protoscience and science gains force. The pioneer work of Joseph Needham with regard to China may well serve as a model for this task.[68]

Preparing the material for *The Human Body* Brown consulted sixty-six of the better known Upaniṣads, establishing not only the physiological but religious and philosophical treatment in these. Out of this grand survey, Brown noticed the major types of reference to the human body, which prove to be,

1) The quasi-scientific.

2) The fanciful, as in multiplying nonexistent parts.

3) The ritualistic and sacramental, containing religious and philosophical considerations.

4) The deistic and animalistic, containing some religious and philosophical considerations.

5) The cosmic correlative, containing philosophical interpretations.

Brown points out that the references to the body are not from a purely physical standpoint except for the late *Yoga Upaniṣads.* Generally the writers are not medical men, but mystics.[69] It is clear

[68] Needham, *Science and Civilisation in China,* 4 vols. Cambridge, Cambridge U. P. 1954–65.

[69] George W. Brown: *The Human Body.* Jubbulpore, Christian Mission Press, 1921, pp. 5–6.

that their interest was primarily in the soul rather than the functioning of the body as such. Insofar as this study goes, the earlier Upaniṣads are more scientifically accurate than the later, one reason for which, Brown avers, is that the animal sacrifice was more common in the earlier period, enabling the writers to gain better knowledge of the body. He says that:

> The early statements of the construction of the body, while not wholly accurate and quite incomplete, at least do not contain much nonsense.[70]

Under the tutelage of *yoga* in later times, "arteries are multiplied and turned into air passages"[71] and certain organs of the body are fancifully described. There are 120 parts of the body mentioned in the Upaniṣads including general terms like blood, bone, sinew and imaginary parts as well as those recognized today by medicine.

Of philosophical interest is that the soul is conceived to lie in the heart, probably in the ventricle, and leaves the body at death, splitting open the skull on the way out, attaining eternal bliss. If it should leave by another route it would not attain bliss. And the heart is also the organ of *manas* (the mind) as well as the keeper of the soul which wanders through the arteries during sleep. By extension, the heart of Brahma is the universe.

How the other organs and limbs are discussed and related to religion and philosophy is also discussed at some length, but this is not the place for such an account, fascinating as it is. We turn next to one of the great popularizers of comparative religion whose work was known to most educated laymen.

Lewis Browne was born in London in 1897 and died in 1949 having lived most of his adult life in the United States. He received his B.A. from the University of Cincinnati, his B.H. from Hebrew Union College and took post-graduate work at Yale University. In 1925 he organized and became president of Newark Labor College, but later taught as a visiting professor at Pennsylvania State College, the University of Hawaii, and the University

---

[70] *Ibid.,* p. 7.

[71] As late as Cartesian times it was believed in Western Europe that air passed through the veins.

of California at Los Angeles. Two of his books are concerned with Indian religion: *This Believing World* (1926) and *The World's Great Scriptures* (1946).

In *This Believing World* [72] Browne wrote an account that was destined to become one of the most widely read books in English containing accounts of Indian religions and philosophy. Treating Brahmanism, Jainism, Buddhism, and Hinduism, it covered nearly fifty pages of text which treated of the development of Indian thought in a breezy style. Of the Upaniṣadic Period he said that the amalgamated Aryans and black aboriginals "threw all the old gods and rites overboard, frankly confessing that they were without essential reality." [73] These people, said Browne, held only one thing to be real—the "Indescribable 'It.' " Man obtains peace by losing himself in the "It." This became at last, Brahman. Browne's comment on this is that:

> One wonders if this nihilistic philosophy of the Upanishads greatly influenced the life of the masses in India twenty-six hundred years ago. Probably it did not, for it must have been far beyond the comprehension of those masses.[74]

This is one of the very few reflections by any of the philosophers and religionists in this volume which deigns to consider the masses. That we have little or no record of their thoughts and feelings, gives to Indian thought a steady view of a tiny elite except for a heretical outburst here and there which is quickly hushed up. Besides such reflections on Brahmanism, Browne's accounts of Jainism, Buddhism and Hinduism are equally pithy and down-to-earth.

A contemporary of Browne, a critic, philosopher, and writer was Waldo Frank (1889–1967) who took his B.A. and M.A. at Yale University and was awarded an honorary Litt.D. by the National University of San Marcos in Lima, Peru. He received some early schooling at Lausanne, lived in Europe and Latin America for a time, and lectured on American culture in Argentina. Considered

---

[72] Lewis Browne: *This Believing World*. New York, Macmillan, 1926. By 1927 it was in its seventh printing.

[73] *Ibid.*, p. 125.

[74] *Ibid.*, pp. 128–29.

an able critic of America, his *In Our America* (1919) was translated into French and received acclaim in France. It is fitting that
mention of him follow the account of Lewis Browne, because each
in his own way was critical of Indian thought as each was skeptical about many paths the intellect had taken throughout philosophical history.

Frank, a believer that man is made by his milieu and not
simply by shared psychic qualities, claimed that although we may
learn from the Hindus, what we can really incorporate from their
experience is strictly limited. He said,

> The Hindus . . . after the Vedic epoch, developed technics for trans-
> figuring man according to the exact principles of their ideal. Their
> ideal, their sense of life, are in no way ours: hence their methods
> cannot be for us.[75]

This must have seemed somewhat heretical to some American
thinkers who hoped for a transvaluation of values from India, but
it seems likely that many familiar with Frank's thesis would not
have disagreed with it. Frank warned Americans that they may be
taken in by mystification and cultism, warned against the "sentimental *mysticalist* who swings from his sense of the absolute
person into the undifferentiated sense of being the Whole-
being" [76] which some like Pitkin would identify with Whitman-
ism. According to Frank, this kind of mystical holism reveals that
the one holding it "has merely transposed his egoism, blown it
into vast dimensions." [77] Here Frank put his finger upon a major
element in American distrust of Indian philosophy and wisdom.
For every Indianophile who learned from Indian philosophy there
were perhaps twenty indifferentists and several openly hostile to
its supposed content and influence. It certainly went contrary to
the behavioristic and positivistic spirit in American philosophy
and against a good deal of realism as well—among the realists only
Santayana and Pratt showed any interest, and as we have seen,
Pitkin was certainly hostile to Indian "mysticism and mystification."

[75] Waldo Frank: *The Re-discovery of America*. New York, Scribner 1929, p. 282.
[76] *Ibid.*, p. 296.
[77] *Ibid.*

Frank believed on the other hand, that transcendental dualism as represented by the Buddha, was a "curse at its best." [78] Frank described this do-nothing dualism as follows:

> This transcendental dualism is the greatest curse of man; it has debauched almost all his highest efforts to know himself and to know life. By means of it, soul and its values are cut off from life and life—the observed—becomes a valueless dominion.[79]

What makes Americans fall for such nefarious doctrines, what makes them even consider them at all? According to Frank,

> As the Mediterranean dogmas grow worn with use, the peace and power hungering soul looks farther afield. America, moving west, comes to the east. So India sends patches of her glorious truth to be woven into modern comforters. The weak soul which cannot master the chaos of our world will be tempted to deny it altogether.[80]

For those Americans who believed that denial of certain Western ["Mediterranean"] values began only with the hippies and students in the 1960's, here is evidence that a similar movement was occurring in the 1920's.

According to Frank "Hinduism is bereft of its organic meanings" when it is incorporated mechanically by Americans— "Breathe *thus*, think *so*—and you will outstrip mankind in the race to Glory or Nirvana." [81] Such practice is foolhardy and is practiced by "impotent Americans." As the behaviorists and positivists would agree, and others besides, "Many of our eastern cults are for dull people, but not all." [82] Frank at least leaves a possible opening here for those who claim to find something different in eastern or Indian philosophy.

Another philosopher who dipped into Indian thought was Joseph Alexander Leighton (1870–1954), for many years professor of philosophy at Ohio State University.

Leighton took his A.B. at the University of Toronto, and his

[78] *Ibid.*, p. 300
[79] *Ibid.*
[80] *Ibid.*, p. 102.
[81] *Ibid.*, p. 103.
[82] *Ibid.*

Ph.D. at Cornell University. In addition he took an S.T.B. at the Episcopal Theological Seminary at Cambridge, Massachusetts and studied in Germany at Tübingen, Berlin and Erlangen universities. Teaching first at Hobart College, he went West to the Ohio State University where he taught from 1910 to 1941. He was a visiting lecturer at the University of Southern California and at the University of California at Berkeley.

He pointed out that there is an

> ultimate similarity between the Idealism of Bradley and Bosanquet and the Indian philosophy of Samkara. I do not say that they are identical but I do say that, in the final position of the finite self, Absolute Idealism is very close to that of Samkara.[83]

Speaking of Buddha's release from individuality, Leighton says:

> What remains, beyond sheer nothingness, I do not understand. I take my stand with western empirical and humanistic affirmation of the central significance of individuality. Give that up and the world becomes a disappearing wraith! [84]

But there Leighton ceases, at least in his writing, to give us a clue to his reading in and thoughts about Indian philosophy.

George Christian Otto Haas (1883–   ) is a philologist and psychologist who took his A.B. at Columbia and his A.M. and Ph.D. at the City College of New York. His major interest has been in psychical research, occultism, and hyperphysical phenomea. He was at one time director of the Institute for Vedic and Allied Research as well as of the Institute of Hyperphysical Research. Haas was also at one time coeditor of the *Journal of the American Oriental Society*. Not the least of his services was his revision of R. E. Hume's *The Thirteen Principal Upanishads* and the Appendix to that work showing the recurrent and parallel passages of the principal Upaniṣhads and the Bhagavadgītā with reference to other Sanskrit texts.

Frances Ruth Grant (1898–   ), the author of *Oriental Phi-*

---

[83] Joseph A. Leighton: The principle of individuality and value. In Clifford Barrett (Ed.) : *Contemporary Idealism in America*. New York, Macmillan 1932, p. 144.
[84] *Ibid.*

losophy,[85] became interested in Indian thought through Indian art as has been the case with a number of Indologists and amateurs alike. Inspired by the Russian Indianophile, Nicholas Roerich, Grant did extensive reading in the Indian classics. Her outlook was not unlike that of the New England Transcendentalists. At one time she was vice president of the Roerich Museum in New York. It is noteworthy that Grant devotes ten pages of her eighty-two page account of Indian wisdom to Jainism, an Indian philosophy that has been grossly neglected by American thinkers, largely, one might guess, because of its extreme asceticism. Americans have their own brand of asceticism, called puritanism, but they have shown little desire to import any other. Grant today has shifted her interests from Asia to Latin America and is today editor of the Journal *Hemispherica.*

Walter B. Pitkin (1878–1953), a product of Columbia University and a philosophy professor for some years before becoming a popular writer of such best sellers as *Life Begins at Forty,* represents to some extent the climatic interpretation of history as it relates to India. He says,

> In India, of course, humid heat combines with overpopulation to the advantage of the submissive mortal. It is so much easier to live long and keep your health in that dreadful peninsula, if you sit stone-still beneath the banyan tree and watch time pass. Thousands of generations have thus multiplied the submissive and, at the same time, enabled the very few surviving aggressive egotists and other power-seekers to intrench themselves.[86]

Pitkin also claims that "There is refuge in the Buddhist monastery [for the intelligent] or the robber's cave, and nowhere else." [87]

During this period American scholars continued to lay a firm groundwork in Indian language study, religion, mythology, and to some extent in philosophy. There was, however, no outstanding academic philosopher like Santayana or Royce who showed sustained interest in Indian thought. Except for the Sanskritists,

---

[85] Frances R. Grant: *Oriental Philosophy.* New York. Dial, 1936.

[86] Walter B. Pitkin: *A Short Introduction to Human Stupidity.* New York, Simon and Schuster, 1932, p. 307.

[87] *Ibid.*

the level of understanding remained relatively amateurish. This situation was to change rather dramatically in the 1940's, 1950's, and 1960's as Indian philosophy became a topic for widespread discussion, writing, and teaching and as Americans began to travel more frequently to Asia—especially to Japan, Southeast Asia, and India after the Second World War.

Chapter IX

INDIAN PHILOSOPHY FROM THE FIRST EAST-WEST PHILOSOPHERS' CONFERENCE TO THE KOREAN WAR

I

FEW OTHER EVENTS in the history of American philosophy have been so bracing for the study of Indian thought as the First East-West Philosophers' Conference held in Honolulu in 1939. Subvented by the Watamull, McInerny, and Rockefeller Foundations and the University of Hawaii under the sympathetic guidance of President Gregg Sinclair, this six-week event focused attention on Asian philosophy and brought together distinguished philosophers from China, Japan, and the United States. It was directed by Charles A. Moore with whom we shall deal at length on succeeding pages.

Prominent Indian philosophers were absent because of the Second World War so that Hinduism and Buddhism were presented by Japanese and American philosophers: Junjirō Takakusu, Daisetz Teitarō Suzuki, Shunzō Sakamaki, William Ernest Hocking, George P. Conger, Filmer S. C. Northrop, and Charles A. Moore. Chan Wing-tsit represented both Chinese and Indian outlooks. For the first time Indian thought was made a public topic of professional concern among American academic philosophers.

The Second East-West Philosophers' Conference in Hawaii in 1949 turned the flickering interest in Indian thought to a warming fire through the presence of D. M. Datta, Swami Nikhilananda, G. P. Malalasekera of Ceylon, P. T. Raju, T. M. P. Mahadevan and C. P. Ramaswami Aiyar. By this time several of the

177

American philosophers had become knowledgeable in Indian philosophy. These included Conger, Northrop, C. A. Moore, E. A. Burtt, W. H. Sheldon, and Charles Morris. With the theme of the conference "An Attempt at World Philosophical Synthesis" Americans confronted Indians with searching questions that led to heat as well as light. The Indian philosophers brought up on a diet of dialectics proved equal to the task of defending their positions within the context of their cultural and educative tradition. American philosophers were faced, some for the first time, with debaters who did not easily succumb to the ground rules tidily taken for granted by those trained in European-American traditions. As a result of the confrontation, some of the Americans repaired to a deeper study of Indian thought and traditions, so that by the Third East-West Philosophers' Conference in 1959 they had made considerable strides from becoming initiates to scholars bordering on expert knowledge. A number of the younger Americans present went to India to study after 1949 and 1959, choosing some facet of Indian philosophy in which to specialize. These included Robert W. Browning, William F. Goodwin, Troy Organ, Bernard Phillips, Dale Riepe, and Thomas Storer. Conger, Burtt, Northrop, and Morris continued their researches into the Indian *Alterzeitgeist* and *Zeitgeist*. Several of the established American philosophers present found it too late or the chase too uncongenial to go on.

II

Before we examine the views of the brotherhood of the East-West Conferences let us turn to a philosopher who at the age of sixty-five began teaching Indian philosophy at the University of Washington in 1940: a life-long friend of the Orientalist H. H. Gowan (1864–1960) and the husband of an Oriental art collector and historian, Hallie Savery.

William Briggs Savery (1875–1945) took his B.A. from Brown University and his Ph.D. at Harvard University. He studied at Berlin on the Sheldon Traveling Fellowship and then took a teaching position at Fairmont College in Topeka, Kansas. From 1902 to 1945 he was chairman of the philosophy department at the University of Washington. Savery studied with three professors who were interested in Indian philosophy: James H. Woods, George Santayana, and Josiah Royce, and was a classmate of two others, William Ernest Hocking and J. B. Pratt. Even William James, under whom he wrote his dissertation, was not totally ignorant of this philosophy, as we have already seen.

Savery taught two courses which dealt with Indian philosophy. They were entitled "The Hindu Philosophies of India" and "Buddhism in India and China." Savery's lectures on the Vedānta systems included Ādvaita, Viśiṣṭādvaita, Dvaita, and Suddhādvaita.[1] There were lectures also on Sāṁkhya, Sāṁkhya-Yoga, and the six Buddhistic Schools: Vaibhāṣika, Sautrāntika, Mādhyamika, Yogācāra, Tien-Tai, and Avatamṣaka. Nāgārjuna was treated at considerable length, indicating, as one might predict, that his logical and epistemological originality would appeal to such a happy dialectician as Savery.

Savery's lecture on the theories of evidence of eight schools of Indian philosophy is one of his more interesting approaches. In it he codifies the Indian systems to conform to his own epistemological approach. Although this appears under the category of logic, it will be seen in its correct perspective if we realize that also under logic are indeterminate and determinate perception, the syllogism, fallacies, categories, universals, and causality. As with Hegel, logic for the Indians is a combination of logic and epistemology in American parlance. In scanning the epistemological views of the different schools Savery shows the following to obtain:

1. *Nyāya:* perception, inference, comparison, revelation, verbal testimony.
2. *Vaiśeṣika:* perception, inference.
3. *Sāṁkhya:*
       perception, inference, revealed word.
   Yoga:
4. *Hīnayāna Buddhism:* perception, inference.
5. *Vedānta:* perception, inference, revealed word.
6. *Prabhākara Buddhism:* perception, inference, comparison, revelation, presumption.

[1] I wish to express my gratitule to the Manuscript Division of the University of Washington Libraries for permission to use the materials of the Savery Collection.

William Savery (courtesy of Garland Ethel).

7. *Kumārila:* perception, inference, comparison, revelation, presumption, and nonperception.
8. *Cārvāka:* perception [Most Indians prefer Lokāyata].

This table separated out the systems that are basically empirical and those which are not; those which are authoritarian, and those that have avenues of knowledge probably unknown in the West, such as presumption and nonperception.

Savery's lectures on Hīnayāna Buddhism were more complete than those on Hinduism. No longer in outline form, he had written complete sentences and paragraphs on the life of the Buddha, the doctrine of *dharma,* the *Saṁgha* (the Buddhist Order), and a conclusion that compared Buddhism with Christianity. This last is worthy of more than passing mention. First of all Buddhism and Christianity differ, said Savery, in that Christianity is monotheism while Buddhism is atheism. In Christianity the Saint [presumably Jesus Christ] is higher than the gods and he rises up after death whereas for Buddhism, there is annihilation or agnosticism in which the Buddha becomes a memory. Whereas Buddhism says "Blessed are the peacemakers," it does not add "For they shall see God." [2]

Turning to ethics, in Christianity the most important virtue is love, while for Buddhism it is renunciation, of not only this world but the next one as well. Buddhistic love, as opposed to the Christian, is goodwill as opposed to passionate, warm affection. Buddhist love is also a less important part of the whole teaching yet wider in scope. This may be seen in the following ways: (1) first, renunciation is more important than love in Buddhism and renunciation is less important than love in Christianity, and (2) much of Buddhistic love is a means to renunciation. "Nevertheless, there is in Buddhism disinterested love also." [3] (3) Buddhistic love is broader than Christian in that it includes all sentient beings.

In his final summation of the differences between the two universal religions, Savery said:

Both religions preach renunciation in this life and Christianity is more or less pessimistic in regard to this life. Buddhism cannot unqualifiedly

[2] Savery, "Unpublished Lectures on Hīnayāna Buddhism," p. 17.
[3] *Ibid.*

> be regarded as pessimistic, for Nirvana is joy and happiness and *it can be attained here.* Buddhism is the *logical religion of pessimism.* [Savery's italics] We are like men on a shipwrecked craft, all that stay on board will perish—it is one's first duty to save himself by abandoning the wreck (retiring from the world) and then to persuade as many others as possible to leave it too. With Buddhism as with Christianity, "to die is to live." [4]

Buddhism is mature and modern in its refusal to discuss "metaphysical questions of no practical import and also in its agnosticism." [5] It is "modern too in its rejection of revelation and in its self-reliance (rejection of help from on high) ." [6]

In summarizing the differences between Hīnayāna and Mahāyāna, Savery pointed out that the earlier school is atheistic while the later is pantheistic [here he crossed out "polytheism" and "theism"]. In the former is virtual annihilation while in the latter, oneness with *nirvāṇa* or Buddha. With regard to renunciation, in the Hīnayāna it led to renunciation and saintship here, while for the Mahāyāna it led to love and Buddhaship hereafter. Finally, it may be noticed that Mahāyāna is much more like Christianity than Hīnayāna.[7] Since Savery's day some twenty-five years ago, there also seem to be scientific and political factors tying Mahāyāna closer to Christianity and spiritualism and Hīnayāna nearer rationalism as may be seen in their differing reaction to Marxist socialism—Hīnayāna showing itself to be more sympathetic.

Savery was more taken with the viewpoint of Nāgārjuna than with that of any other follower of Buddhism except the Buddha himself. Savery was particularly intrigued by Nāgārjuna's argument against the operation of causation in the phenomenal world (*saṁsāra*). He stated the quadrilemma in this way:

(1) Nothing is caused by itself.
(2) *Or* by anything different from itself.
(3) *Or* by itself together with what is different from itself.
(4) Nor is anything uncaused "Like the color and the scent of a Lotus growing in the sky." [8]

[4] *Ibid.*, p. 18.
[5] *Ibid.*
[6] *Ibid.*
[7] *Ibid.*, p. 21.
[8] *Ibid.*, p. 1.

Nāgārjuna stated that there is no energy of production (hence no necessity). The trilemma was stated in this fashion by Savery:

(1) The energy cannot be after the effect.
(2) It cannot be previous to the effect.
(3) *Or*—simultaneous with the effect.[9]

Following this is his statement of Nāgārjuna's double dilemma:

(1) When the cause is, the effect is not, hence it is not a cause.
(2) When the effect is, the cause is gone, hence it is not the cause.
(1′) When the effect is not, it can have no cause.
(2′) When the effect is, it has no cause.[10]

Following this, Savery found that the subsequent reasoning of Nāgārjuna led that dialectician to maintain that (1) Substance is impossible because it contains nothing "real over and above the corresponding sense-data." [11] (2) Predication is impossible. (3) Introspection is impossible, for "consciousness is one thing and the object another" in which

> first case we shall have a double consciousness. But if they are identical, how is then consciousness to be cognized through consciousness? Consciousness cannot apprehend its own self. The trenchant of a sword cannot cut its own trenchant. The tip of a finger cannot touch that very tip. Similarly this consciousness cannot be conscious of its own self.[12]

(4) There is no evidence for an object of consciousness because sensations need not have an object counterpart. (5) Things and relations are impossible "If they are relative (empty or void), they have no real existence." Yet, despite all this "illusions can produce either moral defilement or purification;" [13] it is this that is so amazing in the consequences of the reasoning of Nāgārjuna.

With the possible exceptions of Clarence Hamilton, Karl Potter, and Richard Robinson, few American philosophers seem to have obtained such satisfaction out of the subtleties of Hindu and Buddhist logic and epistemology as Savery. This of course squares harmoniously with his avowed ethics, namely hedonism. He stud-

[9] Savery, "Unpublished Lecture on Nāgārjuna," p. 1.
[10] *Ibid.*
[11] *Ibid.* Savery like E. A. Burtt follows G. E. Moore on "sense-data."
[12] *Ibid.*, p. 2.
[13] *Ibid.*

ied Indian philosophy for the intellectual enjoyment it afforded him and not for occult, cryptic, pious, or other reasons that might be thought of.

Curt John Ducasse (1881–1969), who was born in France, came to New York City as a young man where he ran across *The Science of Peace* by Bhagavan Das.[14] As Ducasse says about it in his "Philosophical Liberalism" written before 1930, it "dealt with the relation of the Individual to the Absolute."[15] Perhaps the only chapter read closely by Ducasse was Chapter VI, which "acquainted me with the existence and some of the thoughts of Berkeley, Hume, Kant, Schelling, Hegel and Fichte; and made me realize the interest which philosophical questions, as conceived by them, had for me."[16]

Ducasse left New York in 1906 and was admitted to the philosophy department at the University of Washington, taking his A.B. in 1908 and his A.M. the following year.[17] After taking the Ph.D. in philosophy at Harvard, he returned to the University of Washington to become the colleague of his teacher, William Savery. He later took a position at Brown University where he stayed until he retired in 1958. He was a visiting lecturer at the University of California at Berkeley and Los Angeles, at Hamilton College, New York University, Radcliffe College, and Boston University. He has been a president of the American Philosophical Association, the American Society for Aesthetics, the Association for Symbolic Logic, and the Philosophy of Science Association.

Like his teacher, Savery, Ducasse found Buddhism congenial, but his interest in that subject was evinced earlier than that of his teacher. In *A Philosophical Scrutiny of Religion*,[18] he devotes a

[14] Bhagavan Das: *The Science of Peace*. London, Theosophical Publishing Society, 1904.

[15] G. P. Adams and W. P. Montague (Ed.): *Contemporary American Philosophy*. New York, Russell, 1962, vol. II, p. 302.

[16] *Letter* to the author, Providence (March 5, 1968).

[17] Ducasse says that "By then, the views of the theosophists had come to seem to me too doctrinaire, and I discontinued membership in the Theosophical Society. *Letter, ibid.*

[18] Curt John Ducasse: *A Philosophical Scrutiny of Religion*. New York, Ronald, 1953. This work, according to Ducasse in a *Letter* to the author, Providence, R. I. (March 15, 1968) says that it "represents the course in the Philosophy of Religion I gave for a number of years at Brown University."

chapter to describing the beliefs and early history of Buddhism. Of this early Buddhism [Theravāda] he says:

> in respect to nobility of teachings, capacity to bring peace of soul to its devotees, and to foster good will and peace among men, it easily ranks with any of these [major] religions and perhaps surpasses some of them.[19]

It is his belief that the original message of the Buddha is of the greatest significance compared to the works of his followers.[20]

Unlike Emerson and Santayana, Ducasse places considerable emphasis upon metempsychosis. His own account of his interest in reincarnation is particularly important, especially in the light of his later concern with psychical research. He says in a letter:

> . . . the idea of reincarnation, which immediately commended itself to me, was first brought to my attention by a lady who was an acquaintance of some member of my family in France. . . . On a short trip to France I took in I think 1903 she showed me a little book that had been published shortly before in that year. The book's title was *La Sagesse Antique a Traverse les Ages,* and its author was a Dr. Th. Pascal. . . . It acquainted me with the views of the Theosophists, which appealed to me, and when I returned to New York I joined the Theosophical Society and was for some time in charge of the library for the New York branch.[21]

As librarian Ducasse read A. P. Sinnett's *Esoteric Buddhism* which, as setting forth the theosophical doctrines as being esoteric Buddhism, made a great impression upon the young philosopher.

He remarks the apparent paradox of the Buddhist maintaining simultaneously the doctrine that one (the "me") has no permanent soul or self and yet holding that something "in" man transmigrates. Naturally it cannot be the body that is resurrected in Buddhism. What occurs, according to Ducasse, is that,

> In Buddhism, the culmination of the long chain of lives, each generating the next, is . . . not described as realization of the identity of *Atma* and *Brahma,* but as extinction of the three "fires"—that is, of craving,

---

[19] Ducasse, *A Philosophical Scrutiny,* p. 35.

[20] *Ibid.,* p. 45.

[21] C. J. Ducasse, *Letter* to the author, Providence, Rhode Island (March 5, 1968).

ill-will, and ignorance—which, as long as they persist, bring about rebirth.[22]

Although Ducasse does not explicitly say that he believes in reincarnation, he does make the strongest possible case for it within the parameter of what he regards as the scientific approach. Although several British philosophers such as John McTaggart, James Ward, and C. D. Broad have taken reincarnation seriously, Ducasse is the only American philosopher I know of to have taken such a strong interest in the problem, although I do recall a conversation with A. E. Burtt in 1949 that seemed to indicate in him more than a passing interest in transmigration and life after death.

III

We now turn to the American philosophers stimulated by the East-West Conferences in Hawaii. First is George P. Conger (1884-1961) who took his A.B. at Cornell University, his B.D. at Union Theological Seminary, and his Ph.D. at Columbia University. After traveling in Germany and France and attending the Universities of Marburg, Berlin, Jena, Heidelberg and the Sorbonne, he returned to the United States. Before settling down to an academic life, however, he served with the Y.M.C.A. in Siberia during the Russian Revolution. Most of his teaching career took place at the University of Minnesota except for interludes of teaching at the University of Hawaii and the University of Calcutta. He visited India three times. In 1954–55 he received the signal honor of giving the S. N. Ghosh Lectures at the University of Calcutta.[23] Like D. M. Datta, his friend Conger, the gentle

[22] Ducasse: *A Critical Examination in a Life After Death.* Springfield, Thomas, 1961, p. 211.

[23] To the best of my knowledge, the first American philosopher-theologian to deliver the S. N. Ghosh lectures was Douglas Clyde Macintosh (1877–1948) of Yale University in 1928. This honor was made possible by S. Dasupta and S. Radhakrishnan who had met Macintosh at the Sixth International Congress of Philosophy held at Harvard University in September 1926. Reference is made in the Ghosh lectures of Macintosh to the following Indian works: Dasgupta's *Hindu Mysticism* (1927), Radhakrishnan's *The Hindu View of Life* (1927), *The Gospel of Ramakrishna, Bhagavad Gītā,* H. Maitra's *Hinduism* (1916), Max Müller's *Ramakrishna, His Life and Sayings* (1898), A. J. Appasamy's *Christianity as Bhaktimarga* (1927). →

bulldog of American philosophy, had great patience in trying to understand an opposing position, but never concluded a dialectical fight until he thought his own position had been fairly understood.

Conger's cosmic naturalism had to make some room for the insights of Indian philosophy. As one of the few American philosophers who paid some heed to the teachings of India, yet who was not idealistic, Conger saw in Indian thought both what was unique and what was common to certain forms of Western thought. Agreeing with J. B. Pratt, who also had the sin of Chicago uppermost in his thoughts, he approached the problem with his usual gruff fairness:

> If we of America would understand India, we need to remind ourselves pointedly of the obvious fact that every social system has its evils as well as its excellences. It scarcely befits an American to expose or deplore the evils of India, unless he thinks also of gangland in Chicago, the divorce merry-go-round at Reno, the false glamour of Hollywood, the long story of injustice to the Negro, and the growing bitterness of American economic conflict.[24]

Americans must also beware lest they approach India from the point of view of some American missionaries, no matter how valuable missionary insights might prove to be.[25]

From a tentative interest in Indian thought fed by his trip to India in 1934, Conger's awareness grew in the 1940's. The conclusion to his "Method and Content in Philosophy" (1946) indicates not only that he has been reading J. B. Pratt's view on India, but

---

Ramanuja's *Commentary on the Vedanta Sutras,* and K. Shastri's *An Introduction to Advaita Philosophy* (1924). His conclusion to the lectures so far as Indians are concerned is that they should "retain all of [their] traditional Indian religion that is in accord with universal ideals of rationality, of beauty, of righteousness, and of truly spiritual love, but do not fail to adopt and incorporate into [their] faith all the additional values that are accessible in this new age." Macintosh: *The Pilgrimage of Faith in the World of Modern Thought.* Stephanos Mirnalendu Lectures. Calcutta, Univ. of Calcutta, 1931, p. 284. This has the flavor of a letter of recommendation which states: "He does well whatever he is qualified to do."

[24] George Conger: Toward understanding India. *The Aryan Path,* VI, 11, 1935, p. 661. Of all the material I have read for this stuly, this alone makes reference to injustice to Negroes, perhaps a commentary on the social concerns of American philosophical Indianophiles.

[25] *Ibid.,* p. 662.

also that he is trying to fit Indian philosophy into his epitomization-structure. He said that,

> Perhaps we may come at last to the fulfillment of the verse of the Bhagavad Gita, where the Blessed One says: "Whatsoever deity any man wishes to worship with faith, to him I render that faith steady." [26]

Three years later, Conger was invited to the Second East-West Philosophers' Conference at the University of Hawaii and there read his paper "Integration." Here his comprehension of Indian thought widened although his focus on contemporary scientific development did not diminish. The following year Conger returned to India. At the annual meeting of the Indian Philosophical Congress in 1950, he read his paper "Some Suggestions Toward a Theory of the Soul." Here he made a cautious suggestion that the Indian view of *mokṣa* may be integrated with the more naturalistic view of goals in the West.

In 1953 he published his naturalistic interpretation of Sāṁkhya-Yoga which goes beyond the interpretation suggested by Santayana some years before. Again he concluded with a plea for integration of Indian and Western views.

Conger wrote "Ṛta: Cosmic Structure and Social Order" in 1954, in which he stated that "Right in the social order is the fulfillment of Ṛta in the cosmic structure." [27] Conger also showed the relationship of levels of integration to integration on the widest cosmic level. Although usually more concerned with the physical and biological aspects of integration and epitomization, Conger gave an analysis of the micro-macro-cosmic development in India from the Vedas to the Medieval mystics in his "Cosmic Persons and Human Universes in Indian Philosophy" [28] as early as 1933.

In the culmination of his work in Indian philosophy, Conger wrote an extremely meaty chapter in *Synoptic Naturalism* [29] entitled "The Religious History of Mankind Epitomized in the

---

[26] Conger: Method and content in philosophy. *Philos Rev,* July 1946, p. 424.

[27] Conger: Rta: Cosmic structure and social order. At Indian Philosophical Congress. Peradiniya, UNESCO, 1954, p. 41.

[28] Conger in *Journal and Proceedings of the Asiatic Society of Bengal,* New Series, XXIX, 1, 1933.

[29] Conger: *Synoptic Naturalism.* Minneapolis, U. of Minn. Lib., 1960.

Ethical Experience of an Individual Person." Conger not only compressed in this a vast amount of Indian philosophy, including Buddhism, but also showed a unique parallelism between religion in general and the religious experiences of the individual person. He here maintained that the ultimate goal of Hinduism and Buddhism is release (*mokṣa*). Eastern religions, he declared, are less aggressive and more composed than Western ones. This generalization was confirmed by Charles Morris in a number of studies relating to characterology. What is of interest here is Conger's life's work culminating in a synthetic overview including a sympathetic understanding of Indian thought as it relates to the total outlook of mankind. He has woven Indian thought into his synoptic system. It might also be mentioned that William Savery had emphasized the need for a "Synoptic Theory of Truth" which would take into account the variegated methods and techniques of mankind in arriving at a knowledge of reality. Conger's final conclusion to this weighty book is that "To exist is to epitomize and to coordinate all Reality." [30] Indeed, it is not Whitehead who has written the last grand-manner metaphysics in the Anglo-American tradition, but Conger himself, Conger who evinced serious awareness that the Indian experience is important to the completion of a description of Reality.

Conger's naturalism was often if not always uppermost in his thoughts when he was dealing with Indian philosophy. He said, for example:

> But if in the West, in spite of current reaffirmations, supernaturalism collapses and idealism evaporates, and if both are succeeded by naturalism, the contribution of India must be quite different. It may be merely prolonged insistence, in the face of overwhelming odds; sometimes it seems as if India's mission were to teach us that, if we are willing to pay the price, we may still maintain our dream-world of the spirit we want it to be.[31]

Not content with this qualified peering into the future of Indian spiritual influence, Conger said,

[30] Conger, *Synoptic Naturalism,* p. 727.
[31] Conger, Outline of Indian philosophy. In C. A. Moore (Ed.) : *Philosophy East and West.* Princeton, Princeton, 1946, p. 22.

> If we cannot evade naturalism, another procedure would be to face it, to look straight into the data of the sciences for empirical indications of kinship between man and nature.[32]

Despite this, Conger is aware that Americans can learn from India, for example in its being engulfed in imperial possessions. Of this he says: "To a Western world too often entangled and stifled by its possessions and its conquests, India shows the deep resources of contentment with little" [33] Conger's usual humane realism seems to have deserted him at this point. Many Indians, judging from their social upheavals, were and are far from content either in the present or in the past. Even the caste system has something to offer, Conger thought, but he does not show the enthusiasm of a Coomaraswamy for it:

> With all the abuses and limitations of the caste system, India shows to a Western world which is engulfed in the flux of its own progress the strength of a structured society and the importance of recognizing the fact that society has a structure.[34]

It seems to me that what Conger is overlooking is that the Western world has just the structure that it requires to carry out its international and domestic schemes. Whereas India is structured partially to feudal agriculturalism and partially to a post-colonial way of life, the structure in "the West" is largely modeled to the interests of international monopolistic capitalism. Perhaps what concerned him was the apparent slipping away of values familiar to him from a "happier" American day. But to fail to see a new structure is not the same as seeing no structure.

Another American stimulated by the East-West Conferences is Edwin Arthur Burtt (1892–　) who took his B.A. at Yale University, his B.D. and S.T.M. from Union Theological Seminary, and Ph.D. from Columbia University. After teaching at

---

[32] *Ibid*. The only idealist to answer Conger, and then indirectly, was Bernard Phillips, a philosopher of religion at Temple University. See his Radhakrishnan's critique of naturalism. In Schilpp (Ed.): *The Philosophy of Sarvepalli Radhakrishnan*, New York, Tudor, 1952.

[33] *Ibid.*, p. 22.

[34] *Ibid.*, pp. 22–23.

Columbia and the University of Chicago he became professor of philosophy at Cornell University where he remained until his retirement. He became president of the American Philosophical Association in 1965. Perhaps best known in the philosophical world for his work on the metaphysical foundations of physics, in *The Compassionate Buddha* (1955) and *Man Seeks the Divine* (1957), he demonstrates his later concern with Indian philosophy. Resembling so many philosophers interested in Indian thought, Burtt, like Emerson, Hocking and Conger, studied for the ministry. Like Conger who also studied theology, and like Sheldon who claims he wished that he had studied theology, Burtt found Indian religion and ethics attractive in a number of ways. Burtt has made several trips to India, his most recent as Ghosh Lecturer at Calcutta in 1968.

First of all Burtt discovered that there is no such concept as "event" in Indian or Chinese philosophy because, as he says, "the separate individual is ultimately illusory rather than real." [35] This is an example, Burtt said, of the kind of appreciative understanding which must be achieved at the philosophical level if we are to understand Indian and Chinese philosophy.

Second, he pointed out that "insofar as American philosophers wish to understand [Indian] methodology, it is difficult for some Westerners [particularly those untrained in theology perhaps] to come to an appreciation of Indian "super-rational intuition, which they distrust." [36] Knowledge in the East, as Burtt saw it, "is the *intellectual aspect of the process* of self-realization, as pursued by one's whole personality. In India this process is a quest for identity with the Absolute Whole." [37] A method conceivable to East and West is cooperative inquiry with impartiality and inclusiveness. Key terms must be used in such a way as to insure "a neutral generic definition of that idea." [38] According to Burtt, "Aristotle managed this when dealing with *causality*, Leibniz with *truth*. It is a serious error to try to reduce all *experience*, for

---

[35] E. A. Burtt: Problems in Harmonizing East and West. In C. A. Moore (Ed.): *Essays in East-West Philosophy*. Honolulu, U. of Hawaii, 1951, p. 107.

[36] *Ibid.*, p. 109.

[37] *Ibid.*, p. 111.

[38] *Ibid.*, p. 116.

example to sense-data." [39] It might also be helpful to develop a universal nonpartisan language by which all people could communicate. Burtt is aware, as other American philosophers dealing with their Indian friends, that the problem of communication via books is simpler although more untrustworthy than through word-of-mouth and the language of gesture and grimace. And yet of all peoples from widely different cultural and geographical settings East and West, only the intellectual Indians and Americans and other English-speaking Westerners have a common language with a relatively long history of use.[40] Ultimately a philosopher may appear who would be "master of all and limited to none." [41] Thus Burtt approached the problem of understanding Indian philosophy in the larger context of world-philosophy, as a sub-region in a greater galactic system.

Ten years passed from the time that Burtt first became concerned about the problem of method, communication, and terminology. Again he faced the Indians across the conference table in Honolulu (1959). He found that the central concept with which the East [India] is concerned is liberation,[42] which four years later Karl Potter was to find the chief axiom of classical Indian thought.[43] Burtt, on the other hand, found the central concept of the West to be rational understanding.[44] The crowning achievement of the classical West was logic; of the modern West it was

---

[39] *Ibid.*, p. 118. Considering the present status of the sense-data hypothesis this is an understatement.

[40] It is true that among Islamic philosophers West of Pakistan the situation may be paralleled with French. This is one of the strongest arguments I know refuting the claim that by clarification of language we can "understand and appreciate" the other point of view. If there is metaphysical, ideological, and aesthetic disagreement to begin with, emphasis upon language seems to increase rather than decrease misunderstanding. The major reason for this is that it highlights those gray areas which give a simulated confluence of seemingly agreeable elements. As soon as they are understood, this hopeful region is eliminated, as we have seen in the shocking disagreements among linguistic philosophers.

[41] Burtt, Problems in Harmonizing . . . , p. 122.

[42] Burtt, A Basic Problem in the Quest for Understanding. In *Philosophy and Culture East and West*. Honolulu, U. of Hawaii, 1961, p. 676.

[43] Karl Potter: *The Presuppositions of Indian Philosophy*. New York, Prentice-Hall, 1963.

[44] Burtt, A Basic Problem . . . , p. 677.

inductive method.[45] Burtt follows this by saying that "so far as I can tell, Eastern thinkers [philosophers] have never quite caught the significance of a general inductive method conceived in this way. . . ."[46]

Burtt's description of the "Religions of the East"[47] includes his usual succinct accounts of Hinduism and Buddhism. For him the Hebrews and Indians had a special "genius" for religion.[48] "To the Indian theologians a theoretical insight is indeed necessary, but the realization as a whole is by no means merely intellectual. It is a remolding of the whole personality. . . ."[49] Included in his account is an attempt to bring out the main features of Hinduism which he finds to be: (1) that Ultimate Reality is a unity transcending all differences, (2) that tolerance and teachableness have been primary,[50] and (3) that the *avatar* has been incarnated as god many times, so that each age may have its own symbol of living Ultimate Reality.[51] Burtt's own religious philosophy underwent a change from the time he began to show marked interest in Buddhism. Whereas an avowed humanist in *Types of Religious*

[45] *Ibid.*, p. 608.

[46] *Ibid.*, p. 680. Many Westerners have held illegitimately that Asians have somehow been bereft of the inductive method simply because no Aristotle or Mill formally laid down rules concerning it. Yet the civilizations of Asia from Turkey to Japan have used it constantly before many Westerners were literate. The history of both deductive and inductive method is part of world history and it is simply nationalistic and continental hubris to suggest otherwise. This has been adequately shown by P. K. Hitti, Joseph Needham, Abdul Rahman, George Sarton, H. E. Sigerist, Charles Singer, and even Lynn Thorndyke in their historical accounts. Results of the painstaking use of inductive method are everywhere apparent to the viewer of Asian antiquities. Think only of Moghul hydraulics, Arab shipbuilding, Indian architecture not to speak of the wonders of Asian agriculture, animal husbandry, and bridge technology. The charming and useful Khwaju Bridge of Isfahan, for example, served not only as a crossing for men and animals, but also for evening strolls, coffee-drinking, symposia, and love-making. The humane and aesthetic dimension were frequently part of Asian inductive consideration.

[47] Burtt: *Man Seeks the Divine*. New York, Harper, 1957.

[48] Facilitated by the caste system.

[49] *Ibid.*, p. 205.

[50] Contrast this with Troy Organ's belief that there must have been a grand period of book-burning in this tradition in his *The Self in Indian Philosophy*. The Hague, Mouton, 1964, p. 40.

[51] Burtt, *Man Seeks the Divine*, pp. 275–80.

Philosophy (1939) his view shifted in *Man Seeks the Divine* to a kind of pantheism. Whether this is attributable to the influence of Indian thought may not be known even by this philosopher himself.

In the "Introduction" to *The Teachings of the Compassionate Buddha* (1959),[52] Burtt gave a clear and sympathetic account of Buddhism written primarily for the layman. His reason for offering the book he said is that since hostility among the great civilized religions has been reduced, we have now

> a magnificent opportunity . . . to participate in that realization and to add to [our] own limited experience and understanding something of the insight achieved by spiritual explorers in other areas of the world.[53]

This mood of synthesis appears often among American philosophers studying India and Buddhism—particularly those who felt this urge expressed in the Second East-West Philosophers' Conference at Honolulu in 1949. Buddhism is usually pleasing to the philosopher, says Burtt, because

> Buddhism is the only one of the great religions of the world that is consciously and frankly based on a systematic rational analysis of the problem of life, and of the way to its solution. Buddha was a pioneering lover of men, and a philosophic genius, rolled into a single vigorous and radiant personality.[54]

Western philosophers can learn some important lessons from Indian philosophy, according to Burtt. They can learn, first, that the main ethical task is not "to find some theoretical loophole in [views of moral progress] which might give an opening to hostile criticism" but rather to give "more understanding." [55] This practical orientation may be called "transcendental" ethics—"the crowning part of Hindu moral philosophy," Burtt avers. He further says:

[52] New York, New Am. Lib.

[53] *Ibid.*, p. 15.

[54] Burtt, *The Teachings of the Compassionate Buddha*. New York, New Am. Lib. 1959, p. 22–23.

[55] Burtt: What can Western philosophy learn from India? *Philosophy East and West*, V, 3, 1955, p. 200. Burtt gives evidence of having been considerably tempered by skirmishes with devotees of linguistic philosophy.

Its role is not just an answer to questions of intellectual curiosity in the field of ethics, it is to provide such wise comprehension of oneself and one's destiny as will give dependable guidance in the responsible task of realizing as rapidly and fully as possible that high destiny.[56]

Second, Western philosophers might learn that "a certain ultimate purpose" is thought "appropriately to guide all of man's quest for knowledge about himself and the world, and therefore to guide his use of conceptual relations and their verbal expression in this quest." [57] A third point Western philosophers ought to note is that:

In its concern for the salvation of all men, with their varying needs and capacities, Indian thought has found that among the most serious obstructions that must be overcome is the dogmatic tendency of people to assume that there is only one way to the saving truth.[58]

Here he mentions particularly the attempt by some contemporary linguistic philosophers to try to force all others to conform to their patterns of understanding. He pinpoints a major source of this tyrannical approach as,

the device of "massive verbal retaliation" after the style of G. E. Moore [which] can be sure of a host of admirers. But it is a terribly slow, wasteful, and cantankerous way of getting ahead in philosophy.[59]

Finally, Burtt believes that the use of fourfold negation can contribute to the flexibility and accuracy of philosophical discussion, putting a new focus on the appropriate role of both P and not $-P$, and neither P or not $-P$.[60] Awareness of the value, especially heuristic, of metaphysical decisions consciously employing four possibilities instead of two would improve a situation brought about by too-scrupulous employment of the either-or cut enthroned by the logical primitivists. This would enable the loosening-up process recommended by John Wisdom whom Burtt cites in this connection.[61] "The great thing we can gain," Burtt

[56] *Ibid.*, p. 201.
[57] *Ibid.*, p. 203.
[58] *Ibid.*, p. 204.
[59] *Ibid.*, p. 206.
[60] *Ibid.*, p. 208.
[61] John Wisdom: *Philosophy and Psychoanalysis*. Oxford, B. Blackwell, 1953, pp. 87 f.

concludes, "is a new and provocative perspective in which to pursue our philosophical thinking." [62] This essay certainly reveals him as without peer in his *entre deux âges* appreciation of Indian thought.

Filmer Stuart Cuckow Northrop, who has attended three of the East-West Conferences, was born in 1893, received his B.A. from Beloit College, his M.A. and Ph.D. from Harvard University. Northrop has taught in various schools from Hawaii to Mexico but has spent most of his productive years as professor of philosophy at Yale University where he was appointed Sterling Professor in philosophy and law in 1947.

Northrop became noticeably interested in Indian philosophy after attending the First East-West Philosophers' Conference at the University of Hawaii in 1939. Since that time he has developed his concern for comparative philosophy, culture, and law and has become the best known American philosopher to deal in these areas. Furthermore, he proved to be the only American philosopher at that conference and the subsequent ones in Hawaii to develop sufficiently simple general hypotheses to explain East-West philosophical differences so as to make an impact on the American nonfiction reading public. His approach, attacked by philosophers from India and American sinologists among others, as implausible, became widely known after his *The Meeting of East and West* (1946) [63] received considerable acclamation.

According to Northrop, the most influential Oriental systems show the following unique characteristics of knowing (epistemology) :

1) immediate apprehension,
2) indeterminate and undifferentiated awareness,
3) embracement of the equally immediate differentiations which come and go with it,
4) undifferentiated aesthetic continuum, which is
5) equivalent to a nominalistic unity of apperception.[64]

[62] Burtt, What can Western philosophy learn from India? p. 210.
[63] New York, Macmillan.
[64] F. S. C. Northrop: Methodology and Epistemology Oriental and Occidental. In Moore (Ed.) : *Essays in East-West Philosophy.* Honolulu, U. of Hawaii, 1951, pp. 151–52.

To be contrasted with this Eastern approach are Western postulational techniques. Postulation can only be verified in a nonintuitive way according to Northrop. Western science reasons deductively from concepts to postulation.[65] On the basis of this differentiation, Northrop maintained that Indian philosophy and Western philosophy are radically different. This is not the end of the discussion for Northrop, however, for he concluded that East and West should borrow from each other's methodology.

Ten years later, Northrop's interest switched to international relations and international law from a concern for methodology. In distinguishing between Western and Indian law his interpretation rested solidly on the foundation of the Laws of Manu.

Northrop's *Meeting of East and West* was written not long after Winston Churchill made famous the phrase invented by the German Nazi propagandist, Joseph Goebbels (1897–1945) : "The Iron Curtain." In contradistinction to Churchill, Northrop, as a man of goodwill, published his work as an indication of the need for a rapprochement between conflicting forces and ideologies in the world, especially in the world of values and ideas. Of all American writers the most like Toynbee with Toynbee's Christianity-panacea, Northrop grasps the sharp antlers of a dozen complex traditions, attempting to make some sense of their reconciliation. Despite all the justified cavils of Asians and Westerners alike, Northrop's attempt cannot easily be robbed of its historical significance. Furthermore, Northrop became overnight one of the few American philosophers since Emerson who found a truly international audience. Northrop's Millian liberal perspective combined with an idealistic epistemology and metaphysics sharpened itself into an international pragmatism appealing to the more advanced thought of the American Establishment.

With the canny ability of a Toynbee to pull together the ragbag of human thought, he ploughed through a vast literature of Indian philosophy as it related to itself and other cultures. Although frequently wrong in detail according to specialists, Northrop yet strove to make some sense out of global philoso-

[65] Northrop: Comparative philosophy and science in the light of comparative law. *Philosophy and Culture, East and West.* Honolulu, U. of Hawaii, 1962, p. 155.

phy.[66] He gave to a hungry American public a thumbnail sketch of world philosophy.

Northrop used as his measuring stick the idea of an *aesthetic continuum* as basic to the Asian outlook. I have heard evangelically-moved Indian, Chinese,[67] and Japanese philosophers deny this thesis. Yet it became a useful, if not totally satisfactory, tool by which to unify a vast field of thought and ideology.

Northrop's account of Hinduism richly combined source material with a profusion of secondary and tertiary works. Few Americans have been capable of such a felicitious result. Yet it is mostly anathema to the expert who is frustrated by the shallowness of the result in specific areas. For popular consumption it seemed to be nearly ideal. And it was for the amateur that he had written it.

It is of interest that Northrop should be one of the few American philosophers to treat of Tantric Hinduism. He went even further by giving economic values in Asia a whole page of consideration. But he sometimes treated culture from the standpoint of psychic determinism, giving his accounts an ephemeral quality.[68] His chapter on social status was congruent with some American sociologizing as it followed the path of nineteenth century thought of a neo-Darwinist direction. His emphasis upon the aesthetic quality of Asian culture was part of his main thesis of the uniqueness of the aesthetic continuum. But the whole lacks impact because it is not based upon a recognizable philosophy of history. There are layers of commentary and exegesis floating like uprooted lotuses. As a result, Northrop's own account of Indian philosophy turns out to be a kind of aesthetic-layered continuum. That all this is pleasing to the casual reader is attested to by the

[66] Another American with a more intimate grasp of Asian thought is now carrying on where Northrop left off. See the account of John C. Plott below.

[67] See, for example, Hu Shih: The scientific spirit and method in Chinese philosophy. In Charles A. Moor (Ed.) : *The Chinese Mind*. Honolulu, East-West, 1967, pp. 104–7. Hu Shih says of Northrop's thesis that it "is unhistorical anl untrue."

[68] An example of this approach is Northrop's contention that: "If one conquers a people politically and exploits them economically while leaving their basic religious and philosophical beliefs intact, one has restrained and harmed their bodies but has not touched their spirit of their souls." Northrop: Why a College Needs a Chapel. *Man, Nature and God*. New York, Trident, 1962, p. 115. It is also his belief that: ". . . we must root our international law in the living beliefs of *all* the religions of the world, not merely in those of our own." *Ibid.*, p. 118.

many laudatory reviews of the book by Americans. The final effect is that the world of ideas is an exciting pluralism in a world too complex to criticize or evaluate—with one exception—Marxism and Communism.[69] But this critique would carry us far afield from our discussion of Indian thought, since Northrop fails to mention M. N. Roy or much of recent contemporary Indian philosophy.

Northrop's outlook is personalistic, idealistic, and indeterministic. At the base of it is his contention that the philosophy of the future must rest on an aesthetic attitude toward human world problems. What the West can learn from the East is precisely this aesthetic attitude towards life. The East, on the other hand, says Northrop, must learn the scientific attitude from the West, learn the controlling significance of concepts of postulation. Indian philosophy then, for Northrop, is an important episode in world thought, largely because it enriches our knowledge of the aesthetic continuum and the aesthetic attitude towards life. Northrop's concern with the aesthetic continuum is constant. The difference between Western and Indian philosophy, he said, consists in:

> that . . . factor in Indian philosophy which transcends the senses . . . [the] immediately apprehended transcendent factor of the aesthetic or existential intuition, not the theoretically conceived transcendent factor of the Western theoretic intuition.[70]

Concerning Oriental civilization as a whole, its genius, said Northrop, consists in having:

> demonstrated the existence of the factor transcending the senses which is immediately apprehended by the . . . existential, aesthetic intuition.[71]

---

[69] Northrop held that, "before Russia can have a *correct ideology* and thereby become a thoroughly safe neighbor for the rest of the world, certain unjustified portions of her Marxian philosophy must be dropped." *The Meeting of East and West*, p. 467. This note should be contrasted with the title of chapter iii of the same work entitled: "The Free Culture of the United States," pp. 66–164.

[70] Northrop: The relation between Eastern and Western philosophy. In Inge (Ed.) : *Essays in Honor of Radhakrishnan*. p. 375.

[71] *Ibid.*, p. 376.

Why then, Northrop asked, have

> the Orientals, both Hindus and Buddhists . . . developed so many
> logically formulated philosophical systems in so many respects similar
> to if not identical with many systems of the West? The answer to this
> query is to be found in two considerations: First, even when the
> Easterner formulates such logically subtle systematic systems, the words
> in these systems for the most part, although not always tend to refer to
> immediately apprehended factors. They are thus concentrating on
> differentiated, transitory factors in the aesthetic continuum rather than
> logically inferred, theoretically formulated, external common sense,
> scientific, or philosophical structures of the Western type having to do
> with the theoretically known component in things.

Second, said Northrop:

> even in the cases in which it occurs, the logical formulation of an
> Oriental system does involve reference to external common sense or
> scientific objects of the Western type, these systems tend to be used not
> as in the West to show what the most important factor in the nature of
> things is, but instead to show what it is not. Consequently, for the
> Easterner even when he develops logically formulated systems contain-
> ing most subtle distinctions and technical concepts, his aim tends to be
> to direct the reader away from the persisting, postulated, determinate
> theoretical component in the nature of things in which the West
> believes, toward the indeterminate, indescribable, ineffable, and imme-
> diately apprehendable aesthetic factor, which neither logical methods
> nor philosophical or scientific theory can convey.[72]

And he continued,

> The logical and the causal order is precisely the reverse of this. Instead
> of the undifferentiated or the differentiated aesthetic continuum being
> projected and known by faculties of the postulated substantial self, or
> modern Western mental substance, the emotionally laden aesthetic self
> and the emotionally laden aesthetic object must be conceived as
> constituted of the irreducible aesthetic continuum. We are conscious,
> emotional, aesthetically luminous creatures not because we are a purely
> spiritual or purely mental, reflexively presupposed, or postulated,
> substance; but because we, like all other aesthetically immediate deter-
> minate things in the universe, whether they be the knowing subject
> (*purusha*), or the known object (*prakriti*), are constituted of the

[72] *Ibid.*, pp. 363–364.

continuum. As the Tantric doctrines puts it, Chit, the "unchanging formlessness" is the source of consciousness in the self.[73]

Karl Potter in commenting on Northrop's interpretation in 1966 said that although it was natural enough to assume this Vedāntic viewpoint, it was not quite accurate. Potter said:

> Northrop's thesis that India has no interest in "concepts by postulation" turns out to be another way of recognizing the Vedantic monopoly of what is available to the casual observer as "philosophy" in India. But those who are acquainted with the full sweep of classical Indian thought know that it is by no means as limited in its inclinations as Vedantists would have us believe. The materials for a revival of philosophy of science in India are there in the traditional texts, and only need the attention of interested scholars to be brought into view.[74]

This will doubtless take some doing if one is confined to the philosophical texts, although turning to the writing that might best be called Indian natural philosophy in eighteenth century Western parlance, there is justice in what Potter says. But Northrop was in no position to dig out this material.

Northrop's account of Indian philosophy kindled the greatest interest when first proposed. It recommends certain hypotheses attempting to explain the differences between India and the United States in the larger context of East-West differences. Whether one can conceive of tests which might prove or disprove these hypotheses is another question. It would appear that no thinker has put forward any suggestions.

An interlude of our account of the view of American philosophers who participated in the East-West Conferences includes a brief discussion of two scholars who in their teaching were influential in spreading Indian thought: F. P. Clarke and J. Wach.

IV

Francis Palmer Clarke (1895) took his A.B. at the University of Colorado, his M.A. at the University of Nebraska, and his Ph.D.

---

[73] *Ibid.*, p. 364.

[74] Ward Morehouse: A four-dimensional problem. *Tech and Culture,* 8, 3, 1967, p. 367.

at the University of Pennsylvania. His interest in Indian philosophy developed under Louis H. Gray who was at Nebraska
(1921–1922) long enough to direct Clarke's M.A. thesis which
was on Hindu philosophy.[75] Although encouraged at the University of Pennsylvania by William R. Newbold to continue in
the Indian field, Clarke did not teach a course in the six systems of
Indian philosophy until 1952. He continued the course until
1956–57. As the demand did not seem to pulse strongly, he let it
drop and it was not until the Dutch linguist-philosopher J. F.
Staal visited Pennsylvania that it was taught again, although in
the meantime W. Norman Brown had been giving a reading
course in the Upaniṣads (in Sanskrit) .

Joachim Wach was born in Germany in 1898, naturalized an
American citizen in 1946, and died in Switzerland in 1955. After
attending the Universities of Munich and Berlin he took his
Ph.D. from Leipzig University where he taught before coming to
the United States. He lectured in this country at both Brown
University and the University of Chicago. His two books that
touched on Indian philosophy and religion were his *Sociology of
Religion* (1944) and *Types of Religious Experience* (1951) .

There is every reason to think that few American religious
scholars have done a more competent analysis of Mahāyāna
Buddhism than Joachim Wach. Reasons for this are that it was
written recently, that it had been aided by recent Japanese scholarship, and that Wach's training in behavioral science, even of
the German academic variety, had given him an edge on American philosophers. Unfortunately his interpretation and evaluation are at a minimum, not unnatural in this sociological school
of comparative religion.

The last section of Wach's account was original. It was a brief
survey of what benefits Christian theologians may derive from the
study of Mahāyāna Buddhism. These are, he thought, as follows:
first are the parallels between Christianity and Buddhism; second
are the sociological affinities between them; third are the decisive
differences between the great religions of Mahāyāna Buddhism

---

[75] Gray later became a professor at Columbia. See Dale Riepe: "Contribution of
American Sanskritists in the spread of Indian philosophy in the United States."
Buffalo Studies, III, 1, 1967, p. 48.

and Christianity. These last are: (1) the difference in the source of authority which consists in the emphasis upon the canonical in Christendom, whereas the emphasis in Buddhism is upon the psychological and epistemological questions: (2) there is nothing comparable to the Holy Spirit in Buddhism whereas in Christianity there is no notion of *karma;* (3) and in Buddhism there is nothing comparable to Christian baptism or the Lord's Supper. While prayer plays a major role in Christianity; meditation has this function in Buddhism. Sacrifice is less emphasized in Buddhism.

Wach concluded his discussion with a worth-repeating quotation from Max Müller. We close this discussion with it.

> I believe the final struggle between Buddhism and Christianity, whenever that comes to pass, will be a hard one, and will end in compromise—there is a prophecy.[76]

Wach maintained that "the first half of this prophecy is not less likely of fulfillment because the second is open to grave doubt." [77] I believe that the quality of Wach's commentary rests on a more secure foundation than seems to be merited by this last reflection.

V

Wilmon Henry Sheldon, another participant in the East-West Conferences, was born in 1875, took his B.A., M.A. and Ph.D. at Harvard University. After teaching at Columbia and Princeton Universities, and at Dartmouth College, he was a professor at Yale University for the remainder of his active teaching career. He also lectured at the University of Indiana, California at Berkeley, and at the University of Hawaii during the Second East-West Philosophers' Conference.

It is interesting to note that Sheldon became quite attracted to Indian thought, especially metaphysics, after attending the Second East-West Philosophers' Conference in 1949. By that time his concern with Thomism had developed extenisvely, perhaps as an outgrowth of his balanced dualism, or his harmonious doctrine of

[76] Joachim Wach: *Types of Religious Experience Christian and Non Christian.* Chicago, U. of Chicago, 1951, p. 131.
[77] One facet of it may be seen in the undeclared Vietnam war.

polarity. As to the origin of this view of Sheldon's it might be related that he first hit on the notion of polarity when he felt it "queer that there were only two kinds of human beings—men and women! My latest conclusions as to this human polarity are in the last published book I wrote, *Sex and Salvation,* which you certainly should read." [78] He also stated:

> In the guise of a (would-be) theologian, I think the outer world revealed to the empirical scientist is much a matter of grace as is the mystical experience or the strength to lead a good life. Do we begin to realize how much is *given* to us, how little we do just by our own power? We don't create the outer world, we don't create the hypotheses that explain the sequence of its events, the artist doesn't create the insight that leads to his production! These all just *occur* to us—all we do is to get the receptive attitude by looking at the facts and welcoming or discarding various ideas that *occur to us!* [79]

> And that suggests something I'd like to say about what I consider my *special* theses in philosophy: (1) chance as an ultimate trait of reality, (2) a new view of time (As a graduate student in Royce's seminar I wrote a paper defending the former—my view has been to a degree verified by the modern notion of statistical law) and (3) the ontological proof of God as the realization of all possibles in *one* being as an absolute logical necessity. All these views are quite unorthodox today, except that the first is getting a tinge of respectability.[80] I'm putting them in a polar synthesis in the book I'm writing now! [81]

Sheldon's comments upon Indian philosophy directly are infrequent in his *magnum opus, God and Polarity.* There he praised Jainism for its openness but attacked it on the ground that it "denies a God, the Atman experimentally verified by the Vedantist." [82] Leaving aside Sheldon's eccentric view of "experi-

[78] *Letter* to Peter Hare, Nantucket, Mass., (August 3, 1960). According to Norman O. Brown: *Love's Body.* New York, Vintage Books, 1968, p. 23: "The prototype of all opposition of contrariety is sex. The prototype of the division into two sexes is the separation of earth and sky, Mother Earth and Father Sky, the primal parents."

[79] *Ibid.*

[80] After writing this letter Sheldon had the pleasure of reading that his third view had been moved into the realm of at least discussion, if not respectability, by Norman Malcolm of Cornell University.

[81] *Letter* to Peter Hare, Nantucket, Mass., (August 19, 1960).

[82] Wilmon H. Sheldon: *God and Polarity.* New Haven, Yale, 1954, p. 431.

mentally verified" it is clear that he found certain aspects of Jainism attractive.

Sikhism, like Jainism, failed according to Sheldon, because it lacked a metaphysical principle of synthesis. It is interesting but not surprising that the only system to satisfy Sheldon is not Indian at all. It is the system of St. Thomas Aquinas, "greatest in ordered articulation, in wealth of detail and panoramic vision." [83]

According to Sheldon the power of Buddhism was shown in its adherence by "the hearts" of Farthest East, yet it too commands less metaphysical respect than Vedānta.[84] Sheldon's subtitle was "A Synthesis of Philosophies" and as such he brought together more different threads of thought than any of his predecessors in American philosophy. His major classifications were monistic idealism, plural or personal idealism, materialism, genuinely synthetic (Thomistic), and ivory-towerism (analysis, semantics, positivism, symbolic logic, and process) philosophy. Although his emphasis was at times like that of Conger, he is not satisfied with Conger's epitomized naturalism.

Sheldon's chapter on idealism contained one of the most sustained accounts of Indian philosophy to be found in American philosophical literature. Here he showed a rich choice of secondary and tertiary sources none of which were available to the American reader until after World War I. What is of exceptional note is that as a venerable emeritus professor, Sheldon contrived to include in his summary of major philosophical hypotheses a considerable body of Indian material, not to speak of Chinese and Islamic. Few American philosophers, not even Hocking, who was two years his senior, have incorporated more Oriental thought into his major work. And certainly none, at so advanced an age, dared look so deeply into ways of thought alien to his American-European tradition. Sheldon progressed rapidly from a neophyte at the East-West Conference of 1949 to *God and Polarity* in 1954.

According to Sheldon, Advaita Vedānta reached the zenith of idealism. Except for *māyā*, all reality is "swallowed up in the One." [85] It is only with the status of *māyā* that doubt and dissen-

[83] *Ibid.,* p. 442.
[84] *Ibid.,* pp. 206-7.
[85] *Ibid.,* p. 188.

sion lie as a poison in the otherwise perfect Vedānta apple for Sheldon.

Charles William Morris (1901–), took his B.S. from Northwestern University and his Ph.D. from the University of Chicago. He has taught at Rice University, the University of Chicago, Harvard University, and is at present a graduate research professor at the University of Florida. Holding the Guggenheim, Rockefeller, and Center for Advanced Studies in Behavioral Science fellowships, he has also been past president of the Western Division of the American Philosophical Association, and has traveled extensively, including in India.

The views of Charles Morris, like those of J. B. Pratt, are unusually broad and hospitable to many different traditions, some of which may be logically incompatible. Following from this he seems to have considerable tolerance for various religious and philosophical viewpoints that may be outside of the pragmatic and positivistic tradition to which he normally belongs. Using William H. Sheldon's typology and characterology as a basis he attempted to describe men's actions and motives through their choice of *paths of life* of which he isolated thirteen that he believed reflect the situation among mankind from East to West and North to South. Of the thirteen paths, the Second Path was that representing the Buddhist ideal, according to Morris. Here,

> The individual should for the most part "go it alone," assuring himself of privacy in living quarters, having much time to himself, attempting to control his own life. One should stress self-sufficiency, reflection and meditation, knowledge of himself. The direction of interest should be away from intimate associations with social groups, and away from the physical manipulation of objects or attempts at control of the physical environment. One should aim to simplify one's external life, to moderate those desires whose satisfaction is dependent upon physical and social forces outside of oneself, and to concentrate attention upon the refinement, clarification, and self-direction of one's self. Not much can be done or is to be gained by "living outwardly." One must avoid dependence upon persons or things; the center of life should be found within oneself.[86]

[86] Charles Morris: *The Open Self.* New York, Prentice-Hall, 1948, p. 75. This description might well be unsuitable for such world-famous Buddhists as G. P. Malalasekera, who believes that nonattachment does not preclude enthusiastic social →

The individual, according to Morris, following the lead of his teacher, George H. Mead, is not simply a consumer who chooses his path of life by looking up at the choices on an illuminated signboard. "Physique, environment, ideas, and culture form a dynamic field of mutually interacting and mutually conditioning factors." [87] Yet there is something about Morris' account that suggests a kind of consumer approach to paths of life and to values. One has a number of paths and chooses one of several of them, although he is conditioned to do this by the various factors which Morris listed and which appear above. Ultimately, the choice of paths of life depends upon our "free choice" if I read his last chapter entitled "Freedom or Frustration?" correctly. In brief, despite all the "mutually interacting and mutually conditioning factors" he still impresses upon us that we can somehow *choose* the path of the open self in an open society. Morris exhorts us to accept at least some of the Buddhistic qualities that soften our aggressive tendencies, for according to him "The new American frontier is human rather than geographical." [88] Furthermore, says Morris,

[the new American frontier] lies wherever an American meets another person, young or old, white or yellow or brown or black, inside our borders or beyond them. Pioneering on the domestic frontier and on the international frontier are now inextricably linked.[89]

In *Paths of Life* [90] (1942) with the subtitle of "Preface to a World Religion" Morris devoted two chapters to Buddhism, the more relevant one being "The Buddhist Path of Detachment from Desire." The other grew out of Buddhist tendencies, entitled "The Maitryan Path of Generalized Detached-Attachment." The importance of early Buddhism, Morris claimed, is that it

offers a position of great significance to those engaged in the religious quest. It presents a path of life and a view of salvation conceived

---

activity. Its ideal is not in a monkish life. Nevertheless, most Buddhists might agree with Morris, particularly the Mahāyānists.

[87] *Ibid.*, p. 46.

[88] *Ibid.*, p. 170. This appears perfectly consistent with American global aspirations. Perhaps he should have said "human *and* geographical" (1968).

[89] *Ibid.*, p. 170.

[90] New York, Harper.

within the limits of human existence, not dependent upon any splitting of the universe into the natural and the supernatural, and not dependent upon any doctrine of the immortality of gods or men.[91]

Another interesting feature of early Buddhism, according to Morris, was that it is "independent of any special system of metaphysics and favorable in principle to any increase of scientific knowledge concerning man or the cosmos." [92] With later Buddhism, however, the quasi-naturalistic view of man was reinterpreted to a view holding that mind or consciousness alone was real, an extreme form of idealism.

Morris' judgment of later Buddhism is contained in a rather longish quotation and represents one of the few incisive critiques of Buddhism to be found in American intellectual literature. He maintains that,

> The difficulties in generalizing the attitude of [Buddhistic] detachment; the hidden affirmations involved in the desire for nirvana for oneself and others; the tendency to metaphysical idealism; the introduction of erotic, magical, and mystical practices; the incipient interests in the techniques for objectively controlling the world in which men live; the vague gropings for an attitude of detachment which is not incompatible with some form of attachment: all of these are witnesses in the history of Buddhism to the inadequacies of detachment from desire as an exclusive way of salvation.[93]

But Morris did not let us forget that "early Buddhism is unique for the sanity and the thoroughness with which it envisaged the essentials of the religious life." [94] Yet Buddhism is not enough, he thought. We must continue on the search for a more adequate path of life.

In a more than superficial sense, but with more sensitivity, Morris exhorts us to carry out the idealistic program of F. S. C. Northrop. Americans cannot leave anyone else alone to go his

[91] *Ibid.*, p. 45.

[92] *Ibid.* Despite certain naturalistic tendencies, Buddhism is generally idealistic north of India. Buddhism is not independent, for example, of the metaphysical doctrine of universal flux despite Sarvāstivādan attempts to modify the notion about 2,000 years ago.

[93] *Ibid.*, pp. 54–55.

[94] *Ibid.*, p. 56.

way. It is our destiny to help others and to help ourselves. "Our social inventiveness must embrace and outpace our physical inventions." [95] Is this a latter-day form of manifest destiny with some philosophical sophistication added? The cause of our difficulties is to be found deep within ourselves, according to Morris, for he has little or nothing to say about social change, structural change, revolutionary change. He is not against change—on the other hand he does not show how it can be brought about except by the determination of the good will of Americans who "will grow strong in crisis." [96] The cause of the crisis is voluntaristic, not structural, economic, political, and so forth. When the demons within people rise up then we are in for trouble. Surely this is an idealistic account of society and the individuals who make it up. The analysis that Morris performs is not inconsistent with the approach of traditional Buddhism to social and institutional crisis, although it does not appear that he derives it from deeply imbibing the Buddhist scriptures. Rather it grows out of the pragmatic tradition of Peirce, James, and Mead. As mentioned earlier there is almost a consumer-approach quality about the dynamics of the paths of life that Morris discusses although he would doubtless deny this. Although he does not completely disregard the structure and motivation of the society in which one or more paths of life prove to be more common than others, there is an air of unreality about such an approach. The economic factor which certainly has as much weight as the psychological, presumably plays no role in his exposition. Although the paths of life are not quite on the level of random questionnaires and popularity polls, there is a kind of superficiality about the whole treatment. In defense of what he has done I should think he would be within his rights to say that after all he is simply making a first attempt to somehow link up ethical research with behavioral science. Emphasis upon body-type or upon the major paths of life (with their religious orientation) is certainly a beginning and for that reason Morris deserves praise rather than reproach. On the other hand, the consumer-preference type of approach seems not only superficial but indeed somewhat regressive today, twenty years

[95] Morris, *The Open Self,* p. 172.
[96] *Ibid.,* p. 173.

later.[97] Nevertheless when Morris began writing there was still much greater hope and confidence expressed in this typical kind of American research with its interesting connections with pragmatism, particularly of the robust voluntaristic "will to believe" type. Another characteristics of Morris' view is that he believes with Bertrand Russell that there are certain innate traits that rise up from the depths by some inexplicable alchemy. He believes, however, that by thinking morally we can control these if we have enough flexibility and good will. Certainly he gives little indication that he thinks that these things rise within a certain type of system, institution or structure. In this sense his social criticism is molar while his views of amelioration are atomic and individualistic. But in this he is certainly in line with much American philosophical thought.

We turn now to the views of the Director of four East-West Conferences, Charles A. Moore (1901–1967) who was born in Chicago and received his B.A. and Ph.D. from Yale University where he was a student of W. H. Sheldon and F. S. C. Northrop. He was professor of philosophy at the University of Hawaii since 1933 when he first became seriously interested in Indian thought under the stimulation of Kalidas Nag who taught at the University of Hawaii in 1933 and W. T. Chan who taught Indian and Chinese philosophy at Hawaii in 1933–1934. Moore was responsible for having made the University of Hawaii a center of East-West philosophy in the Western world. Founder of the East-West Philosophers' Conferences in 1939, 1949, 1959, 1964 with the help of President Emeritus Gregg Sinclair of the University of Hawaii, he dedicated his life to alerting American philosophers and laymen to the rich treasures of Asian thought, particularly Indian. Editor of *Philosophy East and West* since its inception in 1950, he saw it rise to preeminence in comparative philosophy. His grasp of scholarship in a vast variety of Asian philosophical fields made him an editor without technical peer in this area and without

[97] It is easy to forget the aura of optimism in the United States before the official implementation of the Cold War Policy as a way of life. Morris reflects this optimism. Some of the events that he warned against in 1942 have appeared in the United States and are now comfortably absorbed in our way of life. One of these is the inflexibility that makes the United States foreign policy the bulwark against all revolution and the defender of most reactionary *coups d'etats*.

sparing himself the daily detail that excellence in this field demands. With so many different Asian languages involved, his job was herculean. He knew personally nearly every important figure in world philosophy outside the socialist countries. And no other American has been so accredited with encouraging young philosophers to study the wisdom of the Indians.

Moore edited *Philosophy East and West* (1944), *Source Book in Indian Philosophy* with S. Radhakrishnan (1957), *Philosophy and Culture: East and West* (1962), among others. He wrote dozens of articles on Indian and comparative philosophy. In 1947–48 Moore studied at Banaras Hindu University and since then visited India for editorial and conference reasons.

Although most of Moore's work has been as an editor of books and journals, he also wrote a notable body of articles about Indian philosophy. But his concern was twofold: not only to help American philosophers understand Indian philosophy, but also to help Indian philosophers understand Western thought. Nowhere did Moore defend the values of the West so sharply as he did in his critique of Sri Aurobindo's account of the West's alleged defects in philosophy. Moore said:

> The West . . . is not materialistic, is not a slave of science, is not devoted to the limitation that all reality consists of the physical, the vital, and the mental—every one of the very many idealists in the entire Western tradition and in what has been called the "Great Tradition" would deny these allegations and interpretations.[98]

Moore might have added that the naturalists and materialists would also deny them, making the judgment nearly unanimous. Moore continued by pointing out that the West's goal is truth, which goal is just as spiritual as in India. "There are many similar misunderstandings which unjustifiably serve to isolate the West from the East." [99] Everywhere in Moore's work is the theme that the West should understand India, and India should understand the West. No other American has taken it upon himself to

[98] Moore: Sri Aurobindo or East and West. In Haridas Chaudhuri and Frederic Spiegelberg (Ed.): *The Integral Philosophy of Sri Aurobindo*. London, Allen & Unwin, 1960, p. 95.

[99] *Ibid.*

harp on this double tune. Moore was unsparing in his insistence that science, reason, progressivism, humanitarianism, and social service cannot be fairly lumped together as being worldly and materialistic, as held by Sri Aurobindo.

Moore's own philosophical position emerges in his evaluation of what he considers Sri Aurobindo's real significance in bringing about an understanding between East and West. According to Moore,

> [Sri Aurobindo] has shown the world that Indian philosophy *in its fullness* . . . is able to meet not only the problems of man and his destiny in terms of the ultimate spiritual Absolute but also the problems of man's life and experiences in the here and now.[100]

Moore believed that Aurobindo combines the insights of the East with those of the West, but surely this does not include the scientific method. For Aurobindo understands scientific method in a sense not unlike that of a fundamentalist preacher in Mississippi with an 1860 Princeton education. With this interpretation Moore falls squarely into the American idealist tradition. Moore quotes with approval, for example, Sri Aurobindo's rhapsodic statement in his *Renaissance in India* (1951) to the effect that the universe is:

> an infinite, indivisible, existence all-blissful in its pure self-consciousness [as it] moves out of its fundamental purity into the varied play of Force that is consciousness.[101]

That the poet artisan of these words can have an adequate notion of science or its method is difficult to see.[102] That Moore finds in the integration of Aurobindo "the true wisdom of the Indian mind" is surely not intended as irony, but might lead a number of Indian scientists, if not philosophers, to throw up their hands in despair. Moore also calls this a

> worldly as well as other-worldly, personal as well as impersonal, rational as well as intuitive, pluralistic as well as monistic, human as well

[100] *Ibid.*, p. 98.
[101] *Ibid.*, p. 100.
[102] A man may *do* science without presumably understanding it. Perhaps in the same sense that he may play a musical instrument "by ear."

as superhuman philosophy is the true essence of Indian traditional thought.[103]

It is to the everlasting credit of Aurobindo "that he has overcome the error of much limited thinking by pointing out the remarkable richness of the Indian tradition." [104] Moore agreed with Aurobindo that "The fallacy of the West lies . . . in exclusiveness of its ideas and in their limited applicability and validity." [105] That this could be said about any and every culture since the beginning of history scarcely makes it a statement uniquely applicable to the West. One might point out that this is precisely where the strength of the West lies. The great billowing, free-floating contradictory concepts of Aurobindo, sometime with objective reference and often with only imaginative reference, are precisely the form of barbarism that science in the West has attempted to hide in its own vast mausoleum of ancient verbiage and mythology. The chanting of the American Plains Indian such as the Sioux at least refers to probable states of affairs.

In "One Step Beyond" Moore claimed that "the general attitude of Indian philosophy . . . is 'ultimate perspective.' " [106] This implies, Moore believes, that:

> The Indian is willing to think things through thoroughly, whereas Western philosophers in general are, by an ever more iron-clad tradition than India is alleged to have, willing to go only so far and no farther in their speculation.[107]

Among Westerners with this "Indian" perspective are such mystics as Plato and the Neoplatonists. Concern with methodology in the West coupled with technological advance and skepticism of the predictive power of religion have, of course, persuaded some but by no means all of Western philosophers to be inhibited in the free-associative use of speculation. Indian philosophers, Moore said, demonstrate "one step beyond" in metaphysics through *neti*

[103] Moore, *ibid.*, pp. 107–108.
[104] *Ibid.*, p. 108.
[105] *Ibid.*, p. 109.
[106] Moore, *K. Bhatacharyya Memorial Volume*. Amalner, Indian Inst. of Philosophy, 1958, p. 121.
[107] *Ibid.*, p. 121.

neti absolutism; in epistemology through intuition going beyond reason; and in ethics in *karma,* renunciation going beyond the most extreme Western conceptions. Indians also go one step beyond in their views of *ahiṃsā* and *mokṣa.* In ethics these views are part of the supposition in India that the ultimate value is spiritual.[108] That this has been the view of so many Westerners also and that its opponents are still stigmatized in the twentieth century, hardly needs proof in the United States. From a more universal historical standpoint, however, these Indian conceptions are an extension of presuppositions to be found in the West, Moore believed. Whereas the West rests its case "from the empirical point of view only," the Indian outlook makes that one step beyond into the nonempirical realm.[109] My own observation is that many philosophers in the American scene go right along with the Indians into the nonempirical realm, some evidence of which may be seen by reading the present book.

Considering the claim that Indian philosophers do not make Western distinctions between philosophy and religion, and indeed have really a religious philosophy and little distinct philosophy at all, Moore replies in his "Philosophy as Distinct from Religion in India." [110] First of all he claims that philosophizing and religionizing may be indispensable to each other—as theory and practice. "Only reasoned faith can give coherence to life and knowledge." This quotation from Radhakrishnan is cited with approval by Moore.[111] The upshot is, Moore believes, that philosophy is pursued in the West as a search for knowledge and truth.[112]

Moore's article "The Meaning of Duhkha" traces various interpretations of that term which is generally held to mean "suffering" (birth, sickness, old age, death, lamentation). The two basic meanings, Moore believes, are (1) commotion or unrest and (2) phenomenal existence. This establishes in Buddhism, Hinduism, and Jainism, "initial pessimism." Ultimately this pessimism is transformed into ultimate optimism when we realize that *duḥkha*

---

[108] *Ibid.,* p. 131.
[109] *Ibid.,* p. 133.
[110] *Philos East West,* XI, 1 and 2, 1961.
[111] *Ibid.,* p. 23.
[112] *Ibid.,* p. 24.

can be overcome. Yet, the pessimistic view of the Indian about phenomenal life will have to stand, according to Moore.

Ahiṃsā has also challenged Moore as it has other sensitive philosophers in the United States who have known anything about it. Hopkins had emphasized *ahiṃsā* in the Indian tradition as being valuable because it includes all living creatures, and not just man. As technology makes killing ever easier, it is the West which seems most likely to commit this gravest of all Jaina sins. Moore believed that it should be the "supreme principle of ethics [that is, noninjury]" and the only exception to its practice being "the situation in which the unavoidable causing of lesser suffering would be justified in the name of the prevention of greater suffering." [113] This is the principle invoked by President Harry S. Truman in justifying the dropping of A-Bombs on Hiroshima and Nagasaki. Moore believed that "The Indian doctrine of *ahiṃsā* is inadequate because of its concern "exclusively with the inner rectitude of the actor, not in the suffering of the victim." [114] He did not mention that a powerful incentive to its adoption in India rather than the West has been in its connection with the doctrine of transmigration. After all, we do not wish to harm at-present-nonhuman life which may once have been human or may indeed be someone in the family tree. How this will work out for mosquitoes and viruses has not yet been resolved, but Rachel Carson, in her *Silent Spring* (1962), has shown good reason for more pragmatic and selfish concern for ecologically-based *ahiṃsā*.

Moore has received no higher praise than that awarded him by Principal Ramjee Singh of Bhagalpur, Bihar. He says that "Professor Moore has done more in the cause of Indo-American goodwill than even millions . . . of hard-earned American dollars flowing incessantly from the Wall Street through the great White House." [115] I, for one, can agree with this wholeheartedly.

VI

We now turn to two philosophers having no connection with the East-West Conferences: Kurt Leidecker and Walter Stace.

[113] Moore, The Significance of Ahimsa for Ethics, East and West. In *Proceedings of the XI International Congress of Philosophy*, XIV, p. 250.

[114] *Ibid.*, p. 250.

[115] *Letter* to the author from Bhagalpur (April 17, 1962).

Kurt Friedrich Leidecker was born in Germany in 1902. He took his B.A. at Oberlin College and his M.A. and Ph.D. at the University of Chicago. He first became interested in Indian thought by reading Edwin Arnold's *Light of Asia* in German when he was thirteen. His interest in Indian philosophy was fostered at Oberlin by Professor Simon Frazer MacLennan and Ethel M. Kitch. His M.A. thesis on Indian philosophy earned him the Newton Prize. Leidecker studied Sanskrit at Chicago with Walter Eugene Clark under whom he wrote his doctoral dissertation entitled "Noetical Terminology in the Upanishads and the Bhagavad Gita" (1927). It is likely that this is the fourth doctorate in Indian philosophy awarded in the United States.

Leidecker has taught at New Mexico Highlands University, Rensselaer Polytechnical Institute, the Air Force Institute of Technology, University of Southern California, and Mary Washington College of the University of Virginia. A Fulbright research scholar in India from 1951 to 1952, he returned to South Asia from 1955 to 1957 as Cultural Affairs Consultant with the American Embassy and United States Information Service in Bangkok.

He has written three monographs on Indian philosophy: *Josiah Royce and Indian Thought* (1931), some of the material of which has been incorporated into the study of Royce in the present book; *The Secret of Recognition* (*Pratyabhijñahṛdayam*) *A Reviving Doctrine of Salvation of Medieval India* (1938); and *Four Dhama Lectures*. He published *Sanskrit: Essentials of Grammar and Language* in 1934. By 1961 he had also published more than forty articles on Indian thought.

Five years after Leidecker had received his doctorate, Walter T. Stace (1886–1967) was born in London, was appointed to lecture in philosophy at Princeton University, and remained in the United States since that time. Stace was educated at Bath College and Trinity College, Ireland. He first became interested in Buddhism and Hinduism after 1910, in observing the Tamil Hindus and Sinhalese Buddhist, as a member of the Ceylon Civil Service. Of his own work in Indian thought he modestly says: "I am not in any sense a scholar in the languages or religions— merely a dabbler!" [116] This "dabbling" became quite impressive

---

[116] *Letter* to the author, Princeton, New Jersey (February 25, 1965).

in his presidential address before the American Philosophical Association and in such books as *The Gate of Silence* (1952) where he writes poetically of the superior man, *Religion and the Modern Mind* (1960), *Mysticism and Philosophy* (1960), and *The Teachings of the Mystics* (1960). Unlike some other professors of philosophy in the United States, Stace had had a first-hand knowledge of Hinduism and Buddhism in practice before most of them since Royce had become seriously aware of the topic. As early as 1924 he gave evidence of this knowledge when commenting upon Hegel's *Philosophy of History* in his *The Philosophy of Hegel*,[117] particularly when Hegel deals with Indian art and religion.

In the *Teachings of the Mystics* Stace writes about philosophers and religionists who themselves had mystical experiences. He includes writings from the Upaniṣads, Sri Aurobindo, The Prajñā-Pāramitā Texts, and the "Awakening of the Faith" by Aśvaghoṣa. His judgment of Hindu mysticism is that:

> It is the revolt of Spirit against Matter that for two thousand years, since Buddha disturbed the balance of the old Aryan world and dominated increasingly the Indian mind.[118]

All India has "lived in the shadow of the great Refusal" with the implication of abiding in the end, dressed in ascetic garb, Stace claims. This renunciation plays as important a role for mankind as the divine ends served by materialism and is probably more easily understood.[119] The meaning of *nirvāṇa*, according to Stace, may be understood with reference to Tennyson's experience. Tennyson said,

> All at once, as it were out of the intensity of the consciousness of individuality, individuality itself seemed to fade away into boundless being—the loss of personality (if so it were) seeming no extinction but the only true life.[120]

---

[117] London, Macmillan, 1924.
[118] Stace: *Teachings of the Mystics.* New York, New Am. Lib., p. 64.
[119] *Ibid.,* p. 65.
[120] Quoted by Stace in *Teachings of the Mystics,* p. 78.

Stace's latter-day growing concern with the problem of mysticism shows itself in several of his more recent works. His experience in Asia as well as America has made it possible for him to deal sympathetically with "that cosmic Spritual Presence toward which the great world religions all dimly grope." [121] For those who take a dim view of mysticism and its significance, Stace has harsh words:

> I should accept it as a matter of course that conventional professionals will hold conventional professional opinions. But here and there a few rare spirits among the thousands of run-of-the-mill professional philosophers being less hide-bound than their colleagues, may go the length of wondering, or even seriously inquiring, whether the foundations of logic, as now taught with complacent self-assurance in the dogmas of the schools, may not require revision.[122]

Perhaps it is too much to expect a cool detachment from philosophers with logic, without logic, or beyond logic, whose actions consist in skirmishes on the battlefields of dogma and ideology.

Stace's view of Indian thought is most like that of Santayana, though richer in the mundane experiential sense of his having lived in Ceylon. Beginning with naturalistic premises, like Santayana he gives considerable credence to the flights of the human spirit found in the Indian mystics. Few other philosophers in the United States including James, have tried so concertedly to understand the mystical dimension of philosophy. He approaches the problem according to a double typology: extrovertive and introvertive mysticism.[123] As an example of the first he cites Sri Ramakrishna, of the second Aśvagoṣa in his *The Awakening of Faith*. In the first, individuality takes on a heightened form while in the second it is dissolved. What is important about mysticism, however, according to Stace, is whether it aids in the good life. It is his feeling that Hindu and Buddhist mystics have probably not translated their mysticism into quite as much social good as Christian mystics; generally their Indian views have led them to a more tangential effect on society. Yet in spiritual and speculative pro-

[121] *Ibid.*, p. 236.

[122] *Ibid.*, pp. 237–238. This sounds very much like William James just a few years before his demise.

[123] Stace: *Mysticism and Philosophy*. New York, Lippincott, 1960.

fundity "we have to award the palm to the mystics of India." [124]
A more materialistic critic than Stace might retort to this that
they might also receive a palm for imaginative flights of fantasy
which we may well mistake for profundity. According to Stace,
summing up his views in ethics, mystical or otherwise:

> I believe that moral rules simply *are* rules of human happiness. And if
> so, they will be universal and not relative to any culture in exactly the
> same way, and for the same reason, as rules of safety and of health are
> so.[125]

One thing Stace is trying to say, I believe, is that any experience,
no matter how labeled, should be employed towards human happiness. It makes little difference whether one is a naturalist or an
idealist when it comes to this final proving ground.

Time and Eternity [126] is in several ways Walter T. Stace's most
challenging book. In it he attempts to include mystical experience
in the naturalistic outlook, something which J. B. Pratt had also
attempted before him but perhaps with more pantheistic designs.
Stace defines religion as "the hunger of the soul for the impossible, the unattainable, the inconceivable." [127] The disease of things
consists in "their this-or-that-ness, that is, in their very existence."
"No being, no time, no place satisfies the ultimate hunger" [128] for
what is beyond. Therefore, even in a scientific naturalistic universe no one will ever be satisfied. Since this seems too obvious
with regard to hardware, no one will cavil concerning the affairs
of the spirit. From this it follows, according to Stace, that religion
will always hold an important place even in an atheistic society—
if we accept Stace's definition of religion which differs somewhat
from that emphasizing the need for a sacred object. Buddhism is
then clearly a religion because its essence lies in religious experi-
ment just as does Christianity's. Differentiations among religions
occur naturalistically through temporal and material conditions.
Buddhism is important because of its vastly proliferated discus-

[124] *Ibid.*, p. 339.

[125] Stace: *Religion and the Modern Mind*. Philadelphia, Lippincott, 1952, p. 270.

[126] Stace: *Time and Eternity*. Princeton, Princeton, 1952.

[127] *Ibid.*, p. 4. He might have added a category highly recommended by a former
liberal arts dean: that of the "unforeseeable."

[128] *Ibid.*, p. 5.

sions of the negative attributes of divinity, on Stace's view. It has
gone further than any other religion in its "description" of the
negative divine which he concludes is Nothing, because nothing
can be predicated of it.[129] What occurs is an entertainment of
aspects of existence which somehow appeal to the sense of the
incommensurable if saying this kind of thing makes any sense.
Yet, according to Stace the answer to " 'What is God?' is not in a
concept but in experience." [130] One might say that experience
itself is the basis of the concept so that Stace may well be deluding
himself in this kind of logomachy.

Although Stace at first was only slightly concerned with Indian
thought, his interest had grown, reaching its zenith presumably in
the decade before 1960, resulting in the publication of his three
books on religious experience all in the same year.

Most of the philosophers discussed in this chapter were second-
arily concerned with Indian philosophy, which partially explains
the breadth of their approach. In short, as nonspecialists they
gained in perspective what they lost in depth and accuracy. We
next turn to some philosophers who become immersed in Indian
thought at earlier stages in their careers and exhibit greater
control of the Indian material.

In the period we have just considered the large American
foundations and the United States Government both contributed
to the spread of Indian thought. India, by the end of 1948, was
no longer a British preserve. The influx of American philosophers
and other scholars after this year created curricular expansion in
many colleges and universities. Where once only whispers of the
Bhagavadgītā and the Upaniṣads had drifted out of the older
Eastern schools and liberal theological seminaries, now colleges
and universities in New Mexico, Minnesota, Illinois and South
Dakota offered courses in Indian philosophy and religion. A large
band of American philosophers appeared who believed students
and the public should know the fundamentals of Hinduism and
Buddhism.

[129] *Ibid.,* pp. 24–25.
[130] *Ibid.,* p. 86.

Chapter X

DEVELOPMENTS IN THE DIFFUSION OF INDIAN THOUGHT SINCE THE KOREAN WAR

A MONG American philosophers who began serious consideration of Indian thought in the 1950's after termination of the American-Korean War is George B. Burch (1902–   ) who took his B.A. at Harvard and his Ph.D. at the University of Geneva. After studying in France he became an assistant professor at Harvard, then went to Idaho College, and is now a professor emeritus of philosophy at Tufts University. Burch himself claims to have become interested in Indian philosophy at the time of his sabbatical leave taken in India in 1953–54, but it appears from a statement of Mrs. James H. Woods that Burch and his wife were part of a group around Boston meeting weekly to read Indian philosophy which began before the Second World War. He returned to India in 1961 when he taught at Viśva-Bhārati University in Bengal.

Burch's account of contemporary Indian philosophers, including K. C. Bhattacharyya, Kalidas Bhattacharyya, T. R. V. Murti, P. C. Chaudhury, G. R. Malkani, R. Das, D. M. Datta, R. D. Ranade, and others is one of the best that we have in English. As has been usual in India, it is not the Indians alone who have given historically valuable accounts of their philosophies, but foreigners, beginning with the Greeks and Chinese, then the French, Germans, British, Russian, Japanese, and today the Americans. Burch is in several ways an exemplary American to write a monograph on contemporary classical Indian philosophy. He is not hardened against Indian transcendentalism or what many American philosophers would consider the irrationality, illogicality, and seemingly fantastic views of the Vedānta thinkers who have flourished since around the turn of the century. He has not dealt with the younger thinkers who have been influenced by European or Anglo-American trends such as pragmatism, existentialism, Marxism, positivism, phenomenology, and analysis.

Burch does a fine and sympathetic sketch of the philosophy of perhaps India's greatest traditional philosopher of the twentieth century: K. C. Bhattacharyya (1875–1949). Bhattacharyya wrote *Studies in Vedantism* (1901), *The Subject as Freedom* (1929), and two unpublished works: *Philosophy of Kant,* and *Philosophy of Samkhya and Yoga.* He developed his philosophy in three phases according to Burch: (1) subjectivist, completely in the Vedānta tradition, (2) objectivist, culminating in the doctrines of alternative forms of the absolute, which Burch considers his most original contribution, and (3) the third phase which resulted in the generalization of the concept of alternatives into a logic of alternation.[1] This third phase is being elaborated by K. C.'s son Kalidas whose appearance at the Fourth East-West Philosophers' Conference in 1964 was one of the highlights of the meetings. Of Kalidas, Burch wrote,

> His oral style is like that of an inspired prophet, the inspiration being his recollection of his conversation with his father.[2]

Whether he will prove to be as able as Burch contends is still a matter of some conjecture. One is not certain that he will expand the family philosophical capital. The philosopher son of a philosopher is often handicapped by the sheer mountain of half-digested opinion with which he is brought up.

Burch's account of T. R. V. Murti, a Vedāntist of mercurial charm, begins with the observation that for Murti philosophy arises from the desire to escape suffering, and not from wonder.[3] Presumably the "recognition that something is wrong in the

---

[1] George Burch: Contemporary Vedanta philosophy I. *Rev Metaph,* IX, 1956, pp. 487–495.

[2] *Ibid.,* p. 498. No irony is intended here.

[3] Burch: Contemporary Vedanta philosophy II. *Rev Metaph,* IX, 4, 1956, p. 664.

world leads to reflection." [4] From the awareness that something is wrong, we are led by reflection, says Murti, to antinomies. These in turn lead to the apprehension of higher reality. "For this faith in revelation is necessary." [5] Reason cannot of itself prove sufficient to gaining the highest knowledge. The three steps to completion are faith, understanding, and vision.[6]

Burch next examines the philosophy of Pravas Jivan Chaudhury (1916–1965). After teaching physics at Shillong, Assam for two years, he studied aesthetics for two years. In 1953 he was appointed professor of philosophy and department head at Presidency College in Calcutta, a position once held by S. Dasgupta, India's greatest historian of philosophy. His outlook, heavily influenced by physical science, has led to his publication of such works as *The Philosophy of Science* (1955) which more properly should have been called the *Philosophy of Physics*. Chaudhury views philosophy as the explanation of planes of reality. Its two main problems are how to rise to a higher plane and how it is that we fall to a lower plane. We reach the highest plane, the seventh, by insight into reality after a critical analysis of the subject-object relation.[7]

Next Burch examines the views of Ghanshamdas Rattanmal Malkani (1892–   ) who has restated the Sanskrit Vedānta into English in terms of an understanding of the history of Western philosophy. But,

> He carries out the implications of Advaita with a ruthless rationality which surpasses in rigor not only the doctrines of other contemporary Vedantists but even, so far as I know, those of any former ones.[8]

Since 1926 the editor of the *Philosophical Quarterly*, Malkani is also the permanent director of the Indian Institute of Philosophy at Amalner. It contains a liberal arts college, a modern hospital and a temple endowed by S. P. Seth, proprietor of the Pratap

---

[4] A statement strangely reminiscent of Feuerbach.

[5] Burch, Contemporary Vedanta philosophy II, p. 664.

[6] *Ibid.*

[7] *Ibid.,* pp. 678–79.

[8] Burch, Contemporary Vedanta Philosophy, continued, *Rev Metaph,* X, 1, 1956, p. 122.

Cotton Mills. Malkani wrote *Problem of Nothing* (1918), which title has a Nishida-like quality about it.[9] For Malkani the truth is found by means of absolute rationality. Faith gives us psychological truth, but only reason gives us logical truth. "Thinking (*manana*) as understood in Vedānta is the rational analysis of experience," [10] according to him. Ultimately we know that there is no world at all, only the reality of Brahman, he concludes on the basis of his ruthless rationality.

Rasvihary Das (1894–   ) is an agnostic who holds all religion to be superstition, and believes philosophy to be the highest activity. "Love is an ultimate ideal" for Das, "coordinate with the ultimate ideals truth and freedom, these three corresponding with the rational functions of feeling, knowing, and willing respectively." [11]

Dhurendra Mohan Datta (1898–   ) with Ramchandra Dattatraya Ranade (1886–1966) composed an outstanding pair of philosophers who have had a great spiritual as well as intellectual affect on India, according to Burch. Datta, for twenty-five years professor of philosophy at Patna University, lectured at the Universities of Hawaii, Minnesota and Wisconsin in the early 1950's, and was much admired by American students who found him witty, kindly, and an able dialectician. He combines humanity with gentleness and is the only eminent Indian philosopher to have written a major survey of modern Western philosophy, in itself a remarkable achievement for a man who appears in the major tradition of freedom-from-Western-influence. Datta's own philosophy is body-soul-ism (*dehātmavāda*).[12] "This term he points out, is used by materialists to mean that soul is only body, but by him to mean that body is only soul." [13] The path of spiritual progress is the way of extraversion by expanding our consciousness, according to Datta. When we expand it in quantity we are scientists; in quality we are philosophers. If we expand it in power we become tyrants. Only those who expand it in love are

[9] Japan's leading modern idealistic philosopher (1875–1945).

[10] Burch, "Contemporary Vedanta Philosophy II," p. 129.

[11] Burch, "Contemporary Vedanta Philosophy, continued," p. 145.

[12] *Ibid.*, p. 147.

[13] *Ibid.*

the persons of good intentions. Yet we should expand in all four ways. Final expansion is accomplished by seeing all things in their real aspects, Datta believes. As we love and control them we identify ourselves with them.[14]

Ranade gave up his professorship of philosophy to succeed his guru, Amburao, to live in an ashram. He returned to academic life to serve again as professor of philosophy and dean at the University of Allahabad, finally serving as vice-chancellor. Since 1947, when he retired, he has returned to the ashram. Ranade believed speculative philosophy to be of little value. Instead he sought beatificism or self-realization. It is attained through a guru, morality, the company of good people, and meditation. He instructed his disciples according to the level of their presumed comprehension and in addition required them to meditate for three hours each day.

Burch, besides giving us a rare insight into contemporary Vedānta philosophers of the older generation, has also written a detailed account of the "Seven-Valued Logic in Jain Philosophy," [15] which includes the twelve types of theory or -ism (*naya*). Although we shall not reproduce them here, we may say that the exposition is notable for its fairness and clarity.

Another philosopher who has contributed much to the understanding of Indian thought is a Pole who lived in the United States in the role of a United Nations mediator, Arnold Kunst, born in 1903. He received his M.A. at the University of Lvov and his Ph.D. at the University of Warsaw in Indian philosophy. He has taught Oriental philosophy at the University of Lvov and was lecturer in Buddhism and Indian philosophy at the University of London before he settled in the United States as Deputy Director of the Department of Trusteeship and Information of Non-Self-Governing Territories at the United Nations from 1947 to 1963, at which time he returned to teach at the University of London in the School of Oriental Studies.

As a scholar steeped in the literature of India, Kunst roams the field not only of philosophy, but literature as well. In his "The

[14] Burch, Contemporary Vedanta Philosophy, continued, p. 149.
[15] *Intl Philos Quar,* IV, 1, 1964.

Concept of the Principle of Excluded Middle" [16] he develops a theme Clarence Hamilton studied earlier and sets a foundation by quoting the following passage from the *Lankavatara Sūtra:*

> Moreover, Mahatma [you cannot maintain] that Maya [means that things] are irreal (nasti). Since everything has the appearance of coherent [reality] everything becomes Maya-like.[17]

In addition, Kunst quotes from Nāgārjuna, to the effect that:

> Absolute reality cannot be explained unless [the explanation] is based on phenomenal truth; *nirvaṇa* cannot be obtained without realization of absolute reality.[18]

It follows by implication from the content and meaning of these citations that the Buddhist hypothesis of interdependence of two realities (*satya*) does not lend itself, Kunst believes, to the application of the principle of excluded middle. This relativity, he points out, is also found in the Jaina notion of *syādvāda.*

The three types of approach recorded by the expressions *syād asty eva, syān nasty eva, syād asti nāsti ca* remove the logical difficulty by asserting that none of the expressions can be used simultaneously with the other, but they have to be applied in sequence.[19] Hence existence and nonexistence are both valid predicates of one and the same subject. Of phenomena one may assert:

1) neither unity or other than unity;
2) neither both nor not both;
3) neither being nor nonbeing;
4) neither permanence nor nonpermanence.

The first problem in Buddhism is that contradictoriness is not gauged on the basis of objective truth. If this were not sufficient then the principle may be invoked that reality when separated into isolated systems as in formal logic isolates reality from the mind.[20] Kunst maintains that:

[16] *Rocznik Orientalistyczny* Tom XXI, 1957.
[17] *Ibid.,* p. 144.
[18] *Ibid.*
[19] *Ibid.*
[20] The proximity of this view to that of Hegel deserves attention.

Ontological or metaphysical concepts make such a law [excluded middle] heterogeneous even within the framework of a single philosophical school . . . and rules of disputation make it baseless for the purpose of logical analysis.[21]

It may be said for Kunst that he has opened a new window facing the problem of universal logic or comparative logic, a yet unrecognized infant of international study and travel.

Joseph Campbell (1904–   ), a scholar of mythology in the United States, studied at Columbia University, the University of Paris, and the University of Munich. He has been a professor of comparative literature at Sarah Lawrence College since 1934. He says in a letter that "In 1923, I met Jiddu Krishnamurti on a liner sailing to Europe, and so discovered Hinduism and Buddhism [and began] Sanskrit studies with Professor Hans Oertel, at the University of Munich." [22] His interest in comparative mythology led to his intensive study of Indian civilization. As a result of a student's introduction, Campbell met Swami Nikhilananda in 1938, following which he helped the Swami edit his translations of *The Gospel of Sri Ramakrishna, The Bhagavad Gita* and the Upaniṣads.

Campbell met Heinrich Zimmer in 1940. When Zimmer died in 1943, his widow asked Campbell to publish his lecture notes to which work Campbell devoted twelve years, producing *Myths and Symbols* (1946), *The King and the Corpse* (1948) and *The Art of Indian Asia* (1954). When the last of these was finished, Campbell went to India, spending six months there and six months in Japan.

As a result of his German training, Campbell became especially interested in the relationship of Indian philosophy and German romantic thought and by extension, the writings of Jung and Freud.

As early as 1927 the writings of James Joyce and Thomas Mann took hold of me; in 1928 Dilthey and Eduard Spranger; in 1934 Spengler, Goethe, and Schopenhauer, Nietzsche, and sometime later, Ortega Y.

---

[21] *Rocznik Orientalistyczny* Tom XXI, 1957, p. 147.

[22] *Letter* to the author, New York City (January 5, 1965). Oertel later briefly taught Sanskrit at Yale.

Gasset. For a time (ca. 1937–1954) Ananda K. Coomaraswamy meant a great deal to me, but this interest faded after my own visit to India.[23]

As an American writer on comparative mythology, Campbell has published works on the Navaho, James Joyce, edited the *Arabian Nights,* the *Gods of Haiti, Christian Myth and Ritual,* and edited the Bollingen Series entitled *Papers from the Eranos Yearbooks* (1953–64). He also began work on the *Masks of God* upon his return from Asia in 1955, of which the following volumes have appeared: *Primitive Mythology* (1959), *Oriental Mythology* (1962) and *Creative Mythology* in preparation. Several of his papers dealing with India include "Oriental Philosophy and Occidental Psychoanalysis" (1958), "Renewal Myths and Rites of the Primitive Hunters and Planters" (1960), "Primitive Man as Metaphysician" (1960), and "Orient and Occident: Id and Ego" (1964).

Campbell holds that the key to the difference of the Indian [Asian] world to that of the Occident is that between "ultimate extinction of the personality in *nirvana* with the occidental idea of one life and the value for all time of the unique individual." [24] The oriental way of *neti neti* according to Campbell, has been adopted by Karl Jung, James Joyce, and Thomas Mann. Whereas India first influenced the West, it was to China and Japan that the contemporary West looked, particularly to the Tao as in Jung. The reason for this, according to Campbell, is the tendency in Indian thought to try to break out of the context of the universe, whereas the occident insists on "the responsibility of the individual to the field of life-in-being." [25] Campbell is of course talking about only one side of the Indian; the other side being naturalist, realist, and materialist in the tradition of Virocana, Lokāyata, the Mīmāmṣikas, Caitanya, Nehru, M. N. Roy, D. D. Kosambi, and Debiprasad Chattopadhyaya who take as their context life-in-being also.

In *The Hero with a Thousand Faces* (1949) [26] Campbell dis-

[23] *Ibid.*

[24] Campbell: Oriental Philosophy and Occidental Psychoanalysis. *Proceedings of the IXth International Congress for the History of Religion.* Tokyo, 1960, p. 494.

[25] *Ibid.,* p. 495.

[26] New York, Pantheon, 1953.

cusses facets of Buddhistic, Hindu, and Jain mythology of the greatest interest to Westerners. According to the Jains there was a time when all man's needs were supplied by ten wish-fulfilling trees (*kalpa vriksha*), but even before this happy time there was an even happier one. When people died in the earlier days they "passed directly to the world of the gods, without ever having heard of religion." [27] There are many such charming and wise myths reconstructed by Campbell. The time spent reading these will more than compensate for losing a few discussions of later glossosophers who often have lost the sense of myth and magic without bringing any new comparable experience or insight. One of the outstanding characteristics of myths is their obvious lack of both religiosity and philosophical weed-pulling, that is to say, the attacks on the obvious errors of one's opponents, both living and dead.

Another mythologist, and in addition a spiritual advisor, is Christopher Isherwood who, born in England in 1904, became an American citizen in 1946. Educated at Corpus Christi, Cambridge, and the University of London, he has taught as a private teacher of English in Berlin, and lectured on literature at Los Angeles State College, and the University of California at Santa Barbara. He is editor of *Vedanta and the West,* the *Bhagavad-Gita* (with Swami Prabhavanand) *The Crest-Jewel of Discriminations* (with *ibid.*), *Vedanta for the Western World* (1945), and *Ramakrishna and His Disciples* (1965).

Although early primarily a playwright and novelist, Isherwood has been influential in alerting the American public to the Vedānta message. In this he has doubtless as much or more popular influence in the United States than any academic philosopher. A gifted writer, he has outlined the popular philosophy of Vedānta in his "Introduction" to *Vedanta for the Western World.*[28] An example of his forthright style is as follows:

> Judge every thought and every action from this standpoint [Vedānta]. Does it make me freer, less egotistic, more aware of the Reality . . . ? You'll find, in practice, that certain thoughts and actions

---

[27] *Ibid.,* pp. 262–263.
[28] New York, Viking, 1962.

obstruct your progress. Give them up. Other thoughts and actions will assist your progress. Cultivate them.

"Tell me some."

"Chastity, truthfulness, charity towards others."

"Chastity? I'm to give up sex?"

"You'll find you have to, sooner or later."

"Why? It's not wrong."

"I never said it was. But what does it lead to? Attachment to this world of appearance." [29]

Isherwood's best known companions in the Vedanta Society of Southern California were Gerald Heard and Aldous Huxley, the only eminent member of that well-known family to desert science for mysticism. Some of Huxley's essays in *Vedanta for the West* became portions of his *Grey Eminence* and *Time must have a Stop*. Hector Hawton, a saint of the rationalist movement, has said of Huxley's Indianism that:

> Aldous Huxley may cherish the delusion that in industrially backward India men are more spiritual than in Europe and America, but it is doubtful if the real situation can best be judged from the hills of Hollywood. The filth and misery of the Indian masses, under-nourished, malaria-ridden, enslaved to money-lenders, will not be relieved by a return to the spinning-wheel; and it is sheer fantasy to suppose that any but a tiny elite escape this degradation by meditating on the Upanishads.[30]

Heard, another Englishman (b. 1889), was an honors history graduate of the University of Cambridge, has lectured at Oxford, in London, at the New School for Social Research, Rockford College, and Oberlin College. He is the author of such works as *The Third Morality* (1937), *The Eternal Gospel* (1946) and *Is God in History?* (1949).[31]

Isherwood has recently written two books that tackle the problem of making Vedānta meaningful to the West. The first is *An Approach to Vedanta* (1963)[32] and the second *Ramakrishna and*

[29] Isherwood, *Vedanta for the Western World*, p. 6.

[30] Hector Hawton: *The Feast of Unreason*. London, Watts, 1952, pp. 15–16.

[31] For a good account of Heard and Huxley in American Vedantism see Stephen B. L. Penrose, Jr. and Oliver J. Caldwell: Ties that Bind. In Christy (Ed.): *The Asian Legacy and American Life*.

[32] Hollywood, Vedanta Press.

His Disciples (1965).[33] The first book is an autobiographical account of Isherwood's shift from a leftish liberalism to pacifism and his conversion by Gerald Heard and Swami Prabhavananda (who finds bliss within the source of all creation). During World War II Isherwood went to Pennsylvania to work with the Friends who among Christian sects were the most like Vedāntists according to him.[34] The latter half of the same book is his interpretation of the Gītā. Since *An Approach to Vedanta* appeared, he has edited *Vedanta for Modern Man* in 1951.[35]

In a recent answer to the question "Is America a dying country?" Isherwood gave a view of India shared by a number of people who have visited there, although they have attempted to keep it from the general public. He said:

> I think America is in a very bad way. We've simply got to stop the breeding; we've got to control the population. All our evils come from that. There are more people, so we've got to put this hideous building, that dreadful place, this causeway, that freeway . . . that everything! You go to India and you see what America is going to be like soon—a nightmare.[36]

Presumably even the knowledge of Vedānta cannot stop this manifestation of sexual *māyā*, but we rejoice in Isherwood's concern now that the aesthetic *māyā* of California is being replaced by unaesthetic *māyā*.

Archie J. Bahm, born in 1907, after attending Taylor University and Albion College took his doctorate in philosophy at the University of Michigan. He has taught at Texas Technological College, the University of Denver, the University of New Mexico and abroad at the University of Rangoon. His interest in Indian philosophy developed partially as a reaction to Christian protestant fundamentalism. Bahm introduced courses in Asian philosophy and religion at the University of Denver and the University

[33] London, Methuen. Reviewed by Francis Hope in *New Statesman,* April 16, 1965.

[34] Isherwood, *An Approach to Vedanta.* London, Methuen, 1963, p. 46.

[35] New York, Harper. Other contributors to this volume include Gerald Heard; J. B. Pratt; Alan Watts, the American Apostle to Zen; Aldous Huxley, and John van Druten.

[36] *Fact,* II, 5, 1965, p. 52.

of New Mexico. After his stay in Burma, he wrote *Philosophy of the Buddha* (1958), *Types of Intuition* (1961), and *Yoga: Union with the Ultimate* (1961). As a Fulbright research professor at Banaras Hindu University (1962–63) Bahm began working on his *Bhagavad Gita: The Wisdom of Krishna,* not yet published. Bahm is the first American philosopher to publish a newsletter or journal solely devoted to Asian philosophy, but after a year's publication (1950–51) the *Oriental Philosophy Newsletter* merged with the newly-begun *Philosophy East and West* under the editorship of Charles A. Moore.

Bahm's first article on Indian philosophy appeared under the title "Oriental Philosophy" (1950).[37] Since that time he has published another dozen articles, the titles of which include "Jaina Logic and World Peace,"[38] "Jainism and Organicism,"[39] "Buddhist Aesthetics"[40] and the intriguing-sounding "Does Seven-Fold Predication Equal Four-Cornered Negation Reversed?"[41] Bahm points out in his essay on Buddhist aesthetics how such aesthetics differs from that of the European-American tradition. For the Westerner, "beauty is intrinsic value which appears as if embodied in an object,"[42] but for the Buddhist this is not the case. Instead,

> The goal of life, for Buddhists, is aesthetic. It is the enjoyment of life as intrinsic value. How can this be done? By surrounding oneself with art objects? No. At least this is not the most direct way.[43]

Instead one may dispense with objects and achieve *nirvāṇa,* man's aesthetic goal under Buddhism. Bahm quotes from the *Dialogues of the Buddha* to demonstrate this: "Whenever one attains to the stage of deliverance entitled the Beautiful, one is then aware 'Tis lovely.' "[44] Furthermore, what follows from this is, it seems to be, that "line, shape, color, theme and variations, vividness,

[37] Archie Bahm: Oriental philosophy. *Rev Metaph,* IV, 2, 1959.
[38] In *Voice Ahinsa,* I, 1, 1951.
[39] *Ibid.,* V. 8 (August 1955).
[40] In *J Aesth Art Crit,* XVI, 2, 1957.
[41] In *Philos East West,* XII, 3–4 1957.
[42] Bahm: Buddhist aesthetics. *J Aesth Art Crit,* XVI, 2, 1957, p. 250.
[43] *Op. cit.*
[44] Part III quoted in *ibid.,* p. 251.

interestingness, expressiveness, or principles of harmony" [45] may or may not be present in the experience of Buddhist beauty. Bahm holds that:

> They are instruments made to serve those who think of religion as magical rather than as aesthetics . . . if the purpose of magic is to try to force things to be different from the way they are, then anyone who seeks to use magic thereby admits that he is not completely willing to accept things as they are. [Yet] Nirvana is enjoyment of complete willingness to have things as they are, without magic and without pagodas, or, more precisely, with or without magic and with or without pagodas. The Buddhist aesthetician has no objection to magic or pagodas because he has no objection to anything. To object is to be unwilling to accept things as they are, and Nirvana is completely without willingness. [46]

Like Ethel Kitch, Grace Edith Cairns (1907–   ) is associated with Oberlin College and the University of Chicago where she took her doctorate. After receiving her B.A. from Goucher College she took her M.A. at the Oberlin Theological Seminary. She has taught at Rollins College and Florida State University where she is now a professor. She has recently studied Sanskrit at the University of Pennsylvania and the University of Chicago as well as in Banaras. At Banaras Hindu University she was a faculty fellow of the American Institute of Indian Studies.

Cairns has written *Philosophies of History* (1962) and chapters on Hinduism, Jainism, and Sikhism in a book on world religions to appear soon. Her "Unity of Ethical Values in Three Significant Twentieth Century Philosophies of East and West" appeared as a chapter in the Radhakrishnan Souvenir Volume published by *Darshana International* (1964). Besides these she has written "The Intuitive Element in Metaphysics," [47] "The Philosophy and Psychology of the Oriental Mandala," [48] and "The New Being," [49] which is a comparison of Sri Aurobindo, Paul Tillich, and Teilhard de Chardin.

---

[45] *Ibid.,* p. 251.
[46] *Ibid.,* p. 252.
[47] *Philos East West,* IV, 1, 1954.
[48] *Philos East West,* XI, 4, 1964.
[49] *Main Currents Mod Thought,* 19, 4, 1963.

Cairns' *Philosophies of History* (Meeting of East and West in Cycle-Pattern Theories of History) [50] is a monumental work which refers constantly to the Indian experience and contains seventy-five pages directly related to Indian philosophy and mythology. Her third chapter, "Development of the Cyclical View in India: Hinduism," opens with a discussion of the cyclical symbolism of the cosmic dance of Śiva. Discussed are the *kalpa* and the four *yugas*, representing the vast ages of change that are believed to occur in the enormous cyclic order. She says that:

> The present is the Kali yuga, the most corrupt of the four ages. When this epoch ends, a Mahayuga of 12,000 divine years will be completed. [51]

In terms of anthropological time this takes us back 14,000 years so that many *mahayugas* could have been predicated of the time of Pekin man, at 386,000 years. This gives a clue to the difference between Indian and Chinese conceptions of the relation of number to human existence.

In treating of the "Development of the Cyclical View in India: Buddhism," Cairns adopts the account of Buddhaghoṣa's *Visuddhimagga* which divides world time in (1) a period of destruction, (2) a period of the continuation of destruction, (3) a period of renovation, and (4) continuation after renovation. A world cycle perishes by water. What is of interest today, according to Cairns, is that:

> Buddhism has anticipated contemporary Western views in scientific astronomy, *viz.*, such theories as the immensity of the space-time continuum, of the enormous number of galaxies in the continuum, and the similarity in the evolution-dissolution pattern of the universe (spiral nebulae) within each galaxy. [52]

A further account of Jain views and those of the *mandala* (magic circle) carry on the account of later cyclic views which conclude with accounts of Sāṁkhya and Advaita. Her general tendency is not dissimilar to the approach of Joseph Campbell with perhaps more Coomaraswamy in evidence than Campbell would approve.

[50] Grace Cairns: *Philosophies of History*. New York, Citadel, 1962.

[51] *Ibid.*, p. 47.

[52] *Ibid.*, p. 68.

The account of Indian cyclic hypotheses represents a needed broadening of the more commonly-known Western cyclical views as ancient as Pythagoreianism.

Robert Willard Browning, who has recently shown increasing interest in Indian philosophy, was born in 1911. He took his B.A. at the College of the Pacific, his A.M. at the University of California at Berkeley and his Ph.D. at Northwestern University. Teaching first at the University of North Carolina, he soon went to Syracuse University and since 1947 has been a professor of philosophy at Northwestern University. He attended the Second and Fourth East-West Philosophers' Conference and also studied philosophy in India.

Browning's major contribution to Indian philosophical studies is his one hundred-page chapter in the Schilpp Radhakrishnan volume [53] entitled "Reason and Types of Intuition in Radhakrishnan's Philosophy." As Radhakrishnan believes in cognitive intuition it might be useful to notice, says Browning, the use of intuition in various contexts such as processes, products, faculties, capacities or sources that cannot be known in other ways. It may refer to fuller realization of what may be already abstractly known in symbols, dawning in a discoverer, a knowledge of individual things in concreteness, unitive knowledge of the One Real dynamism of thinking. Or it may refer to spontaneous dynamism, an immanent part of discursive thought, incorrigible or infallible thinking, nondiscursive, nonconceptual, rational, part of fundamental nature in the self, or a response of one's whole being.[54] All of these different uses, according to Browning are not only found in Radhakrishnan's writing, but are clear in their separate contexts. There are, Browning says, the following major categories of intuition: sensory, rational, "descrying of complex structures of fact and possible fact," [55] valuational, and integral.

Browning questions the appropriateness of using "intuition' to signify anything cognitive. He also questions Radhakrishnan's view that some intuitions are infallible, while others are not. His final assessment is given as follows:

[53] Schilpp (Ed.): *The Philosophy of Sarvepalli Radhakrishnan.*
[54] *Ibid.,* pp. 177–178.
[55] *Ibid.,* p. 181.

We admire those souls who can rise to relatively universal points of view, and we admire some of the fruits of lives which claim the radically deeper experience of the whole . . . [yet] the hypothesis is always insinuating itself that these may be more the products of relatively local conditions, psychical and cultural, than of the total cosmic, or supra-cosmic object.[56]

In the last analysis the empirical naturalist, according to Browning, is willing to entertain the recorded account of mystical experience but is scarcely willing to go further than William Savery who said that "mysticism always remains a *possibility*" [emphasis added].[57]

Troy Organ was born in 1912. After receiving his Ph.D. from the State University of Iowa and after taking a B.D. from McCormick Theological Seminary, he began teaching at Parsons College where he also served as an assistant dean. He taught at the University of Akron and Chatham College and is at present professor of philosophy at Ohio University. Dissatisfied in his middle years with the metaphysics of Western philosophy, Organ studied in India in 1958 as a Fulbright professor and went to Viśva-Bhārati University in India in 1965–66.

During his stay at Śantineketan in Bengal, Organ began working on *The Self in Indian Philosophy*.[58] His survey covers major views from the Rig Veda to Aurobindo Ghose (1872–1949). Looking with alarm at the preoccupation with the external world in the United States, Organ believes that it is possible that Americans can learn something important from the Indian view of the self. If we wish to be rid of anxieties having their roots in the "concentration on externalities" it would be well to perhaps follow the example of Indians who have made a specialization of looking inward.[59] The genius of India may well lie in this direction, and we Americans, Organ believes, can learn from this genius.

[56] *Ibid.*, p. 276.
[57] *The Philosophy of Sarvepalli Radhakrishnan*, quoted by Browning, p. 259n. "It is possible," Savery held, that "in an ideal future, when all capitalists and dictators have perished, there will always remain a small minority of intelligent mystics."
[58] The Hague, Mouton, 1964.
[59] *Ibid.*, pp. 19–20.

Originally was the Self from which arose the gods, the world, and men.[60] "To identify this self," says Organ, "and to relate man to it is the whole of the philosophical enterprise of India, and perhaps man's most significant quest." [61]

Organ points out an interesting fact about the understanding of the self in India. The self for Indians which is now in tranquillity or in anguish may not be the self that originally opted for the decision that led to its present state since they believe in *karma* and transmigration. Organ has lost considerable faith in the "Western," or better, "scientific," method of explaining the self. He does point out that certain Westerners also tried to explain the self by concentration on the inward through introspective psychology.

Indians have produced ingenious methods of analyzing the self. They have come up with such divisions as lower self and higher self, second self and third self, the self that is I and the self that is not-I, the *māyā* self and the Brāhman self, the self with a little "s" and the Self with a big "S." Movement towards unity could only be consummated in giving up the external world and concentrating on the inward Self. Sāṁkhya-Yoga has a transcendent or true self; the unconscious self is posited by Nyāya-Vaiśe-śika; Sāṁkara held the self to be an unchanging substratum; which cannot be identified with the body, while in Viśiṣṭādvaita there were three selves: (1) those always free, (2) those bound to bodies, and (3) those released through discipline.[62] By the twentieth century many Indian philosophers had read about Western notions of the self. In Sri Aurobindo the self in conceived as the "All-Person of whom all conscious beings are the selves and the personalities." [63] But man cannot find his real self nor the real Self in the world. This self of man "is thus identified with the limitations and exclusions of the ego." [64] Yet truly, for Aurobindo "In our depths we ourselves are that One." [65] There

[60] *Ibid.*, p. 32.
[61] *Ibid.*, p. 32.
[62] *Ibid.*, pp. 127–128.
[63] Organ quoting Sri Aurobindo, *ibid.*, p. 146.
[64] Organ quoting Sri Aurobindo, *The Self in Indian Philosophy*, p. 158. John A. Hutchinson (1912–   ) studied Indian philosophy and religion at Poona in 1966–67 where he prepared the Indian material for his book *Paths of Faith* (1969) .
[65] *Ibid.*, p. 159.

Organ leaves Aurobindo and us. What we are to learn from all these views of the self is up to our own self.

The role of Kenneth William Morgan (1908–   ) has been fruitful in exposing American philosophers and religionists to the recent literature of Indian religion. Of great worth has been his painstaking attempt to vivify this with collections of slides that are valuable aids for Western students' understanding of Hinduism, Buddhism and Islam.

Morgan took his B.A. at Ohio Wesleyan University and his S.T.B. at Harvard University. His administrative services as director of the Council of Religious Education, his work in the Ford, Danforth, and Hazen Foundations, in addition to his teaching as professor of religion at Colgate University, have kept him a constant instigator of investigation into Hinduism and Buddhism. He has edited *The Religion of the Hindus* (1953), statements by contemporary religious leaders in India of their religious views and has written *The Path of the Buddha* (1956).

Born in British Columbia in 1914, but now an American citizen, Richard Abbott Gard is a scholar of Buddhism who has long been acquainted with Southeast Asia and Japan. For example, he has lectured in more than seven Japanese universities on such topics as Theravāda Buddhism. In this connection, he has received the Thai Buddhist Theravāda Award in Bangkok and the Burmese Buddhist Theravāda Award in Rangoon, and has been the United States vice president of the World Fellowship of Buddhists since 1961.

Gard himself believes that the greatest influences upon him have been European political philosophy and Chinese philosophy, especially Buddhist. He has been involved in Japan and Southeast Asia from 1939 and 1954 respectively doing research, teaching, advising and assisting Buddhist institutions with and sometimes through The Asia Foundation and the United States Government. At the present writing Gard is a Foreign Service reserve officer assigned to the Department of State and stationed at the American Consulate General in Hong Kong. His travels take him to Japan, Ceylon, Nepal, and other non-Communist countries.

After working in the department of political science at the University of Washington, he took his M.A. at the University of

Hawaii Oriental Institute in Taoist studies. He began Buddhist studies with Johannes Rahder and Junjirō Takakusu, studying with the latter until 1940, when Gard returned to Seattle. He then moved to the University of Pennsylvania to work under W. Norman Brown, Derk Bodde and Fung Yu-lan for two years. He completed his Ph.D. at Claremont Graduate School in 1951 where he studied with Ernest Richard Hughes (Formerly professor of Chinese at Oxford University) and Ch'en Shou-yi, Ensho Ashikaga, and Daisetz Teitarō Suzuki. After World War II, Gard studied at Kyokoku and Otani Buddhist universities and has since lectured at Kyoto, Tokyo, Seoul, Rangoon, and Bangkok. He moved to Hong Kong after four years at Yale University. A contributor to many collections of work on Asian philosophy, some of his monographs include: *A Comparative Study of Some Japanese and Wagnerian Aesthetic Ideals* (South Pasadena, Perkins, 1949), *Buddhist Influences on the Political Thought and Institutions of India and Japan* (Claremont, Oriental Society 1949), and *Buddhist Political Thought* (Bankok; Mahamakuta University, 1956). His influence may well be greater outside than inside the United States.

Daniel H. H. Ingalls was born in 1916, and began the study of Sanskrit as a junior in college "purely out of curiosity." Later, after completing a major in classics, Ingalls decided to go into a field where "the ashes had not been raked over." As a Harvard Junior Fellow he was sent by the Society of Fellows to India. There he came alive under the splendid instruction of Sri Kālipada Tarkācārya, then chief Pandit in logic at the Sanskrit Research Institute at Calcutta. Although Ingalls had already studied Sanskrit for four years, the impact of this poet-logician on him was inflammatory.

Ingall's main contribution to Philosophy is his *Materials for the Study of Navya-Nyāya Logic*,[66] the first American monograph devoted exclusively to Indian logic, the outcome of his fruitful association with Tarkāchārya. In his introduction Ingalls says:

> A great part of Indian philosophy since the thirteenth century is unintelligible without it. . . . The metaphysical basis of Navya-Nyāya is thoroughly realistic, yet its logic is a formal logic showing an unusual

[66] Cambridge, Harvard, 1951; Harvard Oriental Series, vol. 40.

power of abstraction. Its realism may be seen in its dissatisfaction with the mere analysis of words. The Naiyāyika always tries to push further back, to explain the relation of the things themselves. Thus his logic deals very little with propositions; it deals rather with 'knowledge,' which when valid is said to represent facts as they actually are.[67]

Furthermore, Ingalls maintains,

There are a number of points where Navya-Nyāya appears definitely superior to Aristotelian logic. Among these are its understanding of conjunction, alternation, and their negates, and of the class corollary of De Morgan's law. Navya-Nyāya never confuses the attributes of a class with the attributes of its members. In its concept of number it seems to anticipate mathematical logic by several centuries.[68]

Of Ingalls' claim that Aristotle was confused between predicating of a class and predicating of a member of a class, William Parry says that "Aristotle never held that mortality is predicated of the class of all men:—in fact, he was quite clear that it applied to men individually." [69]

Among the logicians whose work is explicated by Ingalls are Gaṅgeśopadhyaya (13th century), Jayadeva Pakṣadhara (ca. 1425 ca. 1500), Raghunātha Śiromaṇi (ca. 1475 ca. 1550), of whom Ingalls says, "if his works were known outside India [he] would be generally recognized as a great logician." [70]

Not only does Ingalls treat of what we in the West generally call logic, but also of epistemology reminding us that logic has an ontological base when it is applied to the world. In this sense, Ingalls' work is more like that of W. H. Johnson than like that of contemporary Anglo-American symbolic logicians. Ingalls examines types of knowledge as well as the inferential process. The

---

[67] Ingalls, *ibid.*, p. 1.

[68] *Ibid.*, p. 2. It has been noted by the logician William Parry in an unpublished paper entitled "Comments on Ingalls" that what Ingalls says about Aristotelian logic holds only for Aristotle himself. "The Stoic-Megaric logicians (who were not Aristotelians) but Theophrastus and some medievals (who were) has a better understanding of propositional logic than this Indian logician seems to have had."

[69] Parry, *ibid.*, p. 1. Parry thinks that Ingalls may here have been led astray by Russell's "ignorant critique of Aristotle's alleged doctrine."

[70] Ingalls, *ibid.*, p. 2. Parry maintains that this is difficult to see from the twenty lines of Ragunātha that Ingalls has included in his text.

stock example of the five-membered syllogism of Old Nyāya is given as:

1) Theory (*pratijñā*) : [The] mountain possess fire.

2) Cause (*hetu*) : because of smoke.

3) Example (*udāharaṇa*) : Where [there is] smoke there [is] fire, as in a kitchen.

4) Application (*upanaya*) : This [mountain is] similar [*i.e.,* possesses smoke].

5) Conclusion (*nigamana*) : Therefore [it is] similar [*i.e.,* possesses fire].[71]

Every entity in the universe is assigned one of the following seven categories according to Ingalls:

1) substance, such as earth, water, wind, fire, time, and soul;

2) quality, such as color, form, taste, scent, pleasure, pain and knowledge;

3) action;

4) generic character—the *jāti* of horse is horseness;

5) ultimate difference—the principle of differentiation or two-ness in Aristotle;

6) inherence—that something that makes parts related to their substance;

7) absence—this is of two types: mutual and relational.

"Mutual" is denial of identity and "relational" is denial of any relation other than identity.[72]

Of interest also are such notions to be found in Ingalls as "unegatable," "nondeviation," "pervasion types of relation," "absences," and "abstracts." With such an auspicious beginning in interpreting Indian logic for English readers, one hopes that Ingalls will continue this work sometime in the near future since at the moment his interest appears to have lapsed. As he himself has pointed out, the editing of philosophy that he does as editor of the Harvard Oriental Series enables him to keep his hand in this area even though he will be preoccupied with Indian literature for the next five years.[73]

As a leading interpreter of Nyāya, Ingalls has many *apesçu*

---

[71] *Ibid.,* p. 33.

[72] *Ibid.,* pp. 37–38, 54.

[73] *Letter* to the author, Cambridge, Mass., (May 13, 1965) .

concerning the early views of that *darśana* that are of interest. He says, for example, in "Human Effort Versus God's Effort in the Early Nyāya (NS. 4. 1. 19–20) " [74] that:

> It has often seemed to me that the teachings of the early Nyāya might better be called a philosophy of man than an exposition of logic. Certainly the greater part of the *Nyāyasūtra* deals with human problems rather than logical ones.[75]

Ingalls' main concern, however, is to show the role of human effort versus divine effort in accomplishing things. He holds that the old Nyāya believed in the efficacy of human effort without qualification.

> This belief, he says, set in more modest bounds, is common in India. Thus it is generally conceded that the particular body one inhabits and the faculties it possesses are based on the human effort one has exerted in past lives.[76]

The basic problem is this. How can the anthropocentric view of effort be squared with the presence of divine beings? This is answered in different ways by the different commentators from Vātsyāyana to Vācaspati Miśra, in such a fashion that in the earlier years man's effort appears to be stronger than in the later years. In brief, Nyāya becomes more theistic through the passage of time. It is interesting to note, Ingalls says, that "both Nyāya and Vaiśeṣika may have grown out of a more thorough-going materialism. But the *sutras* already represent a compromise with orthodoxy" [77] following the lead of Jacobi, and hence the emphasis upon man's autonomy is gradually replaced by emphasis upon man's need of the ministrations of divine beings.

In "Words for Beauty in Classical Sanskrit Poetry," [78] Ingalls makes an important contribution to comparative aesthetics, a discipline still in its bassinet. His classification includes (1)

---

[74] Ingalls, in *Dr. S. K. Belvalkar Felicitation Volume* (1953?) .

[75] *Ibid.*, p. 228.

[76] *Ibid.*

[77] *Ibid.*

[78] *Indological Studies in Honor of W. Norman Brown.* New Haven, Am. Orient. Soc., 1962.

beauty as affecting the physical senses; (2) beauty as affecting the mind and heart; (3) beauty as power and supremacy; (4) beauty as light or splendor; (5) beauty as wealth, glory, majesty; (6) beauty in motion, that is the beauty that excites or entices as opposed to beauty revealed at rest. I shall reproduce examples of the first three: (1) *sutanu,* of beautiful body or figure, (2) *dhanyā-nām. .ramyas tuṣārāgamaḥ* [*ramya*-delightful], "For the rich the coming of winter is delightful." [79] (3) *cakṣur mecakam ambujaṃ vijayate* [*vijayate*-victorious] "Her eye bears the victory over the irridescent waterlily." [80]

In his summary of words for beauty, Ingalls says that:

> Instead of saying with Wordsworth "It is a beauteous evening, calm and fair," assigning the matter in hand to an objective class of the beauteous, the Sanskrit poet will say that it charms his heart, it delights him, it is dear to him, it wins a victory, over others perhaps, but certainly over himself. Even when an objective statement is made, one finds that often it contains within itself a subjective one.[81]

Ingalls, in holding that realists in the West have usually been stronger than the nominalists, says that we [in Western countries] have objectified beauty as though it were something separated from the individual upon whom it has an effect: "Such notions have played no part in Sanskrit. Beauty is conceived by the Sanskrit poet far more subjectively than in the West.[82] Of this Ingalls has more to say in his *An Anthology of Sanskrit Court Poetry: Vidyākara's Subbāsitaratnakosa.*[83]

Among all the American philosophers dealing with Indian thought, the career of John Culpepper Plott is in many ways the most intriguing. Born in 1916, he took his B.A. at the University of Oklahoma, was a novitiate in Ontario, did graduate study at the University of Chicago, studied and worked in Civilian Public Service Camps under Quaker Administration during World War II, returned to the University of Chicago after the war and repaired to India where he took his M.A. and Ph.D. at Banaras

[79] *Ibid.,* p. 93.
[80] *Ibid.,* p. 100.
[81] *Ibid.,* p. 106.
[82] *Ibid.,* p. 107.
[83] Cambridge, Harvard University Press, 1965, Harvard Oriental Series, vol. 44.

Hindu University. He has also studied at Annamalai and Mysore Universities in India and at Northwestern, Hawaii, and Michigan Universities when he returned to the United States after eight years in India living as an Indian. At present he is a professor of philosophy at Marshall University. Previously he taught at William Penn College and Oakland University.

Plott's dissertation is entitled "Philosophy of Religion in Ramanuja, St. Bonaventura and Gabriel Marcel." His published writing includes "Ramanuja as Panentheist," [54] and "An Appreciation of the Tirunvoimoli of Nammalwar." [85] Included in his unpublished manuscripts are "Jnanartha Sangraha," his two-volume study of "M. N. Roy" (his most interesting philosophical work to date) , "The Transition from Comparative Philosophy to a Globalized History of Philosophy," [86] "What is Meant by Embodied?" [87] "The Razor's Wedge: An Autobiographical Pilgrimage to India: 1949-1957," and a "A Himalayan Journal." Some of these works contain hundreds of pages of fascinating material still requiring editing, but rich in Indian lore and overflowing with psychological as well as philosophical treatment of Indian philosophy and religion.

Plott's views in "A Proposal Concerning the Transition from Traditional Comparative Philosophy to Global History of Philosophy" are extremely useful to an improved history of comparative thought. He claims, for example, that:

> By stricter application of Historical Method, it may be seen more clearly that the History of Indian Philosophy, the History of Chinese Philosophy, the History of Japanese Thought, the History of Islamic Philosophy and the History of Byzantine, Jewish, Western and Latin American Philosophies, have been remarkably parallel in at least two respects: (a) They have flourished most where they have experienced

[54] *Annamalai University Journal,* (1954) .

[85] *Journal of the Vaishnava University of Vrindaban,* U.P. (1956) .

[86] In his "Introduction" to Debiprasad Chattopadhyaya's *Indian Philosophy* (1964) Walter Ruben calls such a history our greatest need in contemporary philosophy, with materialistic rather than spiritualistic underpinnings.

[87] On page 166 of this MS, Plott the poet bursts forth with:
Why, oh Why, do we chop up God,
We, cosmic infants, who would our Engenderer slay
Knowing not that His is the rod
of Life and light and illusion too.

the maximum encounter . . . (b) They have gone through comparable periods, namely, (1) the classical period of the formulation of the Canon (2) the development of varieties and heresies and counter-heresies, emerging in a more-or-less stabilized orthodoxy, especially during the Medieval Period (3) the break-up of this medieval stability along with the break-up of the Political Unity of the Eurasian Land-mass wrought by the period of the ascendency of Islam, and the beginning of "renaissances," reformations, counter-reformations, etc., stimulated by the abrogation of Edicts of Toleration. . . .

Plott continues with two more points which he calls

(4) The Period of Modernization characterized by the use of the vernaculars and (5) the Period of Total Encounter, in which we are still engaged "when no one Tradition may be allowed to dominate over the other, colonialism is condemned, and the impact of the different religions on each other is almost as great as the impact of the revolutions in science, technology, transportation, and communications . . ." [88]

The breadth of Plott's approach makes some of his views supplementary to the narrower parameters laid down by Paul Masson-Oursel, P. T. Raju, Kwee Swan Liat and others. There is a tendency in Plott's approach to overstress the intellectual components and underrate the economic and technological, undoubtedly attributable in part to his allegiance to the suggestion of Toynbee. At this juncture it looks as if Plott will not stand on his head like Hegel, but will recline on his side like the many images of the Buddha in South East Asia and Ceylon.

It is too early to say what Plott's position will be a decade from now because of certain difficulties he presents to publishers, largely stylistic in nature, somewhat reminiscent of the hierophantic James Joyce. But it can be said unqualifiedly that no other American philosopher has written so much in such varied ways, with so much personal experience of India. In addition to this he represents a problem to respectability in academic life: his sincerity, his guilessness, his humor bursting and bubbling irreverently, his sadhu-like modesty. If one can imagine Walt Whitman, whom

[88] Unpublished MS. A Proposal concerning the transition from traditional comparative philosophy to global history of philsophy. 1964? pp. 2–3. There is reason to believe that E. J. Brill will publish some version of it in 1969–70.

Plott reminds me of, embroiled in the frog pond of academic life when he has been living in the ocean of Indian total experience, then one can guess with what trepidation he is greeted by the bureaucracy of American higher education, including potential colleagues and peers shaken by the experience of meeting an open-necked mind instead of a buttoned-down one.

A true wandering scholar in the best medieval sense, Plott combines the protestant social gospel with the sociology of knowledge [89] and a totally encompassing philosophy of culture. Combining erudition with a strong synthetic and syncretic penchant, he is the Toynbee of American philosophy. As has been recognized by Charles A. Moore and Karl Potter, there is no other American philosopher so knowledgeable of Indian philosophy as it is felt and practiced in twentieth century India. His major aim transcends a knowledge of Hinduism, however, because it spreads to the entire gamut of comparative philosophy, religion, and sociology.

From the encyclopaedic quest of Plott-the-all-encompassing, we turn to the examination of Indian naturalistic philosophy by Dale Riepe, who first met Plott while that *sadhu* was hoeing in his vegetable garden on the banks of the Ganges River at Banaras in 1951. Born in Tacoma in 1918, he took his B.A. at the University of Washington where he studied with the Orientalist H. H. Gowen (1864–1960) and William Savery. At the University of Michigan after World War II his concern for Indian philosophy was rekindled by James Marshall Plumer (1895–1960), professor of Asian art there. Riepe had intended to write his doctoral dissertation on the naturalistic philosophy of China, but changed this aim when that country was no longer open to Americans. Instead he decided to examine the evidence for a naturalistic and materialistic philosophy in India, a topic which developed in his thinking while he attended the Second East-West Philosophers' Conference in Honolulu in the summer of 1949.

Riepe studied in India as a Fulbright scholar at Banaras Hindu University and Madras University; in Japan at Waseda University. As a Fulbright Lecturer at the University of Tokyo he was

---

[89] Insightfully described as "Marxism without Marx."

also inspired by association with Indologists at that and other universities in Japan. As a Carnegie Corporation faculty intern he spent a year in the Asian Studies program at the University of Michigan in 1960–61. He attended the Fourth East-West Philosophers' Conference in Honolulu in 1964, coming into association at that time with Hajime Nakamura, Kalidas Bhattacharyya, T. V. R. Murti, and other leaders in the study of Indian thought. Again in 1966–67 he returned to India as a research scholar for the American Institute of Indian Studies, devoting his energy to collecting material for a study on "Contemporary Indian Philosophy." At present he teaches Indian philosophy at the State University of New York at Buffalo.

Riepe's doctoral dissertation at the University of Michigan is entitled "Early Indian Naturalism" which was expanded into *The Naturalistic Tradition in Indian Thought.*[90] Following suggestions of Santayana and Conger, he has written articles on Indian philosophy limning naturalistic trends such as the dualistic development of Indian philosophy. On the one side it has been strongly motivated in the direction of idealism and *mokṣa,* but on the other towards empiricism, sensationism, skepticism, and hedonism. A relatively recent emphasis in the interpretation of Indian philosophy, its other investigators include Walter Ruben, director of the Institute of Indology at East Berlin, Erich Frauwallner at the University of Vienna, and Debiprasad Chattopadhyaya, the Calcutta editor and philosopher. Some of Riepe's publications on India include "Contributions of American Sanskritists in the Spread of Indian Philosophy in the United States,"[91] "Indian Philosophical Naturalism,"[92] "Recent Indian Philosophical Literature,"[93] "Early Indian Hedonism,"[94] and four installments of "India: Terrifying Land."[95]

In defending the thesis that important elements in Indian philosophy have been naturalistic, Riepe examines the Vedas and

[90] Seattle, U. of Washington, 1961.
[91] *Buffalo Studies,* III, 1, 1967.
[92] *Philosophical Quarterly,* Amalner, July 1952.
[93] *Philosophy and Phenomenological Research,* XVI, 2, 1954.
[94] *Ibid.,* XVII, 4, 1956.
[95] *The North Dakota Quarterly,* 27, 2, 1959; *Ibid.,* 27, 4, 1959; *Ibid.,* 28, 1, 1960; *The Little Review,* Spring 1963.

Upaniṣads, the Ājīvikas and Cārvākas, Jainism, Theravāda Buddhism, Sāṃkhya, and Vaiśeṣika. Some of his conclusions are that the views of Uddalaka, Cārvāka, and early Vaiśeṣika are clearly naturalistic, while the views of the Ājīvikas, Jains, Sāṃkhya, and Theravāda and Vaibhāṣika Buddhism are strong in various naturalistic elements. One cause of the decline of naturalism in India is attributed by him to a series of political misfortunes which struck India. First of these was the conflict among the principalities from 500 to 1000, then the Muslim theological supremacy from 1000 to 1650, followed by the Europeanized colonial period from 1650 to 1947. During these phases naturalism in India was nearly totally replaced by various forms of idealism "which tried to make pleasant an imaginary life when the natural one was frequently intolerable." [96]

Our only philosopher concerned with Indian thought to have been born in Russia (1918), Abraham Kaplan, who became an American citizen in 1939, was a student of Charles Morris at the University of Chicago. Taking his B.A. at the College of St. Thomas, he studied at the University of Chicago briefly, and then took his Ph.D. at the University of California at Los Angeles. He has taught at New York University, Harvard University, Columbia University, the University of California at Los Angeles, Wesleyan University, and is now a professor of philosophy at the University of Michigan. Besides his teaching activities, he has been a Rockefeller Fellow and Research Associate, a Guggenheim Fellow, and an Associate at the Second East-West Philosophers' Conference. Recently he was appointed Director of the East-West Philosophers' Conference to fill the position left vacant by the death of Charles A. Moore. His popular lectures, entitled *The New World of Philosophy*,[97] include his thinking about the significance of Indian thought for the American mind. He became interested in Indian thought at the East-West Conference in 1949 and nine years later visited India for a number of months where he was most impressed by the philosophers Kalidas Bhattacharya

[96] Riepe, *The Naturalistic Tradition in Indian Thought*, p. 248.

[97] New York, Random, 1961. Born the same year as Kaplan and Riepe, Howard L. Parsons also looked into Asian and Indian thought in terms of its social and political consequences.

and "the Śānkarachārya of the Madras district." About his visit to India, Kaplan remarks that:

> My overall impression of Indian philosophy was that it is still struggling to accommodate the achievement of its tradition to contemporary lines of thought, especially British, and that for the most part the traditionalists are opposed to any modernization of their thought while the modernists have only contempt for their own tradition.[98]

This is congruent with the outlook of both William Harris and Karl Potter, the second mentioned having tried to discourage the narrow vision of the modernists.

Kaplan includes chapters on Indian philosophy and Buddhism in *The New World of Philosophy*. Since this book is compiled from public lectures, the style is informal and the information relatively untechnical. Deprecating the parochialism of American philosophers regarding Asian thought, he says that:

> Part of the reason for the philosophers' dismissal of oriental thought is what I might call the myth of mysticism. It is the notion that all Asian philosophies are of a piece, and that what characterizes them is a certain obscurantism that makes them inaccessible to clear statement and thus invulnerable to criticism.[99]

Kaplan believes that this is not only an over-simplification, but essentially false. One might even say that "A great deal of philosophy in India today is essentially Western. Indeed, this seems to me to be true throughout Asia—and unfortunately so . . ."[100] It is unfortunate, he says, because "Asians confuse the task of modernization of their cultures with the very different enterprise of Westernizing them."[101]

When Indians approach philosophy, says Kaplan, they have a characteristically Indian viewpoint. It has the qualities of (1) catholicity, (2) individualization of teaching, which is to say that it is recognized that each man has an individual path of life that may change with his *āśramas* (stages on life's way), his talents,

---

[98] *Letter* to the author, Ann Arbor, Michigan (January 6, 1966).

[99] Kaplan, *op. cit.*, p. 201.

[100] *Ibid.*, p. 202.

[101] *Ibid.*, pp. 228–29.

his social condition, and level of progress, and (3) tolerance for differing perspectives. Judged as a whole, "Indian philosophy is as great an expression of the human as to be found in any culture," Kaplan remarks. Furthermore,

> It makes of philosophy not a merely academic pursuit, but a kind of vision of eternal truth—the sort of vision that we find in the West in Plato, Plotinus, Spinoza, and Kant.[102]

Like Ingalls, Alex Wayman performs a philosophical as well as philological role in the diffusion of Indian philosophy in the academic world. He was born in 1921, took his B.A. and M.A. in mathematics at the University of California at Los Angeles. His interest in Indian thought dates back to his reading books on the subject as a lad in the Los Angeles Public Library. He took Sanskrit at the University of California at Berkeley where he studied under Emeneau and F. D. Lessing. Wayman has taught Buddhism and Hinduism at the University of Michigan and Tibetan and Sanskrit as well as Indian philosophy at the University of Wisconsin and is now teaching it at Columbia University. He has written *Analysis of the Śrāvakabhumi Manuscript* (1961)[103] and with F. D. Lessing translated *Fundamentals of the Buddhist Tantras* (1966).[104]

Wayman has written a number of articles of considerable philosophical interest. His illuminating "Conze on Buddhism and European Parallels"[105] is a contribution to comparative philosophy. Not only does he here demonstrate his control of the material, but also shows himself to be a logician *in situ* when pointing out that as yet no good reason has been developed why Buddha and European philosophy cannot be compared. Conze holds a purist position which implies that if there are *any* incongruences, then there can be no valid comparisons. Wayman points out that if this were so then "this poses a discouraging prospect for all future

[102] *Ibid.*, pp. 202–203.

[103] U. of California Pub. in Classical Philology, vol. 17.

[104] The Hague, Mouton.

[105] *Philos East West*, XIII, 4, 1964, pp. 361–64. Edward Conze (1904–   ), a famous and productive Buddhologist, and formerly social philosopher, briefly taught Buddhism at the University of Washington. Since leaving Germany where he was born and educated, he has spent most of his time lecturing and writing in England.

[comparative] philosophical ingenuity and insight." Wayman becomes more specific about his disagreement with Conze in the following manner:

> A remarkable criterion—measuring the amount of supposed disagreement as a test of mutual agreement; for example, 'For pages upon pages Shinran Shōnin and Martin Luther in almost the same words expound the primacy of "faith," and yet in fact their system disagrees in almost every other respect.' [106]

What Conze means, says Wayman, is that:

> If two persons seem to agree on item x, and seem to disagree on items $y_1 y_2 . . . y_n$—it follows they do not agree on x; for if two persons seem to disagree on several things, they do not agree on anything.[107]

This might be called the principle of extended comparison or the principle of most comparative effort. Wayman shows in the thickets of comparative philosophy done with a heavy hand, a presumption of omniscience, and revamping of texts to please the whim of the commentator. Wayman's other philosophical articles are detailed, concise, never dull and if the comparison be not odious, a little like Coomaraswamy's without the latter's moralizing and polemicizing.

Not only has Wayman a keen eye for the pitfalls of comparative philosophy and philology, but also has brought a new depth into American considerations of Indian philosophy. For he has realized the importance of a total naturalistic ecology, from mythology, from totemism, and from climate. His views on the history of ideas are rich and substantial. In this he is comparable to Joseph Campbell and Coomaraswamy at their best, but is superior to the philosophers who have emphasized intellectual structures without giving them firm sociological foundations. This he shows in his fine papers on "Climactic Times in Indian Mythology and Religion," [108] "Totemic Beliefs in the Buddhist Tantras," [109] and "Female Energy and Symbolism in the Buddhist Tantras." [110] His

[106] *Ibid.*, p. 361.
[107] *Ibid.*, pp. 361–62.
[108] *Hist Relig*, 4, 2, 1965.
[109] *Ibid.*, 1, 1, 1961.
[110] *Ibid.*, 2, 1, 1962.

"Buddhist Dependent Origination and the Samkhya Gunas," [111] is more typically philosophical and philological in its treatment at first glance, but immediately upon turning to the second page one discovers that Wayman has found correspondences between the twelve zodiacal signs and the twelve members of Dependent Origination.[112] Some of the credit for Wayman's superior approach is doubtless due to the inspiring teaching of F. D. Lessing, the University of California Buddhistic and Tibetan scholar. There is also good reason to believe that Wayman's grounding in Tibetan will prove a great asset in his continued original conception made clearer undoubtedly by his mathematical training, part of the value of which is seen in his ability to handle astronomical material with assurance. Of particular interest is Wayman's contention that, speaking of correspondences in his "Climactic . . ." essay:

> And the most important conclusion is that if these correspondences be admitted, one can easily see how the idea of rebirth or transmigration arose as a correspondence between the human soul and the sun.[113]

There is every reason to believe that the career of this scholar with his knowledge of mathematics and Tibetan will give a new breadth in the interpretations and assessments of various facets of Indian philosophy.

Concerned with a revitalization of religion stripped of its dross, hypocrisy, and religion-as-usual, William Henry Harris (1922–1966) received his Ph.D. from Boston University, began teaching philosophy at the University of Arkansas and became a professor of philosophy at Southern Illinois University where he taught since 1953. He spent two years in India, one at Madras studying at the University of Madras Graduate School under T. M. P. Mahadevan and another studying at Calcutta at the University and also at the Ramakrishna Mission Institute of Culture in Gol Park. He did special study on Rāmānuja whose philosophy resembled the personalist tradition Harris had known at Boston

---

[111] *Ethnos* (1962).

[112] *Ethnos,* p. 15. A major doctrine of Buddhist moral causation explaining the origin of man's craving.

[113] Wayman: Climatic times in Indian mythology and religion, p. 318.

University under Brightman. Harris was a member of the Third
East-West Philosophers' Conference at Honolulu in 1959.

His early concern with Indian thought was to find in it clues for
spiritual insights which might prove valuable for Americans in
the United States. He said,

> I had hoped that the Ramakrishna Mission represented an indigenous
> reforming force, I find that it is as occupied with institutional aggran-
> dizement as any of the Western religious institutions, which I know too
> well. The cult of Ramakrishna . . . is played down in the West but
> cultivated in India.[114]

This reaction is by no means unique. One receives similar im-
pressions concerning the cult of The Mother at Pondicherry and
cults in other Indian *āśrama*. Harris continued,

> I realize the problems of relating to the profound conservatism and
> obscurantism of Indian culture. But I am distressed by the ignorance
> and self-satisfaction of many of the Ramakrishna swamis and by the
> evidence that they do not even see some of the blemishes of Indian
> society, let alone fight them.[115]

Is it perhaps likely that Harris experience with American clergy
was unusually felicitious? Yet Harris found fanaticism and ob-
scurantism in India more desirable than the brands he rejected
in his own culture, a peculiarly revealing statement with which
a number of Americans might agree. As has happened in the case
of other philosophers recently studying in India, the pilgrimage
had a salutary and chastening effect. Now Harris claimed that he
was "interested in being a philosopher rather than an "Orientalist
or theologian." [116] Yet his religious concerns remained uppermost
in his thoughts.

In "Philosophy in Indian Culture" Harris indicated that he
was concerned to show the relationship of philosophy to culture,

---

[114] *Letter* to the author, Carbondale, Illinois (January 4, 1965). Kenneth Inada,
born in 1923, has very recently focused on problems of Indian philosophy. An expert in Buddhism, he also has a broad training in Western philosophy. His instruction was at the universities of Hawaii, Chicago, and Tokyo. He has also studied
Hindi and Tibetan in Delhi.

[115] *Ibid.*

[116] MS, Philosophy in Indian Culture. *Philosophical Forum,* pp. 1–2.

which he began by pointing out the levels upon which philosophy is done in any culture:

1) level of folklore, proverb, and myth.
2) level of descriptive metaphysics and descriptive moral philosophy.
3) level of normative and constructive philosophy.[117]

The first step of the third level, according to Harris, consists in being aware of one's own cultural assumptions. If one is not so aware he engages in ideology. Another name for ideology is apologetics, said Harris. The value of studying and living amidst Indian culture is that it gives one perspective. "These cultures are far too important to leave in the hands of Orientalists," [118] he claimed.

Harris then gave a resumé of the philosopher's status and function in traditional Indian culture. First of all, the philosopher belongs to the Brahmin caste born to be an intellectual. What results from this is that his philosophy becomes a kind of scholasticism, for his job is largely explication of the text. Among the philosophers the highest honor goes to the *guru* since he has "achieved spiritual realization of the truth." [119] Harris held that,

> Two things give to Indians evidence of the failure of most Western philosophers to find truth. First [is] the fact that they confess that they are still searching for it . . . Second is the fact that Western philosophical speculation has been thought to be for its own sake . . . [it is thus] at best a profession, at worst a game; it is not devoted to a serious attempt to realize the meaning of one's own existence.[120]

Here I believe Harris has stated an important evaluation of Western philosophy that brings home the idea that the philosophical quest has taken on the comfort and shallowness of easy professionalism and that its tendency to be a game is frankly admitted by some logicians, cyberneticists, analysists, and others who merely went halfway with Wittgenstein. "In method, therefore, Hindu philosophy is frankly esoteric." [121] said Harris. Dia-

[117] MS, Philosophy in Indian Culture.
[118] *Ibid.,* p. 3.
[119] *Ibid.,* p. 5.
[120] *Ibid.,* p. 6.
[121] Philosophy in Indian Culture, p. 6.

logue with traditional Indian philosophers is nearly impossible because one cannot have a dialogue between two persons satisfied that they have realized ultimate truth or between a seeker and an unchallenged authority.[122]

Harris concluded his illuminating discussion by pointing out that the *guru* principles permeates all of Indian culture and is a serious factor in its lack of political development. Could it be put another way?: that India's lack of political and economic development allows the *guru* principle to permeate all of Indian culture? Lack of political development is permeated by the undemocratic principle that determines an educated *guru* to announce final and irrevocable truths to the uneducated masses, Harris concluded. Since something like the *guru* principle may be found also in Spain and in Latin American countries in the form of priests, perhaps the socioeconomic explanation does not have unique reference to India. But perhaps Harris also came to a similar conclusion as he since discovered that the spiritual interpretation of history is no longer either factually or aesthetically satisfactory.

Harris' "Swami Vivekananda and Neo-Hindu Universalism" [123] dealt with a topic inadequately discussed by other American philosophers, although probably Isherwood has done the most along this line. Of Ramakrishna, Harris says:

> This capacity to induce mystical ecstacy with the symbols of faiths other than his own seems to have been as far as Sri Ramakrishna went in searching for some kind of trans-cultural truth or good. He never had to face a direct challenge from faiths critical of his own.[124]

Vivekananda, on the other hand, became a vigorous polemicist defending "not only Hindu culture but asserting its superiority over other cultures and religions." [125] Vivekananda, according to Harris, reached the height of pseudosociological absurdity in Detroit when he claimed that Hindus "are the handsomest and finest of feature," [126] in which he combined religious superiority with

[122] *Ibid.*, p. 8.
[123] *The Iliff Review*, XXII, 2, 1965.
[124] *Ibid.*, p. 31.
[125] *Ibid.*, p. 32.
[126] *Ibid.*

nationalism. Upon returning to India at the end of the nineteenth century, Vivekananda stated that

> Unlike the Asiatics, the Westerners are not deeply spiritual. Religious thoughts do not permeate the masses . . . The immorality prevalent among Western peoples would strike the Indian visiting London or New York . . . The lower classes are not only ignorant of their scriptures and immoral, but are also rude and vulgar.[127]

When getting to the more solid foundations of metaphysics, Vivekananda holds that "On metaphysical lines no nation on earth can hold a candle to the Hindu." [128] One year later in 1894, his universalism is shown in the discovery that "all of religion is contained in the Vedanta" [129] which Mme. Blavatsky had discovered, with slight modification, in New York in 1877. Harris drew the following conclusions concerning the proposed universal framework of religious thought of Vivekananda which are sharply summarized as follows: (1) This framework did not serve as a basis for toleration within India itself.[130] (2) Vivekananda's universal scheme did not really transcend Indian ethnic origins.[131] (3) His attack on Western materialism is not to be taken seriously because it is fanatically and clearly uninformed, based mostly upon tertiary sources and wounded national pride. (4) There is little reason to believe that Vedānta is the complete fulfillment of all other religions and systems of thought.[132] In summation, Harris proposed his own critical criteria as depending upon a pluralistic rather than a monistic philosophy: "a genuinely universal philosophy is needed. It will have to account for plurality and uniqueness on more than a provisional basis." [133] One can agree that plurality and uniqueness are worthy of consideration, but it is not yet clear as to the necessities or advantages of "a genuinely universal philosophy." But perhaps Harris' statement is one of comparative philosophy's unexamined shibboleths?

[127] *Ibid.*
[128] *Ibid.*
[129] *Ibid.*
[130] *Ibid.*, pp. 33–34.
[131] *Ibid.*, p. 34.
[132] *Ibid.*, pp. 35–36.
[133] *Ibid.*, p. 36.

Although several Sanskritists in America were born in Eastern Canada, Richard Hugh Robinson (1926–   ) is a native of Alberta, where he grew up on an isolated farm. He became an omnivorous reader by thirteen with a particular penchant for exotic languages. As an undergraduate he majored in economics, but this now cheerful science could not hold his attention so he became an Orientalist largely because of a growing attachment to Buddhism. Working at odd jobs for three years, and reminding us of the dedication of Schliemann, he saved enough money to go to London where he was deeply impressed by the persons and work of Theodore Pulleyblank in Chinese Studies and Arthur Waley the famous translator of Chinese and Japanese classical literature. Returning to Canada, Robinson made himself into a Buddhologist and a competent descriptive linguist, the fruit of which may be seen in his book *Early Mādhyamika in India and China.*[134] Like Potter's *Presuppositions of Indian Philosophy,* this is a work of high quality and represents another breakthrough in scholarship relating to Indian philosophy. Its first chapter indicates a sign of the times, a concern with methodology. Historically such a concern is important because it ties up Indian and Chinese thought, showing that Buddhism, like Christianity and Islam, is of such scope that it cannot be squeezed into the confines of one culture. In addition to the main thesis, describing the introduction of Mādhyamika Buddhism into China are appendices including "Epilogue: The Lineage of the Old Three Treatise Sect," and the translation of ten documents based on, but not completely dependent upon, those of Edward Conze. Among the conclusions gathered by Robinson the following are of considerable importance. They are answers to questions raised in the early pages of his book:

(1) Which aspects are Indian and which Chinese in the writings of the first Chinese who encountered Mādhyamika? *Answer.* The cosmology is India, and the logical element is Indian, while the literary form is Chinese. Concerning the last point Robinson says "Evidently the gentlemen of the time [in China] found it easier to change their religion than their literary taste."[135] The

---

134 Madison, U. of Wisconsin, 1967.
135 Robinson, *Early Mādhyamika,* p. 161.

Indian problematic was not adopted, according to Robinson, because they raise such problems as cause and effect, time, and temporal series, which the Chinese interested in Mādhyamika had not considered. According to Robinson, ". . . it is difficult to understand and assimilate a foreign philosophy if it answers questions that one has never asked." [136]

Robinson also contributes some important hypotheses concerning cultural transmission growing out of his study of Mādhyamika's transport from India to China [esp. 409–401 B.C.]. This requires rather full quotations to do justice to its philosophical and cultural import:

> In the first place, I assume that no smallest and no largest unit of culture need be posited, that neither a holistic view of culture nor an atomistic conception of the individual's world-view is necessary to the inquiry. Consistency and homogeneity within the cultural behavior of individuals and groups may of course be discovered, but should not be presupposed.[137]

Robinson believes,

> secondly, the degree and manner in which different individuals participate in one culture differ greatly. From the individual point of view, any cultural behavior must be learned in order to be inherited, and this learning process proceeds gradually, piecemeal, and imperfectly, whether one is learning an ancient property of one's own society or a recent import from abroad. Usually any one individual masters only a part of a tradition, and forgets parts that he has learned and no longer uses. Generally, only a part of a historic tradition is in vogue at any time. Consequently, it is dangerous to predict a priori that anyone will actually possess any universal trait that has been posited for his culture.[138]

And the third point Robinson makes is that,

> the persisting biases of a cultural community are transmitted chiefly through its institutions of learning. People usually learn first and most from immediate associates and approach the remote through the interpretation of familiar spokesmen. The infants who grew up to be

[136] *Ibid.*
[137] *Ibid.*, p. 7.
[138] *Ibid.*, pp. 7–8.

Chinese dharma-masters were born ignorant of everything Chinese or Indian. They acquired native and imported ways alike by a process of gradual and groping discovery, conditioned by their instruction in the family, by their tutors, and in the Saṅgha. The distinctive biases of certain kinds of families and tutors, and of different monastic schools, are sometimes discoverable in the biographies of eminent monks. To the extent that we understand these factors, we understand perhaps the major circumstances that promoted or inhibited assimilation of novel ideas and practices.[139]

Robinson's particular forte is his ability to swing across two cultures, India and China, which gives his opinions a breadth rather uncommon to most of the scholars and thinkers treated in this book with the exception of Clarence Hamilton, Joseph Campbell, and perhaps a few others. His perspective of Indian philosophy through eyes that wear Chinese spectacles is a valuable asset to contemporary scholarship.

Robinson's "Some Logical Aspects of Nāgārjuna's System" [140] is an examination activated by modern logic, although Nāgārjuna's knowledge of logic "is about on the same level as Plato's." [141] In examining the *Mūla-madhyamika-kārikā,* Robinson finds the principle of contradiction employed by Nāgārjuna as in the example: "For the real and non-real, being mutually contradictory, do not occur in the same locus." [142] The law of excluded middle is also to be found in such examples as "Other than goer and non-goer, there is no third one that goes." [143] On the other hand, the law of identity is not to be found in Nāgārjuna, any more than in Aristotle according to Bochenski.[144]

The hypothetical syllogism is found in two forms in Nāgārjuna, first in the *modus ponens* and second in *modus tollens,* according to Robinson. There is recognition also of the fallacy of antecedent, negation, quantification, the tetralemma, dilemmas, and others. Of particular interest is Robinson's discussion of emptiness and nullity in Nāgārjuna since it is with these that we usually

[139] *Ibid.,* p. 9.
[140] *Philos East West,* VI, 4, 1957.
[141] *Ibid.,* p. 295.
[142] *Mūla-madhyamika-kārikā* 8.7.
[143] *Ibid.,* 2.8.
[144] Robinson, Some Logical Aspects of Nāgārjuna's System, p. 296.

associate his outlook. Then Robinson makes one of the statements
of tolerance that goes far in enabling philosophers to sympathetically encompass the intellectual travail of mankind:

> Nāgārjuna's contemporaries were infinitely less sophisticated than
> Kant's. Their problems were simple, their concepts were fewer, and
> their devices for handling concepts were much cruder. It is not that
> they were worse thinkers than the moderns, but simply that they were
> earlier. It is in this milieu that Nāgārjuna's reasoning should be
> appraised. I believe that when this environment has been analyzed and
> taken into account, his stature will appear greater, and his system
> much less barbarous and baffling than it has seemed hitherto.[145]

This is not Robinson's last word. He now makes an appraisal of
Śūnyavāda as a kind of theory of fictions. "Indeed, the greatest
achievement of Indian Buddhism—[not without an analogue in
Indian mathematics]—," Robinson generalizes, "is its understanding of the process of abstraction." [146]

> For the concept of designation (*prajñapti*) provides a way of handling
> abstracts without concretizing them, or assigning ontological value
> to them.[147]

It would be more valuable, Robinson concludes, to compare
Nāgārjuna with the pre-Aristotelians and William of Ockham
than with Kant or Hegel. Perhaps no one would have agreed
more with this than Hegel himself.

Karl Potter (1927–   ), like James H. Woods, Kurt Leidecker, and Richard Robinson, learned Sanskrit as he learned
philosophy and consequently brings to his studies of Indian
thought a level of specialization rare among American philosophers for the century-and-a-half that they have studied it. This is
evident in the sureness with which he handles the Indian sources
and in the originality he evinces in dealing with problems that
interest him, often of a linguistic nature. He began studying
Sanskrit at the University of California at Berkeley under Emeneau and then finished his doctorate at Harvard University in
Sanskrit and philosophy under Ingalls. He has taught at Carleton
College and is at present a professor of the philosophy department

---

[145] *Ibid.,* p. 307.
[146] *Ibid.*
[147] *Ibid.,* pp. 307–8.

at the University of Minnesota. He was a Fulbright Scholar in India in 1952–53, and a Fulbright Research Fellow in 1959–60, and a fellow of the American Institute of Indian Studies in 1963–64. Recently he has been appointed editor of the comprehensive *Encyclopedia of Indian Philosophies.* He published *The Padarthatattvanirupanam of Raghunatha Siromani*[148] in 1957 and *Presuppositions of Indian Philosophies* in 1963.[149] These two works establish him as a foremost American philosopher specializing in Indian thought. It is noteworthy that he is also the third American philosopher since J. H. Woods[150] to combine competence in an Indian language with a Ph.D. in philosophy which he took at Harvard in 1955.

In a number of ways *Presuppositions of Indian Philosophies* rises above previous American critical works by philosophers. For one thing, Potter is more at home in Indian systems than previous philosophers who either did not know Sanskrit or had begun their studies either in the middle or near the end of their careers or who did not have the wealth of material that threatens to inundate present scholarship. For another, Potter set out on a path that covered a vaster area of philosophy than either the American Sanskritists or philosophers and indeed, showed a willingness to critically attack the traditional approaches bringing much-needed fresh breezes into the subject-matter and treatment. He remained traditionalist however, in his interpretation of "Indian philosophy" as Indian religious philosophy, since he claims that the end of the classical and "sophisticated" systems was "release." Potter claims that:

> What is needed are philosophers who are willing to push to the limit the presuppositions of Indian thought, work along original lines either to refute or to justify them, but at any rate to address them as living ideas and not as dead ones.[151]

A parallel that pops into mind is the attempt of modern Roman Catholic philosophers to do the same for medieval Christian and

[148] Cambridge, Harvard.

[149] New York, Prentice-Hall.

[150] Before him were Ethel M. Kitch of Oberlin and Kurt Leidecker of Mary Washington College.

[151] Potter, *Presuppositions of Indian Philosophies,* pp. 257–58.

earlier Aristotelian and Platonic thought. Perhaps such a scholasticism is historically fruitful. It would appear from Ingalls' work on Indian logic, for example, that the Indian approach is significant for historical understanding, but is not necessarily fruitful in terms of the solution of new problems besetting Western logicians after the nineteenth century, or for the most part, the eighteenth. Contextual demands are such that a civilization and its problems cannot be solved by *philosophiae perennes.* That these are so intertwined with prescientific psychology, anthropology, ecology, physiology, anatomy, to mention only a few, makes it seem unlikely that gems of wisdom applicable today will be uncovered.[152] There is no objection to trying this, but Western neo-scholasticism and the lesson of Needham's *Science and Civilization in China* [153] appear to make the probability of success slight. Whatever we decide about this, Potter's work is suggestive and illuminating in throwing new light on classical Indian thought especially of the idealistic persuasion.

For historical purposes as well as for contemporary assessment, Potter's "fresh classification" of Indian philosophical systems and viewpoints has as its main analytic device, a division of systems into speculative philosophy on the one hand and path philosophy on the other. The two subdivisions of speculative philosophy he calls "leap" and "progress." His development of them is original and exciting. Outside the spectrum of his consideration are the "anti-freedom" Cārvākas and the "fatalistic" Ājīvikas. These are generally speaking naturalistic, skeptical, materialistic, and deterministic, and hence allied with empirical and naturalistic philosophy in the West. Classical Indian philosophy has been, with rare exceptions, embraced by Westerners with theological and idealistic proclivities. Even Santayana, with all his heartwarming defense of naturalism and what he took to be materialism, main-

---

[152] Is the statement of Ernest Gellner too strong? He claims that "philosophies given to inventing spurious vindications of what once was the human image of man, are worthless." *Thought and Change.* London, Weidenfeld and Nicholson, 1964, p. 217. Perhaps William A. Williams makes a more judicious observation when he states that "approaches to knowledge if viewed, or practiced, as a process of reaching back into the past for answers sufficient unto the present and the future" is "misleading." *The Contours of American History.* Cleveland, World, 1961, p. 19.

[153] Joseph Needham, vols. I–IV (1954–1965), Cambridge, Cambridge U.P. See also Kwiat, Masson-Oursel, Piovesana, and Raju.

tained a charming Platonism and a remarkable tolerance for most forms of idealism not proclaimed by those of German birth.

Potter's greatest contribution may well be not unlike that of Colonel Olcott's in Ceylon fifty years ago. Whereas Olcott wished to impress on the people of Ceylon the need to understand, teach, and use their own rich Buddhist tradition, Potter wishes to exhort contemporary younger Indian philosophers to look at their heritage, not as a historical phenomenon, but as a tradition and a knowledge that can be useful in solving current problems and "guarantee the relevance of [Indian] philosophy to a human predicament and longing which does not change through the ages." [154] He wishes to goad the perplexed into examining their classical philosophy with an eye to using its insights today. If this does not occur then "it is hard for a young man to become really engrossed in [classical Indian] philosophy, and one is forced to the realization that the quality of philosophy teachers and scholars in India is steadily declining." [155] Suffice it to say that the quality is changing. Whether it is declining is open to question, but if it is [as many hold that it is in the United States as well] [156] there may be other considerations besides neglect of the classical tradition. The more important historical question is, in any case: *why* is the classical tradition being neglected? Just as the classical tradition is being neglected in the United States, so it is being neglected in India. To answer this question one must have the rudiments of a philosophy of history and considerable information in the area of the sociology of knowledge. Otherwise one is reduced to the impotence of psychical determination and the mystification of the idealistic and spiritualistic history of ideas.[157]

Johannes Adreanus Bernardus van Buitenen (1928–   ) was born in The Hague, studied at the University of Utrecht and

[154] Potter, *Presuppositions of Indian Philosophies*, p. 255. Another American, Ernest Fenellosa, (1853–1908) was largely responsible for the Japanese revival of its ancient and medieval art. See Brooks: *Fenellosa and His Circle with Other Essays in Biography*. New York, E. P. Dutton & Co., Inc., 1962.

[155] *Ibid*.

[156] Although for many years philosophy graduate students made the best showings on the American graduate record examinations, they have now been replaced by graduate students in physics.

[157] I shall try in my next book to indicate why classical studies in India are being downgraded, although there was a flurry of interest in Sanskrit immediately after Independence (1948).

became a candidate for Indo-Iranian Letters as well as Indonesian Letters. His principal subject for the doctorate was Vedic Sanskrit, with secondary emphasis upon Pāli and Modern Persian. His thesis was "Rāmānuja on the Bhagavadgītā." At first assistant to the chair of Indo-European philology at Utrecht, he became subeditor of the Sanskrit Dictionary on Historical Principles at Deccan College in 1954. Receiving a post-doctoral fellowship on the Rockefeller Foundation he came to the United States in 1956, where he soon was appointed assistant professor at the University of Chicago. At present professor of Sanskrit and Indic studies at the University of Chicago, he has since that time also been reader of Indian philosophy at the University of Utrecht.

Besides his thesis work on Rāmānuja, van Buitenen has also written the following monographs: *Rāmānuja's Vedārthasaṃgraha* (1955), *Yāmuna's Treatise on the Authority of Pancarātra* (1965), *The Maitrāyanīya Upaniṣad* (1961), and *A Glossary of Sanskrit from Indonesia* (with J. Ensink, 1965). Among his numerous articles, those dealing with Sāṁkhya and Vedānta are clearly of a philosophical nature. His monograph on Bhāskara's *Sārīrakamīmāmsābhāṣya* will appear in the Harvard Oriental Series in the future.

Edwin Gerow, a student of van Buitenen, was born in 1931. After taking his B.A. in philosophy at the University of Chicago he then went into linguistics, Indo-European, and finally Sanskrit. He studied a year with Louis Renou at the Institut de Civilisation Indienne of the University of Paris and then a year at the University of Madras, both on Ford Foreign Area Training Fellowships. At Madras he studied with V. Raghavan and Pundit K. L. Vyasaraya Shastri. His work at Chicago was carried on under George V. Bobrinskoy and van Buitenen. He has written *Notes and Appendix to S. K. De's Tagore Memorial Lectures* ("Sanskrit Poetics as an Aesthetic" (Berkeley, University of California Press, 1963) and "An Intellectual History of Indian Poetics" in *Introduction to Indian Literature,* edited by Dimock and van Buitenen (New York, Columbia University Press, 1965), and *A Glossary of Indian Figures of Speech,* Dissertation Series of the Department of Near and Middle East Languages of Columbia University (New York, Columbia University Press, 1966).

James Hoyt Knapp Norton (1931–   ) took his B.S. at Yale University, his B.A. at Oxford University, and his M.A. and Ph.D. at the University of Madras. He has been a Ford Fellow in India, a fellow of the American Institute of Indian Studies in Madras, and is now an assistant professor of religion at Wooster College. A specialist on Viśiṣṭadvaita (that the spirits of men have a qualified identity with the one Spirit), he has written on that theme and other aspects of contemporary Indian philosophy.

One of Norton's helpful studies is "Theological Presuppositions," [158] which assumes that "faint flashes of the divine . . . are far brighter than the dim glow afforded by human reason." [159] That the existence of God must be assumed rather than proved is especially promulgated by the Advaita Vedānta, according to Norton. Advaita holds that:

> Philosophy by its very inability to verify the existence of Brahman, demonstrates the transcendence of the reality which is presupposed to it.[160]

Viśiṣṭādvaita proposes a slightly different approach: Brāhman cannot be logically demonstrated, yet He is seen as the basis of our experience of the world. Brāhman is intuited upon the basis of our experience according to Rāmānuja. From this it follows that philosophy has a divine function as shown in the work of Rāmānuja's fourth generation disciple, Atreya Rāmānuja in *The Sharp Spear of Reason* (*Nyāyaklīśa*).

Atreya Rāmānuja's commentary on the proofs for the existence of God are of special interest to Norton and linguistic philosophers. The argument from efficient causality he calls inconclusive because the argument implies a creator who has a body, who has temporary knowledge, and who creates as we humans do. A body is required so that visible action can occur. But if it does occur, the cause of the action is the body of a creator. On the other hand, since Brahman is Immutable, Imperishable, and One, there can

---

[158] *Essays in Philosophy Presented to Dr. T. M. P. Mahadevan on His Fiftieth Birthday.* Madras, Ganesh, 1962. Another Indologist philosopher who studied at Madras and received his doctorate under Mahadevan is the Dutch scholar J. F. Staal, recently appointed at the University of California at Berkeley.

[159] *Ibid.,* p. 43.

[160] *Ibid.,* p. 45.

be no motion in Him, and hence "Creative activity . . . does not have-its-source in His divine essence in so far as He is the efficient cause of the universe," [161] according to Norton. From whence does our knowledge of God come, if it cannot come from the speculative argument on efficient cause? It must come from the Vedas which are revealed. If rational demonstrations do not contradict the Vedas, then they may be used to interpret and validate them. Norton continues this examination which leads to a discussion of the ontological substratum of language. This discussion is of considerable concern to contemporary American philosophers. They may not all approve of Atreya Rāmānuja's conclusion that:

> What happens is that, in order and according to their own (expressive) power, God causes common words, as well as Vedic words, to be used just as they were in previous eons.[162]

This pre-established linguistic harmony, if it could be believed, would have saved Wittgenstein a great deal of bother.

In summary, the argument of Atreya Rāmānuja is that although one cannot rationally talk about Him, nevertheless He has made discourse possible through preestablished linguistic harmony.

Another theologically trained scholar with language training in India is Herbert P. Sullivan, who was born in 1932, received his B.A. and B.D. from the University of Chicago. He took his Ph.D. in Indic Studies at the University of Durham after which he studied at Banaras Hindu University for a year on a Spalding Fellowship. Since returning to the United States he has taught the history of religion at Duke University where he is now an associate professor.

Sullivan first began reading Indian religion and philosophy while he was in high school. He turned to Indian studies as a result of listening to the lectures of Joachim Wach and worked under him until Wach's death in 1955. At the University of Durham he studied with Arabinda Basu under whom he wrote his doctoral thesis on the philosophy of Sri Aurobindo Ghose. In-

---

[161] *Ibid.*, p. 49.
[162] Norton, Theological Presuppositions, p. 53.

cluded in his writing are three articles on Indian religion for the *Encyclopedia Britannica,* the "Development et expansion du Bouddhisme," "The Nature of the Individual Self in Shankara, Ramanuja and Sri Aurobindo," "A Re-Examination of the Religion of the Indus Civilization, and "Reality and Illusion: The Problem of Phenomenal Existence in Indian Philosophy." Sullivan's work at this stage is largely exegesis upon the leading Indian religious philosophers, although he does criticize Radakrishnan's interpretation of Śaṁkara's doctrine of illusion. An important point that he makes in this is that one cannot hold that a thing can be both an illusion and eternal. For the

> **Nature of an illusion** is that it *is* not eternal since it can and does cease to be; it is exhaustible and exhausted by an act of knowledge. For example, the illusion of the world-existence may be beginningless in time, but it is not eternal since it ceases "to be" when the eternal truth of Reality is known . . . If the world is eternal, then it must also be real, for only the real can never cease to be. If it is real, it cannot also be illusion. And so forth. It is this confusion of Shankara's two levels or standpoints which leads Radhakrishnan into all manner of *non-sequitur.*[163]

And it might be hypothecated that Śaṁkara himself deserves credit for many more *non sequiturs* and hence volumes of commentaries on them. The whole doctrine of illusion and illusionism outside the field of aesthetics and advertising appears to lead to the most incredible logical excrescences.

Upon the death of Charles A. Moore in 1967, the editorship of *Philosophy East and West* was taken over by Eliot Deutsch (1931–   ). Deutsch took his B.S. at the University of Wisconsin and his Ph.D. at Columbia University. He has taught at Rensselaer Polytechnic Institute, the University of Chicago, and is now professor of philosophy at the University of Hawaii.

---

[163] Herbert Sullivan: Reality and illusion: the problem of phenomenal existence in Indian philosophy. *Sri Aurobindo Circle,* XVI (n. d.), p. 42. W. Norman Brown reminded me at this point of the following limerick:
> "There was an old man of Cadiz,
> Who said the world is what it is,
> For I long ago learnt
> If it were what it weren't
> It couldn't be that which it is."

Deutsch was a fellow of the American Institute of Indian Studies in India in 1963–64. He returned there in 1967–68 as a New York State Faculty Scholar in international studies. Since that time he has been at Honolulu.

Deutsch has written two books: *The Bhagavad Gita* (1968), which he translated and wrote a commentary on, and *A Reconstruction of Advaita Vedanta,* which was due to appear in 1969. Among his articles of greatest interest is "The Nature of Divine Action in Advaita Vedānta," [164] which explores the basis for the advaitin's denial of any activity in Brahman and the ascription of a special kind of creative activity to this same Brahman. This involves,

> a consideration of the concept of *līlā,* or creative activity as sportive play, and the manner in which Brahman, seen in māyā as Iśvara or God, is caught up in the law of karma and is, in a sense, limited by it.[165]

What is so joyful about the act of creation in this context is that it is "Spontaneous, without purpose—and no *karmic* consequences attach to it. . . . Līlā, or God's sportive play, is precisely different in kind from all action which yields results that are binding upon, and which determine, the actor." [166] It is God's nature to create in this fashion just as it is man's nature to breathe in and out. From his nature is removed all motive, purpose, and responsibility when engaged in this creative act. Consequently, Deutsch points out,

> Having no need to create and having no consequences attach [ed.] to his action, God cannot be held responsible for the actions which arise subsequently within the field of His creation. Theologically, *līlā* avoids thereby any problem of evil of the sort associated with Judeao-Christian theism, and it sets aside as meaningless any question of why God creates in the first place. There can be no "why" to creation.[167]

[164] *University Seminar on Oriental Thought and Religion,* Columbia University, April 1965.

[165] *Ibid.,* p. 1.

[166] *Ibid.,* p. 10.

[167] *Ibid.,* p. 11. This is extremely suggestive of the possibility of an additional chapter to the concept of "oriental despotism." Administrative irresponsibility here perhaps reaches an unprecedented height in human affairs.

It is no accident that Deutsch is concerned with the dance or play for of all the American philosophers with whom we deal, his aesthetic concerns are most apparent. This shows in another article entitled "Śakti in Medieval Hindu Sculpture," [168] which he claims is the central category in the interpretation of medieval Indian sculpture. Duetsch says,

> *śakti* is that which informs the creation of the world: it is the energy whose creative release as a play or sport (*līlā*) gives rise to the manifold things of the world. . . .which informs the psychophysical organization of an organism: it is that energy which underlies as essence, and constitutes as form, the lifeforce or breath (prāna) which sustains an individual's existence.[169]

This is but one instance of the fact that Indian art cannot be interpreted within the framework of Western or European aesthetics. When we take it for granted, Deutsch holds, that universal norms may be set up, we are simply mistaken. Instead, the Western aesthetician should take for granted only what the Indian artist takes for granted.

Another interest of Deutsch's is recent Indian metaphysics. In "Sri Aurobindo's Interpretation of Spiritual Experience: A Critique," [170] he attempts to verify Aurobindo's "spiritual evolutionary theory." Obviously, one cannot use scientific method to verify it because, as Aurobindo himself says,

> Scientific theory is concerned only with the outward and visible machinery and process, with the detail of Nature's execution, with the physical development of things in Matter and the law of development of life and mind in Matter.[171]

Instead of such a merely external method of verification, one must use another kind. What is it? According to Sri Auribindo, spiritual experience can only be verified by those who have the capacity for inner methods. Deutsch approaches this problem by referring

[168] *J Aesth Art Crit,* **XXIV,** 1, 1965.
[169] *Ibid.,* pp. 81–82.
[170] *Intl Philos Quar,* **IV,** 4, 1964.
[171] Quoted by Deutsch from *The Synthesis of Yoga.* Pondicherry, Sri Aurobindo Asharm, 1955, p. 744.

to experiences of the mystics both East and West. "There does seem to be a unity of vision fundamental to them all" [172] from Plotinus to St. John of the Cross and from the Upaniṣads to Śaṁkara. Verification will then depend upon a theory of ascent. According to Deutsch, the principle of integration itself cannot be verified:

> If the ideal of a divine-manhood put forward by Sri Aurobindo is to be attained, a principle of integration, as he describes it, is no doubt indispensable. However, it does not seem to be verified in experience or to be capable of verification as something inherent in the evolutionary structure of nature.[173]

Another principle, that of descent, must also be considered. The descending spirit and its powers penetrate being and consciousness so that the person receiving it is remolded and transmuted.[174] Deutsch believes that since this is a nonrational process so far as explanation is concerned, it must remain an "ideogram." [175] The only verification that could take place would be the shifting one of a seer comparing his experiences with another through confessional dialogues. Deutsch concludes,

> Our major criticism, then, is that Aurobindo commits what we might call the "fallacy of misplaced certitude"—the fallacy of translating, without proper qualification, the special kind of certitude obtained in spiritual experience to what one theorizes *about* the experience. The confounding of theoretical, explanatory concepts with spiritually grounded symbols is precisely what has brought about to a great extent the "obscurantism prejudicial to the extension of knowledge." [176]

Certitude is proper to the realm of the spirit, and here Deutsch leaves Sri Aurobindo's attempt to reduce the "unknowable" to the "known." [177]

And with this account, our discussion of contemporary Ameri-

---

[172] Sri Aurobindo's Interpretation of Spiritual Experience: A Critique, p. 587.
[173] *Ibid.,* p. 588.
[174] See Sri Aurobindo: *The Life Divine.* New York, Dutton, 1951, p. 811.
[175] Sri Aurobindo's Interpretation of Spiritual Experience: A Critique, p. 589.
[176] *Ibid.,* p. 591.
[177] *Ibid.,* p. 594.

can philosophers working on the vast reach of Indian thought is complete.

Although I have tried to include the views of all philosophers, religionists, and other intellectuals in this book, certain omissions are inevitable if regrettable. Yet the story is not complete even with them. Subsequent research will fill the recognizable gaps.

One may discern a movement among several of the younger American experts in Indian philosophy to change the style of research. This was first noticeable in Potter's *Presuppositions* which perhaps can serve as a model of the impending change. In India, as might have been anticipated, the traditionalistic Sanskritists and philosophers were both fascinated and horrified by his treatment of Indian philosophy. The younger linguistic philosophers applauded what he had done and others found that they were not quite sure what he had intended nor what he had achieved. It was a mixed affair. It would appear that Potter's impact will be greater and more immediate in the United States, especially since he is now the only expert in Indian philosophy in a position to grant advanced degrees in a philosophy department with the exception of his teacher, Ingalls.

This latest direction has probably been set by the members of a new organization. This is the Society for Asian and Comparative Philosophy, established in 1968. Its first national meeting was held in Philadelphia March 1968 in conjunction with the Association for Asian Studies. Karl Potter was elected first president, and Chung-ying Cheng the first secretary-treasurer. Eliot Deutsch joined them to make up the executive committee. The second meeting was held in Boston in the spring of 1969 at which time the Society sponsored a panel on the topic "Referring Expressions." This topic indicates the direction of the Society at the present time to translating problems of Indian philosophy into linguistic philosophical terms. Whether this direction will continue for long will depend partly upon the future viability of linguistic philosophy in general. A considerable thrust in this direction may be seen in India as well as in the United States although it is far from being a dominating expression in either country. One finds it difficult to imagine a country more suited to its expansion than traditional India, which long before Europe was greatly concerned with the problems of language. The future may well bring a stronger focus on the linguistic achievement of Indian philosophy.

The philosophers surveyed in this chapter have all studied in India, most are familiar with one or more Indian languages, and some have made Indian thought their major specialty. A few know Chinese, Japanese, and Tibetan in addition to Sanskrit and modern Indian languages. American Indological philosophical scholarship may now be said to have a firm, although still narrow, base in the United States.

American philosophers are still embued with concern for ancient or medieval Indian thought, rather than modern or contemporary. This may well mean that fruitful intercourse between American and Indian philosophers about current problems will be too often intercepted by classical considerations. One must hope for a partial shift in emphasis. A dialogue between contemporaries should awaken them both to current global philosophical problems.

Chapter XI

CONCLUSION

I

INDIA HAS HAD more influence on American philosophic thought than any other non-Western culture. Judeo-Christian "Asian" thought has been incorporated into the West for 1500 years, so hardly serves as a counterexample.

In the past hundred years the intellectuals of three great nations have been particularly influenced by Indian thought: Germany, Japan, and the United States. These have also been outstanding in intellectual cosmopolitanism during the time span which begins with the Japanese Meiji Era in 1868 to the present. The Japanese by their particular ties to India through Buddhism have paid heed to Indian thought over many centuries. Germans have studied it since Schlegel in the early years of the nineteenth century. Americans since Emerson's manhood in the 1830's have found it worthy of attention. The intellectuals of all three nations, particularly the philosophers, have been concerned with somewhat differing aspects of speculation in the subcontinent in Asia: the Japanese primarily with ethics, the Germans with metaphysics, and the Americans with epistemology and ethics.

As the United States outgrew the restricted colonial empirical outlook during the periods variously called the flowering of New England, the Rise of Romanticism, or the Growth of Independent Mercantilism, another vector of lively awareness appeared. This dimension was often romantic, speculative, holistic, and spiritual in its concern. Part of this was conditioned by the impact of German thought. German thought infused British empiricism and realism with speculative trends emphasizing not only what

273

man is as an object and commodity, but what he should be and could be as a subject. German romanticism touched Britain just as it did the United States, in the first quarter of the nineteenth century. But whereas it petered out in Britain except among the British Hegelians and R. G. Collingwood, it was sustained in the United States in part by the German immigration. It was Alfred North Whitehead's opinion that the ethnic superiority of the American to the British scene lay in its German immigration. Of importance also was the impact of German higher education on American thinkers before the founding of Johns Hopkins University and even afterwards. In the late nineteenth century intellectually alert Americans preferred to study in Germany although we did have graduate facilities in this country. American philosophers still considered it *de rigueur* to spend a year in a German university between World War I and the Great Depression. I dwell on the German influence because it has been a major source of American awareness of Indian thought.

II

The development of interest in Indian thought in the United States showed the following trends. Before 1800 very little was known beyond what Priestley was able to publicize. From 1830 onwards a steadily increasing flow of translations, histories, and other monographs from Europe made much wisdom, literature, philosophy and religion known. Institutions dealing with the questions of Indian thought were founded, among them the Vedanta Centres. The impact of Indian thought in the twentieth century markedly changed in both quantity and quality. Americans wrote monographs on Indian thought, translated treasures of Hinduism and Buddhism, and spread knowledge of Indian speculation and philosophy in major universities and many colleges. Doctoral programs in Indian thought were instituted. For college undergraduates and even high school honors students, numerous courses of academic study responded to the ever-widening concern with India. For the general public a host of paperback volumes on Indian philosophy, culture and history appeared. The center of foreign Indian studies shifted from Europe to the United States. Many of the ablest Indian philosophers have now taken up temporary or permanent residence in American universities. A half-dozen of the finest collections of books and manuscripts from India are now in the United States.

III

What were the circumstances contributing to American concern for Indian thought? Six factors were largely responsible. First, the economic expansionism of the United States from 1812 onwards pressed American claims to all corners of the globe, including India. Since having recently taken over the mantle of Britain, although less with military than economic occupation, official American policy has encouraged intellectuals to become proficient in knowledge of foreign cultures, not least of all Indian. The largest A.I.D. Program, for example, is that in India. This same factor, American expansionism originating in the nineteenth century, has intensified interest in older cultures. Sometimes this was a result of a certain bitterness generated by the consequences of the expansionism itself. One reaction to the violence, alienation, and social fragmentation that have intensified since militarization has been in the direction of the Indian repertoire of ideas. Gandhism and the integralism of Sri Aurobindo provided reinforcement of innocuous solutions to the official encouragement of foundations and foreign aid policy. That the aim of American official policy was often contrary to that of the intellectuals is not here germane.

But even before official American interest in Asia there were intellectuals disillusioned with the so-called Judeo-Christian tradition. This is a second factor. The disenchantment with that tradition was increased by the alliance between the Judeo-Christian conservatism and the ethos of pragmatic expansionism. Science, for example, became increasingly the handmaiden of the needs of the expanding industrial state and the armed forces needed to protect it. Instead of searching for the causes of this sacred-secular amalgamation, the romantic Indianophiles looked for other options and thought they had found some in Indian ethics and metaphysics. Socioeconomic analysis of the situation was much less attractive than imaginative and idealistic flights into the golden past of India.

A third factor, one that could be satisfied for increasing numbers, was the desire for novelty. Often novelty was inspired by the means to get it, that is, by fast travel. After 1900, Americans, at first by the hundreds, visited India. A few even studied there. Between 1950 and 1970, from the beginning of the Fulbright Program in India, thousands of Americans and perhaps a hundred philosophers and religionists among them, taught, studied, and did research in India. Others went to India on subventions provided by private foundations and the U. S. State Department. An unprecedented speed of travel and expansion of higher education led increasingly numerous Americans to international tastes in everything from food to philosophy.

Discontent with the state of American philosophy itself was a fourth factor. If a contemporary American wished to get spiritual consolation, a view of a better perspective of community life, a critique of American civilization, to what contemporary American philosopher could he turn after World War I? Where were the philosophical consciences of America? Where were the Emersons, Thoreaus, Bellamys, or Howells? They were not often visible among the philosophers, especially not those in academic philosophy. There were some who showed concern. But philosophers like Royce, Santayana, and William Ernest Hocking never went to the heart of the matter, dominated as they were by spiritualistic and idealistic conceptions of causation. It is true that Hocking went the farthest towards a critique of American civilization. The sharpest critiques of American civilization were to come, not from the Indianophiles so much, as from those conversant with German theory and historicism—Thorstein Veblen, John Dewey, Lewis Mumford, and C. Wright Mills. Although Veblen took his doctorate in the philosophy of Kant, and Mills and Mumford were avid readers of philosophy, only Dewey could be considered a professional philosopher. Yet all four were irritated by the supine attitude of American philosophers to problems of justice, fair distribution of social production, and planned amelioration. The more tender-minded philosophers, on the other hand, looked into the Indian display hoping to find solutions to the problems being raised by American business civilization.

A factor, finally, that cannot be underestimated was that of language. Communication between Indian and American intellectuals and educated people in general was made possible by the colonial activities of the British in India. America reaped a harvest from what was meant primarily to serve commercial interests. It is possible for Americans with no knowledge of a foreign language to live and work in India, even to do research. This would be impossible in any other major Asian civilization. It could not have occurred in China, Japan, Iran, or Southeast Asia. Widespread communication between Indians and Americans was possible. It is a rare moment that an American philosopher finds an Indian thinker who cannot express himself in English, frequently with considerable skill and sometimes with originality. Some have even suggested that English is *the* language of intellectuals in India. What a powerful recommendation this has been to the study of Indian philosophy and religion cannot be accurately gauged. Yet it must be considerable. One can surmise that its influence has been enormously greater than if a knowledge of one of the great Indian languages like Hindi, Bengali, Tamil, or Marathi must have been mastered first. These were the major reasons for the impact of Indian thought on American thinkers.

IV

No matter how much certain American philosophers were intrigued with Indian philosophy, no one could make their Americanism vanish. We have heard critical comments about it beginning with Emerson and continuing down to the present. Americans have grown up with the scientific attitude, with gadgets, with skeptical views about the efficacy of spiritual practices, with doubts concerning contemplation, and a general contempt for anything which gets in the way of speed and production. These cannot be easily erased. First of all there is the faith that salvation will appear in scientific garb. Right now it is hoped that the computer will somehow reverse the chaotic situations in life. There is also the faith that if only we construct the right model much will be improved. This faith is centered around game-theory. Most of the philosophers interested in India cannot reject these possibilities out of hand. Their scientific faith makes it almost unthinkable. The attendant optimism keeps bubbling up. Therefore a constant chord struck against Indian thought is that it is too negative, that it is too passive, that it is even supine in its consequences. If only the Indians would *do* something! Critics who say that Indian philosophy is not *really* negative and passive have not been generally convincing even to sympathetic American thinkers. There is no reason to think that the situation will always remain so. If the American empire meets with the fate of the British, if Americans cannot resolve their life-and-death struggle with the intelligent use of technology, if the alienation in American society cannot be alleviated, then a new attitude may gradually replace the 300-year reign of optimism. Such eventualities may lead to more philosophers turning to contemplation, meditation, and increased poring over the Hindu and Buddhist scriptures. But there is yet no strong trend in this direction except among a handful of poets, religious devotees, and philosophers. There is still an attempt to fit Indian thought into the optimistic and pragmatic American temper.

V

What have American thinkers gained by their study of Indian philosophies and religions? I believe that the following are noteworthy. First, they discovered new technical philosophy of undreamed complexity and ingenuity. The latest rich deposits to be noticed from the viewpoint of linguistic philosophy concerns the Indian contributions to semantics. There are thousands of notions recognized as contributions to philosophy, such as *syādvāda* (perspectivism), *ahimsā* (noncruelty or noninjury), *sphoṭa* (symbolism), *ākāṅkṣā* (syntactic expectancy), yoga (unity of the mind and body), and *śūnyatā* (somewhat comparable to *das Nichts*).

Second, knowledge of Indian thought led to expanded interest in the philosophies and religious systems of China and Japan. Indian thought, it was discovered, is to subsequent Asian thought what Greek thought is believed to be in relation to subsequent European, Semitic, Islamic and American thought. When one investigates an alien system his appetite is also whetted by its web of relations to what is already known. One thus has increasing awareness of the vast complexity and also similarity of human thinking.

As a result of studying Indian thought, third, some American intellectuals have been led to attempt studies which encourage the spirit of cooperation and understanding among peoples. This effect may be seen in the work of W. E. Hocking, G. P. Conger, E. A. Burtt, F. C. S. Northrop, and C. S. Morris.

Fourth, the resources of Indian philosophy have provided American thinkers, long dominated by European and Judeo-Christian traditions, with historical and cultural perspectives that have sociopolitical as well as humanistic consequences. The rich treasures of the time-honored Indian museum of speculation have provided previously unimagined perspectives. As these are revealed in their "skeletal and physiological" interconnections with the socioeconomic aspects of Asian history their fuller meaning has enlarged man's understanding of himself. The embryonic development of philosophical anthropology in the United States depends somewhat upon Indian resources. Also the American studies in the philosophy of history are increasingly beholden to the Indian tradition.

And finally, is a consideration dear to the hearts of jaded or romantic philosophers everywhere. That is the discovery of and pleasure in the *curiosa* of philosophy. Recently a young practitioner of the analytic philosophy returned from a conference with Indian and Chinese philosophers. He was excited, flushed as he talked, over the treasures of thought (by which he meant linguistic philosophy) that Indian experts had revealed to him. Indian philosophy has expanded the enjoyment and subtlety of the European-dominated mind in a way parallel to the expansion of his palate following an introduction of Indian cooking: delicious curries like the monistic *vedānta, chappaties* and *parathas* like *yoga* and *vaiśeṣika;* soups like *bauddha; chutneys* like *nyāya.* If these can be thought of as symbols they represent a richness and novelty that is unparalleled in our history. They have expanded the imagination, increased the number of categories, made possible new studies in the history of logic, revealed new sensations, and driven the mind back to its origins and out to its possibilities.

BIBLIOGRAPHY

ADAMS, BROOKS: *The Law of Civilization and Decay: An Essay on History*. London, Sonnenshein, 1895.

ADAMS, HENRY: *The Education of Henry Adams: An Autobiography*. Boston, Houghton, 1918.

ANDERSON, JACK: The Washington merry-go-round. *Buffalo Courier Express,* February 22, 1964.

ANDERSON, PAUL RUSSELL: *Platonism in the Midwest*. New York, Temple U., 1963.

ANDERSON, PAUL RUSSELL and FISCH, MAX HAROLD: *Philosophy in America from the Puritans to James*. The Century Philosophy Series, Lamprecht, Sterling P. (Ed.) New York, Appleton, 1939.

ARBERRY, A. J.: *Oriental Essays*. London, Allen & Unwin, 1960.

ARCHER, JOHN CLARK: Hinduism. In Jurji, E. J. (Ed.): *The Great Religions of the Modern World*. Princeton, Princeton, 1947.

ATKINS, SAMUEL D.: Notes [on Harold Herman Bender]. *Language,* 27, 1951.

ATKINS, SAMUEL D.: The meaning of Vedic *aktú. J Amer Orient Soc,* 70, 1, 1950.

ATKINS, SAMUEL D.: The meaning of Vedic *Páktú. J Amer Orient Soc,* 85, 1, 1965.

ATKINS, SAMUEL D.: *Pūṣan in the Rig-Veda*. Princeton: 28 Edwards Place, 1941. [Doctoral Dissertation 1935].

ATKINS, SAMUEL D.: Pūṣan in the Sāma, Yajur, and Atharva Vedas. *J Amer Orient Soc,* 67, 4, 1947.

ATKINS, SAMUEL D.: RV. 2.38: A problem hymn. *J Amer Orient Soc.* 81, 2, 1961.

BABBITT, IRVING: *The Dhammapada Translated from the Pāli with an Essay on Buddha and the Occident*. New York, Oxford U. P., 1936.

BABBITT, IRVING: *Literature and the American College*. Boston, Houghton, 1908.

BABBITT, IRVING: *The New Laokoon; an Essay on the Confusion of the Arts.* Boston, Houghton, 1910.

BABBITT, IRVING: Romanticism and the Orient. *On Being Creative and other Essays,* Boston, Houghton, 1932.

BAHM, ARCHIE: Buddhist Aesthetics. *J Aesth Art Crit,* XVI, 2, 1957.

BAHM, ARCHIE: Does Seven-Fold Predication Equal Four-Cornered Negation Reversed? *Philos East West,* XII, 3–4, 1957.

BAHM, ARCHIE: Inconsistencies in Naming Patterns in the Bhagavad-gītā. Banaras Hindu U., IX, 2, 1964.

BAHM, ARCHIE: Jaina Logic and World Peace. *Voice Ahinsa,* V, 8, 1955.

BAHM, ARCHIE: Oriental Philosophy, *Rev Metaph* IV, 2, 1951.

BARBU, ZEVEDEI: *Problems of Historical Psychology.* London, Routledge & Kegan Paul, 1960.

BARROWS, JOHN HENRY: *The World's Parliament of Religion,* 2 vols. Chicago, Parliament, 1893.

BENDER, ERNEST (Ed.) : *Indological Studies in Honor of W. Norman Brown.* American Oriental Series, Vol. 47, ed. E. H. Schafer (Ed.). New Haven, Am. Orient. Soc., 1962.

BENTLEY, WILLIAM: *The Diary of William Bentley, D. D.,* 4 vols. Salem, Essex Institute, 1905.

BHATTACHARYA, S.: Daniel H. H. Ingalls on Indian logic. *Philos East West,* V, 2, 1955.

BIERCE, AMBROSE: *The Collected Works of,* Vol. XI. New York, Neale, 1912.

BIERCE, AMBROSE: *The Devil's Dictionary.* Cleveland, World, 1942.

BIERCE, AMBROSE: Immortality. *The Shadow of the Dial and Other Essays.* San Francisco, Robertson, 1909.

BIGELOW, WILLIAM STURGIS: *Buddhism and Immortality,* The Ingersoll Lecture, 1908. Boston, Houghton, Riverside Editions, 1908.

BLAU, JOSEPH: *American Philosophical Addresses 1700–1900.* New York, Columbia, 1946.

BLAVATSKY, H. P.: *Collected Writings 1883.* Los Angeles, Philosophical Res. Soc., 1950.

BLAVATSKY, H. P.: *Isis Unveiled: A Master-Key to the Mysteries of Ancient and Modern Science and Theology,* 2 vols. New York, Bouton, 1877.

BLOOMFIELD, MAURICE: Brahmanical riddles and the origin of Theosophy. *International Congress of Arts and Science,* ed. Howard J. Rogers, IV, London, University Alliance, 1906.

BLOOMFIELD, MAURICE: *The Religion of the Rig Veda*. New York, Putnam, 1908.

BOAS, GEORGE: *Never Go Back*. New York, Harper, 1928.

BOCHEÑSKI, I. M.: Review of D. H. H. Ingalls, Materials for the study of Navya-nyāya logic. *J Sym Log* 17, 2, 1952.

BONDURANT, JOAN V.: *Conquest of Violence: The Gandhian Philosophy of Conflict* Princeton, Princeton, 1958.

BOSE, SUNDHINDRA: Sir Rabindranath Tagore at the State University of Iowa. *Modern Review,* XXI, 2, 1917.

BOURNE, RANDOLPH: Paul Elmer More. *War and the Intellectuals.* New York, Harper, 1964.

BRIDGMAN, RAYMOND L.: *Concord Lectures on Philosophy,* Cambridge, Moses King, 1883.

BRIGGS, GEORGE WESTON: *Gorakhnāth and the Kānphata Yogīs,* The Religious Life of India Series. Calcutta, Y.M.C.A., 1938.

BRIGHTMAN, EDGAR SHEFFIELD: Personalistic metaphysics of the self: its distinctive features, in W. R. Inge, *et. al.: Radhakrishnan: Comparative Studies in Philosophy Presented in Honor of His Sixtieth Birthday.* New York, Harper, n.d. [1952?].

BRIGHTMAN, EDGAR SHEFFIELD: Radhakrishnan and mysticism. *The Philosophy of Sarvepalli Radhakrishnan.* New York, Tudor, 1952.

BROOKS, VAN WYCK: *Fenellosa and His Circle With Other Essays in Biography.* New York, Dutton, 1962.

BROOKS, VAN WYCK: *The Flowering of New England 1816–1865.* New York, Dutton, 1940.

BROOKS, VAN WYCK: *The Times of Melville and Whitman.* New York, Dutton, 1947.

BROOKS, VAN WYCK: *The World of Washington Irving.* New York, Dutton, 1944.

BROWN, GEORGE WILLIAM: *The Human Body in the Upanishads.* Jubbulpore, Christian Mission, 1921.

BROWN, W. NORMAN: An American View of Gandhi, In Martin Deming Lewis (Ed.) *Gandhi: Maker of Modern India?* Boston, Heath, 1965.

BROWN, W. NORMAN: The Basis for the Hindu act of truth, *The Review of Religion,* V, 1, 1940.

BROWN, W. NORMAN: The creation myth of the Rig Veda, *J Amer Orient Soc,* 62, 1942.

BROWN, W. NORMAN: Biographical Memoir: Franklin Edgerton (1885–1963). *Year Book American Philosophical Society,* Philadelphia, Am. Philos. Soc., 1965.

BROWN, W. NORMAN: *The Indian and Christian Miracles of Walking on the Water*. Chicago, Open Ct., 1928.

BROWN, W. NORMAN: *The Mahimnastava or Praise of Shiva's Greatness*. Poona, Am. Inst. of Indian Studies, 1965.

BROWN, W. NORMAN: The Rig Veda equivalent for hell. *J Amer Orient Soc*, 61, 1941.

BROWN, W. NORMAN: *The Saudaryalaharī or Flood of Beauty*, traditionally ascribed to Saṅkarācārya. Harvard Oriental Series, Vol. 43. Cambridge, Harvard, 1958.

BROWN, W. NORMAN: South Asian studies in the United States. *Indian Studies Abroad*, Indian Council for Cultural Relations. New Delhi, 1964.

BROWN, W. NORMAN: Theories of creation in the Rig Veda, *J Amer Orient Soc*, 85, 1, 1965.

BROWNING, ROBERT W.: Reason and Types of Intuition in Radhakrishnan's Philosophy. *The Philosophy of Sarvepalli Radhakrishnan*. New York, Tudor, 1952.

BUITENEN, J. A. B. VAN: Dharma and Mokṣa, *Philos East West*, VII, 1–2, 1957.

BURCH, GEORGE: Contemporary Vedanta philosophy, I. *Rev Metaph* IX, 3, 1956.

BURCH, GEORGE: Contemporary Vedanta philosophy, II. *Rev Metaph* IX, 4, 1956.

BURCH, GEORGE: Contemporary Vedanta philosophy, continued. *Rev Metaph* X, 1, 1956.

BURCH, GEORGE: The definite and the indefinite. *Krishna Chandra Bhattacharyya Memorial Volume*. Amalner, Indian Inst. of Philosophy, 1958.

BURCH, GEORGE: A Footnote to K. C. Bhattacharyya's philosophy. *Brahmavidya*, The Adyar Library Bulletin and Research Center, Adyar, Madras 20 Vols. XXXI–XXXII, 1967–68.

BURCH, GEORGE: The Hindu concept of existence. *The Monist*, 50, 1, 1966.

BURCH, GEORGE: Principles and problems of Monistic Vedānta, *Philos East West*, XI, 4, 1962.

BURCH, GEORGE: Recent Vedanta literature. *Rev Metaph* XII, 1, 1958.

BURCH, GEORGE: Search for the Absolute in Neo-Vedanta: the philosophy of K. C. Bhattacharyya. *Intl Philos Quar*, VII, 4, 1967.

BURCH, GEORGE: Seven-Valued Logic in Jain Philosophy. *Intl Philos Quar*, IV, 1, 1964.

BURKE, MARIE LOUISE: *Swami Vivekananda in America, New Discoveries.* Calcutta, Advaita Ashrama, 1958.

BURNOUF, E.: *Introduction a l'historie du Buddhisme Indien.* Paris, 1876.

BURTT, E. A.: Basic problems of method in harmonizing Eastern and Western Philosophy. In C. A. Moore (Ed.) : *Essays in East-West Philosophy.* Honolulu, U. of Hawaii, 1950.

BURTT, E. A.: General introduction, in E. A. Burtt (Ed.) : *The Teachings of the Compassionate Buddha.* New York, New Am. Lib., 1959 [1955].

BURTT, E. A.: The problem of a world philosophy, in W. R. Inge, *et. al.: Radhakrishnan: Comparative Studies in Philosophy Presented in Honor of His Sixtieth Birthday.* New York, Harper, n.d. [1952?].

BURTT, E. A.: *In Search of Philosophic Understanding.* New York, Am. Lib., 1967.

BURTT, E. A.: *Types of Religious Philosophy.* New York, Harper, 1939.

BURTT, E. A.: What can Western philosophy contribute to Eastern? *Philos East West,* V, 4, 1956.

BURTT, E. A.: What can Western philosophy learn from India? *Philos East West,* V, 3, 1955.

BURTT, E. A.: What happened in philosophy between 1900–1950? *Essays in Honor of A. R. Wadia.* Madras, G. S. Press, 1954.

BUTTERFIELD, HERBERT: Delays and paradoxes in the development of historiography. In K. Bourne and D. C. Watt (Ed.) : *Studies in International History.* New York, Longmans Green, 1967.

CAIRNS, GRACE E.: *Philosophies of History.* New York, Citadel, 1962.

CAMPBELL, JOSEPH: Editor's Foreword. In Heinrich Zimmer, *Myths and Symbols in Indian Art and Civilization.* New York, Harper, 1962 [1946].

CAMPBELL, JOSEPH: *The Hero with a Thousand Faces.* Bollingen Series XVII. New York, Pantheon, 1953.

CAMPBELL, JOSEPH: *The Masks of God: Primitive Mythology.* New York, Viking, 1959.

CAMERON, KENNETH WALTER: *Companion to Thoreau's Correspondence.* Hartford, Transcendental Books, 1964.

CAMERON, KENNETH WALTER: *Emerson the Essayist: An Outline of his Philosophical Development Through 1836.* Hartford, Transcendental Books, 1945.

CAMERON, KENNETH WALTER: *Ralph Waldo Emerson's Reading.* Raleigh, Thistle Press, 1941.

CARDIFF, IRA D. (Ed.) : *Atoms of Thought: An Anthology of Thoughts from George Santayana.* New York, Philosophical Lib., 1950.

CARUS, PAUL: *Buddhism and its Christian Critics.* Chicago, Open Ct., 1897.

CARUS, PAUL: *The Dharma, or The Religion of Enlightenment: An Exposition of Buddhism.* Chicago, Open Ct., 1896.

CARUS, PAUL: *Fundamental Problems: The Method of Philosophy as a Systematic Arrangement of Knowledge.* Chicago, Open Ct. 1903.

CARUS, PAUL: *God: An Enquiry into the Nature of Man's Highest Ideal and a Solution of the Problem from the Standpoint of Science.* Chicago, Open Ct., 1908.

CARUS, PAUL: *The Gospel of Buddha according to Old Records.* Chicago, Open Ct., 1894.

CARUS, PAUL: *Karma, A Story of Buddhist Ethics.* Chicago, Open Ct., 1903.

CARUS, PAUL: *Nirvāna, a Story of Buddhist Psychology.* Chicago, Open Ct., 1902.

CARUS, PAUL: *Nirvāna, a Story of Buddhist Philosophy.* Chicago, Open Ct., 1896.

CARUS, PAUL: *Philosophy as a Science.* Chicago, Open Ct., 1909.

CARUS, PAUL: *The Surd of Metaphysics.* Chicago, Open Ct., 1903.

CHANG, MING HUI: *Yeats and Indian Philosophy.* Seattle, U. of Wash., 1952.

CHARLTON, D. G.: *Secular Religions in France 1815–1870.* London, Oxford, 1963.

CHARVAT, WILLIAM: *The Origins of American Critical Thought.* Philadelphia, 1936.

CHRISTY, ARTHUR E. (Ed.) : *The Asian Legacy and American Life.* New York, John Day, 1945 [1942].

CHRISTY, ARTHUR E.: *The Orient in American Transcendentalism, A Study of Emerson, Thoreau, and Alcott.* New York, Columbia, 1932.

CLARK, WALTER EUGENE: *The Indian Conception of Immortality.* Cambridge, Harvard, 1934.

COHEN, MORRIS RAPHAEL: *American Thought: A Critical Sketch.* New York, Collier, 1962.

COMMAGER, HENRY STEELE: *The American Mind: An Interpretation of American Thought and Character Since the 1880's.* New Haven, Yale, 1950.

CONGER, GEORGE P.: Cosmic persons and human universes in Indian philosophy. *J Proc Asiatic Soc Bengal,* New Series, XXIX, 1, 1934.

CONGER, GEORGE P. Epitomization and epistemology. *The Monist,* 1933.

CONGER, GEORGE P.: *The Horizons of Thought.* Princeton, Princeton, 1933.

CONGER, GEORGE P.: The implicit duality of thinking. *J Philos* XIX, 9, 1922.

CONGER, GEORGE P.: Integration. In C. A. Moore (Ed.) : *Essays in East-West Philosophy.* Honolulu, U. of Hawaii, 1951.

CONGER, GEORGE P.: Method and content in philosophy. *Philos Rev,* July, 1946.

CONGER, GEORGE P.: A naturalistic approach to Sāṁkhya-Yoga. *Philos East West,* III, 3, 1953.

CONGER, GEORGE P.: A naturalistic garland for Radhakrishnan. In W. R. Inge, *et. al.: Radhakrishnan: Comparative Studies in Philosophy Presented in Honor of His Sixtieth Birthday.* New York, Harper, n.d. [1952?].

CONGER, GEORGE P.: Nature and reality. *Actes du Xiéne Congrés International de Philosophie,* Vol. III. Bruxelles, North Holland, 1953.

CONGER, GEORGE P.: An Outline of Indian Philosophy. In C. A. Moore (Ed.) : *Philosophy—East and West.* Princeton, Princeton, 1944.

CONGER, GEORGE P.: Radhakrishnan's World. In P. A. Schilpp (Ed.) : *The Philosophy of Sarvepalli Radhakrishnan,* New York, Tudor, 1952.

CONGER, GEORGE P.: Ṛta: cosmic structure and social order. Peradeniya, UNESCO, 1954.

CONGER, GEORGE P.: Some suggestions toward a theory of the soul. *Indian Philosophical Congress,* 1950. Madras, Associated Printers, 1951.

CONGER, GEORGE P.: *Synoptic Naturalism.* Minneapolis, U. of Minn. Lib. 1960.

CONGER, GEORGE P.: Toward Understanding India, *The Aryan Path,* November 1935.

COOMARASWAMY, ANANDA KENTISH: *Asiatic Art.* Chicago, New Orient Soc. of America, 1938.

COOMARASWAMY, ANANDA KENTISH: *The Bugbear of Literacy.* London, Dennis Dobson, 1949.

COOMARASWAMY, ANANDA KENTISH: *Eastern Religion and Western Thought,* reprinted from *Rev Relig,* January 1942.

COOMARASWAMY, ANANDA KENTISH: *Hinduism and Buddhism.* New York, Philosophical Lib., n.d.

COOMARASWAMY, ANANDA KENTISH: Primitive mentality. *Quar J Mythic Soc,* 31.

COOMARASWAMY, ANANDA KENTISH: Recollection, Indian and Platonic and on the one and only transmigration. *Supp J Amer Orient Soc,* 3, 1944.

COOMARASWAMY, ANANDA KENTISH: *The Religious Basis of the Forms of Indian Society and Indian Culture and English Influence and East and West.* New York, Orientalia, 1946.

COOMARASWAMY, ANANDA KENTISH: Speech delivered at his 70th birthday, Harvard Club at Boston, August 22, 1947.

CORY, DANIEL, (Ed.): *The Letters of George Santayana.* New York, Scribner, 1955.

CORY, DANIEL: *Santayana: The Later Years.* New York, Braziller, 1963.

COUSIN, VICTOR: *Course of the History of Modern Philosophy,* 2 vols. W. W. Wright, trans. New York, Appleton, [1852?].

DAVIDSON, ELIZABETH: Americans look to India. *Prabuddha Bharata,* March 1945.

DEUTSCH, ELIOT S.: The justification of Hindu 'polytheism' in Advaita Vedānta, *East-West Ctr Rev,* I, 3, 1965.

DEUTSCH, ELIOT S.: Karma as a 'convenient fiction' in the Advaita Vedānta. *Philos East West,* XV, 1, 1965.

DEUTSCH, ELIOT S.: Levels of Being. *Darshana International,* V, 4, 1965.

DEUTSCH, ELIOT S.: The nature of divine action in Advaita Vedānta, *University Seminar On Oriental Thought and Religion,* Columbia U., April 1965.

DEUTSCH, ELIOT S.: The nature of scripture. *Vedanta Kesari,* LI, 9. 1965.

DEUTSCH, ELIOT S.: Śakti in Medieval Hindu Sculpture. *J Aesth Art Crit,* XXIV, 1, 1965.

DEUTSCH, ELIOT, S.: The self in Advaita Vedānta. *Intl Philos Quar,* VI, 1, 1966.

DEUTSCH, ELIOT S.: Sri Aurobindo's interpretation of spiritual experience: A critique. *Intl Philos Quar,* IV, 4, 1964.

DEUTSCH, ELIOT S.: Ways of thinking of Eastern peoples: India, China, Tibet, Japan. A review. *J Philos,* LXII, 22, 1965.

DEWEY, JOHN: Emerson. *Character and Events.* New York, 1929.

DEWEY, JOHN, and ALICE CHIPMAN DEWEY: *Letters from China and Japan* London, Dent, 1920.

DEWEY, JOHN: On Philosophical Synthesis. *Philos East West,* I, 1, 1951.

DILLIARD, IRVING: Philosopher with a pen that stabbed. *St. Louis Post-Dispatch,* December 30, 1964.

DUBOIS, ABBÉ: *Hindu Manners, Customs and Ceremonies,* 3 ed. Oxford, Clarendon Press, 1943.

DUCASSE, CURT JOHN: *A Critical Examination of the Belief in a Life After Death.* Springfield, Thomas, 1961.

DUCASSE, CURT JOHN: *A Philosophical Scrutiny of Religion.* New York, Ronald, 1953.

DUNHAM, BARROWS: Paul Elmer More. Unpublished MS to appear in *The Massachusetts Review,* Winter, 1966.

DUTT, K. GURU: *Existentialism and Indian Thought.* New York, Philosophical Lib., 1960.

EASTON, LOYD: *Hegel's First American Followers.* Athens, Ohio Univ. Press, 1966.

EDGERTON, FRANKLIN: *The Beginnings of Indian Philosophy.* Cambridge, Harvard, 1965.

EDGERTON, FRANKLIN: Did Buddha have a system of Metaphysics? *J Amer Orient Soc,* LXXIX, 1959.

EDGERTON, FRANKLIN: Edward Washburn Hopkins. *J Amer Orient Soc,* LII, 1932.

EDGERTON, FRANKLIN: Dominant ideas in the formation of Indian culture. *J Amer Orient Soc,* LXII, 1942.

EDGERTON, FRANKLIN: Maurice Bloomfield (1855–1928). *J Amer Orient Soc,* XLVII, 1928.

EMENEAU, M. B.: Franklin Edgerton. *Language,* 40.

EMERSON, RALPH WALDO: *The Complete Works of Ralph Waldo Emerson, with a Biographical Introduction and Notes,* 10 vols. Boston, Houghton, 1875.

EMERSON, RALPH WALDO: In Stephen Whicher and Robert Spiller (Ed.): *The Early Lectures of,* Vol. I. Cambridge, Harvard, 1959.

EMERSON, RALPH WALDO: In Edward Waldo Emerson Forbes (Ed.): *Journals of,* 10 vols. Boston, Houghton, 1909.

EMERSON, RALPH WALDO: Veeshnoo Sarma (July 1842). *Uncollected Writings.* New York, Lamb, 1912.

EWING, ARTHUR H.: The Hindu conceptions of the functions of breath. *J Amer Orient Soc,* 22, 2, 1901.

EWING, ARTHUR H.: *Theosophy Examined.* London, Christian Lit. Soc., 1905.

FERGUSON, ALFRED R. (Ed.): *The Journals and Miscellaneous Note-*

books of Ralph Waldo Emerson, 4 vols. Cambridge, Belknap, Harvard, 1964.

FISKE, JOHN: *Essays Historical and Literary,* 2 vols. New York, Macmillan 1902.

FOERSTER, NORMAN: *Nature in American Literature: Studies in the Modern View of Nature.* New York, Macmillan, 1923.

FRANK, WALDO: *The Re-discovery of America.* New York, Scribner, 1929.

GABRIEL, RALPH HENRY: *The Course of American Democratic Thought: An Intellectual History Since 1815.* New York, Ronald, 1940.

GARAUDY, ROGER: *From Anathema to Dialogue,* trans. Luke O'Neill. New York, Vintage Books, 1968.

GARRATT, G. T.: Indo-British Civilization. *The Legacy of India.* Oxford, Clarendon Press, 1938.

GOODWIN, WILLIAM F.: Sāṁkhya and the philosophy of Santayana: some parallelisms. In S. Radhakrishnan, *et. al.* (Ed.) : *A. R. Wadia Essays in Philosophy Presented in His Honor.* Madras, G. S. Press, 1954.

GOODWIN, WILLIAM F.: Theories of consciousness and liberation in the Samkhya philosophy and the philosophy of George Santayana. *Philos Quar,* XXVII, 1955.

GRANT, ELLIOTT MANSFIELD: *French Poetry and Modern Industry 1830–1870.* Cambridge, Harvard, 1927.

GRANT, FRANCES: *Oriental Philosophy.* New York, Dial, 1936.

GRAY, LOUIS HERBERT, (Ed.) :*The Mythology of All Races.* Boston, Jones, 1917.

GROSSMAN, MORRIS: A glimpse of some unpublished Santayana manuscripts. *J Philos,* LXI, 1, 1964.

GUÉNON, RENÉ: *East and West.* London, Luzac, 1941.

HAAS, WILLIAM S.: *The Destiny of the Mind.* New York, Macmillan, 1956.

HAHN, E. ADELAIDE: Franklin Edgerton, Personal Reminiscences. *J Amer Orient Soc,* 85, 1, 1965.

HALL, FITZEDWARD: *Index: A Contribution Towards an Index to the Bibliography of the Indian Philosophical Systems.* Calcutta, 1959.

HAMILTON, CLARENCE H.: *A Psychological Interpretation of Mysticism.* Chicago, U. of Chicago Lib., 1916.

HAMILTON, CLARENCE H.: *Buddhism: A Religion of Infinite Compassion.* New York, Liberal Arts Press, 1952.

HAMILTON, CLARENCE H.: *Buddhism in India, Ceylon, China and Japan.* Chicago, U. of Chicago, 1931.

HAMILTON, CLARENCE H.: Buddhist Philosophical Systems. In Ferm, Vergilius (Ed.) : *A History of Philosophical Systems,* Ames, Little-field, 1958.

HAMILTON, CLARENCE H.: Buddhistic idealism in Wei Shih Er Shih Lwen. In T. V. Smith and William K. Wright (Ed.) : *Essays in Philosophy.* Chicago, Open Ct., 1929.

HANSEN, HARRY, (Ed.) : *World Almanac.* New York, New York World Telegram, 1962, 1963, 1964, 1965, 1966, 1968) .

HARE, PETER: The emergence and submergence of polarity in the phi-losophy of Wilmon Henry Sheldon. M.A. Thesis, Columbia U., 1962.

HARMON, FRANCES B.: *The Social Philosophy of the St. Louis Hegel-ians.* New York, Columbia, 1943.

HARRIS, WILLIAM HENRY: Human values in a non-technical culture. *Main Currents Mod Thought,* 14, 2, 1957.

HARRIS, WILLIAM HENRY: India and Western spirituality. *Quest,* 37, 1963.

HARRIS, WILLIAM HENRY: Philosophy in Indian culture. Boston, Bos-ton U. Graduate School, 1965.

HARRIS, WILLIAM HENRY: Swami Vivekananda and Neo-Hindu Uni-versalism. *Iliff Review,* XXII, 2, 1965.

HARRIS, WILLIAM HENRY: The third way. *Unitarian Reg,* 139, 3 1960.

HARRISON, JOHN S.: The ascendancy of Platonism. *The Teachers of Emerson.* New York, Sturgis & Walton, 1910.

HARTSHORNE, CHARLES: Introduction: The development of process philosophy. In Douglas Browning (Ed.) : *Philosophers of Process.* New York, Randon, 1965.

HAY, STEPHEN N.: Rabindranath Tagore in America. *Amer Quar,* XIV, 3, 1962.

HAY, WILLIAM H.: Paul Carus: a case-study of philosophy on the frontier. *J Hist Ideas,* XVII, 4, 1956.

HEARD, GERALD: *Is God Evident?* London, Faber & Faber, 1950.

HEARD, GERALD: *The Human Venture.* New York, Harper, 1955.

HEARD, GERALD: The third redemption of Man. *Is God in History?* New York, Harper, 1950.

HEARD, GERALD: *The Eternal Gospel.* London, Faber and Faber, 1946.

HEARD, GERALD. *Is God in History?* London, Faber and Faber, 1949.

HEARD, GERALD: *The Third Morality* New York, William Morrow, 1937.

HOCKING, WILLIAM ERNEST: *Human Nature and Its Remaking.* New Haven, Yale, 1918.

HOCKING, WILLIAM ERNEST: Living religions and a world faith, In

Arthur E. Christy (Ed.) : *The Asian Legacy and American Life.* New York, John Day 1945.

HOCKING, WILLIAM ERNEST: *The Meaning of God in Human Experience.* New Haven, Yale, 1934.

HOCKING, WILLIAM ERNEST: Mind and Near-Mind. In Edgar S. Brightman (Ed.) : *Proceedings of the Sixth International Congress of Philosophy.* New York, Longmans, Green, 1927.

HOCKING, WILLIAM ERNEST: *Strength of Men and Nations.* New York, Harper, 1959.

HOFSTADTER, RICHARD: *The Age of Reform.* New York, Vintage Books, 1955.

HOPKINS, E. WASHBURN: *Ethics of India.* New Haven, Yale, 1924.

HOPKINS, E. WASHBURN: *The Great Epic of India.* New Haven, Yale, 1920 [1901].

HOPKINS, E. WASHBURN: *The History of Religions.* New York, Macmillan 1918.

HOPKINS, E. WASHBURN: The Holy Numbers of the Rig-Veda. *Oriental Studies,* Oriental Club of Philadelphia (Ed.) Boston, Ginn, 1894.

HOPKINS, E. WASHBURN: Mythological aspects of trees and mountains in the Great Epic, *J Amer Orient Soc,* XXXI, IV, 1910.

HOPKINS, E. WASHBURN: On the Hindu custom of dying to redress a grievance. *J. Amer Orient Soc,* XXI, 1900.

HOPKINS, E. WASHBURN: Indic and Indian religious parallels. *J Amer Orient Soc.* XXXVII, 1, 1917.

HOPKINS, E. WASHBURN: *The Origin and Evolution of Religion.* New Haven, Yale, 1923.

HOPKINS, E. WASHBURN: The sniff-kiss in ancient India, *J Amer Orient Soc,* XXVIII, 1907.

HOPKINS, E. WASHBURN: Yoga-techniques in the Great Epic, *J Amer Orient Soc,* XXII, II, 1911.

HUME, ROBERT ERNEST: *The Thirteen Principal Upanishads.* Madras, Goeffrey Cumberlege, Oxford, 1941.

HUME, ROBERT ERNEST: *Treasure-House of The Living Religions,* Selections from Their Sacred Scriptures. New York, Scribner, 1932.

HUME, ROBERT ERNEST: *The World's Living Religions.* New York, Scribner, 1924.

HUMPHREYS, CHRISTMAS: *Development of Buddhism in England.* London, 1937.

HURST, JOHN FLETCHER: *Indika.* New York, Harper, 1891.

INDIAN COUNCIL FOR CULTURAL RELATIONS: *Indian Studies Abroad.* New York, Asia Publishing House, 1964.

INDIAN COUNCIL OF WORLD AFFAIRS: *India and the United Nations National Studies on International Organization.* New York, Manhattan Pub., 1957.

Indian Studies in Honor of Charles Rockwell Lanman. Cambridge, Harvard, 1929.

INGALLS, DANIEL H. H.: A reply to Bhattacharya. *Philos East West,* V, 2, 1955.

INGALLS, DANIEL H. H.: Bhāskara the Vedantin. *Philos East West,* XVII, 1–4, 1967.

INGALLS, DANIEL H. H.: Human Effort versus God's Effort in the Early Nyaya. (NS 4.1 19–21) *Dr. S. K. Belvalker Felicitation Volume.* Banaras, N. Banarsi Dass, 1957.

INGALLS, DANIEL H. H.: The heritage of a fallible saint: Annie Besant's gifts to India. *Proc Amer Philos Soc,* 109, 2, 1965.

INGALLS, DANIEL H. H.: *Materials Toward a Study of Navya-Nyāya Logic.* Harvard Oriental Series Vol. 44. Cambridge, Harvard.

INGALLS, DANIEL H. H.: Walter Eugene Clark. *Harvard University Gazette,* October 28, 1961.

INGALLS, DANIEL H. H.: Words for Beauty in Classical Sanskrit Poetry. *Indological Studies in Honor of W. Norman Brown.* New Haven, Am. Orient. Soc., 1962.

ISHERWOOD, CHRISTOPHER: *An Approach to Vedanta.* London, Methuen, 1963.

ISHERWOOD, CHRISTOPHER: *Ramakrishna and His Disciples.* New York, Simon and Schuster, Inc., 1965.

ISHERWOOD, CHRISTOPHER: *Vedanta and the West.* New York, Harper, 1951.

ISHERWOOD, CHRISTOPHER: *Vedanta for the Western World.* New York, Viking, 1962 [1945].

JACKSON, SAMUEL MACAULEY, (Ed.) : *The New Schaff-Herzog Encyclopedia of Religious Knowledge,* 12 vols. New York, Funk, 1909, Vol. V.

JAGADISWARANANDA, SWAMI: *Hinduism Outside India.* Rajkot, Shri Ramakrishna Ashram, 1945.

JAMES, HENRY: *Partial Portraits.* London, Macmillan, 1888.

JAMES, WILLIAM: *Essays in Radical Empiricism A Pluralistic Universe.* New York, Longmans, Green, 1943.

JAMES, WILLIAM: *The Varieties of Religious Experience.* The Gifford Lectures in 1901–1902. New York, Modern Lib., n.d. [1902].

JEFFERSON, THOMAS: *The Writings of,* Albert Ellery Burgh (Ed.) Washington D. C., Thomas Jefferson Mem. Assoc., 1907, vols. XIII, XIV.

JOHNSON, ALLEN, and DUMAS, MALONE: *Dictionary of American Biography,* 20 vols. New York, Scribner, 1931.

JOHNSON, HELEN M., (Ed., trans.) : *The Triṣaṣṭiśalākāa-puruṣacarita or The Lives of Sixty-Three Illustrious Persons* by Ācārya Śrī Hemacandra, 6 vols. Baroda, Oriental Inst. 1962.

JONES, ADAM LEROY: *Early American Philosophers.* New York, Ungar, 1898.

JURJI, EDWARD J.: *The Great Religions of the Modern World.* Princeton, Princeton, 1947.

KAPLAN, ABRAHAM: *The New World of Philosoiphy.* New York, Random, 1961.

KASEGAWA, KOH: Thoreau and the Bhagavad-Gita. *Thoughts Current in English Literature* [Japan], XXXVI, 1963.

KENNEDY, GAIL, (Ed.) : *Pragmatism and American Culture.* Boston, Heath, 1950.

KITCH, ETHEL MAY: *The Origin of Subjectivity in Hindu Thought.* Philosophical Studies of the Department of Philosophy, Number 7. Chicago, U. of Chicago, 1917.

KONVITZ, MILTON, and STEPHEN WHICHER: *Emerson: A Collection of Critical Essays.* Englewood Cliffs, Prentice-Hall, 1962.

KOSAMBI, D. D.: *Myth and Reality: Studies in the Formation of Indian Culture.* Bombay, Popular Prakashan, 1962.

KRAUS, MICHAEL: Science and curiosity. *Intercolonial Aspects of American Culture on the Eve of the Revolution.* New York, Columbia, 1928.

KRIPPNER, STANLEY: Hypnosis and creativity. *Gifted Child Quar,* IX, 3, 1965.

KRUSÉ, CORNELIUS: What contribution can philosophy make to world understanding? *Proc and Addresses of Amer Philos Assoc 1947–1948,* XXI.

KUNDARGI, G. N.: God's finger touched him and he slept *Fulbright Newsletter,* XV, 1, 1967.

KUNDARGI, G. N.: In memory of the late Dr. William Henry Harris. Unpublished MS at Southern Illinois U. Philosophy Department, 1967.

KUNST, ARNOLD: Indian studies in Poland: Stanislaw Schayer. In Indian Council for Cultural Relations (Ed.) : *Indian Studies Abroad.* New York, Asia Publishing House, 1964.

KUNST, ARNOLD: Another catalog of the Kanjur. *Bull School Orient Afric Studies,* University of London, XII, I, 1947.

KUNST, ARNOLD. The concept of the principle of excluded middle in Buddhism. *Rocznik Orientalistyczny,* XXI, 1957.

KUNST, ARNOLD: Kamalaśila's commentary on Śāntarakṣita's Anumana-parikṣa of the Tattvasangraha. *Des Melanges Chinois et Bouddhis-ques,* L'institut Belge Des Hautes Etudes Chinoises. Bruges, St. Catherine Press, 1947.

KUNST, ARNOLD: Stanislaw Schayer. *Rocznik Orientalistyczny,* XXI, 1957.

KWIAT, JOSEPH J.: Thoreau's philosophical apprenticeship. *New Eng Quar* XVIII, 1, 1945.

LAL, CHAMAN: *Hindu America.* Bombay, Bharatiya Vidya Bhavan, 1960.

LANMAN, CHARLES ROCKWELL: *The Beginnings of Hindu Pantheism.* Cambridge, Charles W. Sever, 1890.

LANMAN, CHARLES ROCKWELL: India and the West with a plea for team-work among scholars. *J Amer Orient Soc,* XL, 1920.

LATOURETTE, KENNETH SCOTT: Far Eastern studies in the United States: retrospect and prospect. *Far East Quar,* November 1955.

LEIDECKER, KURT: Emerson and East-West snythesis. *Philos East West,* I, 2, 1951.

LEIDECKER, KURT: *Yankee Teacher: The Life of William Torrey Harris.* New York, Philosophical Lib., 1946.

LEIDECKER, KURT: Oriental philosophy in America. In Winn, Ralph B. (Ed.) : *American Philosophy.* New York, Philosophical Lib., 1955.

LEIDECKER, KURT: Sunyata and Christian Kenotic speculations. *A. R. Wadia Essays in Philosophy Presented in His Honor.* Madras, G. S. Press, 1954.

LEIGHTON, JOSEPH ALEXANDER: The principle of individuality and value. In Clifford Barrett (Ed.) : *Contemporary Idealism in America.* New York, Macmillan, 1932.

LIND, BRUNO: *Vagabond Scholar: A Venture Into the Privacy of George Santayana.* New York, Bridgehead Books, 1962.

LONG, O. W.: William Dwight Whitney. *New Eng Quar,* II, 1929.

MASIN, MARIANNA: What Vedanta means to me. *Vedanta and the West,* No. 125. Hollywood, Vedanta Press, 1957.

MASSON-OURSEL, PAUL: *Comparative Philosophy.* London, Kegan Paul, Trench, Trubner, 1926.

MATHER, COTTON: *India Christiana.* Boston, B. Green, 1721.

MAYER, FREDERICK: *A History of American Thought.* Dubuque, W. C. Brown, 1951.

MILLARD, BAILEY: Rabindranath Tagore Discovers America. *Bookman,* XLIV, 1916.

MILLER, PERRY, (Ed.) : *The American Transcendentalists.* New York, Doubleday, 1957.

MILLER, PERRY: *Jonathan Edwards.* New York, Meridian, 1959.

MILLS, CHARLES D. B.: *The Indian Saint or Buddhism and Buddhism.* Northampton, Journal and Free Press, 1867.

MILLS, CHARLES D. B.: *The Tree of Mythology.* Syracuse, C. W. Bardeen, 1889.

MOORE, ADRINNE: *Rammohun Roy and America.* Calcutta, Satis Chandra Chakravarti, 1942.

MOORE, CHARLES A.: Ahimsāa (non-cruelty) as the supreme ethical principle. *A. R. Wadia Essays in Philosophy Presented in His Honor.* Madras, G. S. Press, 1954.

MOORE, CHARLES A.: An attempt at world philosophical synthesis. In Charles A. Moore (Ed.) : *Essays in East-West Philosophy.* Honolulu, U. of Hawaii, 1951.

MOORE, CHARLES A.: Cohen on the role of philosophy in culture. *Philos East West,* V, 2, 1955.

MOORE, CHARLES A.: Filosofía Comparada y Perspectiva Mundial. trans. Maria Luisa Oehler, *De Notas y Estudios de Filosofia,* IV, 13. San Miguel de Tucuman, Enero-Marz, 1953.

MOORE, CHARLES A., (Ed.) : *The Indian Mind.* Honolulu, East-West, 1967.

MOORE, CHARLES A.: The meaning of Duhkha. *Proceedings of the International Congress of Philosophy,* XI, IV, 1953.

MOORE, CHARLES A.: Metaphysics and Ethics in East and West. In Charles A. Moore (Ed.) : *Essays in East-West Philosophy.* Honolulu, U. of Hawaii, 1951.

MOORE, CHARLES A.: La pensée de Sri Aurobindo à l'égard des rapports de l'Orient avec l'Occident. *Synthèse,* 20, 1965.

MOORE, CHARLES A.: Philosophy as distinct from religion in India. *Philos East West* XI, 1–2, 1961.

MOORE, CHARLES A.: Pluralistic Aspects of Indian Philosophy. *Darshana* I, 3, 1961.

MOORE, CHARLES A.: One Step Beyond. *Krishna Chandra Bhattacharyya Memorial Volume.* Amalner, Indian Inst. of Philosophy, 1958.

MOORE, CHARLES A.: The significance of Ahimsa for ethics, East and West. *Actes du Xieme Congres International de Philosophie* XIV. Amsterdam, North-Holland, 1953.

MOORE, CHARLFS A.: *Spirituality in the West.* Chandigahr, Unesco Centre, 1965.

MOORE, CHARLES A.: The West as not materialistic. Bangalore, Indian Inst. of World Culture, 1958.

MOORE, GEORGE FOOT: *History of Religions,* vol. I. New York, Scribner, 1947 [1913].

MOORE, GEORGE FOOT: *The Birth and Growth of Religion.* The Morse Lectures of 1922 at Union Theological Seminary. New York, Scribner, 1924 [1923].

MOREHOUSE, WARD: Confronting a four-dimensional problem: science, technology, society, and tradition in India and Pakistan. *Tech and Culture,* 8, 3, 1967.

MORGAN, ARTHUR E.: *The Philosophy of Edward Bellamy.* New York, King's Crown Press, 1945.

MORISON, SAMUEL ELIOT: *The Intellectual Life of Colonial New England.* Ithaca, Great Seal Books, 1956 [1936].

MORRIS, CHARLES: Comparative strength of life-ideals in Eastern and Western cultures. In Moore, C. A. (Ed.) : *Essays in East-West Philosophy.* Honolulu, U. of Hawaii, 1951.

MORRIS, CHARLES: *The Open Self.* New York, Prentice-Hall, 1948.

MORRIS, CHARLES: *Paths of Life: Preface to a World Religion.* New York, Harper, 1942.

MOORIS, CHARLES: *Varieties of Human Value.* Chicago, U. of Chicago, 1956.

MOZOOMDAR, P. C.: *Lectures in America and Other Papers.* Calcutta, Navavidhan, 1955.

MOZOOMDAR, P. C.: *Sketches of a Tour Round the World.* Calcutta, Navavidhan, 1940.

MUKHERJEE, S. N.: Sir William Jones and the British attitudes towards India. *J Royal Asiatic Soc,* 1–2, 1964.

MÜLLER, GUSTAVE E.: *Amerikanische Philosophie.* Stuttgart, Fr. Frommanns Verlage, 1936.

MUMFORD, LEWIS: *The Golden Day.* New York, Norton, 1926.

MUMFORD, LEWIS: *The Human Prospect.* Boston, Beacon, 1955.

MUMFORD, LEWIS: *Sticks and Stones,* Second Rev. Ed. New York, Dover, 1955.

MURWITZ, HAROLD M.: Tagore in Urbana, Illinois. *Indian Literature,* 4, 1961.

The National Cyclopaedia of American Biography, 53 vols. New York, James I. White, 1924.

NORTHROP, F. S. C.: Comparative philosophy and science in the light of comparative law. *Philosophy and Culture, East and West.* Honolulu, U. of Hawaii, 1962.

NORTHROP, F. S. C.: The complementary emphases of Eastern intutive and Western scientific philosophy. In C. A. Moore (Ed.) : *Philosophy East and West*. Princeton, Princeton, 1946.

NORTHROP, F. S. C.: *Man, Nature and God*. New York, Trident, 1962.

NORTHROP, F. S. C.: *The Meeting of East and West*. New York, Macmillan, 1960 [1946].

NORTHROP, F. S. C.: Methodology and Epistemology, Oriental and Occidental. In C. A. Moore (Ed.) : *Essays in East-West Philosophy*. Honolulu, U. of Hawaii, 1951.

NORTHROP, F. S. C.: The philosophical roots and validity of Tagore's Genius. *World Perspectives in Philosophy, Religion and Culture: Essays Presented to Professor Dhirendra Mohan Datta*. Patna, Bharati Bhawan, 1968.

NORTHROP, F. S. C.: The theory of types and the verification of ethical theories. C. A. Moore (Ed.) : *Essays in East-West Philosophy*. Honolulu, U. of Hawaii, 1951.

NORTHROP, F. S. C.: The undifferentiated aesthetic continuum. *Philos East West*, XIV, 1, 1964.

Notes and Personalia [Rev. George William Brown]. *Language*, IX, 1, 1933.

OLCOTT, HENRY S.: *The Buddhist Catechism*. London, Theosophical Publishing House, Adyar, Madras, 1915 [1897].

OLCOTT, HENRY S.: *The Spirit of Zoroastrianism*, Adyar Pamphlets No. 23. Adyar, Theosophical Publishing House, 1913.

OLMSTEAD, CLIFTON E.: *Religion in America Past and Present*. Englewood Cliffs. Prentice-Hall, 1961.

O'NEILL, EDWARD H.: *Biography by Americans*. Philadelphia, U. of Pa., 1939.

ORGAN, TROY: *The Self in Indian Philosophy*. The Hague, Mouton, 1964.

ORIENTAL CLUB OF PHILADELPHIA 1888–1894: *Oriental Studies*. Boston, Ginn, 1894.

PADOVER, SAUL K.: *Jefferson*. New York, New Am. Lib., 1955.

PANNIKAR, SARDAR K. M.: *Hinduism & the West*. Chandigahr, Panjab Univ., 1964.

PARAMANANDA, SWAMI: *Emerson and Vedanta*. Boston, Vedanta Centre, 1918.

PARKER, THEODORE: Man in his religious aspects. *Lessons from the World of Matter and the World of Man*, sel. Rufus Leighton. Chicago, Charles H. Kerr, 1887.

PARRY, WILLIAM T.: Unpublished notes on Ingall's materials for the study of Navya-nyāya logic. Buffalo, May 26, 1965.

PARSONS, HOWARD L.: Review of Grace E. Cairns' philosophies of history: meeting of East and West in cycle-pattern theories of history. *Philos East West*, XII, 4, 1963.

PEDERSON, HOLGER: *Linguistic Science in the Nineteenth Century*, trans. from Danish by J. W. Spargo. Cambridge, Harvard, 1931–35, VI.

PEIRCE, C. S.: In Charles Hartshorne and Paul Weiss (Ed.) : *Collected Papers*. Cambridge, Harvard, 1931–35, VI.

PELL, JOHN H. G.: *Ethan Allen*. Boston, Houghton, 1929.

PENROSE, STEPHEN B. L. JR., and OLIVER J. CALDWELL: Ties that bind. In Arthur E. Christy (Ed.) : *The Asian Legacy and American Life*. New York, Day, 1945.

PERRY, CHARLES M.: Philosophy of the early century. *Henry Philip Tappen: Philosopher and University President*. Ann Arbor, U. of Mich., 1933.

PERRY, RALPH BARTON: *The Thought and Character of William James*. Cambridge, Harvard, 1948.

PERSONS, STOW: *Free Religion: An American Faith*. New Haven, Yale, 1947.

PHILIPS, C. H.: *The East India Company 1784–1834*. Manchester, Univ. Press, 1961.

PHILLIPS, BERNARD: Radhakrishnan's Critique of Naturalism. In P. A. Schilpp (Ed.) : *The Philosophy of Sarvepalli Radhakrishnan*. New York, Tudor, 1952.

PITKIN, WALTER B.: *A Short Introduction to Human Stupidity*. New York, Simon and Schuster, 1932.

PITT, WILLIAM: *Introducing Hinduism*. New York, Friensdhip, 1958.

PLOTT, JOHN: An appreciation of the Tirunvoimoli of Nammalwar. *Journal of the Vaishnava University of Vrindaban*, U. P., 1956.

PLOTT, JOHN: A Himalayan Journal. Unpublished MS.

PLOTT, JOHN: Janartha Sangraha. Unpublished MS.

PLOTT, JOHN: M. N. Roy. Unpublished MS.

PLOTT, JOHN: Philosophy of Religion in Ramanuja, St. Bonaventura, and Gabriel Marcell. Doctoral dissertation, Banaras Hindu University, 1956.

PLOTT, JOHN: Ramanuja as Panentheist. *Annamalai University Journal*, 1954.

PLOTT, JOHN: The razor's wedge: an autobiographical pilgrimage to India: 1949–1957. Unpublished MS.

PLOTT, JOHN: Transition from comparative philosophy to a globalized history of philosophy. Unpublished MS.

PLOTT, JOHN: What is meant by embodied? Unpublished MS.

POCHMAN, HENRY A.: *German Culture in America*. Madison, U. of Wis., 1961.

PORTER, NOAH: Philosophy in America. In Friedrich Ueberweg: *History of Philosophy from Thales to the Present Time*, 2 vols., trans. G. S. Morris. New York, Scribner, 1893, Vol. II.

POTTER, KARL: Dharma and Mokṣa from a conversational point of view, *Philos East West*, VIII, 1–2, 1958.

POTTER, KARL: Freedom and determinism from an Indian perspective. *Philos East West*, XVII, 1–4, 1967.

POTTER, KARL: The logical character of the causal relation in Indian philosophy. *World Perspectives in Philosophy, Religion and Culture: Essays Presented to Professor Dhirendra Mohan Datta*. Patna, Bharati Bhawan, 1968.

POTTER, KARL: More on the unrepeatability of the Guṇas. *Philos East West*, VII, 1–2, 1957.

POTTER, KARL: *Presuppositions of India's Philosophies*. Englewood Cliffs, Prentice-Hall, 1963.

POTTER, KARL: The naturalistic principle of Karma. *Philos East West*, XIV, 1, 1964.

PRATT, JAMES BISSETT: *India and its Faiths: A Traveler's Record*. Boston, Houghton, 1915.

PRATT, JAMES BISSETT: *The Pilgrimage of Buddhism and A Buddhist Pilgrimage*. New York, Macmillan, 1928.

PRATT, JAMES BISSETT: *Reason in the Art of Living*. New York, Macmillan, 1949.

PRATT, JAMES BISSETT: Recent developments in Indian philosophy. *J Philos*, 30, 1933.

PRATT, JAMES BISSETT: Study of Indian Philosophy. In Christopher Isherwood (Ed.) : *Vedanta for Modern Man*. New York, Harper, 1951.

PRESTON, WHEELER: *American Biographies*. New York, Harper, 1940.

PRICE, LUCIEN: *Dialogues of Alfred North Whitehead*. Boston, Little, 1954.

PRITCHARD, EARL H.: The foundation of the Association for Asian Studies 1928–48, *J Asian Studies*, XXII, 4, 1963.

RADBILL, SAMUEL X.: The autobiographical annals of Robley Dunglison, M. D. *Transactions of the American Philosophical Society*. Philadelphia, Am. Philosophical Soc., 1963.

RADHAKRISHNAN, SARVEPALLI: The philosopher replies. *The Philosophy of Sarvepalli Radhakrishnan.* New York, Tudor, 1952.

RAO, E. NAGASWARA: The American in India. *East-West Ctr Rev,* I, 1, 1964.

RAO, E. NAGASWARA: Thoreau and Gandhi: A Comparison. *Aryan Path,* XXXVII, 8, 1961.

REID, JOHN T.: Indian influence in American literature and thought. *Hyphen,* November–December 1962.

REISCHAUER, AUGUST KARL: Buddhism. In E. J. Jurji (Ed.) : *The Great Religions of the Modern World.* Princeton, Princeton, 1947.

RENOU, LOUIS (Ed.) : *Hinduism.* New York, Braziller, 1961.

RENOU, LOUIS: L'influence de l'Inde ancienne sur la pensee Francaise. *Sanskrit et Culture.* Paris, Payot, 1950.

RIEPE, DALE: The all-India seminar in East-West philosophy. *Philos Phenom Research,* XXVIII, 2, 1967.

RIEPE, DALE: Contributions of American Sanskritists in the spread of Indian philosophy in the United States. *Buffalo Studies,* III, 1, 1967.

RIEPE, DALE: Emerson and Indian Philosophy. *J Hist Ideas,* XXVIII, 1, 1967.

RIEPE, DALE: The Fourth East-West Conference. *Philos Phenom Research,* XXV, 3, 1965.

RIEPE, DALE: The Indian influence in American philosophy: Emerson to Moore. *Philos East West,* XVII, 1–4, 1967.

RIEPE, DALE: Influence of Indian thought upon that of the United States. *World Perspectives in Philosophy, Religion and Culture: Essays Presented to Professor Dhirendra Mohan Datta.* Patna, Bharati Bhawan, 1968.

RIEPE, DALE: Indian Philosophical Literature 1955–57, *Philos Phenom Research,* XVIII, 3, 1958.

RIEPE, DALE: Influence of Indian thought since the Civil War. *Proceedings XIII International Congress of Philosophy,* Thema II. Mexico City, National Univ., 1963.

RIEPE, DALE: Josiah Royce's transaction with Indian philosophy. *Personalist,* 48, 2, 1967.

RIEPE, DALE: *The Naturalistic Tradition in Indian Thought.* Seattle, U. of Wash., 1961.

RILEY, ISAAC WOODBRIDGE: *American Thought from Puritanism to Pragmatism.* New York, Holt, 1915.

RILEY, ISAAC WOODBRIDGE: *American Thought from Puritanism to Pragmatism and Beyond.* New York, Peter Smith, 1941.

RILEY, ISAAC WOODBRIDGE: *American Philosophy: The Early Schools.* New York, Dodd, 1907.

ROBINSON, RICHARD H.: *Early Mādhyamika in India and China.* Madison, U. of Wis., 1967.

ROBINSON, RICHARD H.: Some logical aspects of Nāgārjuna's system. *Philos East West,* January 1957.

ROBINSON, RICHARD H.: Mysticism and Logic in Seng-Chao's Thought. *Philos East West,* VIII, 3–4, 1958.

ROGERS, ARTHUR KENYON: *English and American Philosophy Since 1800.* New York, Macmillan, 1922.

ROLLAND, ROMAIN: *Mahatma Gandhi.* New York, Century Press, 1924.

ROLLAND, ROMAIN: *Prophets of the New India,* trans. E. F. Malcolm-Smith. London, Cassell, 1930.

ROSS, FLOYD H.: *The Meaning of Life in Hinduism and Buddhism.* Boston, Beacon, 1952.

ROYCE, JOSIAH: *The Philosophy of Loyalty.* New York, Macmillan, 1930 [1908].

ROYCE, JOSIAH: *The Religious Aspect of Philosophy.* Boston, Houghton, 1891 [1885].

ROYCE, JOSIAH: *The Spirit of Modern Philosophy.* Boston, Houghton, 1899.

ROYCE, JOSIAH: *The World and the Individual,* 2 vols. New York, Macmillan, 1904.

RYDER, ARTHUR WILLIAM: *The Bhagavad Gita.* Chicago, U. Chicago, 1929.

RYDER, ARTHUR WILLIAM: *The Little Clay Cart,* Harvard Oriental Series, Vol. 5. Cambridge, Harvard, 1905.

RYDER, ARTHUR WILLIAM: *Panchatantra.* Chicago, U. Chicago, 1925.

SALTUS, EDGAR: *The Anatomy of Negation.* New York, Scribner, 1896.

SALTUS, EDGAR: *The Philosophy of Disenchantment.* New York, Bel-, ford, 1885.

SANTAYANA, GEORGE: *Character and Opinion in the United States.* New York, Scribner, 1921.

SANTAYANA, GEORGE: *Dominations and Powers.* London, Constable, 1952.

SANTAYANA, GEORGE: *Egotism in German Philosophy.* London, J. M. Dent, n.d. [1916].

SANTAYANA, GEORGE: *A Hermit of Carmel.* New York, Scribner, 1901.

SANTAYANA, GEORGE: *Idea of Christ in the Gospels.* New York, Scribner, 1946.

SANTAYANA, GEORGE: In Daniel Cory (Ed.) : *The Idler and His Works.* New York, Braziller, 1957.

SANTAYANA, GEORGE: *Interpretations of Poetry and Religion.* New York, Scribner, 1911.

SANTAYANA, GEORGE: *Lucifer.* Cambridge, Dunster House, 1924.

SANTAYANA, GEORGE: In Justus Buchler and Benjamin Schwartz (Ed.) : *Obiter Scripta.* New York, Scribner, 1936.

SANTAYANA, GEORGE: On the False Steps of Philosophy, In Daniel Cory (Ed.) : *J. Philos,* LXI, 1, 1964.

SANTAYANA, GEORGE: *Persons and Places.* New York, Scribner, 1944.

SANTAYANA, GEORGE: In P. A. Schilpp (Ed.) : *The Philosophy of George Santayana.* The Library of Living Philosophers. Evanston, Northwestern U., 1940.

SANTAYANA, GEORGE: *Poems.* New York, Scribner, 1923.

SANTAYANA, GEORGE: *Realms of Being.* New York, Scribner, 1942.

SANTAYANA, GEORGE: *Reason in Society, The Life of Reason,* vol. II. New York, Scribner, 1924.

SANTAYANA, GEORGE: Review of James Haughton Woods, The value of religious facts. *New World,* IX, 1900.

SANTAYANA, GEORGE: *Scepticism and Animal Faith.* New York, Scribner, 1923.

SANTAYANA, GEORGE: *Some Turns of Thought in Modern Philosophy.* New York, Scribner, 1933.

SANTAYANA, GEORGE: *Sonnets and Other Verses.* New York, Duffield, 1906.

SARADANANDA, SWAMI, (Ed.) : *Notes of Some Wanderings with The Swami Vivekananda by Sister Nivedita of Ramkrishna-Vivekananda.* Calcutta, Brahmachari Gonendra Nath, 1913.

SAURAT, DENIS: *Literature and Occult Tradition: Studies in Philosophical Poetry,* trans. from the French by Dorothy Bolton. London, G. Bell, 1930.

SCHERMERHORN, R. A.: When did Indian materialism get its distinctive titles? *J Amer Orient Soc,* L, 1930.

SCHLEGEL, FRIEDRICH: *The Aesthetic and Miscellaneous Works of,* trans. E. J. Millington. London, Henry G. Bohn, 1860.

SCHNEIDER, HERBERT W.: *A History of American Philosophy.* New York, Columbia, 1946.

SELLARS, ROY WOOD: Essence and existence for critical realism, In E. S. Brightman (Ed.) : *Proceedings XI International Congress of Philosophy.* New York, Longmans, Green, 1927.

SHELDON, WILMON HENRY: *America's Progressive Philosophy.* New Haven, Yale, 1942.

SHELDON, WILMON HENRY: *God and Polarity*. New Haven, Yale, 1954.

SHELDON, WILMON HENRY: Main contrasts between Eastern and Western philosophy. In C. A. Moore (Ed.) : *Essays in East-West Philosophy*. Honolulu, U. of Hawaii, 1951.

SHELDON, WILMON HENRY: *Process and Polarity*. New York, Columbia, 1944.

SHEPARD, ODELL, (Ed.) : *The Journals of Bronson Alcott*. Boston, Little, 1938.

SINGAM, S. DURAI RAJA: *Homage to Ananda Coomaraswamy*. Kuantan, Malaya, n.p., 1952.

SINGH, MAN MOHAN: *The Influence of Hindu Maya on Emerson*. Master's Thesis, Department of English Literature. Boulder, U. of Colo., 1943.

SMITH, GROVER, (Ed.) : *Josiah Royce's Seminar 1913–1914*. New Brunswick, Rutgers, 1963.

SMITH, T. V., and WILLIAM KELLEY WRIGHT, (Ed.) : *Essays in Philosophy*. Chicago, Open Ct, 1929.

SNIDER, DENTON J.: *The St. Louis Movement*. St. Louis, Sigma, 1920.

SNYDER, HELENA ADELL: *Thoreau's Philosophy of Life with Special Consideration of the Influence of Hindoo Philosophy*. Heidelberg, n.p., [1900?].

SOPER, EDMUND DAVISON: *The Religions of Mankind,* 3rd. ed. rev. New York, Abingdon, 1951.

SPILLER, ROBERT E., (Ed.) : *Literary History of the United States, 3* vols. New York, Macmillan, 1948.

STAAL, J. F.: *Advaita and Neoplatonism,* Madras University Philosophical Series, No. 10. Madras, U. of Madras, 1961.

STACE, WALTER TERENCE: *The Concept of Morals*. New York, Macmillan, 1937.

STACE, WALTER TERENCE: *The Gate of Silence*. Boston, Beacon, 1952.

STACE, WALTER TERENCE: *Mysticism and Philosophy*. Philadelphia, Lippincott, 1960.

STACE, WALTER TERENCE: *The Philosophy of Hegel*. London, Macmillan, 1924.

STACE, WALTER TERENCE: *Religion and the Modern Mind*. Philadelphia, Lippincott, 1952.

STACE, WALTER TERENCE: *The Teachings of the Mystics*. New York, New Am. Lib., 1960.

STACE, WALTER TERENCE: *Time and Eternity*. Princeton, Princeton, 1952.

STEIN, WILLIAM BYSSHE: *Thoreau's First Book, A Spoor of Yoga: The*

Orient in "A Week on the Concord and Merrimack Rivers." Hartford, Emerson Society, 1965.

STEIN, WILLIAM BYSSHE: Thoreau's *Walden* and the Bhagavad **Gita**. *J Lib Arts,* Topic 6, 1963.

SULLIVAN, HERBERT P.: Reality and illusion: the problem of phenomenal existence in Indian philosophy. *Sri Aurobindo Circle,* XVI, n.d., p. 42.

TAGORE, RABINDRANATH: Nationalism in the West, *Atlantic Monthly,* CXIX, 1917.

TEIGNMOUTH, LORD: *Memoirs of the Life, Writings and Correspondence of Sir William Jones.* Philadelphia, Wm. Poyntell, 1805.

THOBURN, JAMES M.: *The Christian Conquest of India.* New York, Young People's Missionary Movement, 1906.

THOMAS, WENDELL M.: *Hinduism Invades America.* New York, Beacon, 1930.

THOREAU, HENRY DAVID: *Journal,* ed. Bradford Torrey and Francis H. Allen. Boston, Houghton, 1949, 14 vols.

THOREAU, HENRY DAVID: *Walden.* New York, Grosset, 1910.

TINDALL, WILLIAM YORK: Transcendentalism in contemporary literature. In Arthur E. Christy (Ed.) : *The Asian Legacy in American Life.* New York, Day, 1945.

TODD, EDGELEY W.: Philosophical ideas at Harvard College 1817–1837. *New Eng Quar,* XVI, 1943.

TOWNSEND, HARVEY GATES: *Philosophical Ideas in the United States.* New York, American Book, 1934.

TSIEN, T. H.: Asian studies in America: a historical study. *Asian Studies and State Universities,* Proceedings of a Conference at Indiana University. Bloomington, 1959.

UNDERWOOD, A. C.: *Contemporary Thought of India.* New York, Knopf, 1931.

UNITED STATES INFORMATION SERVICE: Thoreau and India. New Delhi, 1962.

WACH, JOACHIM: The Study of Mahayana Buddhism. *Types of Religious Experience Christian and Non-Christian.* Chicago, U. of Chicago, 1951.

WALLER, GEORGE M., (Ed.) : *Puritanism in Early America.* Boston, Heath, 1950.

WARREN, AUSTIN: The Concord School of Philosophy. *New Eng Quar,* II, 1929.

WARREN, HENRY CLARKE: *Buddhism in Translations.* Harvard Oriental Series, Vol. III, ed. C. R. Lanman. Cambridge, Harvard, 1909 [1896].

WARREN, SIDNEY: *American Free Thought, 1860–1914.* New York, Columbia, 1943.

WAYMAN, ALEX: Buddhist Dependent Origination and the Samkhya gunas. *Ethnos,* 1962.

WAYMAN, ALEX: The Buddhist 'Not This, Not This.' *Philos East West,* XI, 3, 1961.

WAYMAN, ALEX: Conze on Buddhism and European parallels. *Philos East West,* XIII, 4, 1964.

WAYMAN, ALEX: The meaning of unwisdom. *Philos East West,* VII, 1–2, 1957.

WAYMAN, ALEX: The Yogācāra idealism. *Philos East West,* 15, 4, 1965.

WELLEK, RENÉ: Emerson and German philosophy. *New Eng Quar,* XVI, 1943.

WERKMEISTER, W. H.: *History of Philosophical Ideas in America.* New York, Ronald, 1949.

WHATELY, RICHARD: Historic Doubts Relative to Napoleon Bonaparte. In Huston Peterson (Ed.) : *Essays in Philosophy.* New York, Pocket Books, 1959.

WHITNEY, WILLIAM DWIGHT: *The Roots, Verb-Forms and Primary Derivatives of the Sanskrit Language.* Leipzig, Breitkopf and Hartel, 1885.

WHITTEMORE, ROBERT CLIFTON: *Makers of the American Mind.* New York, Morrow, 1964.

WHITTEMORE, ROBERT CLIFTON: The relevance of Indian philosophy. *South J Philos,* IV, 1, 1966.

Who Was Who in America. Chicago, Marquis Who's, 1962, 1963, vols. I, II.

WIDGERY, ALBAN G.: Review of H. N. Spalding's civilization in East and West. *Rev Relig,* V, 1, 1940.

WILD, JOHN: Certain basic concepts of Western realism and their relation to Oriental thought. In C. A. Moore (Ed.) : *Essays in East-West Philosophy.* Honolulu, U. of Hawaii, 1951.

WINDISCH, ERNEST: *Geschichte der Sanskrit-Philologie und Indischen Altertumskunde,* 2 vols. Berlin, Walter de Gruyter, 1920.

WOODS, JAMES HAUGHTON, (Ed., trans.) : *The Yoga-System of Patanjali,* Harvard Oriental Series, Vol. 17. Cambridge, Harvard, 1927 [1914].

WRIGHT, CALEB: *Lectures on India,* 5th ed. Boston, Caleb Wright, 1851.

INDEX

Index